Rosemary Bailey was born in Halifax, Yorkshire. She has lived in the French Pyrenees for seven years. Her previous book, the bestselling *Life in a Postcard*, also published by Bantam, describes her life in a mountain village and her attempts to restore a Romanesque monastery. Her account is skilfully interwoven with the poignant history of the monks and villagers who once lived there, adding a rich vein of history to a personal and contemporary tale.

Bailey has been a travel writer and journalist for many years. In 1997 she wrote the acclaimed *Scarlet Ribbons: A Priest with AIDS*, the story of her brother, Simon Bailey, and the remarkable support he received from his Yorkshire mining village parish. Bailey is married to the biographer Barry Miles, and has one son, Theo, who plays his own part in this book.

D1080620

Also by Rosemary Bailey

National Geographic Traveller Guide to France
Scarlet Ribbons: A Priest with AIDS
Life in a Postcard: Escape to the French Pyrenees

THE MAN WHO MARRIED A MOUNTAIN

A journey through the Pyrenees

Rosemary Bailey

BANTAM BOOKS

LONDON • TORONTO • SYDNEY • AUCKLAND • JOHANNESBURG

To Theo

THE MAN WHO MARRIED A MOUNTAIN
A BANTAM BOOK : 0 553 81523 7

First publication in Great Britain

PRINTING HISTORY
Bantam edition published 2005

1 3 5 7 9 10 8 6 4 2

Copyright © Rosemary Bailey 2005

Extract from *Mountains of the Mind* by Robert Macfarlane published by Granta
Publications. Reproduced by permission of Granta Publications.
Every effort has been made to obtain the necessary permissions with reference to
copyright material, and should there be any omissions in this respect we apologize and
shall be pleased to make the appropriate acknowledgements in any future edition.

Set in 12/14pt Erhhardt by
Falcon Oast Graphic Art Ltd.

Bantam Books are published by Transworld Publishers,
61–63 Uxbridge Road, London W5 5SA,
a division of The Random House Group Ltd,
in Australia by Random House Australia (Pty) Ltd,
20 Alfred Street, Milsons Point, Sydney, NSW 2061, Australia,
in New Zealand by Random House New Zealand Ltd,
18 Poland Road, Glenfield, Auckland 10, New Zealand
and in South Africa by Random House (Pty) Ltd,
Endulini, 5a Jubilee Road, Parktown 2193, South Africa.

Printed and bound in Great Britain by
Cox & Wyman Ltd, Reading, Berkshire.

Papers used by Transworld Publishers are natural, recyclable
products made from wood grown in sustainable forests. The
manufacturing processes conform to the environmental
regulations of the country of origin.

Acknowledgements

I would like to express my appreciation of the libraries and individuals who helped in my research for this book. The Musée des Pyrénées in Lourdes proved the best source of nineteenth-century English texts as well as French. Thank you to Genevieve Marson and Agnes Mengelle. Christine Juliat, archivist of the public library in Pau, provided me with information on the history of Pau and located a key text, Joseph Duloum's *Les Anglais dans les Pyrénées*. The Cauterets public library supplied several useful references. Jean-Marc Boirie, Secretary of the Société Ramond in Bagnères-de-Bigorre was very helpful in sending archive copies of articles. A very special thank-you to Marie-Jo Delattre and the libraries of Mosset and Thuir, who supplied me with books and waited patiently for many months for their return.

I would like to thank librarian Margaret Ecclestone and the Alpine Club library for considerable assistance, including sending material to me in France. The London Library was as ever a treasure trove and also obliged by sending me books when needed. The British Library was invaluable, especially the periodicals division of the Oriental and India Office and the Rare Manuscripts division. The Sheffield Sports Library also proved a good source of nineteenth-century mountaineering books, and the Calderdale Central Reference Library in Halifax found unpublished material on Anne Lister. I would also like to thank Gerard Coupinot and the staff of the Observatoire du Pic du Midi, Didier Lacaze, Jean Ritter, Baroness de Lassus, Louis Bergugnat, the Cercle Anglais of Pau, Nicholas Inman and Clara

Villaneuva, Rory and Mini Constant, Edward and Angelika Rich, Mme Laterrade at the Hôtel des Voyageurs in Gavarnie, Mme Vergez at the Hotel du Cirque, M. René Rose, mayor of Borcé, the Reverend Richard Eyre, former chaplain of St Andrew's church in Pau, and the family of Henry Russell, who kindly supplied me with documentation. A special thank you to André Labarrère, mayor of Pau, for his interest in the project and for the umbrella.

Thanks also to Chris and Anita David for sending a precious volume from the USA, to Jo Goldsworthy for historical research, and to Lucy Irvine for the support only a fellow writer can give. For walking, talking and appearing in the book thank you to Thérèse Caron, Fiona and Gary Peters, Caty Friloux, Gerard van Westerloo, Henri Sentenac and especially Monique Didier-Mereau.

I owe a huge debt to Paul Mirat and the mairie of Pau, who welcomed me to Pau so graciously, and kept me supplied with information and encouragement throughout the project. Mirat's knowledge of Russell's work and his own research into the history of Pau and the Wright Brothers was invaluable. My thanks go to him, his wife Pascale, and his children, Pablo, Mathilde and Martin for their generous hospitality.

On the home front, my husband Barry Miles was as supportive as ever. We could hardly have diverged further in our respective writing; as I pursued the high romantics of the nineteenth century he was writing about Frank Zappa and modernist music, but he supported me as graciously as ever and edited the book with his usual scrupulous taste and attention. Thank you most of all to my son Theo for coming with me.

Author's Note

In most cases the French translations are my own. Spellings of place names is something of a minefield with often several possibilities for one place (or even several names for one place . . .) both sides of the frontier; Spanish and French, Aragonese, Catalan, Béarnais etc, as well as nineteenth-century French (or indeed English) spellings of Spanish places which may never even have been written down before . . . Most spellings have been rationalized according to current maps; Spanish places spelled in Spanish and French in French, with a few exceptions such as Mont Perdu, which despite being in Spain is in fact famously known as Mont Perdu (Perdido).

If you asked me why I live in these green mountains
I would laugh to myself. My soul is at rest.
Peach blossoms float in the gushing streams:
Another heaven, another earth lies beyond our own.

Li Po (701–762)

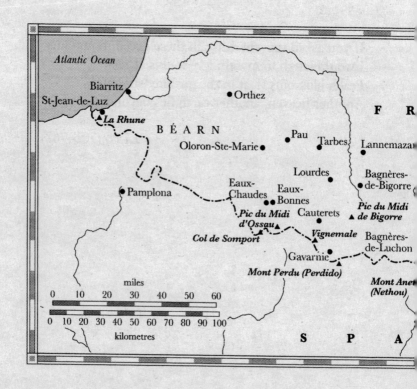

Atlantic Ocean

Biarritz
St-Jean-de-Luz
▲ *La Rhune*

● Orthez

B É A R N

Oloron-Ste-Marie ●

Pau ●
Tarbes ●
Lannemaza

F R

Lourdes ●

Bagnères-
de-Bigorre ●

● Pamplona

Eaux-
Chaudes
● ●
Eaux-
Bonnes

*Pic du Midi
d'Ossau* ▲

Cauterets ●

*Pic du Midi
de Bigorre* ▲

Col de Somport

Vignemale ▲

Bagnères-
de-Luchon

Gavarnie ●

▲

Mont Perdu (Perdido)

*Mont Anet
(Nethou)*

miles

0   10   20   30   40   50   60

0   10 20 30 40 50 60 70 80 90 100

kilometres

S   **P**   **A**

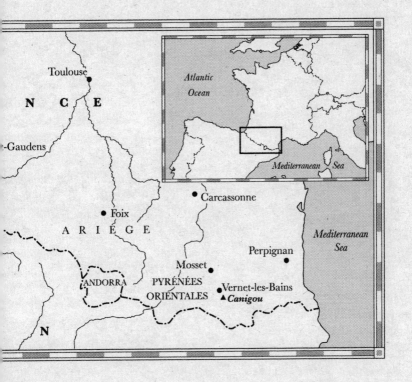

Contents

Count Henry Russell (1834–1909)

Prologue

The Pyrenees: summit of Vignemale (3298 metres), 26 August 1880

'Having chosen my site, and with supplies, two determined and devoted men, my sheepskin sleeping bag, and the probability of a serene calm night, I decided to pass it in the open air on the summit of Vignemale. Nothing could be more wholesome or moving.'

After more than twenty years of climbing all the highest peaks of the Pyrenees, Count Henry Russell-Killough, Baron of Ulster, had decided that a few brief moments spent on the summits was not enough. To fully savour the experience he must become a mountain dweller, and in order to stay at high altitudes for longer periods he needed to select a perfect site and devise an ideal shelter. The mountain was already chosen: the Vignemale with its great glacier, the fourth highest peak in the Pyrenees, and the highest on the French side. It was the mountain to which he had been most attached since he was a child.

He and his guides had made the climb in seven hours from Gavarnie and arrived at dusk. From the summit Russell surveyed the view: the immensity of snowy peaks unfurling to the east and west, France to the north and Spain to the south.

They all drank hot punch, followed by a glass of Chartreuse, then, while Monsieur le Comte sat and smoked a cigar, the men dug a ditch as long as a tomb.

They buried him there, snug in his sheepskin sleeping bag, under a pile of stones and earth, leaving only his head exposed. The guides were persuaded to descend about fifty metres to the north-west of the summit, where they huddled in the shelter of a large rock. 'Without any cover it would have been barbaric to make them sleep with me on the summit,' observed Russell magnanimously. After three solemn *bonsoirs* he was alone.

Night came quickly and the moon appeared at about eleven o'clock. 'There I was alone in darkness on one of the wildest coldest peaks of the Pyrenees. Three hundred metres below was an immense ocean of clouds from which rose islands of snow or granite, which seemed to quiver in the subtle light of the moon. There was an unnatural deathly silence. Without being able to see the horizon, it seemed as if I had left the earth.'

Despite the cold and tension he finally slept, so profoundly that he did not notice when the men climbed up twice to see how he was faring. He was snoring, his hat and goatee beard white with frost. 'I have often asked myself since had an unfortunate tourist seen me there, a human head without a body on the summit of Vignemale! He would have taken me for a torture victim, his hair would have stood on end with fear, he would have gone mad. How his terror would have doubled if he had noticed that this fantastic head was not dead, but moved from time to time, became livid and blue and opened its eyes spasmodically. I wish I could have seen myself.' His gruesome speculations have all the fantastic detail of Tibetan Buddhist meditation visions. He woke around 3 a.m., and checked his thermometer: minus three degrees centigrade. The peak was illuminated by chilly, silver moonlight. 'It seemed to me I felt the night and heard the silence. I saw God everywhere.'

Never had dawn taken so long. But finally, at 4.30 a.m., he saw a golden band streaking the dark horizon in the east, and at 5 a.m. he received at last a ray of sun. 'What joy. One of the greatest physical joys of my life.' He recalled his journey across the plains of Siberia twenty years before. 'Sunrise was so beautiful there, but it was no consolation when it was still nearly 40 degrees of cold.' But in the Pyrenees, despite the surrounding snow, he was soon warm. 'The view alone of the sun was enough to warm the blood, the grand glacier empurpled and the rivulets of water melting like the imploring music of Chopin. What poetry. Once tasted how can one ever say goodbye to the mountains.'

Henry Russell had met his destiny on Vignemale. 'She will become my spouse,' he declared, and began to wonder how he could gain legal possession of the summit. When the guides appeared to say good morning, they boiled up a bottle of Bordeaux and all slept in the warmth of the sun before descending to Gavarnie. Not a moment too soon, since Vignemale immediately exploded in a series of terrifying storms that raged around the summit for several days: 'a veritable hell of snow from which we would not have emerged alive if we had stayed one day more.'

1

Canigou: sacred mountain of the Catalans

'There is something magical and supernatural in hill land-scape which entrances the mind and the senses. One forgets everything, one forgets one's own being.'

Jean-Jacques Rousseau

Mountains get in your blood. After seven years of living in the Pyrenees I miss their familiar contours when I go away. I am used to their monumental presence, the way they seem so secure in their immutability yet offer a mercurial visage that is constantly changing. Nothing else seems quite so satisfying. Every day the first thing I do is look at the mountains, the unfolding hills to the west that herald the beginning of the Pyrenees, and most of all Canigou, our own mountain.

'Did you see Canigou today?' is a common greeting in our little community, the lodestone by which all is measured. For the farmers its appearance is a presage of the weather that dominates their lives: the rain that might ruin the crops of peaches or lettuces, the fierce cold that might affect the newborn calves, or the dry winds and fire that can spell disaster for many hectares of upland pasture. In winter these farmers sit snug by the woodstove, in summer in dim cool darkness shuttered against the heat. They express astonishment at our big windows, our rooms flooded with sunshine, our table on the terrace positioned so we can admire the view. After a day in the fields they have no need to contemplate nature when they get home.

When we first thought of living in the Pyrenees we wanted to escape the noise and pollution of the city, find somewhere with space and beauty for our child to grow up. We wanted to discover a new culture and our son to grow up speaking more than one language. We had fallen in love with a Romanesque monastery complete with its own frescoed chapel and surrounded by peach orchards; my desire for escape combined inexorably with my husband's passion for medieval buildings. We bought the building and spent many years slowly restoring it to its former beauty.

When we first came we were in search of the sweet pleasures of summer, and thought only of pretty white-washed villages, hillsides scented with herbs snoozing in the sunshine under a shutter-blue sky. I anticipated a community of medieval peasants wedded to the earth, who would teach me their frugal, humble ways, their knowledge of the land and the rhythms of nature; who would leave me crates of peaches and eggs in baskets of straw.

There were a few such, peasants from central casting with their berets and baguettes, planting by the phases of the moon, and plotting next year's wood supply, but they regarded us with deep suspicion. It soon became clear that I would quickly run out of subjects for conversation, rapidly exhaust the possibilities of the crops and the weather, and that they would never, ever, tell me the best places to find mushrooms.

Instead I was drawn to all the dreamers, the escapees from city life like me, who found in the mountains a source of inspiration and beauty. They had a familiarity with the mountains that I wanted to share, spending days trekking with donkeys over forgotten smugglers' paths, riding over mountain plateaux, picnicking beside still clear lakes, skiing through the forests, collecting wild herbs, dancing by moonlight and sleeping under the stars.

Once we came to live in the dilapidated monastery we now call home, I discovered that we were part of a second wave of travellers who had fallen in love with these mountains. For the English of the nineteenth century the Pyrenees were as much the South of France as the Riviera, a region of romance and adventure that they colonized as thoroughly as they did the Mediterranean. Our generation was not the first to discover mouldering chateaux in Gascony, spy out ruined chapels, gush over the fresh produce in the markets or the cheapness of the wine; it had all been done before.

The Pyrenees were never very easy to get to and were rarely included in the eighteenth-century Grand Tour of Europe, a sort of finishing school for young English gentlemen, visiting the famous artworks and monuments of France and Italy. Most of the Grand Tourists skipped through France via Paris, Burgundy and the Rhône Valley and struggled over the Alps into Italy, heading for Rome and Venice. A few adventurers made their way via the coastal routes to Spain, but that was far from being a popular choice.

However from the mid-eighteenth century on, a steady trickle of British, Americans and other foreigners did come to the Pyrenees in search of the Sublime, the Picturesque and the Beautiful, exclaiming over the landscape, sketching the peasants and striding up glaciers and snowy peaks in tweed jackets and hobnailed boots, with porters bearing wine, sides of beef and a good supply of cigars.

Mountain exploration was still dominated by the Alps, with macho members of the Alpine Club battling with the forces of nature and competing bitterly for first ascents of unvanquished peaks. The spirit of Pyrenean exploration was different, characterized more by a quest for knowledge and an appreciation of beauty than by a desire for conquest. The Pyrenees were gentler, greener, more feminine mountains. The *pyrénéistes* were always more likely to carry a book than an ice axe.

I wanted to understand what had drawn so many of these travellers to the Pyrenees and I wanted to see for myself the glorious landscapes and high distant mountains that had inspired them. I soon came across the greatest dreamer of all, the character that loomed most spectacularly from that distant past, the legendary Count Henry Russell-Killough, a man with, literally, his head in the clouds – or *dans la lune*, as the French would say. His passion for the Pyrenees, his lifetime spent exploring and climbing the entire chain, seemed the key to appreciating it for myself. He was Irish and French, both country lover and urbane socialite, a great traveller, a fine writer and musician, but most of all he was a *montagnard*, a mountain dweller, who not only buried himself on a mountain top but dug caves from the rock to enable him to live for long periods at the highest possible altitudes. Finally he was even granted a lease on his favourite summit, so he could symbolically marry his mountain. His book, *Souvenirs d'un Montagnard* (*Memories of a Mountain dweller*) published in 1888, is the classic text of the Pyrenees, a lyrical, passionate account of his adventures. 'Few mountaineers have more deeply felt or more delicately expressed the poetry and above all the romance of mountain solitudes,' said the *Alpine Journal* in his obituary.

Of all those who sought the Sublime and the Beautiful in the Pyrenees it was Henry Russell who found it. The romantic Byronic spirit of adventure and escape that inspired the youth of the time found expression in a sturdy Gascon, born and bred in the mountains, and able to find a physical outlet for his philosophy.

He combined a wild Irish spirit and thirst for travel and adventure with a typically French attachment to his own *pays*, his own corner of France, where he felt his roots to be. Nevertheless, in his youth he travelled widely, first crossing the high seas to America, and then journeying through Siberia in winter and crossing the Gobi desert twice, visiting China, Japan, Australia and New Zealand (where he got lost for two days without food or water). He wandered India for a year, and after an absence of three years finally returned to his beloved family in the Pyrenees. He never again travelled further than Paris or Britain (the Alps once) and spent the rest of his life seeking adventure in the land he loved best.

He climbed every peak on both sides of the Pyrenees, often many times, striding up the mountains on his long legs at an astonishing pace. He made numerous first ascents and was regarded with awe by his peers. He would spend days at a time sleeping out in his trusty sheepskin sleeping bag, often alone, sometimes accompanied by one or two faithful friends or guides. Finally he fell in love with Vignemale, the mountain where he was buried all night on the summit, and in order to spend more time up there had seven caves blasted out at different altitudes. He became known as the hermit of Vignemale, and as his fame spread he became a sort of Harold Acton of the snows, attracting hundreds of fans and admirers to huddle in his remote eyrie. He organized the celebration of mass on the peak of the mountain, and held sumptuous dinners with fine wine and food and Persian rugs spread over the glacier.

Russell's life was in the world above the clouds, an undulating white ocean that cut the peaks off from the earth, his own heavenly kingdom. He lived for wild storms, glorious sunsets, dazzling snow fields, coruscating Spanish sun that left him burnt and exhausted and deep dark nights punctuated by a thousand stars. He was like a lover, completely obsessed with the object of his love, to which he submitted totally. He followed his own songline, listening to different music from everyone else.

For him nature was not a pastoral view to be captured in a watercolour and neatly framed. He revelled in great horizons and impressive spectacles, stormy waves crashing on rocks, frozen forbidding glaciers, dawn illuminating the peaks. The awesome elements that had terrified the valley-dwellers in the past were what Russell loved.

Get to know your own mountain was his advice, and I have. After seven years of seeing Canigou almost every day, I felt I knew its contours and ravines like the palm of my own hand. To know that it would always be there, has been there for millions of years, made me humble.

I have seen it in all its guises: blushed pink by the dawn, sidelit by the sunset as it basks in the final rays from the next valley when we are already in shade, sharp and clear after a wild cleansing wind, etched harshly against the sky, a deep navy blue in the intense southern light. When the inky lines of its contours are encircled by clouds it is reminiscent of a Chinese painting. Sometimes on a clear night it is so brightly illuminated by the moon, it looks as if it has its own electricity supply. Other times we wait for the peak to reappear after days of low cloud obscure it completely.

I see it as I emerge from the supermarket with a groaning trolley or pause in the village as I deposit glass at the bottle bank, which happens to have one of the best views I know. Our first Christmas here we modelled our cake icing on Canigou, with my perfectionist husband studying the Ordnance Survey maps to get the shape exactly right.

The Catalans revere Canigou as their sacred mountain. We have watched them carry their flaming torches from a fire lit specially on the summit every midsummer's eve, a bright trail winding its way down the dark mountain, a beacon to be taken all over French and Spanish Catalonia as far as Barcelona. Hilaire Belloc called it 'the mountain which many who have never heard the name before have been looking for all their lives'.

When we land at Perpignan, it rises ostentatiously over the plain of Roussillon, visible from head to foot, one of the most picturesque peaks of the Pyrenees, needing only vapour puffing out of the top to seem as dramatic as Mount Etna. Driving back from Spain we glimpse it like an old friend, a beacon visible across the great plain of the Empordà. Canigou has always been a lighthouse for mariners and I love to see it floating ghostly in the sky from the shores of the Mediterranean.

Often we drive around the narrow roads which hug its sides, winding through craggy ravines to reach the valley on the other side of the mountain. Or we climb up to the Romanesque monasteries, Saint-Martin-du-Canigou and

Serrabone, holy sanctuaries perched on its rocky flanks.

Our nearest town is Prades, which lies at its foot. I have always liked a town with a mountain at the end of the street. From here Canigou seems close, almost intimate, the red-roofed houses, schools and supermarkets spread commodiously at its base. It looks as if you could stride up in a moment. It has tantalized me, finally taunted me, for years. Though my own natural inclination was more in line with Ruskin, who much preferred to paint and philosophize about the meaning of mountains than actually climb them, I knew I had to get to the top.

I set off with my twelve-year-old son Theo, after several years of French school as French as he is English, early one fresh summer morning. It was still cool at 7 a.m. but we were in the middle of a heatwave and the day would soon be hot. Still I carried a heavy pack with fleeces and water, sunscreen, egg sandwiches, apples and dried apricots, maps, notebook, camera, and binoculars. No Chartreuse.

We travelled by jeep for the first few kilometres of the journey. To walk from the bottom would take at least five hours, and I knew a ten-hour round walk was beyond us. There are several possible routes of varying degrees of difficulty, and driving partway up is dependent on the weather. The snow stays till well into June and then the piste has to be cleared. It is still a very bumpy road requiring considerable skill to negotiate vast potholes and ridges, and sometimes to pass another vehicle with sheer drops to one side and overhanging rocks to the other.

We left from Estoher, a tiny village where the road stops at the foot of the mountain, whose water comes straight from the glacier. My friend Polly lives there, a long-legged Englishwoman who quite frequently strides halfway up the mountainside on walks with her dog. We followed the Llech valley up to Prat-Cabrera, where there were the ruins of an old stone *bergerie* and an astonishing view of the vineyards and limestone cliffs of the Fenouillèdes, slashed by the Galamus gorge and sentinelled with Cathar castles.

Climbing so quickly, the change in vegetation was easily apparent. I have heard it said that mounting Canigou is the best way in France to observe the stages of vegetation at different altitudes, as if making a long voyage from south to north along the same meridian. The difference is most apparent in early spring when the Roussillon features its most characteristic sight, pink peach blossom in flower, while the upper reaches of Canigou are still blanketed with snow.

At its foot oranges and lemons and palm trees grow in sheltered gardens, and there are fields of olives, vines, peaches and plums. At 420 metres the olive is abandoned, at 500m there are no more vines. Beyond 800m the chestnut stops growing and at 1320m the first rhododendrons appear. Beyond 1500m there are no more ferns, asphodels or purple irises.

At 1640m there are still umbrella pines, ash, firs and silver birch, but they are becoming smaller because of the cold, wind and snow. The last forest of fir trees is at 1950m, drawing its water from the granite of the massif, the light clear and luminous, the temperature dropping now, despite the rising sun.

After about an hour and a half we arrived at the refuge of Cortalets at 2100 metres, built by the Club Alpin Français in 1899. During the war it was a sanctuary for local Resistance fighters, whose intimate knowledge of the mountains created many remote and inaccessible hiding places. Still, the refuge was finally attacked by the Germans and left for many years as a burnt-out shell. Now it is restored and again provides a comfortable and substantial refuge for walkers and climbers, with beds and meals available. It is set in a shady area of scattered trees with a wide shallow river running through it, a gentle dreamy space to linger. Beyond is a muddy little lake where wild horses and cows graze. Tiny little yellow birds were hopping and piping around us as if they felt they had nothing to fear from these visitors.

Above us towered the grey pyramid of the summit, and the ridge that curves round and back to its little sister, Pic Joffre, two peaks which make it look as if Canigou has two heads. It is about two hours' climb to the summit, first over grass, then shale and rock. We wended our way, zigzagging slowly, adjusting to the altitude and the effort of climbing, round large boulders and the occasional trickling stream. Soon the scrubby pine trees, gnarled and knotted and clinging to the rocks, ceased, and there were no more rhododendrons, cistus, wild lavender or thyme.

Among the rocks, though, were still tough little juniper bushes, fragrant when rubbed, and a lawn of tiny alpine plants, little stars of pastel pink, purple and cornflower blue. Then only rock. Only rock! I paused, astonished. The rocks are deep red; there is iron in this mountain. 'The magnetic mountain!' said Theo, remembering the stories of planes crashing into it, their instruments sent awry by the magnetism. After that it became a silver mountain, the granite glittering with a silvery patina, and then a golden mountain, mica threaded with quartz. The path was quite beautiful.

It became steeper and narrower as we followed a ridge

running along the side of the mountain. I was glad it was not windy; it felt as if we could easily be blown off. We could not see the summit, only had to believe it was there. It seemed very far away. Theo was wearing sandals, since we only discovered at 6 a.m. that he had left his sneakers at the beach, and had bruised his foot. Grateful for the excuse, I offered to give up. 'It is not that important we get to the top . . .' But he insisted we go on.

'I am not giving up now,' he said. 'I want to do it for you.' But I wanted him to do it for himself.

We compromised by eating some of our egg sandwiches, and I fished out the binoculars from the enormous backpack that was weighing me down at every step. The view was extraordinary, right down the valley to Vernet and to Prades. We could see the blue oval of the lake of Vinça, and with the binoculars peer right up our own Castellane valley to the village of Mosset. We could actually identify our house, the red roof of the monastery, the faint curve of the chapel apse, even, just, the bell tower. How often had I looked this way from there. I imagined my husband, Miles, in his library, listening to Frank Zappa as he wrote his biography. While I pursued the story of a nineteenth-century romantic in the wilds of the Pyrenees, he was writing about one of the high modernists of the twentieth century who spent his life in the urban desert of Los Angeles. It seemed hardly possible that we could find more divergent subjects.

The path wound back and forth round the steep cone of the summit, stones held in place with iron bars and nets. The height felt dizzying, and I was climbing, gasping for breath, with hands as well as feet. Theo was ahead of me, brown legs twinkling along, his golden hair shining in the sun. He waved gleefully from the top as I struggled the last few metres.

One hundred and twenty-two years after Russell's summit burial, I too found myself on top of a mountain, the last great peak before the Pyrenees plunge into the Mediterranean, at 2785 metres a shade lower than Vignemale, but a respectable height none the less. I couldn't stop tears, of relief and triumph.

It was a hot and unusually clear day for summer. The view was all it could be, a god-like 360-degree panorama of our world. We could see right along the coast, the shore a dim blue line, the sea an endless expanse. The view swept down to the Albères, the last low hills before the Pyrenees drop into the sea. Beyond was Spain.

Immediately west is the Cady valley, where there is a steep precipice, and we could see birds swooping below us in complicated aerial games. They were *chocards*, little cousins of the *corbeau*, who live in mountain cavities, and the male feeds the female all year. To the west the Pyrenees begin, blue peaks disappearing into the distance, beginning with Mount Carlit, higher than Canigou though it never looks it, and Madrès, the mountain called mother.

Two hundred years ago you had to climb a mountain to see such an all-encompassing view. These days we take such a lofty perspective for granted, as we fly casually over continents. When I fly over France I love to see the country laid out like a geography book, the coastlines of the Mediterranean and the Atlantic, the secret volcanic valleys of the Massif Central, the granite folds of the Pyrenees, the golden rivers splashed like mercury across the hillsides in the setting sun.

The peak is crowned with an orientation table naming

the winds, in Catalan of course, and all the places in a 360-degree radius, from Toulouse to Barcelona. The other permanent fixture is the iron cross, festooned with the yellow and red striped Catalan flag. It is a replacement for the cross dragged up here by the Resistance after the peak suffered the ignominy of being renamed Pic Pétain at the height of the Vichy government.

That day the summit, not much larger than a couple of parking spaces, was crowded with German tourists eating lunch and taking photos. Theo regretted he had forgotten his *Beano*, which has a regular feature of kids reading the comic in unlikely places. We too ate our remaining sandwiches, crouched on the loose rocks that formed the peak and guiltily pocketed fragments to take home.

I thought then of Russell buried on his mountain top, the Vignemale, a secret mountain in the centre of the Pyrenees. I thought of all the other mountain lovers I knew tucked into the myriad folds of these hills. Of Caty with her menagerie of animals on her windswept plateau above Mosset, Hubert guarding the cows on the Col de Jau, the pilgrims from Lourdes worshipping the Cirque de Gavarnie, the star-watchers on the Pic du Midi, the botanists, geologists, and all the walkers and climbers exploring hidden valleys and deep ravines, refreshing themselves at abundant waterfalls and dipping into icy green tarns.

Unlike Russell I had no intention of spending the night buried on the summit, though I regretted not being able to stay for sunset. Oddly, the first person to record passing the night on the summit of Canigou did so the same year that Russell spent the night on Vignemale, in 1880. He was a Catalan priest, Mossen Frances, who spent the night sheltering in a small stone hut as a storm raged around him. He saw the sun rise like a great red disc out of the sea, and could hear the distant sound of the Angelus calling the faithful to prayer far below. He got out his prayer book and said the first office of the day, high up there on the mountain top.

Theo abandoned trying to phone home on my new mobile phone, and, already wise to the ways of the world, enquired, 'Why are you writing about Henry Russell, mum? He's not famous.' I tried to explain how intrigued I had become by this character.

'I thought by writing about Russell I could understand the Pyrenees better, and understand why people love mountains so much,' I began. I too wanted to share in the Romantic poets' joy on the mountain tops, the great epiphanies of sunsets and wild winds, lose myself cloud-gazing, focus my full attention on the flight of the butterfly or the sound of the wind.

I was also intrigued that Russell was both French and Irish, and wondered how much this combination had affected his personality; what elements of both nation-alities had combined to produce a character so rich and strange. I had brought my son to France aged six, and was watching and wondering how the experience of two cultures and double-track languages would affect and maybe enrich his life.

I asked Theo once if he felt English or French. He said, 'I think I have an English heart,' which seemed a terribly French thing to say. Then he added that he felt more English in France and French in England. He relishes cartoons and films in both languages and seeing a favourite character take on a whole different persona in French.

Football is difficult; he never expresses support for any national side. I think he prefers to hedge his bets, though he did wear an England football T-shirt after the French won the World Cup.

There were other reasons too for my interest in Henry Russell and his mountain tops. I had long been intrigued by the idea of retreat, the desert fathers living in caves far from the world, the hermit who had once lived in our very own chapel down below, the monks who had built the monastery there, tucked into a quiet remote valley. I had tried to write about our monks, tried to understand the monastic experience, their ability to separate themselves from the world, and to enter fully into their contemplations. It seemed to me that there were echoes of their retreat in Russell's escape to the mountains, as he literally rose above the world. His desire for remote caves resonated with those of the desert fathers in Egypt, St Francis in his rocky retreat, even of the hired hermits in the follies of eighteenth-century English gardens.

I thought too of my brother, who until he died of AIDS had been a parish priest, sustained by regular retreats to the holy islands of Iona and Bardsey, who liked nothing better than to sit and contemplate the sea and the sky for hours on end. What did he find there? My own desire to escape city life and live in the wilderness had been partly motivated by such a desire. To try to appreciate beauty with such full attention, and to find out what was left when everything else was taken away. Who would be left. I suppose it was a test of strength.

It was time to descend. I found it hard, noticing the altitude as I tried to catch my breath, developing a headache from the strong sun despite my hat, aware that solar radiation is twice as intense at 1800 metres as at sea level. Next day my legs were neatly sunburnt between my shorts and my socks.

Behind us we could hear careful instructions being given. 'Step here, stone there, right a bit, *tout droit, tout droit*, more stones . . . big step.' I turned to see a white stick and realized a blind man was being guided down the mountain. We wondered about his experience, how intense it must be without sight, the sense of space, the abyss below, the smells, the caress of the wind, stones crunching underfoot, the sound of the birds. Later we both tried walking a few metres with eyes shut to see how it felt. But I was going so slowly even with my eyes open that the blind man overtook me in the end.

'It looks like the Paramount Pictures logo, floating above the clouds like that,' observed Miles of Canigou, as cynical as I am romantic, as we sat on the terrace later that week with a glass of wine. I sat in smug contemplation of the summit in the distance, while Miles equally typically was facing the building, eyeing the Romanesque arches of the cloister, blocked up with stones since the monastery became a farm after the Revolution, still waiting to be opened and restored. Our conversation turned inevitably to jobs still to be done. It was windy, and the newspaper blew off the table and across the garden. 'How wonderful to rebuild the cloister walls,' said Miles wistfully. 'That would stop the wind.' Then we had our usual argument about what height the walls would have been. Already some of the trees had grown tall enough to partly obscure the view of Canigou. I argued that the monks would have wanted to see it, that contemplation of beauty would have been part of their meditation. Miles disagreed. 'Surely the point of a cloister is that they were cut off from the world, concentrating on spiritual things, not picturesque views. Anyway, I thought people used to be afraid of mountains?'

2

There be dragons

'The immensity of the aerial summits excited, when they suddenly burst upon my sight, a sentiment of ecstatic wonder not unallied to madness.'

Percy Bysshe Shelley.

It was true. Mountains were not always considered beautiful. There are times when Canigou does indeed look forbidding and I can imagine that medieval peasants were afraid of the immense mysterious monster looming above them. During one cold winter we went to have dinner with our English academic friends, Gary and Fiona Peters, who spend their holidays in Fillols, the village at the highest altitude on Canigou. We dined well on Fiona's excellent roast *gigot* of lamb and made serious inroads into Gary's wine cellar, and ended up staying the night rather than drive the dark and treacherous road back home again. Next morning we went for a hangover walk under a granite grey sky threatening rain, a chilly wind sending us all back for gloves and hats. In the street we encountered their neighbour in her flowery pinafore, voluble about the weather, and eager to present them with her latest apricot jam. As we left the village and surmounted a ridge, accompanied by several of the village dogs, we could see the lower contours of Canigou, scarred with bare rocks and gouged by gloomy ravines. It did not look beautiful, I had to concede. Gary, a lecturer in aesthetics, with cropped silver hair and neatly trimmed beard, shivered and shoved his hands deeper into the pockets of his black leather jacket. Oblivious to the noise of yapping dogs, or indeed his own children tumbling around him, he began to explain theories of landscape, that it all depended on who was looking at it. Mountains, he averred, were neither ugly nor beautiful. It was all in the eye of the beholder.

'Someone's response to beauty, to landscape, depends on what they are looking for. Things are not inherently beautiful, it depends on how you experience them,' Gary explained. We watched a lone orange tractor heading up the steep slope opposite. 'Canigou as a spectacle is just a mountain. To experience beauty you have to put yourself into the picture. It's about your response.' He had not always taken pleasure in country scenery, he said with a rueful laugh. 'After I left school I worked on a farm for four years, and then I hated the country. I certainly couldn't see any beauty in it!'

Until about two hundred years ago it was a common idea that mountain peaks harboured horrors of all kinds, from dragons to vengeful gods; they inspired terror not romantic notions. One bishop believed the devil had been allowed to add mountains to the world after the fall of man. The idea of mountains being enjoyed for their beauty is recent; they were useless for agriculture, difficult and dangerous to cross, certainly harboured villains if not dragons and were generally thought to be ugly, referred to as deserts and 'horrible precipices'. The peaks did not even have a word in peasant vocabulary. 'Alps' referred only to the slopes. (Even today the sherpas of Nepal have no word for the summit of a mountain.)

To climb mountains for inspiration or pleasure was considered thoroughly outlandish if not downright wicked. The Italian poet Petrarch is usually credited with the first recorded ascent of a mountain expressly to see the view, when he climbed Mount Ventoux in Provence in 1336, but Pierre III of Aragon made an ascent of Canigou a century earlier, an expedition considered so outrageous he made his two companions swear an oath of secrecy before they set off. An account of the climb, by monk Fra Salimbene, preserved in the Vatican, begins, 'Mons Canigosus. This mountain, never has man inhabited it and never has the son of man dared to climb it, so great is its height, so difficult and painful the ascent thereof.' He describes the terror of their journey up, the thunder and lightning, wind and hail. Eventually Pierre's companions were so terrified they collapsed and Pierre went on alone. He threw a stone into a lake near the peak, from which, he reported, there appeared 'an enormous and terrible dragon, which flew, obscuring the air and covering the whole mountain in shadow'.

But surely not everyone had been afraid of mountains? Did those monks who chose such magnificent locations for their monasteries really only have practical considerations in mind, a remote eyrie, a source of water, good pastures? Were they blind to beauty? There was plenty of evidence of mountains as potent religious symbols; the early Christian mystic Theodoros said 'a mountain is the image of the soul rising in meditation'. Muhammad sought the quiet and solitude of the hills for his meditations.

In the Far East mountain landscapes have always been revered. Mount Fujiyama has always been considered sacred in Japan. Thousands of pilgrims still climb to the

3728m summit every year. In China landscapes were painted on scrolls, kept in carved chests and only taken out on special occasions, so it was a fresh experience every time they were looked at. Mountains were worshipped as gods and the tallest mountain was believed to be the god of the country. The Chinese phrase for 'going on a pilgrimage' means literally 'paying one's respects to the mountain'. The Chinese Taoist poet Li Po was only one of many mountain hermits who sought poetic inspiration in landscape, and believed in living in harmony with nature.

The Hindu religion is full of stories of dwellers on high mountains, mahatmas – 'great souls' – devoting their time to contemplating the universe, far from the emanations of ordinary mortals. They believed that the air circulating round the tops of mountains of great altitude was very pure and thus improved the mahatmas' spiritual vision. Native Americans believed that the earth was the mother and the sky the father and that mountains united the two.

Henry Russell fits into this ancient tradition; he was closer to the Chinese Buddhist monks than to the Victorian explorers who were his contemporaries. He had no desire to dominate the natural world; he understood that he was a part of nature.

Still, it was well into the eighteenth century before most Westerners regarded mountains and the natural landscape as something to be marvelled at and sought out for pleasure or inspiration. Rousseau, one of the eighteenth century's bestselling authors, started it all with his celebration of natural beauty, rustic pleasures, and especially mountain scenery. The Romantic poets caught on fast. Lord Byron, for one, said he tried 'to lose my own wretched identity in the majesty, and the power, and the glory, around, above and beneath me'. Wilderness became all the rage, and carefully laid out English gardens became infested with lakes, rocky crags, grottoes and even resident hermits.

Most of the poets were just looking, however. It was still rare and eccentric to actually try to climb the mountains, so most people had no idea of the view of the earth from above. It was not until 1783 that the Montgolfier brothers made their first balloon ascent, causing the spectators to embrace each other and weep, and feel as if a path had been opened to the heavens.

The Enlightenment desire for knowledge based on experience rather than scripture stimulated a wave of exploration, and climbing mountains offered the opportunity to explore virgin territory. Poetry and science were not natural enemies in those days, and hand in hand with the focus on the natural landscape as a suitable subject for painting and poetry went the development of interest in natural science, the study of plants, geology, and the strange slow-moving rivers of ice called glaciers that nobody could figure out. (They were regularly exorcised by the bishops to be on the safe side.) People began to investigate nature for themselves, setting out armed with microscopes and barometers to collect specimens of flowers and beetles, study rock strata and analyse the components of the air.

However, observation from reality was often considered subversive since in the process it cast doubt on sacred ideas and theories enshrined in church doctrine. For anyone who has ever yawned over diagrams of U-shaped glacier valleys or ox-bow lakes it is hard to believe that only two hundred years ago the new subject of geography was considered blasphemous. Geology presented another challenge, since it was difficult to combine theories about the gradual evolution of the earth's crust with the biblical theory of Creation-in-a-week which was accepted without question by most people until late into the nineteenth century. An Irish bishop, James Ussher, worked out by counting generations back from the birth of Christ that God had begun creating the world at 9 a.m. on Monday 23 October, 4004 BC.

To establish scientifically the formation of the earth, the slow processes of erosion and upheaval, compression and explosion, was difficult when all subscribed to the biblical account of the Flood, and the idea that the entire earth had then been covered in water. To imply that glaciers might have done more than God to create the world fatally undermined fundamental Christian beliefs.

Genuine attempts to get to the tops of mountains only really began towards the end of the eighteenth century with Horace-Bénédict de Saussure, professor of natural history in Geneva, who started the Alpine craze. From an early age he was obsessed with the peaks he could see from his home town, and Mont Blanc in particular, which he believed was the highest mountain in Europe, if not the world. Saussure spent thirty years travelling in the mountains, though mainly by mule in the valleys, smartly turned out in a purple silk frock coat. His observations, published as *Voyages dans les Alpes* in 1786 and 1796, were to be enormously important, despite his problems trying to combine geology and the Bible.

Saussure began his climb of Mont Blanc on 2 August 1787, and made it to the summit the next day. It was a propitious moment in the history of mountain exploration

since the very same day in the Pyrenees Louis-François
Elisabeth-Ramond de Carbonnières was climbing the Pic
du Midi, and was about to launch the same passion for the
mountains on the southern border of France as Saussure
had inspired for the Alps to the east. As the first to write
about all aspects of the Pyrenees, scientific, geological,
botanical and cultural, Ramond is regarded as the father of
pyrénéisme, the Saussure of the Pyrenees.

He came from Strasbourg, studied to become a lawyer
and had a distinguished political career, but he also liked to
travel and met Goethe, Voltaire and the naturalist Buffon,
developing a taste for both nature and literature which was
to stay with him all his life. Early excursions to Switzerland
gave him a taste for mountains, and he was as intrigued by
the glaciers as he was by the lives of the mountain dwellers.
His translation of Coxe's *Tour in Switzerland* was well
received, and William Wordsworth cites Ramond's own
annotated observations of nature as a primary inspiration
for several verses about the Alps.

Ramond became secretary to Cardinal Rohan, archbishop of Strasbourg and a close intimate of Louis XVI; he
led a life of political intrigue and high luxury in Paris and
Versailles, abruptly brought to an end when Rohan fell
from favour and was banished to the recently fashionable
spa of Barèges in the centre of the Pyrenees. While the
cardinal took the waters, Ramond seized the chance to
abandon his powdered wig and lace ruff, and explore the
mountains. Above Barèges is the Pic du Midi de Bigorre,
standing proudly forward of the main chain of the
Pyrenees and thus long thought to be the tallest mountain
of the range. (Canigou and the Pic du Midi were long
rivals for the accolade, since both stand alone and give

the appearance of being taller than the peaks behind.)

The maps available at the time were often merely fanciful, none were quite the same, and some included peaks that did not exist, or put them in the wrong place. 'Maps of Japan are as accurate as maps of the Pyrenees published by the Academy of Sciences,' Ramond grumbled. 'There are valleys represented as mountains, enormous mountains substituted by valleys and dozens of lakes forgotten.' No-one knew anything about the mountains beyond what they could see from the plain, or from the few narrow passes which led over into Spain. Only the shepherds and smugglers knew the paths.

Ramond was deeply affected by his climb of the Pic du Midi. He was a man of his time, of the *siècle des lumières* as the French call the Enlightenment, ready to think for himself and challenge the accepted ideas of the past. He grasped eagerly the chance to broaden his knowledge and understanding of the world and realized the value of the perspective he gained from the mountain summit.

The experiences of Saussure and Ramond could hardly have been more different. Mont Blanc was of course 2000 metres higher, and therefore a more dangerous and expensive challenge. Inevitably much more planning and equipment were required. But the key difference was in the spirit of the attempts.

When he reached the summit of the Pic du Midi Ramond made a momentous discovery. 'One look was sufficient. The chaos was unravelled, and I had no longer any doubt as to the relative height of its various mountains, or the road towards the principal elevations. Many ranks of mountains rise in succession, like a vast amphitheatre, from the Pic du Midi as far as the frontiers of Spain.'

Seeing before him the snows and gleaming glaciers above the Cirque de Gavarnie he realized that there were many peaks higher than the one on which he stood. He saw Mont Perdu, which he was convinced must be the highest of the chain, and determined to climb it. The name alone, the lost mountain, conveys how little it was known at that time, regarded with awe and terror from afar.

Ramond on his mountain top was immediately smitten by a feeling of 'vague content, that lightness of body, that agility of limb, and that serenity of mind, which are all so sweet to experience, but so difficult to paint'. He resolved to write about the Pyrenees as Saussure had done for the Alps, and, accompanied by local guides, clambered all over the centre of the chain, opening up new routes and climbing peaks as yet unknown.

His botanical observations were invaluable and the collection of dried plants he assembled remains a precious relic, preserved in the museum at Bagnères-de-Bigorre, specimens of flowers and herbs all carefully labelled in brown ink, the French script clearly readable two hundred years later. The *Ramondia myconi*, a rare violet primula with yellow stamens that grows on limestone between 600 and 1900 metres, was named after him.

Every evening he cut himself a new quill pen and mixed his ink, and carefully noted his observations, from the colour of the grass to the taste of Spanish wine, the quality of milk given him by a shepherd, or the beauty of a gentian. Nothing escaped his curiosity. He was enraptured by country life, and had a romanticized picture of peasant existence, their simple, self-sufficient life striking him as a fine model for the free, liberated being that Enlightenment and Revolution had promised. He writes with the wide-eyed enthusiasm of a back-to-nature *soixante-huitard*, as the French survivors of the student revolution of 1968 are affectionately known. The scenes he describe sound like the rococo drawings that figured on the *toiles de Jouy* fabrics popular at the time: the scented grass, warm sun and sheep in the shade watched by jolly shepherdesses. He even abandoned his crampons and took to climbing barefoot in imitation of the country folk.

His *Observations dans les Pyrénées* was published in 1789, not an ideal publication date in retrospect, but it was nevertheless very popular, combining his detailed observations of nature with the romantic spirit of Rousseau. It became the Bible of the Pyrenees. The book was translated into English in 1813 and his romantic depictions of the landscape were to inspire a whole generation of mountain lovers, both French and English, not least Henry Russell. Fifty years later Russell and his friends would found the Société Ramond, devoted to the discovery of the Pyrenees and named in honour of the pioneer explorer.

That, at least, is the French version. But while Ramond was pontificating on the Pic du Midi, the English were already busily exploring for themselves. Despite Ramond, the French were a long time in taking up the challenge and for the next sixty years or more it was the British who really discovered the Pyrenees, as it was the British who first developed the Riviera and the Alps.

So British was Pyrenean exploration during the nineteenth century that the Société Ramond itself (established in 1864, predating the Club Alpin Français) was overwhelmingly British when it was founded. Of the founder members two were British, the barrister explorer Charles Packe and the aptly named photographer Farnham

Maxwell Lyte; the third was anglophile Emilien Frossard, who was married to an Englishwoman. The fourth was Count Henry Russell-Killough, Le Grand Russell himself, who was mahatma, Ramond and Saussure rolled into one.

Henry Russell took the quest for the Sublime to the ultimate. He was determined to fully experience the awe and fear which according to Edmund Burke in his classic treatise, 'A Philosophical Enquiry into the Origin of Our Ideas of the Sublime and the Beautiful', was the essential combination of the Sublime. It was, said Burke, 'tranquillity tinged with terror', resulting from intense experiences that were 'productive of the strongest emotion which the mind is capable of feeling'. As the Sublime became fashionable in the eighteenth century, travellers began to seek out volcanoes, glaciers, raging rivers and waterfalls, oceans and deserts, dramatic sights that would arouse such emotion, preferably from a safe vantage point.

When we returned to the cosy philosophers' house in Fillols that winter's day, for *café au lait*, warm *croissants* and the neighbour's luscious apricot jam, Gary explained what was meant by the Sublime. 'Beauty is about being in a certain harmony with the world, imposing order on it. It is essentially communicable, something we can share. But the Sublime goes beyond what we know. Immanuel Kant put it this way: "Beauty charms, the Sublime moves." ' Gary continued talking as he rescued his small son Francis, who was teetering dangerously on a tall kitchen stool in an attempt to reach the sweetie jar. 'The idea of the sublime experience, pleasure mixed with pain, goes back to Aristotle. The Sublime is something that is overpowering, that exceeds our comprehension. Beauty is pleasurable because it is containable, understandable. The Sublime is excessive, unsettling, a bit like vertigo. Something you can no longer grasp.'

He laughed. 'It's like the attraction of philosophy for me – I am most interested in thinking myself to a point where things don't make sense any more.' Gesturing out of the window, to the skeletal trees and grey clouds hovering over the hillside, he added, 'It is like a horizon, a fascination with the other side, getting to the edge of what you know. The post-modernists love the Sublime, because it is all about blasting open rational Western thinking, the idea that you can truly know anything.'

Daunted by philosophy, one chilly winter evening I curled up with a novel in an old leather armchair by the woodstove in the monks' fireplace. It was no ordinary novel, mind, indeed a novel from a time when reading fiction was considered a distinctly racy occupation, never indulged in before lunch. *The Mysteries of Udolpho* by bestselling author Mrs Radcliffe, was first published in 1794. It was the Peter Mayle of its time, one of the first novels to be set in the Pyrenees, its romantic descriptions of the mountains inspiring many readers to travel. *The Mysteries of Udolpho* had it all: gloomy chateaux, hidden treasure, sinister forests, deep mountain gorges and remote monasteries. The lonely heroine, who suffers an interminable series of misfortunes, sits dreaming at her casement window, playing her lute and composing poetry. The landscape is constantly invoked to create an atmosphere of Gothic horror, and the distant and mysterious Pyrenees made a perfect setting.

It was one of the most popular novels of its time and is still in print after two hundred years. Mrs Radcliffe and her genre became a cliché, often inspiring other writers and poets. After her novel *The Italians* was published, cloaks, slouch hats and black whiskers were fashionable for a while among young gentlemen. It was even rumoured that Byron had modelled himself on one of Mrs Radcliffe's sultry heroes. Jane Austen parodies her style in *Northanger Abbey* where the hero pours scorn on Catherine Morland's preference for romantic novels. In *Sense and Sensibility*, Edward despises Marianne's romantic taste in novels: 'She would have every book that tells her how to admire an old twisted tree.'

The Mysteries of Udolpho had many imitators, among them *The Abbot of Montserrat or The Pool of Blood* by William Child Green, *The Romance of the Pyrenees* by Catherine Cuthbertson and *The Maniac of the Pyrenees* by John Shipp. In 1796 the *Critical Review* remarked acerbically, 'Since Mrs Radcliffe's justly admired and successful romances, the press has teemed with stories of haunted castles and visionary terrors; the incidents of which are so little diversified, that criticism is at a loss to vary its remarks.'

But Mrs Radcliffe's novel had one major drawback. Mrs Radcliffe never went anywhere near the Pyrenees or even to France. Her descriptions of the landscape, the yawning abysses, rushing waterfalls and awesome peaks, were based entirely on Ramond and his *Observations*, which she must have read in the original French edition.

For Mrs Radcliffe and for a generation of English voyagers the Pyrenees was a romantic adventure. It was a country of the mind, a Gothic backdrop for the English imagination. Only when I began to read her book, snug in my very own crumbling monastery, did I realize that I had succumbed, rather late, to the nineteenth-century passion for romantic ruins in the Pyrenees. I had, it seemed, bought the whole package: the frescoed chapel echoing with the lost anthems of the monks, the stone arches of the cloister in the moonlight, the dim dappled forest grove, the cypresses and olives framing a picturesque view of the mountains.

Perhaps somewhere there exists a faded watercolour or carefully penned description of our monastery as it was at the beginning of the nineteenth century. How delicious would those Victorian wanderers have found this ancient building had they chanced upon it one day. After the French Revolution, when church property was confiscated by the state, the monks had fled, abandoning the monastery to be torn apart by the villagers. What a frisson of delight and shivers of horror would they have felt at the sight of the skeletal cloisters, the bats darting between the smashed arches, the bell tower silent, its bells melted down. How they would have shivered at the thought of the ghosts in the cemetery, or peered hopefully into the remains of the crypt and contemplated the possibility of buried treasure, or listened to the peasants' tales of secret passages connected to the ancient church on the other side of the river. It would have answered all their romantic longings at a stroke, as it did mine, almost two hundred years later.

I had no idea when I wrote about my own escape to the Pyrenees that I was part of a publishing genre of such antiquity. It was only as I began to investigate this first wave of English ex-pats that I discovered there were dozens of nineteenth-century versions. In the 1830s and 1840s a new book was published almost every year on travelling in the Pyrenees. I burrowed deep into the dusty bowels of the London Library, handled precious volumes tied up with pink ribbon in the Rare Manuscripts Room of the British Library and even made occasional hits in the Internet world of antiquarian books, though most of the volumes were rare and expensive.

Books by women and leisured reverend gentlemen predominated. Mrs Boddington, Lady Chatterton and Selina Bunbury had wandered far and wide, botanizing, sketching and patronizing the natives, sometimes carried by sedan chair to astonishing precipices. Anglican clergymen brandished Bibles and lamented the pagan state of the French, while investigating archaeological sites and pocketing rock crystals. Among my favourites were *A Peep at the Pyrenees* by a Pedestrian, an author too modest to reveal his name, and *Travels in the Pyrenees* by V. C. Scott O'Connor, with its photos of picturesque peasants washing clothes on the river banks and barefoot gypsies with monkeys on chains. The one I most coveted was *The Pyrenees. A Description of Summer Life at French Watering Places* by Henry Blackburn with its illustrations by Gustave Doré, gloomy engravings which perfectly captured the brooding mystery of the mountains.

Gradually my bookshelves filled with nineteenth-century travel books, my walls with maps of the Pyrenees and even more photographs of sunsets and mountains. My defiantly cerebral husband's contribution was a French surrealist text on climbing an invented mountain. I struggled through hair-raising accounts of death-defying climbs in English and French, several decades of the journal of the Société Ramond and the Alpine Club journal, in pursuit of the English in the Pyrenees and, most of all, Count Henry Russell himself.

3

A peek at the Pyrenees

'Such as are not acquainted with the mountains of the first order, can have no idea of that golden and transparent hue, which tinges the highest summits of the earth.'

Ramond de Carbonnières

There were plenty of contemporary mountain lovers in our little village, I discovered. Mosset is a typical Pyrenean village, still remote from the world, perched on the side of the fertile Casterllane valley, terraced with peach and cherry orchards, cow pastures and stone farms and cottages. To the west the valley narrows, the sides are thickly forested and the rounded hills beyond seem to enclose it. Henry Russell would have known many such villages in the nineteenth century, as he wandered over the mountains, stopped to dine in a small *auberge*, at a wooden table beside a smoky fireplace, picked up supplies – legs of lamb, bread and bottles of wine – and hired his guides.

In those days, though, Mosset would have been much busier, supporting a population entirely dependent on the land, with several iron forges on the banks of the fast-flowing river and a constant stream of goods transported up the valley by mules. Until recently such villages had changed little since the Middle Ages, the peasants raising livestock and growing food for themselves with a bit extra to sell. In winter they huddled by the fireside, in summer headed off to the hills to graze the animals, sheltering in the *cortals*, rudimentary shacks of wood and stone.

Like many of these villages today Mosset is hanging on to its identity with a frail but tenacious grasp. There are still peasants in Mosset, old folk who tend their vegetable gardens religiously, slaughter a pig from time to time and can occasionally be seen scything the grass in the old way. The *transhumance* is still practised, when in spring the cattle follow ancient trails to pasture in the high mountains, and in the autumn are brought back down to the lower valleys again, though now it is subsidised by the EU, as part of an effort to keep these mountain communities alive.

Until a few years ago the village seemed to be in inevitable decline. Young people had abandoned the harsh rural life and left for the city, shops and cafés had closed, the population had dropped and many of the houses were shuttered most of the year. In the last few years, however, it has seen signs of revival, with a healthy leavening of incomers seeking a simpler country life, free from pollution and surrounded by mother nature. Retired people have returned to the village of their childhood and taken up walking, exploring old footpaths, and rediscovering the abandoned ruins and ancient dolmens where they once played. Idealistic young families have arrived with their children, and saved the little village school from closure. Up in the hills are modern hermits looking after refuges, guarding sheep, growing vegetables, their lives as simple and primitive as medieval peasants'. Then there are the foreigners, the artists, potters, carpenters, photographers and writers who have also helped to keep the village alive with art exhibitions, a village library, farm accommodation and donkey trekking. Mosset prides itself on the number of nationalities represented: Spanish, Dutch, Belgian, Swiss, Swedish, English, Spanish, even Chileans – refugees from Pinochet's regime, who have found consolation in these mountains for the Andes of their homeland.

I sat with some of my Dutch friends on the café terrace one evening just as the sun was sinking behind us and bathing the valley in a golden reflected glow, catching the tip of Canigou like an ice cream cone. Gerard, an artist who has been here almost thirty years, expressed his appreciation of the view and ordered wine. As Mosset's first foreigner he is something of an institution, and is responsible for one of the most astonishing transformations in the village, growing a splendid verdant municipal garden on what was the building site surrounding the new *mairie* (town hall). I often see him, his compact form still lithe, though his skin is deeply tanned and lined from years of sun and wind, crouched over a tender new plant. 'Of course I find mountains exciting,' he said when I asked. 'I'm a Dutchman!' He poured red wine from a small earthenware pitcher. 'There is so much more surface, so much more variety. At every turn there is another view.' Lettie, the Dutch potter, with her streaked blond topknot and rosy face, who always looks to me as if she has walked out of a Vermeer painting, agreed with Gerard. 'Holland is so flat. My friends say there are no stones left in Holland now. So when they come here they take stones back home with them,' she says mournfully.

Strolling up the village street was Skall, followed by several faithful dogs. Skall was now living in the *cortal* high up on the hillside where Gerard had spent several years alone, a basic stone shack with no water, no electricity and no road, used originally in the summer when cows were taken up to the high pastures. Skall, an Austrian nomad, is fired by the enthusiasm and vague goodwill of the rainbow tribe, a loose coalition of ecologically minded hippies, determined to live self-sufficiently in harmony with the earth, right down to his clothes, which are an extraordinary patchwork of leather he has tanned and stitched himself. Now he has been joined in his mountain refuge by several others, living in tepees, growing their own vegetables and baking bread in a primitive outdoor oven they constructed themselves.

Later I had dinner with my friends Henri and Monique, in Monique's tiny Hansel and Gretel house with its turquoise shutters and lace curtains. Over a meal of leek soup, and pork with a sauce of morel mushrooms, gathered by Henri (known as the Emperor of Cèpes hereabouts) and bottled by Monique, they told me about their mountain walks, showing me photographs of high windblown ridges and views to stretch the eyes. When I told them of my interest in Henry Russell, Henri rushed off to find books for me, returning with well-thumbed copies, bound in vellum cream and red, of works by the Frères Cadier, a crack team of five mountaineering brothers who were protégés of the famous Count, whom they honoured as 'the eagle of the Pyrenees'.

Monique and Henri walk in the mountains for the sheer pleasure of it, rarely with a specific peak in mind, but simply to revel in the air and light and freedom of the high slopes. It is an experience that unites them like no other, these two, from opposite ends of France. Henri is a Catalan, stocky, bullish and argumentative, chestnut brown from his years working in the vineyards around Perpignan. Monique, a social worker in our local town of Prades, is a cool blonde northerner from the Vosges, who likes her mountains snowy, preferably on skis. They are *pyrénéistes* not *alpinistes*, more interested in exploring than enduring. 'It's nice to get to the top,' said Monique, 'but that's not why you do it.' After an hour or so at table Henri was restless, keen to be active, to get back to his dogs, his vegetable garden and chickens or best of all to go hunting, for *la chasse* (hunting) is his great passion. 'In the mountains he is a like a man unchained,' laughed Monique.

Henri poured the last of the wine, and confided with the tone of a true connoisseur, 'It tastes so much better on a mountain top!'

So that was why Henry Russell never climbed without a couple of bottles of good Bordeaux.

I wanted to learn more about these mountain lovers and about Henry Russell; it was time for me to leave my little corner, my fireside and my own mountain, and head west. I planned a trip to Pau and Béarn in the Western Pyrenees, epicentre of *les anglais* in the nineteenth century and where Count Henry Russell was based for most of his life. Travelling by train to Pau, from one end of the Pyrenees to the other, offers in good weather a view of the mountains almost as good as a plane's, and it unfolds more slowly. The journey provides an excellent geography lesson, more vivid than any I experienced at school, as we cross France from east to west, from the gentle Grande Bleue of the Mediterranean sea to the powerful waves and vast horizons of the Atlantic ocean.

It was clear I needed a basic grasp of the geography I

had once studied so reluctantly. For that matter, I realized with a sinking heart, as Miles patiently explained theories of plate tectonics yet again, I probably needed the history of geography. Once people began to relinquish the biblical Flood theory, new ideas about mountain formation, glaciers and the age of rocks grew up and have been vigorously debated ever since. I had begun reading one of the old travel books from my shelves, the *Book of the Pyrenees* by Sabine Baring-Gould, published in 1907, enjoying its red binding embossed with gold, thick ivory pages and faded nineteenth-century black and white photographs. Baring-Gould was a prolific writer and wrote numerous books on France, not to mention the biographies of 3600 saints and the words to 'Onward Christian Soldiers'. (His name had a nagging familiarity until I remembered I must have seen it many times when I studied the hymnbook during boring church sermons as a child.) He visited southern France as a boy; near Pau he uncovered some mosaics, paying the workmen out of his own pocket money. While his book was hardly up to date, Baring-Gould explained the geography in a clear if ponderous style I could understand.

The Pyrenees resulted when two continental land masses crashed against each other over 65 million years ago, a violent process which lifted the land mass several thousand metres. Marine fossils have been found on the limestone cliffs of Gavarnie and the summit of Mont Perdu, proving that these heights were once under the sea. The dramatic action also compressed the lumps of granite, now smoothed by time, which form the backbone of the range. The limestone sediment which once lay on the seabed was carved by powerful rivers into the gorges which divide the range into steep valleys and the high plateaux which are now protected national parks, the Parc National des Pyrénées on the French side and the Parque Nacional de Ordesa y Monte Perdido in Spain.

There is still some seismic activity in the Pyrenees – this I know from personal experience after an early visit to Mosset, staying in a friend's house, a converted mill on the riverside. I was woken by the bed shuddering dramatically, and it felt as if the house was about to take off. I thought at first that the gas tank in the kitchen had exploded but Miles woke up and mumbled with typical British phlegm, 'Oh, it's probably an earthquake,' and went back to sleep. It turned out that it had been quite a dramatic tremor, wrecking houses in the epicentre of nearby Saint-Paul-de-Fenouillet.

The Pyrenees run at an angle from north-west to south-east so to talk of Spain to the south and France to the north is not strictly accurate, but perhaps the early mapmakers can be forgiven for getting so much of it wrong. The chain effectively cuts off the Spanish peninsula from France, with only the coastal routes and a few neighbouring passes providing easy communication.

The two sides of the chain, which is about 450 kilometres long, are quite dramatically different, even more so than the contrast between east and west. On the Spanish side the mountains spread further and when they do flatten out the plains are still high, so there is less sense of drama in the contrast, and no view from Spain as spectacular as the view from France. Nevertheless, about two-thirds of the 55,000 square kilometres of the area covered by the Pyrenees are actually in Spain.

The climate either side is also very different. The

French side gets plenty of rain from the north-west Atlantic winds and is thus more verdant, with snow, ice, waterfalls, meadows and forests, and according to Baring-Gould with his distinct preference for the north, 'hillsides that sparkle with villages smiling in prosperity'.

The Spanish Pyrenees is one of the dryest places in Europe. Baring-Gould writes: '. . . on the southern slope the eye ranges over barren rocks, sun-baked, scanty pastures, and here and there at long intervals occur squalid clusters of stone hovels, scarce fit to shelter goats, yet serving as human habitations'. To see the baked red plain of Spain from one of the high passes of these mountains is to understand why it has always been said that Africa begins at the Pyrenees.

The mountains do not form an unbroken range but rather two with a gap in the middle which encloses the Valle de Arán, an odd anomaly of a place, technically on the French side of the watershed but due to one of the many dodgy deals between distant potentates now part of Spain. Its geography has kept it still one of the most remote and unspoilt valleys of the Pyrenees, without road access until 1948, and with one of the richest collection of Romanesque churches anywhere. Even now throughout the Pyrenees the jumbled complex of valleys, massifs and peaks, high plateaux and mountain pastures, and silent beech, fir and pine forests keep many secrets.

On the northern side strong river torrents have cut deep valleys, plunging down to the plain, where they become important rivers, the Aude, the Garonne and the Adour, and wind their way, fertilizing the plain and eventually pouring into the Atlantic and the Mediterranean. On the Spanish side of the watershed it is more complicated since the valleys tend to run parallel to the main axis and are thus more inaccessible. The rivers wander east and west until they arrive at the Ebro plain in the middle of Spain.

The passes over the natural frontier of the central ridge have always been of critical importance, crossed for centuries by traders, smugglers, pilgrims, soldiers and refugees. But the *ports*, as they are called, are high, there are few natural breaches in the chain and rare is the pass lower than 2000 metres. Even today only a handful are accessible by road and still remain subject to the rigours of the weather, the automobile vanquished by the Pyrenean winter.

Travelling across France from east to west the vegetation changes, the crops vary and the traditional architecture reflects the available local material, from the terracotta tiles and ochre mortar of the Mediterranean coast to the grey schist slates and stone of the central Pyrenees and the low-roofed cobblestone farms of the Basque country.

The train left Perpignan, Mount Canigou clear above the coastal plain, with the pale limestone ridge of the Albères, the eastern end of the Pyrenees, rising out of the Mediterranean. First stop is Rivesaltes, its name synonymous for me with the sweet white Muscat wine for which it is famous. The train hugs the coast of the Mediterranean, traversing a narrow track right through the saltwater lagoons, which dazzle the eyes with reflected light. Wind ripples the broad flat expanses of water bordered by tenacious marram grass. Here and there are the attenuated silhouettes of herons, and rose-tinted flamingos defying the laws of nature as they perch on one leg and crane long necks into the waterbed, seeking the shrimp that turn them pink. Piles of rough granular salt indicate salt works and horses graze beside the track. Gulls swoop over the oyster and mussel beds, and only a thin shadowy line divides the lagoons from the open sea.

The houses are all pale ochre and cream and exotic with palm trees. Inland are the hills of the Corbières, bare and scrubby and scarred with white quarries. Fractured castle ruins are reminders of its past as a frontier land and the bloody history of the beleaguered Cathars to whom it offered hopeless sanctuary. A faded sign on a building beside the tracks, Hôtel de la Poste, is a reminder of the days before the railway came when everyone travelled by horse and carriage, changing horses at the posting houses along the way. The fields in between are serried ranks of vines, in winter pruned down to twisted stumps with a strange sculptural beauty. Above the hills I can still see Canigou, now miles away, its distinctive white summit clearly silhouetted against the pale blue sky, beyond it the scalloped border of further snowy peaks.

Ramond's description of two hundred years ago was still a perfect rendering of the view I could see unfurling before me. 'The Pyrenees are seen from a vast distance, and, whatever aspect they present, appear like the Alps to be a stupendous mass of sharp, ragged, and pointed summits, partaking either of the whiteness of the clouds or of the azure of the sky, as they reflect the light or are covered with shadow. Nothing can be more striking than the eastern part of the chain. Situated on the borders of the sea, it unfolds itself as it were in the view of all Languedoc.'

After Narbonne the train turns west towards Carcassonne, the cypresses give way to poplars and the roads are lined with plane trees. Here and there are glimpses of the Canal du Midi, a gentle tree-shaded road of water, its somnolent passage an echo of the slower speed of the past. Still Canigou is visible. It seems even taller seen from a distance, and I understood why the inhabitants believed it to be the highest of all the peaks of the Pyrenees.

As we travelled west patchwork fields of barley, maize and sunflowers appeared. I glimpsed the pepperpot towers of Carcassonne glinting in the sun like a Disneyland castle, then Castelnaudary, a pretty bustling town on the banks of the Canal du Midi, most famous as a contender for the cassoulet crown – Ford Madox Ford claimed the cassoulet he ate in Castelnaudary 'had sat on the fire for the last three hundred years' and I rather regretted not being able to stop for lunch.

Beyond Carcassonne is the Lauragais, a fertile plain of wheat and maize studded with prosperous farms and turreted Renaissance chateaux. Already we have crossed the climatic boundary between the Mediterranean and the Atlantic, marked by Mount Carlit to the east of the Pyrenean chain, the transition between the dry winds and rocky outcrops of the Med and the heavy rains and green pastures of the Atlantic region.

At Toulouse I had to change trains for Pau, so I decided to break the journey to look for Henry Russell's birthplace. The train guard announced the station in the rich accent of the Midi, a final flourish adding a whole extra syllable to the name: 'Toulous-A.' On the platform a young man and woman were kissing in a passionate embrace in the style of Doisneau's famous Paris photo, though I noticed the young man was still clutching his mobile phone in one hand.

It was a clear day and I could still see the Pyrenees, visible on such a day from Toulouse, though the locals remark cynically that if you can see the mountains there will be rain within forty-eight hours. It was nice to think of the great *pyrénéiste* being born within view of his beloved mountains. Perhaps it was one of the first significant sights of his life? His mother was a great walker and mountain lover herself, and would surely have pointed out the distant peaks to her young son.

Russell was born on Valentine's day, 14 February 1834, at no. 25 rue du Cheval Blanc, now rue Mazaret, the name changed in honour of a mayor of Toulouse who perhaps took over the house as well. Certainly his is the only plaque today. On the corner of rue Mazaret and rue d'Astorg is a solid square redbrick town house with white shutters and balconies, with worn iron-barred wooden doors into what would have been a stableyard on the ground floor. It is close to what were once the original ramparts of Toulouse and the church of St Etienne. In those days the house was probably surrounded by vegetable gardens, chickens and stables, and in 1834 St Etienne was a ruin, its statues smashed in the Wars of Religion and the building itself torn down during the Revolution, hardly a pretty sight for ardent Catholics and Royalists like Russell's family. The church also has a monument to salt-tax baron Paul Riquet, ancestor of Russell's mother, who went broke constructing the Canal du Midi, a prodigious engineering work which in 1681 finally linked the Atlantic Ocean and the Mediterranean Sea via the Garonne river. It passes through Toulouse and when Russell was born, before the railways arrived in the south, would still have been a critical, bustling waterway for commercial traffic, especially the transport of wine and wheat.

Henry's birth was registered at the *mairie* in the place du Capitole at the centre of the city, a short walk along the rue de Pomme, a winding street of redbrick dwellings. The baby was named Henry Patrick Marie Russell. (The French spelling of Henri and the double-barrelled Russell-Killough were later affectations.)

In 1834 France was once more a monarchy; Louis Philippe, the bourgeois king, had replaced the Bourbons of the Restoration after a further revolution in 1830. French society was torn between many opposing factions, the socialist revolutionaries, the Royalists and diehard Catholics like Russell's family, and the Romantic painters and poets revelling in the tension and heightened passions of the times.

Henry's parents no doubt appreciated the monarchist sympathies of Toulouse. His father was registered as an Irish gentleman, M. Thomas John Russell. He had left Ireland for France in 1820 at the age of twenty-two, fleeing the oppression of Irish Catholics, and attracted by the restoration of the Catholic monarchy in France after the fall of Napoleon. France was a traditional bolthole for Irish Catholics and the French–Irish connection has resulted in such legacies as Hennessy brandy, and the Bordeaux vineyard of Chateau-Brown.

Thomas John Russell must have been an adventurer and courageous too, to leave his native country and settle in a foreign land. Such actions must have influenced his first-born son. His first wife had died childless, and he then married Henry's mother, Ferdinande Clémentine Aglae Marie Joséphine de Grossolle de Flamarens, a nomenclature indicating her aristocratic origins. Her double name (and double 'de's) allied her with the aristocracy of France and of Belgium, where she had been born during the emigration of French royalists after the Revolution. For the French the 'de', called the *particule*, is of critical importance, denoting an aristocratic background. Critically *de* means from, an attachment to a place, and implies the ownership of land, whereas for the English the important thing is the family name, with or without a title. The key thing is to be member of the clan. The family of the artist Henri de Toulouse-Lautrec, southern French aristocrats who were known to the Russells, thus laid historical claim to two different places, Toulouse and Lautrec. Ferdinande's clutch of names must have comforted Thomas John, who deeply resented his own lack of title, despite claiming descent from the illustrious Russell family, albeit an obscure Irish branch.

These days the strongest foreign influence in Toulouse is Spanish, with late night tapas bars and lots of flamenco. There are a few Irish bars, but then there always seem to be Irish bars. The only remaining taste of old England I could locate was a shop selling pink duffel coats and a bar called the Frog and Rosbif, which had a quiz night and a curry and beer night, sold fish and chips, brewed its own beer and had Sky Sports on the TV. It wasn't quite the kind of history I was looking for, though I had already decided I liked a town where the buskers sang opera and a beggar cuddled a pet rabbit instead of a dog.

After Toulouse the train headed south-west towards Saint-Gaudens, Lourdes and Tarbes. I could still see the mountains in the distance, glaciers glinting in the rays of the sun. In the foreground was a fertile plain of cow pastures, small villages with ox-blood red shutters and witch's hat churches, as peaceful as it had always been. With such a barrier beyond there was little reason for development, and it was so well watered that here agriculture still reigned supreme. At one point an escaped cow trotted along beside the train as if it meant to climb aboard. At Saint-Gaudens a solitary factory looked strangely exotic with its one clump of chimneys belching smoke into the fresh air.

For Ramond the approach to the Pyrenees from the north was the most dramatic, with the Pic du Midi at its most visible, somehow less grandiose than Canigou, despite competing with it to claim, falsely in both cases, to be the highest peak of the Pyrenees. The Pic du Midi looks more as a mountain should, like a child's drawing or as if it has been dumped by an ice cream scoop. The buildings of the famous observatory are visible on the summit, as well as the chains and wires of the cable car, which Hilaire Belloc said made the mountain look as if it was in harness.

Lourdes announces itself early with signs for la Grotte de Bernadette, promises of miracles and hotels offering peace and sanctuary in neon lights. All that can be seen from the train, however, is the *château fort de Lourdes*, a grim thirteenth-century pile which dominated the fortunes of the little village of Lourdes long before Bernadette was persuaded to see visions. Lourdes was the stronghold of the Black Prince in the Hundred Years War, and for centuries after the inhabitants were disparagingly referred to as *les petits-fils* (grandchildren) *des anglais*.

My pilgrimage to Lourdes had a different purpose from most. The château of Lourdes now houses the Musée Pyrénéen, a collection of local artefacts lovingly assembled by Louis le Bondidier, a friend of Henry Russell. Within its stone walls is a huge assemblage of costumes, tools and furniture, precious evidence of centuries of local life from kitchen bowls to cowbells, shepherd's knives to woollen shawls. There is also a small collection of memorabilia from the early Pyrenean mountaineers, a few portraits and busts and several well-worn alpenstocks, the wooden poles which were essential pieces of equipment, about seven or eight feet in length, good for surmounting glaciers, and sometimes used as a glissading pole to slide down slopes, or horizontally as a trapeze over snow bridges. Here too were Russell's own water gourd and compass.

Best of all is the library, which has an unparalleled collection of books on the Pyrenees in both French and English. It yielded almost all of Henry Russell's works, some of them now very rare: guidebooks in English to Pau, the Basque country, and the Pyrenees, *Les Grandes Ascensions*, a guide to climbing the peaks which was among the first of its kind for the Pyrenees, and an early edition of his masterpiece, *Souvenirs d'un Montagnard*.

I sat at a desk overlooking the town and the sanctuary of Lourdes below, the river curving round it, and a helpful library assistant in climbing boots and a thick Aran sweater, who quite clearly would prefer to be marching up mountains than cataloguing them in dusty archives, brought me piles of precious volumes. I loved their leather-tooled bindings and gilt lettering, thick creamy pages, maps and engravings protected by flimsy sheets of tissue paper.

I spent the night in Lourdes, and before supper went to see the sanctuary itself. I ran the gauntlet of souvenir shops, stuffed with Bernadette snow globes, medallions, rosaries, crucifixes and Lourdes holy water in every conceivable container, from large plastic jerry cans to tiny pendants, and cafés with menus in seven or eight languages. I especially relished the Hôtel de Solitude, in a particularly garish noisy street. I found myself walking down to the river which loops round the town. The traffic of nuns and invalids on crutches and in wheelchairs was all heading the same way. A group of miners from the north of France all wore white plastic pit helmets to identify each other. Above us the vast golden basilica glittered in the late sun. For many people a trip to Lourdes is the experience of a lifetime, and despite my natural cynicism I felt overwhelmed by the atmosphere, the feeling of hope and grace in the air.

The sanctuary itself, the rocky grotto by the river where Bernadette saw her visions of the Virgin Mary, is as humble as the basilica is grand. I was amazed by how serene it was, people in prayer by a peaceful wide flowing river, with just the sound of birdsong as a long line of supplicants filed past the rock, touched it and genuflected, kissed it and lit candles.

In the café where I had breakfast to the sound of Cliff Richard and Jimmy Cliff singing 'Many Rivers to Cross', I heard English accents. Two retired policemen from Wythenshawe in Manchester were drinking beer and discussing council house restoration and property prices. On an adjacent table a group of London taxi drivers were waiting for their devout wives and expounding the Knowledge of London geography with a chap from Hong Kong who was trying to recall the address of his old club in Curzon Street. All agreed that Lourdes was very cosmopolitan. 'You can even buy the *Sun*.'

When I talked to the hotel receptionist, a young man named Michel with a crewcut and gold earring above his white shirt and black bow tie, I asked him what he thought of the efficacy of the water of Lourdes. He grinned at me, and said he knew nothing about it, but then added, 'In the World Cup 2002 the Italian team manager scattered Lourdes water on the pitch at a desperate moment – and they scored a goal!' Then, clutching my photocopies of nineteenth-century travellers, and a bottle of Lourdes water, just in case, I continued on my way to Pau and Béarn.

The train track followed the Gave de Pau (*gave* is the local name for river), its wide waters pounding along as it rushes down from the mountains, tumbling rocks and cobbles with it to scatter across the plain, to be painstakingly gathered to build peasant dwellings. Here and there bright orange kayaks swept by, betokening a more recent, leisured class. It was hard to imagine this peaceful region as the scene of bloody fighting between French, English and Spanish at the beginning of the nineteenth century when the British 'freed Spain from the yoke of Napoleon', and as a bonus caught their first sight of the Pyrenees. By 1808 Napoleon had extended his imperial ambitions to Spain, where intermarrying to protect the line had produced a king of Spain who was an idiot, Charles IV. Napoleon replaced him with his own brother, and thus the next Spanish war began, a morass of factional fighting which devastated the country. The English, led by Wellington, joined in, determined to drive the French out of Spain, which was rapidly reduced to plague and famine.

It was a monstrous conflict. I had recently seen the series of engravings by Goya, *The Disasters of War*, in the museum of Castres to the east of Toulouse, and nothing, bar Picasso's *Guernica*, depicts the sheer horror and futility of war with more passion. Goya doggedly drew it all: piles of corpses rotting by the roadside, mutilated bodies, raped women and despairing conscripts.

By 1809 the English appearing in Béarn were most likely to be soldiers staggering into Pau from the horrors of the war. Some were hospitalized there, including several wives, some with new babies born en route, who had accompanied their husbands on the campaign. Apparently sixty women, legitimate wives or picked up on the way, were allowed to accompany each British battalion in the field, though they often ended up in a pitiable state, sometimes forced into prostitution to feed themselves and their children. Some practised a morbid serial monogamy, marrying another soldier if their original husband was killed.

Wellington's army finally crossed the Pyrenees in 1814, driving Napoleon's French army before it. Wellington then occupied most of Aquitaine, where he was welcomed as a liberator by the local populace, who still smarted under French control and resented Napoleon's army. There remained too a folk memory of the *lou tems dous angles*, the time of the English, the fourteenth century when all of Aquitaine was under the control of England. The southwest had remained stoutly Royalist and many harboured hopes of restoration of the old regime. When the troops marched through the streets of Tarbes they cried, '*Vivent les anglais! Vive l'Angleterre!*'

It seems that the English preferred accommodation to pillage. They were well disciplined compared to the Spanish and Portuguese elements of the army, paid for the food they took and were ready to negotiate mutually beneficial terms with the local populace. Bayonne's banker trotted over to see Wellington in Saint-Jean-de-Luz to offer his services.

The British soldiers even discovered the local delicacy of *confit d'oie*, preserved goose, in the course of searching for food in an abandoned village in the midst of the battleground. They needed fat for frying and found pots of it, which when opened turned out to contain entire preserved geese and chickens. A welcome change, after the chickpea diet of Spain.

The English felt as if they had landed in Paradise. After a six-year war marching about six thousand miles across the dry, baked plains and freezing plateaux of Spain, they arrived in Béarn, a land of gentle green pastures, fresh flowing rivers and cool, shady forests. One smitten officer wrote, 'It is so beautiful. I could live here for ever and forget England.' It reminded many of them of their own land. Or rather perhaps the England they had created in their fevered imaginations, an imaginary bucolic England with no industrial revolution filling the skies with smoke. Even in winter, indeed especially in winter, the sun shone on the pristine white peaks of the Pyrenees and the air was as clear as pure water.

How curious though that women stayed at home, stultified by their limited lives, and read titillating tales of fantasy horror set in the Pyrenees, and their menfolk arrived there in reality, escaping real horror, the actuality of war, and found peace and solace.

In letters home the soldiers often complained that they did not have enough time to see the sights. As a change from warfare they began fox-hunting– Wellington always travelled with his own pack of hounds. 'Hunting, that beautiful school of energy and of courage, affords the best training for war,' he declared. They found Béarn perfect for the sport, galloping over hedges and ditches with wild enthusiasm. Just outside Orthez, where one of the last great battles of the war was staged, a group of French cavalry discovered some English officers in full cry. They joined in the chase and together pursued the fox. Once the quarry was despatched they returned to the matter in hand and set to fighting each other.

Napoleon was finally vanquished at Waterloo, and the weary veterans returned to England and the Industrial Revolution. They thought fondly of Béarn and the Pyrenees, and, like so many British in the years to come, many decided to retire to France. Apart from the attractions of the landscape there was cheap accommodation and abundant fresh food available from the local markets. Moving to the Continent was generally seen as a cheap option for cash-strapped gentry at the time. Not so different from today, then.

After a quarter of a century of limited travel due to the Napoleonic wars, the British poured onto the Continent, which for them now included the Pyrenees. Apart from the memories of battle-worn troops, they were also encouraged by the works of Ramond and by the novels of Mrs Radcliffe and others. Most visitors came for the spas, to drink and bathe in the thermal waters of the mountains, combining the promise of health benefits with a cool retreat in the summer months. The more adventurous explored the neighbouring valleys, and made excursions to famous sights like the Lac de Gaube and the Cirque de Gavarnie, admiring the mountains from afar. A few of the more intrepid climbed the Pic du Midi. Some ventured as far as the spa of Bagnères-de-Luchon in the Central Pyrenees and climbed up to Vénasque, the high pass from where they could catch a glimpse of the red earth of Spain – still the exotic 'other' – and shiver at the snow and glaciers of the far and terrible mountains of the Maladetta.

A few made it as far as the Eastern Pyrenees and Andorra, the Ariège and Roussillon, visiting Perpignan and the baths of Vernet-les-Bains. They climbed Canigou and explored the flower-strewn plateau of the Cerdagne, but since there were few roads and the passes were high and difficult to cross, access remained difficult from the west.

They travelled either via Paris, or most often by boat to Bordeaux as recommended by the Murray Guide and Galignani's Travellers' Guide. Some made the grand tour via the Rhône and Provence, especially to get to the eastern end of the Pyrenees, down the Rhone as far as Avignon, and then across country by stagecoach, or via the recently constructed Canal du Midi.

To get from Bordeaux to Pau and the Pyrenees required a combination of steamboats on the Garonne, followed by the *diligence*, the public horse-drawn carriage, or a variety of smaller vehicles. If at all possible it was preferable to travel in one's own carriage, fully equipped with servants and provisions. There was no guarantee of food at the *auberges* on the way, which were often dirty and ridden with lice and vermin. Restaurants in any modern sense only really began after the Revolution, started by the unemployed chefs of equally if more habitually un-employed aristocrats, and were still practically unheard of in the south.

As the border with Spain came nearer, traces of the war were evident, and always noted by the travellers: the site of a battle ground or a ruined village, and most of all the cemeteries of English dead. Thomas Clifton Paris, a Cambridge professor who set out to explore the mountains in top hat and tails (and invariably got lost), was told that the bed in which he slept near Orthez was the deathbed of a young British officer. 'Absolutely consoling information for a traveller alone and ill,' he noted morosely in his *Letters from the Pyrenees*.

Gradually, despite the trials of the journey, British army officers and men began to arrive to settle in Pau with their families. Tarbes was popular for a while, but Bayonne was considered too expensive and was still recovering from the depredations of wars. There was a small English colony in Tours in the Loire valley, but Pau soon became the most significant English colony in France and Henry Russell one of its most flamboyant characters.

As we approached Pau across the plain, my new mobile phone rang; Miles calling with news of Mosset. The horses from the neighbour's field had invaded the garden again, the cherries were beginning to ripen, and battle lines had been drawn over plans for a housing estate outside the village. I thought of the distance between us, and the huge variation I had already observed between the Eastern and Western Pyrenees. It is still a slow business travelling from one end to the other, five or six hours by road, and more by train, and neither extreme seemed to have much idea of the other. Few people in Mosset had even visited the Central Pyrenees let alone the Atlantic coast, and I met people in Pau who clearly had no idea where Perpignan was.

Russell's comparison of the different regions of the

Pyrenees is that of someone who has surveyed it all from the dizziest heights. 'The three sections are so distinct they seem to be parts of different continents,' he wrote. The Mediterranean Pyrenees, our own chosen land, he compared to Africa: '. . . they shine like the sun, the limestone arid like the sands of the desert. The light is intense, the sky stays blue for weeks at a time.' For Henry himself there was no contest: 'The Pyrénées Centrales is the most splendid region of the Pyrenees, a sublime country of snow and glacier and clouds, the promised land for passionate mountaineers who always come back there.' He acknowledged, however, that the west was the most popular, 'Why do so many foreigners come to live in the south-west? It is the region with the most charm and tenderness, with a great variety of climates, inhabitants, colours, vast forests, still almost virgin, rivers for all tastes, from the most soporific to the wildest torrents.'

It is as true today as it was in the nineteenth century that the British overwhelmingly favour the verdant Western Pyrenees, finding small castles and manor houses tucked into the gentle valleys of the foothills, which they say remind them of England, or at least the long-lost English countryside of their fantasies, a beauty that they can understand and agree upon, that is safe and familiar, unchallenging. The Pyrenees remain at a safe distance on the horizon.

4

Pau: ville anglaise

'The English have spoilt it all. They want to make it into
an English garden which you cannot enter except in a
carriage with six horses and servants in livery. I never want
to see another Englishman.'

Eugène Viollet-le-Duc, 1833

When the Russell family moved to Pau in 1841 there was
still no railway and they would have arrived by horse-
drawn carriage bumping over deeply rutted roads. Henry
was six by then; perhaps he was permitted to sit beside his
father and the coach driver, eager to feel the wind on his
face and see the mountains.

Happily for me there were now railways and I arrived at
the station just below the great Boulevard des Pyrénées,
elegantly fringed with palm trees. I was met by Paul Mirat,
responsible for international relations for the *mairie* of Pau,
who bounded up with a huge smile and shining bald pate
to shake me by the hand. He had responded with enthusiasm to my e-mail, expressing great interest in Henry
Russell, whose work he had rediscovered and published
during many years running his own publishing company.
M. Mirat had described himself as an anglophile, though
the main evidence seemed to be a rather elderly Burberry
raincoat and a passion for fox-hunting. We took the antique
funicular railway up into the centre of Pau, and already I

liked a town where a Frenchman was prepared to abandon his car and ascend slowly by public transport, with plenty of time to shake hands and enquire after the health of the driver.

On Place Royale we paused to look over the railings while Mirat pointed out the peaks one could see from Boulevard des Pyrénées. It is probably the best place for a long view of the Pyrenees, a view that the poet Lamartine avowed was as beautiful as the Bay of Naples. Russell always loved it. 'Is there anything in Europe more beautiful than the astonishing panorama of the Pyrenees from the Place Royale?' he exclaimed.

The Pyrenees at this point are only about thirty kilometres away and there is nothing in the broad valley of the Gave de Pau to interrupt the view of the range of shimmering peaks. The river itself, which has tumbled and roared down from the cold glaciers of Gavarnie, snakes gracefully across the plain. Pau stands on a ridge running east to west high above the river, facing the mountains to the south. An orientation table identifies each of eighty-three peaks across a horizon of a hundred kilometres or so, from the western Pic du Midi d'Ossau, looking like an upturned whale's head or a bishop's mitre, east as far as the Pic du Midi de Bigorre. Only the Vignemale is hard to discern, tucked away in the middle, like a shy king surrounded by courtiers. Perhaps its obscurity and remoteness was one reason why Russell eventually favoured it above all others. I was privileged to be granted such a view on a day of clear luminous light.

The air was very still, and almost immediately I could understand the attraction of this calm for the English. It was so soothing it was like being wrapped in a cashmere shawl and fed camomile tea by Peter Rabbit's mother. There is almost never any wind in Pau, a geographical phenomenon which Russell explained in one of the guide books he wrote in English, *Pau and the Pyrenees*, published in 1871. The Pyrenees themselves break most of the wind, he says; 'the north wind blows over Pau without sinking to its surface; the southern scirocco is broken and cooled by the Pyrenees, the lofty trees of the Park are a protection to westward, and the easterly wind very seldom blows at all.' He too concludes, 'There is something peculiar and un-accountable in the quality of the air.'

Mrs Sarah Ellis, one of the first to write about the health benefits of Pau, put it exquisitely in her book, *Summer and Winter in the Pyrenees*, published in 1841: '. . . there is so little wind in this climate that not a leaf is seen to move . . . There appears at first a sort of mystery in this universal stillness. It seems like a pause in the breath of Nature, a suspension of the general throb of life.' When I checked Mr Baring-Gould I found he was more sceptical. 'The climate does not agree with all constitutions. It is enervating, a land of lotus-eaters,' he sniffed.

When I commented on how gentle it seemed, the im-mediate contrast I felt between Pau and the wild and windswept Roussillon that I inhabited, Mirat nodded approvingly. 'Even the swallows don't migrate from Pau,' he said, 'they stay at the chateau,' which he pointed out at the end of the Boulevard des Pyrénées. It is the only grand building in Pau, a thirteenth-century medieval castle, with a façade added in the Renaissance and an interior restored for Napoleon III on his one visit.

The chateau is surrounded by the old town, a maze of medieval streets with houses of stone or half-timbered *colombage*. Place Royale is a classical eighteenth-century square, overlooked by the *mairie*, and my suitcase on wheels bounced noisily over the cobblestones as we walked under the dappled shade of pruned limeflower trees. At the centre of the shady square stands the statue of Henri IV, 'Our Henry, that's what we call him in Béarn,' said Mirat proudly. 'He was a jolly good chap,' he added in his excellent but oddly dated English.

All I knew about Henri IV, or Henry of Navarre as we called him in my English history lessons, was that he wanted 'a chicken in every pot', in France, which made him sound wonderfully pragmatic. He is the most famous son of Béarn, which until the Middle Ages was a large and independent kingdom straddling both sides of the Pyrenees and including Navarre in Spain. It did not become part of France until Henri IV became king, or, as the béarnais always put it, 'Béarn annexed France'. Henri IV was brought up in Béarn, his lips smeared with garlic and Jurançon wine when he was born, in the local tradition, to ensure his continuing loyalty. As a child Our Henry lived a country existence, playing barefoot with local children, and helping out in the chateau kitchen. He always had a lusty appetite and was famous for his forty-four mistresses. (The chateau guides announce this with distinct pride.)

He retained a great attachment to his native Béarn, but sadly his descendants, Louis XIII and Louis XIV, the Sun King, did not. The intrigues of Paris meant they neglected their progenitor's region and the rest of France as well. By the time of the Revolution, Pau was capital of what was then the Basses Pyrénées, but otherwise a sleepy and unimportant provincial town. It is now capital of the

Pyrénées-Atlantiques department, which encompasses the Basque country and the ancient territory of Béarn.

I was disappointed that there was not even one hotel with a view of the Pyrenees (since then two new hotels have opened, Hôtel du Parc Beaumont and Hôtel Villa Navarre, both with just such views) but I was mollified when I arrived at Hôtel Roncevaux to be greeted by a chicly dressed receptionist with a strong Lancashire accent. She had come from Burnley about six years ago. 'I only came for a couple of months,' she explained, 'but then I stayed. Pau is like that.'

Later I met Mirat at the Café Bouzom, once a centre of ex-pat life in Pau, where English ladies, Parisian beauties and Russian countesses would meet for afternoon tea, to gossip over their fans in rustling silk and chiffon dresses and hats of ostrich feathers and flowers. The famous *patissier* even initiated them in his special art, teaching the future last Tsarina of Russia and the future Empress of Prussia how to make macaroons and scones. As in so many small towns in France, there are a few streets of Pau which could easily be a luxurious Paris *arrondissement*, with smart shoe shops, truffle and *foie gras* emporiums and artistic window displays of chocolates. Elegantly dressed women in high heels and red lipstick stride purposefully by, and plump-looking executives with after-lunch cigars try to drive their SUVs up the steps of narrow streets. Just a few streets away the town reverts to its true self, its medieval heart, the market hall full of butchers and vegetables, and local people with shopping baskets and the ubiquitous flat tartan caps.

Mirat spread out a map on the table next to the teapot of Earl Grey, and indicated the vestigial evidence of the once huge English colony: rue des Anglais, rue Buckingham, avenue Norman Prince, rue O'Quinn, avenue Ridgeway and rue Alexander Taylor. A stroll round the neighbouring streets soon revealed shops selling golf equipment, hunting gear, an English pharmacy, and the Brunswick Billiard Shop. I particularly liked Sir Shop and Lady Shop, and a new establishment rather unfortunately entitled 'Best & British', which sounded to me like a choice between the two.

'We still have the Cercle Anglais,' Mirat announced proudly, 'though all the members are French now. Count Russell was an honoured member, of course.' As he offered more tea, Mirat explained his own English connections. 'All the English like tea! My great-grandfather was a horse breeder and he taught himself English because there were so many Brits around. Then he opened up a big shop in the centre of Pau, A la Ville de Londres, selling furniture, carpets, all brought from England.' His son, Mirat's grandfather, went to work as a fashion designer for Swan and Edgar's department store in London. 'Everything from England was perfect – they had such admiration for England!' Mirat in his turn went to work for Marks and Spencer's wine department and then set himself up in business as a wine importer. 'I fell totally in love with London and stayed for nearly ten years. It was jolly amusing!'

But finally Béarn called. 'I have my roots here; I missed my mountains! Some days it was painful. The mountains and the accent. I understand why Russell stayed here. Here Russell found everything: glaciers, deserts, forests.'

It soon became clear that despite his declared Anglophilia, Mirat's true passion was reserved like most

Frenchmen's for his own *pays*, his own little corner which he firmly believed was the best place on earth to live. As did Henry Russell. 'What a country is Béarn! One would have nostalgia for it in heaven!'

I asked Paul how he had ended up publishing Henry Russell.

He beamed. 'Ah yes, that's a very good story.' He explained that he had begun selling sealing tape for wine boxes to the French, then printing it with his customers' names. This evolved into a printing business and finally he ended up publishing, though he was clearly as maverick as I was in his interests. His first book was by a priest who wrote poetry: 'One of my former teachers, the only one who didn't beat me!' He had attended a seminary, and was severely beaten one day when, asked what his ambition was, he said he wanted to be Pope, which seemed a reasonable goal for a potential priest. 'At least I know how to say the mass in Basque!'

The priest's book, astonishingly, won the Academie Française award for poetry, and got huge publicity. The priest himself gave away his entire prize money of 100,000 francs in one day. It didn't take Mirat much longer to spend the profit. He published the illustrated diaries of an American living in Pau in the 1900s, followed by works by Henry Russell. Now Mirat is Pau's authority on its colonial history. 'I became the one who knew.' Every five minutes his mobile phone would ring with someone seeking information or contacts. Walking around Pau was a hazardous affair as he greeted everyone with enthusiastic handshakes. He almost stopped a friend riding past on a bike in order to shake his hand. When I commented on how long all this was taking, he grimaced. 'I know, I know.

My children refuse to come to town with me any more!' I caught a glimpse of the tightly woven network of family and friends, of obligations and debts, that entwine the community of these small provincial towns. I felt a wave of envy for such involvement and security, quickly followed by distinct doubts about such suffocating intimacy.

Henry Russell spent most of his life in Pau, and though he loved to stride off to the mountains at every opportunity he was also a very social creature, deeply involved in the life of the small town, and became one of its most recognizable characters as he strolled along the boulevard or caught a breath of air by the river. After he died a street was named after him.

The following day I had lunch at the Pau golf club with Mirat. We were served the *plat de jour*, *blanquette de veau*, which although a French dish seemed to embody in its name and blandness a certain English pallor. The club is a black and white timbered mock Tudor building, modelled on the one in Calcutta, itself modelled on the original golf club in St Andrews, Scotland. And all for a game which evolved from sticks and stones and rabbit holes. In the club room I flicked through bound copies of *Field, Farm and Garden* and *The Gentleman's Newspaper* and saw photos of the club's Scottish founders in their tweeds and plus fours, Colonels Hutchinson and Anstruther, Major Pontifax and Archdeacon Sapte, who laid out the first golf course in Europe here in 1856.

In Pau library we met the archivist, Christine Juliat, petite and smart in a brown cord trouser suit and a silk scarf tied as only Frenchwomen know how. She showed me a vast cache of old black and white photographs she had just received, of Americans in Pau at the turn of the nineteenth century: the parties, the hunts, the dogs. She also produced triumphantly the book I had been looking for everywhere, Joseph Duloum's *Les Anglais dans les Pyrénées*, a mine of information on the English in the Pyrenees, which I scanned eagerly. When I expressed my interest in Russell, Madame Juliat said, 'But you must meet M. Ritter. He is also writing about Russell. He is right over there.' At one of the library tables an elderly white-haired gentleman was poring over bound copies of a nineteenth-century newspaper, *Le Mémorial des Pyrénées*, and once we were introduced Mirat whisked us both off to see the Palais Beaumont, a grand villa and casino in a magnificent park at the eastern end of the Boulevard des Pyrénées. It has recently been restored by the *mairie* of Pau, with the glass atrium of the winter garden resplendent with giant palms again, though the fruit machines did not fulfil my visions of a casino full of dinner jackets and diamonds.

M. Ritter turned out to be only one of at least three people writing biographies of Russell, and since the only one I had managed to find so far was a hagiography from 1925 I wanted to know more. Ritter's elderly gait belied his sharp mind, and he questioned me closely, particularly curious to know my religious affiliation, still an important factor for a traditional Frenchman. I muttered something about lapsed Protestant, which seemed to suffice. He explained that the Villa Beaumont was where the Russells first stayed in Pau when they arrived in 1841. Like many of their class at that time, large families traipsed about the country to wherever somebody had managed to inherit a large house.

After Toulouse the Russells had moved to Normandy, where Mme Russell's elder brother conveniently had a castle near Vernon-sur-Seine. By the time they left the north they had four children, Frank and Christine born in Vernon in 1836 and 1837, and Ferdinand born in Paris in 1841. The peripatetic Russells arrived in Pau after a trip to Italy to visit another wealthy relative, a cousin of Mme Russell, who owned the Palais Beaumont, then a magnificent private mansion with its own stables, vegetable gardens and orangery full of fruit and flowers. A faded early photograph shows a grand Palladian-style white-stuccoed villa with shady veranda surrounded by its own tree-filled private park. Tall upper windows looked out over a view of the mountains.

By 1841 Pau already had a substantial British community. From the 1820s on there were forty or fifty English families in the town, living in rented apartments in the centre, boarding houses or villas further out in Jurançon or Billère. Hotel accommodation at that time was limited to the Hôtel de la Poste, the Hôtel d'Europe, and the Hôtel de France, which always had loyal British clientele.

Among early visitors to Pau were the ramshackle Burton family, whose father Joseph, was another Irish landowner, looking for an easier, cheaper life of hunting, shooting and fishing in France. His son, Richard Burton, born in 1821, was to become famous as an explorer, writer and translator of *Arabian Nights*. Like Russell he grew up partly in France, mainly in the English colony of Tours but also spending summers in Pau, running wild with his brother, terrorizing tutors, serving maids and local lasses alike. The passion for languages that he developed and perhaps his sense of rootlessness contributed to his restless desire to travel. Burton, with his fierce demeanour, long curling moustache and sabre scar across his cheek, was the epitome of the hard-drinking, swashbuckling, whoring adventurer. The young Russell would no doubt have heard of his exploits in India, America and darkest Africa, where he went to seek the source of the Nile.

Most of the English visitors to Pau, however, were of a gentler disposition, and most found it all delightful. Artist Marianne Colston, travelling on her honeymoon in 1821, described the chateau and park of Pau in her *Journals*, accompanied by her exquisitely detailed watercolours. 'The lofty and venerable trees offer a canopy almost impervious to the sun's beams, and every opening gratifies the eye, with a new and beautiful vista, resembling but surpassing the shifting scenes of a theatre.'

Mrs Boddington writes even more romantically of the market in *Sketches in the Pyrenees*: '. . .the market folks were coming in with the fresh country air on them and the sweet garden bloom on their fruit, as if it had dropped gently into their baskets without the impression of a finger.' As if.

Mrs Ellis made a drawing of Pau on her visit in 1840 to illustrate her *Summer and Winter in the Pyrenees*. It looks idyllic, the towers of the chateau dominating the bluff. Beyond is the gentle verdant valley of the *gave* and the mountains sketched with a soft pencil in the background. In a wooded glade in the foreground are two well-dressed ladies, complete with bonnets, one holding a small child by the hand.

Though Napoleon himself had suggested a promenade for Pau back in 1802, when there was still a wall blocking the view from the Place Royale, the Boulevard des Pyrénées did not reach its full extent till the end of the nineteenth century. In those early days visitors strolled on the sunny parterre at the foot of the chateau and in the wooded park of oaks and beech on the long slope overlooking the river. Mrs Ellis described the scene: 'Here are to be seen travellers from almost every country ... Spaniards, with their long dark cloaks, lined with red, and gracefully thrown over one shoulder, Italians, Scotch, and Irish, officers of different ranks, soldiers, Béarnais peasants, monks, and nursemaids, and a tide of respectable and fashionable-looking English people. Nor was there wanting the usual proportion of dandies, still evidently English, notwithstanding all the pains they had taken to look French ...'

The Reverend William and Mrs Ellis were missionaries, who had spent many years in Polynesia and Madagascar with the London Missionary Society, travelling in rough canoes and preaching about the evils of cannibalism beneath the banana trees of Tahiti. They visited Pau for the winters of 1839 and 1840 with the dual purpose of converting the French heathen (Catholics anyway) and curing Reverend Ellis of lung disease.

Sarah Ellis was very much the missionary's wife, and she brings her strict, moralizing tone to observations of the natives, the lodgings, the food, the behaviour of the servants and the moral level of the natives. She records the deprivations of the early days, complaining that the accommodation offered was very cold and bare, and rarely had carpets. She strongly advised visitors to bring their own soap. By English standards the houses were very dirty, the floors and stairs were never cleaned and the entrances were like stables. (This hardly seems surprising since they were stables, with horses and carriages accommodated on the ground floor of most buildings.)

Happily for Mrs Ellis she found an apartment of which the previous resident had been an Anglican clergyman, who had conveniently left a few rugs behind. She concludes, however, that the reason the English lived more cheaply elsewhere than in England was that they accepted the lack of things they usually considered necessities. The servants she believed were too familiar, though at least they never showed any sign that they felt themselves the equals of their masters.

To make proper tea was an almost insurmountable enterprise. It was impossible to find a kettle (still is, actually) and the virtues of boiling water were apparently unknown in Pau. Tea had to be purchased in Bordeaux or Toulouse. (When the Ellises did offer tea to visitors, it was usually served already sweetened due to the propensity of the French to pocket the sugar.) Nor were the English fond of French bread, which they reckoned had a bitter taste. Fortunately most of the palois bakers had learnt to make the English kind, and one Christmas *les mince pies* made a first appearance in the shops. On the whole, though, the English found the food more than acceptable and on occasion would even try local dishes.

Transportation was difficult, and Mrs Ellis complains of the lack of carriages available. There were balls but no way of getting to them with unmuddied skirts. In the early days of the colony French and English society mixed easily, despite the fact that few of the béarnais spoke English. The English did try to speak béarnais. *A Grammar and Vocabulary of the Language of Béarn* was published in 1888, 'for the many English and American visitors to the south of France who are anxious to hold intercourse with the kindly and cheerful peasantry of this sunny land'. Not to mention give instructions to their servants. Actually the proud indigenes preferred to speak béarnais, and rather looked down on people speaking French at all.

But already by 1840 Pau was becoming a town of invalids, as an increasingly significant component of its visitors came for their health, in particular those suffering from tuberculosis, then an incurable scourge. It was a horrible wasting disease as the lungs slowly collapsed, resulting in a final dramatic haemorrhage. Oddly, as the victims declined the more convinced they became that they would survive. Attracted by the supposed benefits of the gentle climate, the invalids presented a melancholy spectacle as they took their morning and afternoon walks. Pale, solitary individuals strolled slowly along the sunny terrace below the chateau. Some were accompanied by anxious families, desperate to cure their loved ones.

I was invited to dinner with the Mirat family at the family house in Meillon, a small village just outside Pau. I had acquitted myself well, I thought, speaking tolerable French to Mme Mirat and the children and restraining my wine consumption to that of a Frenchwoman, until we came to the cheese course. I was offered the plate first, and sliced the end off the slab of *brébis*, a pungent local cheese of sheep's milk. There was consternation – 'You can't do that to the cheese!' – and I was instructed in the proper appreciation of a Pyrenean cheese, how to slice it from rind to centre in order to taste the full range of its flavour. Their attitude epitomized for me what I loved about the French, this ability to maximize pleasure, whether it is in amorous flirtation or eating a piece of cheese.

Paul's father, the mayor of the village, told me the story of the first British invalid of distinction to discover the beneficial climate of Pau, though I must say it took me a while to understand his pronunciation of Selkirk. Thomas Douglas, Earl of Selkirk, was a philanthropist and pioneer, who bought lands in Canada to settle poverty-stricken emigrants from northern Scotland and Ireland, and is now best known as the founder of the state of Manitoba. Sadly, by the time he left Canada in 1819 and returned to Scotland he was already suffering from advanced tuberculosis.

He arrived in Pau in September 1817, on his way to Spain, accompanied by his doctor, family and servants in a retinue of several carriages. He was so taken with Pau, warm and golden on a calm October day, he decided to spend the winter there. He particularly enjoyed the stunning prospect of the Pyrenees, and the fact that although winter was fast closing in the sun still shone every day. The Selkirks were among the first British families of distinction to stay in Pau, where they rented an elegant seventeenth-century mansion, Hôtel Larriu, on Place Royale. It had a wide enough staircase for the invalid earl to be transported in a sedan chair in order to enjoy the view. In his account Selkirk's doctor describes the decline of his patient throughout the winter, not helped by the weather, which despite Pau's benign reputation was terrible, with fierce storms that uprooted trees and tore off roofs and chimneys. Local doctors simply shrugged their shoulders and pointed to the Pyrenees covered in snow and asked why in the name of heaven the family had decided to winter in Pau. They recommended Marseille or at least Toulouse. Selkirk died in the spring of 1820. His wife lived a further fifty years, which may say something for Pau after all.

But it was Dr Alexander Taylor, another Scotsman, who really established Pau as a health resort. He had been with the British forces in Vittoria in Spain, where he contracted typhus. When he recovered he spent his convalescence in Pau, and established a consultancy there. An anonymous caricature of M. le Docteur shows a Victorian gentleman in all his glory: muttonchop whiskers, large paunch, tail coat, high white stock collar, and glossy top hat. He exudes the kind of pomposity that must have inspired confidence in his patients at that time. He was more than anyone responsible for changing the fortunes of Pau. (And he too has a street named after him in gratitude.)

In 1842 he published *The Climate of Pau*, recommending the town and the surrounding region as a remedy for all sorts of ailments, in particular tuberculosis. He included a table of longevity which seemed to prove that of all cities in the world Pau was the one where people lived longest, and cited a remarkable number of béarnais living to over a hundred still in perfect health. This was borne out when I went to look for the Russell family grave in Pau. The family tomb, guarded by a low iron rail in a corner of the cemetery, holds the remains of Henry and his family, their names inscribed in stone. Henry lived till he was 75, and of his two brothers Ferdinand lived till he was 98, and Frank till he was 99.

Dr Taylor also noted that Béarn was one of the few regions of the west to escape the terrible plague of 1348, and the influenza epidemic that ravaged Spain in 1837. He stressed the low crime rate, pointing out that between 1827 and 1840 only two people had been condemned to death.

Russell later confirmed this opinion, 'Violence is a thing almost unknown. Only nineteen heads fell here in the atrocious days of the great French Revolution; and at the present day there is no place so safe at all hours of night or day as Pau and every corner of Béarn.'

Taylor even had an answer for Pau's rainy reputation: although there was more rainfall in Pau than in England there were, he claimed, fewer rainy days; 109 per year compared to 178 in London. And anyway, he argued, the soil of Pau had a special quality which meant it drained quickly so the air was never damp. He cited as proof the fact that ladies' coiffures held better in Pau; even after several days of rain their curls did not drop out.

Taylor could not have done a better PR job for Pau. He emphasized how much conditions in the town had improved. 'Twenty years ago one searched in vain for *le confort*', the houses had no carpets, there were no carriages to rent, nor even any pavements, but by 1840 the hotels and boarding houses were fully cognizant of the needs of the English, there were plenty of churches, and there was even a Club Anglais supplied with English newspapers.

He proposed a programme of improvements for the town, many of which were eventually realized, including the Boulevard des Pyrénées, a horizontal promenade to extend from the Parc du Château to the Place Royale and beyond where invalids could easily stroll and take the sun. He described all the attractions of the region, the pleasures of riding, walking and fishing. The joys of the hunt were particularly stressed, with an abundance of quail, partridge, duck, isard and foxes. You could even go bear-spotting.

While invalids sought health, therefore, the other

members of the family could find plenty of amusement. They toured the Pyrenees, climbing, botanizing and sketching and writing prolifically about their experiences. Many of their entertainments already had an oddly British flavour. In 1841 Pau had its first steeplechase (an event still celebrated in 2003 with horses and riders pounding through the streets of Pau and applauded by a new generation of *les anglais*). Taylor did add a note of warning with regard to the quality of fox-hunting, however, and recommended, 'Any English sportsman wishing to hunt with the Pau hounds, should bring out horses from England.'

There was some scepticism about Taylor's hyperbole, notably in a review in the *Lancet* by Lefevre, who had been Lord Selkirk's doctor. Though he too sang the praises of Pau he expressed, not surprisingly given the demise of his own patient, some doubts about the precise health benefits of the climate, and accused Taylor of wearing rose-coloured spectacles.

Still, Taylor's book was a great success with good reviews in the *Athenaeum* and the *Spectator*. A French translation soon appeared and by 1844 it had been translated into several other European languages. The trickle of invalids turned into a flood, mainly from Britain but also from France, the rest of Europe and even St Petersburg.

Climate as a cure was all the rage and the reputation of Pau and the Pyrenees grew rapidly. The early 1840s, when the Russells arrived, were the turning point. Apart from Dr Taylor's, several other books were published, and Mrs Ellis's *Summer and Winter in the Pyrenees* became a best-seller. The development of cheap lithographs meant every middle-class English dining room could have a drawing of the waterfalls of Gavarnie on the wall. It was the beginnings of mass tourism.

As the English colony grew it became clear that they needed spiritual solace as well. Pau soon had several non-Catholic churches, starting with the first Anglican church in 1841. There was never any lack of sermons since there were plenty of clergymen available, determined to evangelize the French, distributing religious tracts and holding services in hotel bedrooms.

There is still an Anglican church in Pau, and the chaplain, the Reverend Richard Eyre, offered 'to initiate me into the mysteries of St Andrew's'. I found the church on rue O'Quinn, named after a famous mayor of Pau of Irish descent. St Andrew's is a classic nineteenth-century neo-Gothic stone building with stained glass windows, like so many small English parish churches, complete with a neatly turreted presbytery next door. Sadly the animal cemetery with its headstones inscribed to the dogs and cats of the English colony is no more.

Reverend Eyre greeted me with a twinkle in his eye, and a plummy '*Bonjour*'. He was tall with thick silvery grey hair and bushy eyebrows, and a small silver cross on top of his woolly jumper. 'I'm really retired,' he explained, as we stood admiring the Gothic carving of the rood screen, 'only here for a couple of years, you know.' He used to be Dean of Exeter cathedral, and clearly a brief sojourn in south-west France had its appeal. He pointed out the altar triptych, a crucifixion flanked by the figures of Joan of Arc and St George. 'Now look at the background. The horizon is a panorama of Pau – the chateau, even St Andrew's.' He chuckled. 'The faces are probably portraits of members of the congregation,' and it was true, both St Joan and St

George had a very pale English look about them. 'Pity about the stained glass, though. Nobody liked the stained glass, not even Mr Acland-Troyte himself – and he founded the church.'

All around the walls were plaques to the English and increasingly American community that worshipped there: to the memory of Reginald Morris Post, born Pau 16 November 1879, died South Bend, Indiana, 1908 age twenty-eight; Cornelia Remsen Kane born NY 1841 died Pau 1912. Here too were all the familiar signs of an English church, the cleaning rota, the flower rota, *Hymns Ancient and Modern*, and a dusty collection of books including Trollope, Browning, a biography of George VI, Wellington's campaigns, various sermons and the Ladybird Book of Saints.

When I tried to leave Pau was living up to its reputation for abundant rainfall, and I had no umbrella. Reverend Eyre insisted on lending me his enormous golfing umbrella, and I struggled back to my hotel trying not to skewer too many palois on the way. I promised to return it before Divine Service the following Sunday. However, my walk home included several shops and a café, and somehow I lost it. I dreaded telling Reverend Eyre, who had stressed that it was a very special golfing umbrella. When I confessed the following Sunday he was forgiving, and reassured me with a tale of his own: how he borrowed the curate's car on his first day in Pau and ignorant of *la priorité à la droite* caused £800 worth of damage.

I joined in the singing of 'All People that on Earth do Dwell', and noted that the communion service was printed in both English and French. (I was intrigued to note that Almighty God is addressed as 'tu'.) The congregation was small but not pitiful: several men in gold buttoned blazers, ladies in smart flowered dresses and hats, and even a Sunday School which acted out a scene from Daniel in the Lions' Den. Over tea and biscuits after the service, I chatted to the faithful, *les fidèles*, as Reverend Eyre called them in quotation marks. I was introduced to Mrs Lily Carter, a fragile but perspicacious elderly lady of ninety-eight and an honoured member of the old English colony, whose husband had been proprietor of the bespoke tailors, Old England, on Place Royale. She came to live in Pau after the Second World War. 'My husband told me it was always summer until Christmas here!' she whispered, leaning on her daughter's arm. She settled into a life of winters in Pau and summers in the shop in Luchon in the mountains, and brought up her three children in France. She never thought of leaving when her husband died. She smiled. 'But I'm still as Irish as the pigs in Drogheda!'

The small British community of Pau continued to grow, with about a hundred and fifty families by 1846. After 1845 the Second Empire of Napoleon III resulted in greatly improved Franco–British relations, and as more military personnel arrived in Pau life became more colonial and social life more circumscribed by protocol. More and more grand soirées were held, as well as *les garden parties* and concerts, including a charity concert given by composer Franz Liszt in 1844, when Liszt himself took the collection. The English particularly liked to participate in carnival festivities, and all remembered the brilliant celebrations in 1846, which included the costume ball given by Dr Alexander Taylor. At least half the guests arrived disguised as Lord Byron or Sir Walter Scott.

The new railways facilitated travel for more than just the

very rich, and by 1860 Thomas Cook (himself originally a Baptist minister) was organizing foreign tours. Once the railway arrived in Pau in 1863 there were 2000 foreigners in a town with a population of 20,000. By 1880 there were 6000 foreigners of whom 2000 were British and 500 American.

The English brought England with them. There were English tutors for the children and a school called Imperial College. There were three English pharmacies, any number of doctors, and of the five dentists in Pau, one was English, the other American. It was not long before you could buy essentials like decent tea, mince pies and Christmas puddings. Shops like Old England and Ville de Londres, established by Mirat's family, supplied English clothes and tailoring, furniture, sporting equipment and the like.

There was a vice-consul appointed by the Foreign Office, George Musgrave-Clay, who doubled as the head of l'English Bank, several churches and the inevitable estate agency. English cottages and large mansions were built for the newcomers, *les Insulaires* (the Islanders, as the British were known). Family hotels and boarding houses sprang up, with names like Angleterre, Bristol and Victoria. Increasingly these were expected to have running water, bathrooms, even toilets. Further luxuries were also required: billiard rooms, reading rooms, tennis courts and croquet lawns.

Every Thursday and Sunday a brass band played 'God Save the Queen' and 'Rule Britannia' in the Place Royale. It was all a great boost to the Pau economy, with increased employment for servants in houses, clubs and hotels, and increased demand for horses and carriages, dressmakers and suppliers of food, wine and other commodities.

Pau responded to this growing popularity, restoring the chateau and improving the Place Royale (Dr Taylor, to whom Pau was so grateful for his indefatigable promotion of the town, was invited to plant the first limeflower tree in the Place in 1878). The Parc Beaumont was created after the Villa Beaumont was donated to the town, and plans were made to imitate the Promenade des Anglais in Nice and extend the Boulevard along the bluff facing the Pyrenees. Even the sewers were improved after a controversial article in *The Times* suggested Pau was actually rather smelly.

Ironically, as Franco–British relations improved politically, the social worlds of Pau became more separate. The English, in the heyday of the Empire, were increasingly snobbish and only invited a small proportion of the more anglicized locals. The first Cercle Anglais social club which was formed around 1840 was dissolved due to certain problems between the French and English members and thereafter it was reserved for English and Americans only. There was a certain amount of misunderstanding and bruised sensitivities, partly because the French often failed to understand the existence of non-titled nobility in Britain. Despite the French Revolution, or perhaps because of it, the possession of a title in France was considered very important. Anyone who could, called themselves Baron. If an Englishman could not claim to be a Lord or a Sir the French took him for a bourgeois. While at first just finding the tea was the problem, all too soon it became more a question of with whom one could take it, my dear.

This was a problem for Henry Russell's father, who was deeply frustrated by his lack of a noble title. He had signed affidavits from the archives of Dublin castle to prove the nobility of his birth but still had no aristocratic prefix to his name. He was enraged by a French publication which confused the English aristocracy with the bourgeoisie and in 1847 published a long vehement letter in the Pau press protesting the distinction, and terming himself 'l'un des Barons d'Ulster'.

His prayers were finally answered in 1862 when the title Comte was bestowed upon him by the Pope, in recognition of the services of his son Frank, who served in the Papal army, commanding an Irish regiment. The title was granted to Thomas John and his heirs and thus did Russell become entitled to call himself le Comte Henri Russell, in France at least. He stuck to Henry Russell in England, where they didn't have counts anyway.

This all made Henry's father sound remarkably stuffy for such an unconventional son, so I warmed to another story of his habits in Pau, which indicated an entirely different side to his personality. Apparently he obtained permission from the town to establish on the banks of the river a kind of bathing machine, a cylindrical tube of waterproof fabric in which he would enclose himself every morning and have his valet throw buckets of glacial water over him. It was typical of the British at the time (there were public baths in Britain where they boasted of how cold the water was) and of the Russell family; Henry too always had a peculiar predilection for cold climates and leaping into cold rivers.

The Russells found accommodation in Pau, but they were used to a nomadic existence; both parents were familiar with a life of exile, and relative insecurity and deprivation. Such a history must have contributed not only to their son's desire to travel but also to the way he so carefully cultivated a grand and aristocratic image. In any case, Pau failed to hold them entirely and indeed they may have been dismayed by its sudden popularity. Soon they were spending much of their time in the spa town of Bagnères-de-Bigorre, by then second only to Pau for the number of English residents.

Before I left Pau I had one last appointment – with the mayor. André Labarrère is an intriguing man, a socialist who has held power for thirty years in a thoroughly patrician manner. He has also been openly homosexual all that time, perhaps one reason why Pau has a substantial gay community. Nobody seems to mind; they are much more concerned that he is one of them, a true béarnais, than about his sexual orientation or indeed his precise politics. He is a tall, elegant man with smooth silver hair, comfortably ensconced in his splendid office overlooking the Place Royale and the mountains. I expressed my appreciation of his town, as he showed me with enormous pride the view he enjoyed from his balcony.

Then with a grand flourish and a twinkle in his eye he whisked a long package from behind his enormous desk and to my astonishment presented me with an umbrella. I had told Paul Mirat about losing Reverend Eyre's precious golf umbrella, and also expressed an interest in the Pau umbrella shop, the only shop in France where you can still buy the traditional shepherds' umbrellas of the Pyrenees, made of strong blue cloth with wooden spokes that won't conduct lightning. For centuries these umbrellas have sheltered the shepherds in the mountains from sun and storms, and even now in my own village I sometimes see one of the old shepherds sitting under a tree with his black and white sheep dog and his faded blue umbrella. It would serve me well on my future forays into the country of the shepherds.

5

Bagnères-de-Bigorre: the Athens of the Pyrenees

'I have thought for a long time of the Pyrenees as a region where I would find this union of the beautiful, the picturesque and the sublime, that I have searched for in vain elsewhere.'

H. D. Inglis

I wanted to see all the romantic sights of the Pyrenees, so Theo and I set off one golden day towards the end of the summer holidays to drive through the High Pyrenees. As we stopped at the Col de Jau for a last glimpse of Canigou we waved to Hubert, our very own cowherd, a distant figure on the hillside in blue jeans and spectacles. Hubert is young, and used to work in the bar in the village. But he hated it, craved solitude and is now happy to spend most of his days wandering the mountainside with responsibility for three hundred cows. He lives in a small shepherd's hut hewn of granite stones for most of the summer, till the autumn *transhumance* when the cows are brought down to winter pastures and hay. He only returns once a week or so for shopping (and maman to do the washing). It is not such a hard life these days; he has a car of sorts, though no blue umbrella, but the job still requires the same self-reliance and fortitude it always did.

The pass above Mosset, the 1500m Col de Jau, is the boundary between the Pyrénées Orientales and the Aude, and there is an immediate change in vegetation and climate. As soon as you descend the other side of the col you leave the south behind, the red-roofed villages and air pungent with Mediterranean herbs, and plunge into a cooler forest of chestnuts and tumbling rivers.

We wound down through the amazing gorges of the upper Aude valley, vertiginous ravines through what seems like a sheer mountain wall, on through Foix and the Ariège, where the valleys open out at the foothills of the Pyrenees and there are wonderful caves and prehistoric paintings to be seen. Corn was waving sheer gold and ripe in the fields. From the vale of Lannemezan we caught our first glimpse of the legendary Monts Maudits across the Spanish frontier. Finally we arrived in Bagnères-de-Bigorre and the Vallée de Campan. It was here that Henry Russell spent much of his childhood, his mountain apprenticeship.

The Vallée de Campan, snoozing in the late sunshine, entirely lived up to its Arcadian reputation, its richly cultivated slopes and well-watered meadows the subject of numerous eulogies in nineteenth-century English travel memoirs. There are more houses now, electricity wires and thankfully a petrol station, but otherwise it seems much the same. It is a glacier valley, and thus broader than some of the deep gorges that characterize the river valleys of the Pyrenees; there is good grassland, pine and beech woods on the slopes, solid farmhouses with balconies and slate roofs and churches with pointed spires. The trees were already turning gold and brown, and the light had that mellow soft quality only the first days of autumn in the Pyrenees can impart.

For many early visitors the Vallée de Campan was the most perfect place they could conceive. This may have had something to do with the fact that it was easily accessible (even by carriage) from the spa town of Bagnères-de-Bigorre. The English always seemed to regard the Pyrenees as a landscape designed for their benefit, as if every tree or hilltop ruin was placed there for them to sketch. They exclaimed over the happy grouping of copses of trees giving variety to the scene and the tasteful mix of colours, yellow corn and green meadows so exquisitely balanced.

Picturesque peasants were added for visual effect. Mrs Ellis confessed herself astonished by the number of women she saw doing their washing in the rivers. 'I have been accustomed to think that English artists in drawing continental scenery put in the washerwomen and linen by way of effect.' Actually, she was not far wrong, since in at least one artist's sketches the same group of rustic peasants has been added into several different landscapes.

Their artistic efforts were not always well received; Thomas Clifton Paris was challenged by police when he tried to sketch a village, and taken for a spy. At Vénasque on the Spanish border beyond Luchon, one diligent artist was stoned. In 1823 Marianne Colston records drawing the citadel at Bayonne, where she attracted a hostile crowd. The spectators mocked her English speech, then began to mimic the action of drawing, and finally threw water at her and tried to turn her chair over. Finally the gallant Mr Colston had to arm himself with his umbrella to protect her.

We too had brought sketchbooks and paintboxes, a romantic notion on my part since I hardly knew one end of the brush from the other. We found conveniently placed rocks to sit on and spread out our painting materials, weighting the paper down with pebbles. Theo painted the trees in several shades of green, while I struggled simply to catch the outline of the mountains with a pencil. I concentrated hard, looking with an intensity I never usually feel whether I am making notes, taking photos or simply contemplating a beautiful view. I realized the truth of Ruskin's conviction that drawing could teach us to see. Before photography the only way to memorize a scene was to paint it or write it; the act of drawing requires one to look with a level of observation and attention we have almost entirely lost.

In those days few people knew what the Pyrenees looked like. For those at home visual impressions could only be gleaned from the descriptions or drawings of early travellers. We are so used to the familiarity of foreign landscapes gained from film, TV and photographs (and tourism itself), it is hard to imagine a time when there were none of those things. Even cheap lithographs came later, so the occasional original sketch or watercolour done on the spot was all there was to convey some sense of the majesty of the far mountains.

We shared a *montagnard* picnic, fresh baguette with rough garlicky sausage (cut with an Opinel knife, of course, the hunter's friend: a sharp blade which folds into a wooden shaft). Theo told me that the French do indeed have their own word for picnic, *saucissoner*, to eat sausages. We added a few sweet, ripe tomatoes, fresh figs and apples, and a chunk of *brébis* (sheep's) cheese we had bought in the *épicerie*. This time I cut it correctly, passing on my newly acquired knowledge of cheese paring to Theo, who it must be said was far more interested in the knife and the sticks he could whittle with it.

Activities in the Pyrenees haven't changed much in two hundred years either, give or take a few more roads and a prodigious quantity of barbed wire. Most of the full-time inhabitants are still farmers or shepherds, though they may supplement their income with work in the ski stations in the winter months. Driving over the Col de Tourmalet once we saw an old man in his beret and blue overalls scything hay in a field, stolidly oblivious of the seats of the ski lift which were swinging over his head. Visitors are still regarded with only mild curiosity, as of little use to them, and less interest. They still assume we must be rich.

Certainly in the nineteenth century it was assumed that all the English were wealthy. (And indeed that all visiting foreigners were English.) Many inns had two tariffs, one for the French and a higher rate for *les anglais*. As far as they were concerned anyone who could afford to travel so far for their health or pleasure must be rich, especially if, like authoress Lady Chatterton, they arrived in their own carriage accompanied by servants and explored the Pyrenees by sedan chair carried by four porters.

Unless they could afford their own carriage, most tourists travelled by public carriage or by horse. For more inaccessible places donkeys or mules and guides could be hired, and sedan chairs were always popular as transport both to the spa waters and further afield. The visitors often drew a crowd of curious observers. Lady Chatterton describes waiting for her carriage wheel to be mended. 'The maimed carriage in which I am writing is surrounded by numbers of peasants and some soldiers staring at every part of it.'

Many of the visitors were landed gentry, the wealthy middle classes of England spawned by the Industrial Revolution, and they came to the spas for the prestige and the elegant lifestyle as much as for health reasons. Others were bourgeois families travelling for their health, and hoping to live more economically on the Continent than in England. They were often Anglican clergymen, with or without their families. In those days every second son sought a living in the church and once he had acquired it often forsook his parish in order to travel. The proximity of Spain, which was considered practically pagan, offered the prospect of evangelization and the London Missionary Society was particularly zealous.

Rich, bourgeois, army families, modest ladies or Anglican clergymen, the English wanted to see everything: picturesque sites, agriculture, industry, art and archaeology. They were avid souvenir hunters and loved to collect rare flowers and plants for their English rock gardens. Philosopher John Stuart Mill (1806–1873), for example, was an enthusiastic botanist. He turned up in 1820 at the age of fourteen with botanist George Bentham, nephew of philosopher Jeremy Bentham, who owned a property in the south of France. John Stuart Mill lived with them for a year and began a lifelong passion for collecting plants. (His precious collection of pressed flowers and plants is now in the natural history museum in Avignon.)

Archaeology was another new discipline and there was ample opportunity for discovering Roman mosaics and other fragments. Author and hymn writer Sabine Baring-Gould discovered a dolmen in the Val d'Ossau in 1850, covered in carvings. Lacking a notebook, he sketched the drawings on his shirt cuff. But when he returned only three weeks later to make a better drawing it had already been broken up by the road menders.

Every Victorian home worthy of the name boasted collections of ammonites and fossils along with the deer antlers in the hall, and amateur geologists chipped away industriously at the rocks, and took handfuls of crystals from the caves they explored. Sometimes these early tourists were destructive in their quest for original souvenirs for their drawing rooms back home. The Grottes de Campan were rapidly denuded. 'They want to take everything home, not just little fragments of crystal, but entire columns. They would take the entire cave if they had pockets big enough,' grumbled an aggrieved French writer. Some souvenirs were quite bizarre; James Erskine Murray was very proud of the knife which had belonged to the assassin of a muleteer at the Brèche du Roland. The Misses Brown, Jones and Robinson found a bugle abandoned by Spanish soldiers at the Port de Gavarnie on the frontier and bore it back to England in triumph.

Theo seems to have continued this tradition quite naturally, assembling collections of animal bones in the garden, hammering away at rocks and crystals, and making artful arrangements of pebbles, fossils, chunks of glittering quartz and mica. One day he discovered an ancient coin with Arabic markings in the field in front of the monastery.

After my own years of solitary travels, I was encouraged to discover how many women travelled alone, even then. They were like creatures from another world. Selina Bunbury, for example, a widow, travelled by horse with only a local servant, brandishing her prayer book and sniping about the inattentive Pyrenean congregations. Come to think of it, perhaps brandishing a Bible might have saved me from some of the compromising situations in which I have found myself, from the lecherous Greek captain whose small boat was the only way out of a small Cretan coastal village to the moment I threw feminism to the winds and chose a man with a bed over a beach with rats.

The impecunious Mary Eyre, travelling alone, writing for money, and grumbling a lot, was the one with whom I most identified. She published *A Lady's Walks in the South of France* in 1863 (for her the south of France was most definitely the Pyrenees). In the preface she explains that she left England 'intending to try whether the south of France was really, as I had been told, a cheaper place of abode than England. I travelled (for a lady) in rather a peculiar fashion, for which I took with me only one small waterproof stuff bag, which I could carry in my hand, containing a spare dress, a thin shawl, two changes of every kind of underclothing, two pairs of shoes, pens, pencils, paper, the inevitable "Murray" and a prayer book.' (Murray's handbook to France was the invaluable guide-book, listing everything from hotels to the price of horses, that most travellers took with them after the series began in 1843. The France guide went through nineteen editions, and is an indicator of the popularity of the region at that time; the Pyrenees section expanded until 1875, and then diminished.) Miss Eyre also took with her a Scottish terrier named Keeper for company.

'Extremely slender means compelled me to travel humbly, and to mix a good deal with the people.' She claimed to have thus acquired a much better knowledge of French life than most of the English, 'who look at everything in the countries through which they travel from an

English point of view'. She was nevertheless extremely critical of conditions, particularly the lack of cleanliness and number of fleas she encountered. Indeed, asked one day by a group of peasants how they compared to their English peers, she chided them for their slovenliness and dirty houses. But she made acute observations of peasant life, their houses, costumes, farming implements and food preparation, and she included lots more recipes than the men, including one for *pot au feu*, which she applauded because it was so economical, using up all the remnants of vegetables, meat and bread and adding wild sorrel and such gathered from the hedgerows. She liked to botanize, revelling in the pretty nosegay of 'scabious, giant bindweed, a stray honeysuckle, some wild marjoram, hare-bells, and one or two beautiful fringed pinks' she gathered out walking one day.

To save money she had meals brought to her room, rather than eat at the *table d'hôte*, the usual arrangement at most *auberges* where everyone shared the same meal. Mostly she drank fresh milk and 'lived on bread and yellow peaches and grapes', but added gloomily, 'In the winter I shall need meat.' She even did her own shopping, though this had its pitfalls; one day she discovered the bakers naked to the waist as they kneaded the dough. 'I drew back in dismay, and ever after bought my bread at the bakeress's next door.'

In Bagnères-de-Bigorre, a sleepy little spa town in the Vallée de Campan, I hoped to find some evidence of its English heyday and Russell's childhood. Russell always retained a special affection for the little town, and in the first of his guidebooks, published in 1868, *A Fortnight in the Pyrenees*, he described it as 'one of the prettiest, cleanest and gayest towns in France', of which the advantage was 'to be at the foot of the Pyrenees, and not in them'. It was called, rather improbably, 'the Athens of the Pyrenees'.

Returning to Bagnères as an adult Henry Russell had always stayed in the Hôtel d'Angleterre, but even from the lobby it looked to us the kind of place that had leaky bathrooms shoe-horned into corners. The Trianon Hôtel seemed more promising, a long low building with a grey slate mansard roof, white shutters and wrought iron balconies. It was once a private villa, and is still surrounded by a shady park and gardens. We searched in vain for the proprietor, quite happily exploring the entire place including its colonnaded restaurant and mahogany panelled reading room before we finally found him, fast asleep with his dog. When we managed to wake him up and ventured to ask for a room he was delighted.

When we went to bed that night I tried to read Tennyson, one of the few English poets who had written about the Pyrenees. He loved dramatic landscapes and his poems were often inspired by the beauty he experienced in the mountains. I had brought my brother's copy of *In Memoriam*, which somehow seemed appropriate. Theo meanwhile watched a terrible French game show, gratified to find he could see the TV from his bed.

Tennyson's first visit to the Pyrenees in 1831 as a Cambridge student has always been clouded in mystery, though it ultimately inspired *In Memoriam*. He travelled with his close friend Arthur Hallam, an elegant romantic youth, also a poet, portrayed most memorably in a sketch sitting in a window playing his lute. They were discreetly recruited to assist the rebel cause in Spain, after the Napoleonic wars and the restoration of the Spanish monarchy. Ferdinand VII had turned out to be very reactionary, abolishing the elected parliament and reintroducing the Inquisition. Many Spaniards went into exile to escape him, including Goya, and many of them came to London, where liberal England rallied to their cause. Tennyson and Hallam were given the job of couriers with coded instructions to take funds to the rebel leader Ojeda across the Pyrenees from Cauterets, a difficult journey since there are no direct roads. They apparently met at the Pont d'Espagne; Tennyson was shocked on meeting Ojeda, who as soon as the money was handed over declared, 'Now we are going to cut the throats of all the priests!'

Tennyson and Hallam lingered in the mountains, which Hallam evoked beautifully in a letter to his brother: 'We remained at Cauterets, and recruited our strength with precipitous defiles, jagged mountain tops, forests of solemn pine, tavelled by dewy clouds, and encircling lawns of the greenest freshness, waters in all shapes and all powers, from the clear runnels babbling down over our mountain paths at intervals, to the blue little lake whose deep, cold waters are fed eternally from neighbouring glaciers, and the impetuous cataract, fraying its way over black, beetling rocks.'

They visited many of the famous sights, and Tennyson was haunted by the grandeur of the landscape. He wrote his poem *Oenone*, while he was there, which, though a story about classical Greece (where he had never been), draws on the shadows of the mountains, the caverns in the rocks, 'the snowy columned range divine' of the Pyrenees. He noted the substitution disingenuously: 'In the Pyrenees, where part of this poem was written, I saw a very beautiful species of Cicala which had scarlet wings spotted with black. Probably nothing of the kind exists in Mount Ida.'

The two friends returned on the steamer to Dublin. But only two years later, in 1833, Hallam died suddenly, on a trip to Vienna. Tennyson was devastated and took many years to write *In Memoriam*, deepening his sadness at the death of a dear friend into a long poem on love and loss and memory. It was finally published in 1850, the year he became poet laureate.

Later, in 1863, the Tennyson family returned to France, travelling by carriage to the Auvergne and the Pyrenees, including Bagnères-de-Bigorre, with Alfred bumping along beside the driver on the outside of the coach, wrapped in his shabby Inverness cape, the pockets crammed with books. Hallam, Tennyson's eldest son and first biographer, who was nine at the time, later recalled the excitements of the trip. They climbed the Pic du Midi and visited Bagnères, where they saw a storm worthy of Russell, 'forked lightning of different colours striking the mountains on either hand'. From Luchon Tennyson walked to the Port de Vénasque and into Spain, to the Lac d'Oô, and the Lac Vert, and rode a white pony along the Vallée du Lys.

They met up with the Victorian poet Arthur Clough on their travels. Clough was wandering round France in an attempt to improve his health, which was exhausted from overwork with Florence Nightingale and her charity for the training of nurses. He had bumped into the Tennysons in the Auvergne, at the café in Mont-Dore-les-Bains, and promised to follow them to Luchon as soon as he got his boots back from the cobblers.

They all met again in Gavarnie, which Tennyson declared 'still the finest thing in the Pyrenees'. They climbed to the Lac de Gaube, a clear still lake among fir woods, and Tennyson climbed on to the Lac Bleu, where he confirmed that the water was marvellously blue except where the shadow of the mountains made parts of the lake purple. Clough observed how silent Tennyson was and how absorbed by beauty of the mountains. They spent the evenings reading poetry together and Tennyson recalled years later how Clough had broken down in emotional tears over one of his own poems. Clough himself wrote one poem on the Pyrenees, *Currente Calamo*: 'Quick, painter, quick, the moment seize / Amid the snowy Pyrenees . . .' It is not regarded as his best work. Sadly for Clough, his days were numbered, and after meeting up with his wife and new baby he travelled on to Florence, where he died, probably of a stroke, only six weeks later.

On 6 August, Tennyson's birthday, the Tennysons arrived at Cauterets, always the poet's favourite valley in the Pyrenees. His son Hallam recalled, 'Before our windows we had the torrent rushing over its rocky bed from far away among the mountains and falling in cataracts. Patches of snow lay on the peaks above, and nearer were great wooded heights glorious with autumnal colours, bare rocks here and there, and greenest mountain meadows below.' Here, on 1 September, Tennyson wrote *In the Valley of Cauteretz*, 'after hearing the voice of the torrent seemingly sound deeper as the night grew', in memory of his first visit there with Arthur Hallam.

By the mid-nineteenth century Bagnères was second only to Pau for the size of its English colony. It too had a gentle climate, sheltered from the wind and considered the best place for consumptives in summer. It was also relatively clean; Richard's guide to the Pyrenees of 1852 remarked that it was as if a king of France had bought Bagnères from Holland to serve as a model for his southern subjects.

It had been a spa since Roman times, and originally had several different private establishments for bathing and drinking the therapeutic waters. There were fountains dispensing water everywhere. Then in 1823 the town created a thermal quarter and the advent of the English and other foreigners triggered a building boom: villas, hotels, *pensions*, shops and, naturally, churches. Finally there was even a railway station. Henry Blackburn in his 1867 book on the spas of the Pyrenees observed the genteel English atmosphere of the town: 'How curious to find the English language spoken continually, to hear the click of croquet, to see cricket bats, and to be asked in English at the shops if we will buy any Pale Ale.'

When the public *diligence* or private carriages arrived in Bagnères, they were always surrounded by an excited crowd, unloading the trunks and hatboxes, offering rooms with the greatest *confort* and the best views and horses and donkeys for hire. Peasants hovered, offering to launder the travellers' linen, and cards in French and English were thrust into hands or pockets.

It is not like that now. Bagnères has never recovered from the departure of the English. The population had dwindled by the end of the nineteenth century as the focus shifted to Biarritz and other coastal resorts, and two world wars sent the remnants scuttling back home. Now Bagnères is a quiet, sleepy town, where it is easy to find a parking place and no-one offers to wash your linen for you.

The railway has long gone, and every other house seems to be a doctor or a homeopath.

There are a few vestiges of its glory days: here the elaborate glass and wrought iron canopy of a hotel, there an elaborately carved wooden balcony painted turquoise, set off by red geraniums, shaded loggias and shutters of pink, pale blue and red. There is a pharmacy with a shelf of cream and gold ceramic jars, the cold cream labelled in English script. A bold sign under the gables of one building declares Hôtel des Américains in Thirties lettering, though below it is nothing but the town urinal.

You can still sit and stroll under the plane trees on Place Coustou, and I found one of the original private fountains, the *buvette de Lassère*, which still promised relief for the stomach, intestines, liver and haemorrhoids. We found a lovely old restaurant for lunch, with patterned clay tiles on the floor, a curved mahogany and glass screen dividing the dining room from the bar, and wine *à volonté* poured by the chef himself.

The Société Ramond still holds meetings here and I met M. Jean-Marc Boirie, the secretary, in the Musée Salies, where he showed me an exhibition of Ramond's very own plant collection, each tiny dried flower carefully labelled in flowing copperplate. M. Borrie was delighted by my interest in Ramond, and when he explained that the Society had always been intended for anyone with an interest in the Pyrenees, mountaineers or not, I resolved to join, and became the first English member they had recruited in quite some time.

By the time the Russells arrived in the 1840s, the English colony was already well established. They lived in Maison

Lacroutz on the rue des Pyrénées on the route up towards the Pic du Midi. It was a typical Bagnères house, entered by a wide passage, large enough for a carriage, with kitchens on the ground floor opening onto a flagged court-yard. Large salons and bedrooms were on the first floor. A family of the Russells' distinction would have had several servants, a cook and perhaps a coachman.

Though Bagnères received plenty of French visitors, society was dominated by the English or Anglo-French marriages and both communities got together to celebrate the anniversary of the return of the king to France in 1824. Relations between the French and English were not always cordial, however. There was the famous duel in 1822 which arose from a contretemps in the public library. An English officer came across an account of the battle of Toulouse which he deemed too favourable to the French, and he pro-ceeded to annotate the margin of the book with his version of events. When this was discovered he was challenged to a duel, and most unfortunately killed his French opponent.

Social life in Bagnères followed strict rules and Mary Eyre typically fell foul of them, failing to pay her respects to the English residents and wearing the wrong dress to a glittering costume ball in honour of the Prince of Wales's marriage. 'I absolutely went to it in my plain black *mousse-line-de-laine* dress, for I had no other.' Her drab appearance led her to be dubbed ever after 'the lamentable Miss Eyre' by her unfeeling compatriots. She did take tea with the celebrated Mrs Alexander, famous for her deeply moving hymns. Her *Hymns for Children* had gone through thirty-two editions, Mary observed in admiration. Mary Eyre always enjoyed remembering the hymns she knew as she sat on a mountainside contemplating the view.

Everyone's preferred physician was Irish Dr Bagnell, known as 'Old Bag', who always departed from Pau for the summer season in Bagnères in great style, as his niece recalled in an article for the Société Ramond. 'We left early in the morning in his large landau with two beautiful black Russian horses, given by one of his admirers, and driven by Jules, who like his master wore a high hat with a large cockade, the better to increase his minuscule stature. We took with us a trunk full of chickens, ducks and rabbits for food in the summer, plus fresh eggs and conserves. It was as if we were going to the north pole.' It took all day to get there, with pauses for picnics and siestas.

In Bagnères the English made their regular morning promenade along the Allées des Coustous and de Thermes, and paid regular visits to Dr Bagnell, who would prescribe gargles for sore throats. Bagnell himself made quite a spectacle on his way to take the waters, riding a donkey called Infanta, decked out in brocade, colourful pompoms and little gold bells, the reins in one hand, in the other a long crook, with which he prodded the donkey. On his knee he carried two grey Skye terriers he had been given by Lady Brooke. Completing the cavalcade was Rob Roy, the donkey's foal.

By far Bagnères's most famous English denizen was Field Marshal Lord Alanbrooke, chairman of the Chiefs of Staff under Churchill in the Second World War. He was born Alan Francis Brooke in 1883 in Bagnères. His father was Sir Victor Brooke, a contemporary and great friend of Henry Russell. He was the classic Great White Hunter, like a character from Rider Haggard, six feet tall, broad-chested, with curled moustache and full black beard, who liked to shoot big game, tigers, leopards and elephants in

India and Africa. He came to the Pyrenees for the health of his wife and finally settled in Pau and Bagnères. There he became the premier sportsman of the Pau colony and was Master of the Pau Hunt from 1884 to 1888. Alan was the youngest of his eight children.

Henry Russell's early life in Bagnères must have been similar to Alanbrooke's: a rustic childhood close to nature, with considerable liberty. Bagnères was very rustic; one anecdote has Alan skinning a vulture using Lady Brooke's scent spray to keep away the lice. Alan began life speaking French and also spoke béarnais with the servants and peasants they met as they rode about the country. Like Russell he always said he felt as if he had two countries, and would embrace like a Frenchman, though the finer points of English grammar and spelling always eluded him. In 1940 a story appeared in the French regional press of an English commander who could speak gascon; Alanbrooke had met a local regiment from the Pyrenees elsewhere in France, and had spoken to the soldiers in their own language, much to their delight.

It was around Bagnères–de–Bigorre that Henry Russell had his first experiences of the Pyrenees. He writes about taking his first steps on the banks of the Adour river, and it was here that he was first introduced to the mountains by his mother.

She was clearly an extraordinary person: very tall, and rather masculine, and by all accounts a prodigious walker. She often walked from Pau to Oloron, a distance of over thirty kilometres, and continued to walk considerable distances well into old age. She was always respectably dressed, as if out to pay a formal visit, in a neat bonnet with a cashmere shawl wrapped around her shoulders, and carried an overnight bag in case she was obliged to spend the night in a hotel.

When the children were still young she would stride off after breakfast with a pack of provisions and a water gourd strapped across her body. They would walk for hours, and when the youngest got tired his mother would carry him on her shoulders. Henry was always ahead, a keen climber from an early age, and already exhibiting remarkable endurance, never affected by thirst or heat, to the dismay of his siblings.

I love to think of them all together, exploring the woods and valleys in view of the surrounding mountains. I like to think Mme Mère, as she was called, would sometimes take off her bonnet and shawl and join her children bathing in the rivers. The image I treasure above all others from our own years in the Pyrenees is a photograph of Theo aged about nine, crouched on a rock beside a waterfall. He is a black silhouette against a great wall of stone smoothed by the constant action of the water tumbling over it, and coloured with mineral shades of vermilion and marcasite. The light catches the glittering cascade and the waves of the pool below churned by the impact of the water. A minute later he leapt in. 'The most amazing thing was being on the other side of the waterfall,' he told me later with shining eyes.

I always loved paddling about in the river with him, under the dim green canopy of overhanging trees, leaping barefoot across stones dappled by rays of sunlight. We would construct dams of twigs and pebbles, slide off large mossy boulders to bathe in cool clear pools, soft mud squishing through our toes, watch tiny silver trout darting round us and wait for iridescent dragonflies to skim the surface of the water.

They must have been thought eccentric, the Russell family, since in those days walking for pleasure was considered distinctly odd. Murray's handbook for travellers is very clear about this in the section on passports: 'Englishmen, especially *pedestrians*, travelling in remote parts of France, or entering by a distant frontier, may arouse the suspicions of the local police and run the risk not only of *detention, but even of rough treatment*, if they cannot produce a passport.' The natives found it hard to understand why anyone would travel simply for pleasure and experience, with nothing to sell.

In *A Peek at the Pyrenees* by a Pedestrian, published in 1867, the Pedestrian records the astonishment of the hoteliers in Les Eaux-Chaudes when he rejects the omnibus to travel the five miles to Eaux-Bonnes. 'They were quite sure we must feel tired after walking about so much; and we had some difficulty in explaining to them that the reason of our coming a distance of 1000 miles was not for the purpose of riding in an omnibus, as that was a thing we could do every day in London, but in order to see the country.'

Ever after Henry was always to hold a particular affection for Bagnères, the gentle hills echoing with cowbells and caressed by harmonious breezes, the murmuring of the river Adour, and 'the gracious mountains with elegant contours, grouped by a divine hand around the Pic du Midi'. It seemed to encapsulate his nostalgia for his childhood haunts, where more than anywhere he felt the tug of humanity drawing him back to earth from his lofty summits. The 'distant sounds of the world that come to us at the summit of mountains' made him realize that nature alone was not enough. 'All sailors at sea know the charm of the least sigh, the least melody coming from the land.'

My friend Gerard too spoke like that of his experience living alone in his *cortal*, one of many simple summer stone cabins constructed by the villagers up in the mountains, and used until well into the 1950s, until recently falling into ruin but now being given a new lease of life by the Mosset rainbow tribe. Gerard explained how important it was that though he was almost an hour's walk from the village, ' I could always hear the sounds of the valley. It was always important to be aware of the world below. I needed to know it was there.'

I was reminded of a TV programme I once saw on Nazi mountain climbers in the 1930s, whose passion for health and fitness was harnessed for the Fatherland; one of them said that the greatest moment was not in getting to the peak, but in returning to civilization and how beautiful it all looked, and how wonderful it was to be welcomed by humankind again, to see flowers, and faces again.

I had read in a 1950s bulletin of the Société Ramond that the tombs of the English could still be seen in the cemetery of Bagnères. But when I went to investigate not only was there no longer an English cemetery, there were no English graves. I found the cemetery keeper, clad in faded blue municipal dungarees, leaning on his broom, chatting to two old ladies with vases of flowers on the way to tend their husbands' graves. He was anxious to help, assuming I was searching for a long lost relative. '*Vous cherchez votre famille, madame?*' he murmured sympathetically, and took me into the chilly little gatehouse, where he thumbed ancient yellowed burial ledgers inscribed in brown ink, scratching his thatch of grey hair in puzzlement. Finally he directed me to one bedraggled corner of the grounds, where two crumbling crosses with the name of Gardner were just discernible, labelled by the *mairie* for imminent removal due to lack of interest. Apart from that there was just a mass grave where all the English had been put together under a simple polished granite slab. The lightly incised lettering had already almost faded away. Only when I mentioned Alanbrooke did the guardian of the dead perk up, and remember singing hymns and dancing outside the Brooke villa after the Second World War. Now the only remaining reference to the English is the avenue Marshal Alanbrooke.

6

The Lac de Gaube and a picturesque death

'And all along the valley, by rock and cave and tree,
The voice of the dead was a living voice to me.'
Alfred Lord Tennyson, *In the Valley of Cauteretz*

For the young Henry Russell his visit to the Lac de Gaube
at age six was his first real experience of the High Pyrenees
and his first view of the Vignemale, the mountain that was
to dominate his life. The Lac de Gaube was one of the most
celebrated sights of the period; a deep cold lake high in the
mountains above the spa town of Cauterets.

It is just as awe-inspiring today, as we discovered. We
followed the traditional route from Argelès-Gazost, south
of Lourdes, to Pierrefitte-Nestalas by car instead of horse-
drawn carriage, and up to Cauterets through a deep
wooded gorge along a road which snakes around the
mountainside hundreds of feet above the river. Even now it
seems a prodigious feat of road building. Its savage
grandeur astonished early visitors as they rattled along in
carriages and open landaus across great arched bridges
spanning the deep abyss.

The narrow defile opens out into the green gentle valley
of Cauterets, the little town nestling in the lee of a thickly
wooded massif. At least, that day it nestled, but Cauterets
is a town of many moods, and when we had visited once

before in late autumn in pouring rain the mountain seemed to loom over it threateningly. Out of season the town was dead, the hotels closed, and the only restaurant open served Swiss melted cheese *raclette* in anticipation of skiers to come. Now, though, it was a hot July day, bustling with a mixture of *curistes* and climbers, each in their own pursuit of health, some discussing their schedule of treatments, others describing perilous snowy scrambles. A carousel tinkled merrily on the promenade, a lacy iron confection built by Eiffel for the Universal Exhibition of 1889 and bought by Cauterets to enhance its attractions. The town's curious wooden train station has the same provenance, starting off as the Norwegian Pavilion for the same Exhibition, and would be quite at home in Disneyland. We stayed in the Hôtel de Paris, one of the Belle Epoque hotels with a jolly terrace on the main square, its beds as authentically of the period as the architecture.

While Theo played crazy golf I visited the museum, accommodated in what was once the sumptuous Hôtel d'Angleterre. The collection is arranged in tableaux of models wearing the fashions of the time: gowns of satin and silk, bonnets and feathers, men in immaculate evening suits; nineteenth-century ghosts clustered round the grand piano and tables set for dinner with the finest crystal and silver. In later years Russell had been a celebrated visitor to the hotel, and his eccentric adventures were always recorded by the local press.

In the latter half of the nineteenth century Cauterets was one of the most fashionable spas in Europe, hosting crowned heads and poets from Victor Hugo to Lord Tennyson, George Sand to Alfred de Vigny. The English naturally were early visitors – the frontispiece of a French volume on the history of Cauterets is illustrated with a drawing by Marianne Colston from 1821. It shows a tiny town of mainly wooden buildings clustered round the church and bridge over the river. Several spa establishments catered to the *curistes*; at first they were simple wooden shelters over the sulphurous hot springs out in the open countryside, to which the wealthier invalids were carried in sedan chairs, and the poorer classes trundled along in wheelbarrows.

As the town developed more hotels and houses were built of stone, with tiled roofs, marble doorways and wrought iron balconies. Elegant gardens and promenades were laid out, and grand *thermes* buildings constructed with marble terraces, baths and fountains for water drinkers. The healing waters were administered in every imaginable way, as showers, massages, gargles and inhalations; most practised at the time was the vaginal douche (no doubt a reflection of the prevalence of venereal disease). When the waters were drunk the sulphurous taste was ameliorated with barley sugar and the *curistes* could be seen walking up and down outside the bath-houses with long yellow sticks protruding from their mouths.

It had all become far too civilized, as Henry Blackburn observed in his 1867 guide to the spas of the Pyrenees: 'Our thoughts are not so much of the mountains and of the pine forests that overhang its streets, as of smooth lawns and parterres; not of torrents, but of the prettiest artificial cascades . . . everything was civilized at Cauterets, they had civilized a bear; and nothing will leave a more mournful memory, not even the tragedy at the Lac de Gaube, than the picture of this dancing bear performing almost in sight of his comrades looming down from the mountains.'

*

It must have been a relief for Henry and his nature-loving mother to escape the town and set off for the high mountains together. I don't know if they had guides but I like to think they were alone. Mme Mère drew a portrait of Henry at that time (he was six in 1840) leaning on a table next to a curtained window from which the light fell on him. He looks relaxed, one hand in the pocket of his soft pantaloons, his shirt loose with wide-cuffed voluminous sleeves. Most noticeable is his height, his long legs, and long delicate fingers. His hair is still uncut, curling round his ears, his eyes gazing down at his seated mother.

They had a strong relationship and she was a deeply religious woman, inspiring an abiding faith in all her children. Henry's sister Christine later became a nun, and his brother Frank joined the army of the Pope. Henry often writes of feeling closer to God on the mountain tops. According to Frank it was his attachment to his mother which prevented him from simple nature worship: '. . . all that was good, strong and generous he had from her. Never had a woman exercised over her son an influence more strong or more enduring, never has a son had such tender affection for his mother.'

It was grey and hazy when Theo and I left Cauterets, with a thick mist veiling the tops of the mountains. The coach driver who skilfully navigated six miles of hairpin bends to the Pont d'Espagne assured us that it was beautiful weather higher up. Even in 1840 the Pont d'Espagne was a favourite resting point; early sketches show shelters of wood and pine branches, chairs and tables laden with bottles. Ladies with parasols were offered *dégustations* of fresh milk by the shepherds, who kept it cool in the river.

There are even more tourists today (though now the Pont itself is closed to traffic and all vehicles are corralled in a large car park) but no amount of visitors could diminish the astonishing sight of the waterfalls. Here two rivers meet, the Gave de Gaube and the Marcadau (*marcadau* means walking place in béarnais, a practical language). They pound down the mountainside, through a forest of tall dark pines and huge boulders, crashing and boiling into thunderous cascades.

We wandered among them, crossing a network of bridges (the Pont d'Espagne itself is now a substantial stone bridge, but in Russell's day was still a simple structure of wooden tree trunks thrown across the chasm) and negotiating large stepping stones, awed by the noise, mesmerized by the power of the water, the torrent a deep blue-green, the spray foaming white, with here and there river rainbows caught in the spray.

These days you can swing up the mountain by *télécabine* (closed cabins) and *télésiège* (open seats intended primarily for skiers) and though we eschewed the former, Theo could not resist the latter. (Personally I found being suspended over the void in an open chair almost as scary as the mountain ride at Disneyland.) There was a lot to be said, in the absence of sedan chairs, for arriving at 1725 metres without trudging up a steep rocky path.

Two valleys meet at the Pont d'Espagne, one leading to the Lac de Gaube, the other via the Marcadau valley into Spain. Thomas Clifton Paris, the Cambridge professor who explored the Pyrenees in 1842 in top hat and tails, typically got lost here, missing the path to the Lac de

Gaube and ending up in Spain. Happily now the paths are marked and the area is part of the Western Pyrenees National Park, a meticulously protected environment, abounding in wild flowers and butterflies. It was exhilarating to walk among the high peaks, under a clear blue sky, on a still warm day, surrounded by the scent of pine and herbs, exclaiming at the flowers: purple irises, yellow poppies, aconite, pink clusters of saxifrage and gentians. We found tiny little *fraises des bois* cool under shady fern leaves, and ate them by the handful. It was very heaven and as Theo slipped his hand into mine I thought of Henry and his mother walking together to the lake.

It was not far to the *lac*, a perfect mountain basin of emerald green water, with steep rugged sides of shale and scree, anchored by scrubby pines. At the far end, framed in a Y of flanking hills, with a cascade pouring down the middle, the Vignemale presents itself, as symmetrical a view as Ruskin could have wished: the beauty of the lake reflecting the forbidding crags of the massif, the grey forbidding north face of the Vignemale, with its glacier glinting in the sun. I sat on a large smooth rock of granite jutting out into the water, rippling into waves with a gentle breeze, and felt it really would be better to sketch it all rather than look for words.

For people as religious as the Victorians mountains inevitably inspired a spiritual response, and visitors to the Lac de Gaube wrote of 'astonishment and religious fear' and 'awful splendour'. For Mrs Boddington visiting in 1837 in a procession of four sedan chairs with sixteen chairmen, it was 'filled with the solemn music of the gale as it sweeps over its waters . . . lonely, and melancholy in its loneliness, but not repelling'.

Gustave Flaubert was more enthusiastic about the trout he ate at the *auberge* than the acclaimed beauty of the lake. He sniffed at the entries in the visitors' book: 'You will see only two kinds of exclamations in it: one about the beauty of the Lac de Gaube, the other about how good the trout are . . . which means that only fools or gluttons have picked up the pen to sign their names and their thoughts.' The trout we ate were as overpriced as Murray's guide warned its nineteenth-century readers, but very good none the less, the white flesh tender around a feathery spray of fennel, the skin grilled crisp, with a chilled glass of dry white Jurançon to wash it down. Theo said it was complemented just as well by Coca-Cola.

As we sat safely ensconced under white umbrellas in the restaurant beside the lake, so smooth and innocent, I described to Theo the great tragedy that had unfolded here. I pointed out the green painted rowing boat moored by the shore, both picturesque and inviting. Had I been invited to row across the lake, however, I think I would have declined.

On 20 September 1832, a few years before Russell's first visit, the Lac de Gaube had been the scene of a terrible accident. A young English couple on their honeymoon had visited the lake, carried there in sedan chairs. Young Mr Pattison, a Lincoln's Inn lawyer, had persuaded Susan, his twenty-six-year-old bride, to take a boat across the lake. About half a mile out he stood up in the boat, and it immediately capsized. He sank into the cold waters at once but his wife's skirts buoyed her up until she too drowned. Neither could swim and neither could their porters, who listened helplessly to their piteous cries from the shore. The actual depth of the lake is about forty metres though it used to be thought much deeper. Victor Hugo claimed you could build six cathedrals of Notre Dame on top of each other though no doubt this was poetic licence. (His own daughter Leopoldine also drowned on her honeymoon, in 1843, only days after Hugo had visited the Lac de Gaube. The megalomaniac Hugo sometimes wondered if the power of his poetry actually made things happen.)

Such a tragedy adds a certain piquancy to any tourist attraction, and the Lac de Gaube soon became one of the most exploited sites in the Pyrenees. More scandalous accounts embroidered the tragedy, suggesting it had been a double suicide pact, supposedly brought on by the English affliction of 'spleen' and the desire for a picturesque death. Stories written in pamphlets were sold by the lake for years afterwards. ('A lying romance, grafted on their sad story,' warned Murray's Guide, 'destitute of all truth, is sold on the spot – let no-one buy it.') Soon there was a marked tendency to people other Pyrenean lakes with drowned English folk. Visitors recalled being told the story, and almost in the same breath asked if they would like to take a row across the lake.

By the time the Russell family arrived there was a marble memorial to the couple, and a scurrilous pamphlet to read. The boat was still there. In 1943 the English monument was destroyed by German troops, and has not been replaced. The event has been almost forgotten. When I asked the waiter at the restaurant about the famous story he looked completely blank.

Henry's first view of Vignemale made a profound impression. While they were at the lake they saw a terrifying storm break over the mountain, one of those Pyrenean storms of such power and menace that it could only have added to the glory and terror of the mountain looming above the child. He never forgot it and ever after he revelled in dramatic Pyrenean tempests. He described in his *Souvenirs* a storm he experienced in 1877, descending from the Pic de Cambales between Vignemale and Balaitous. He and his guides had stopped for the night at a shepherds' cabin just below the snow line, and while the shepherds stayed in the hut, laughing and joking around the fire as they prepared their soup, Henry went outside to watch the storm. 'It was one of the most beautiful storms I ever witnessed in my life,' he wrote. 'All the furies fell on the Vignemale and the great orifice of Port de Marcadau. The lightning did not stop. When it flashed it was like daylight behind the vast mountains, in between reigned impenetrable night.'

Pyrenean storms have lost none of their intensity. I too have a weakness for them, though I prefer to draw up a chair to the French windows for the performance. A storm can arrive so fast – one minute the sky is clear and cloudless, then little clouds gather at the head of the valley, higher branches of the trees start to rustle, then suddenly it is as if there are four winds at once, bending the trees and whirling dust and leaves into the air like a tornado. Within half an hour the sunny valley is a howling wilderness of moaning wind and rolling thunder. The mountain tops go dark, momentarily thrown into silhouette by flashes of lightning, sheet and forked, so close you duck even at a window.

Then the rain comes in sheets, as if someone has upended a bucket. Sometimes there are hailstones as big as snooker balls cracking onto the skylights, pulverizing the grapes and peaches in the fields. Water floods under doors, and through any available cracks. Just as suddenly after half an hour the rain stops, the mist clears, and the clouds drift away elsewhere, leaving the valley awash with torrents of water, silver pools shining in the emerging sun, the river muddy and turbulent with floating debris everywhere, devastated trees and shattered branches. The sun's rays streaming through the clouds add a weird quality to the light, as if a great holocaust has passed. The process is cleansing, almost biblical in its intensity, as if we have been purged, as if a giant hair dryer has been turned on the valley, blasting away every mote of dust and cloud. Then it moves on to the next valley, like the helicopter which patrols overhead, watching for fires, and we see the lightning flashing away behind the hills.

Recounting the tragedy of the Lac de Gaube years later in of one his guidebooks, Russell added, 'They were English of course.' It is an enigmatic remark, but this fact must have struck him even then, as a child, aware of his own dual identity, already trying to make sense of the different threads of his background. Though he always spoke French with his mother (she never spoke a word of English) and spent his first years in France, he was also deeply influenced by his father's insistence on his aristocratic British lineage.

Russell was always known nevertheless as *l'anglais*, the Englishman (even if he was actually Irish). He clearly enjoyed his dual identity, playing up his Englishness to the French, and no doubt vice versa. His name was conveniently adaptable too, and he used a variety of signatures in hotel visitors' books. Sometimes he was Henri Russell, sometimes Henry Russell-Killough. And once his father received his papal title he could even call himself count.

Henry, like Henry IV and Field Marshal Lord Alanbrooke, must also have spoken the regional language of béarnais, a version of gascon, which is related to occitan and provençal. Until the end of the nineteenth century when French became compulsory in schools and there was a deliberate campaign to eliminate regional languages, most of the peasantry spoke little or no French. A woman of the region like Mme Russell would have spoken béarnais to her servants and to the peasants she met on her walks. In later years Henry would have spoken patois as well as French with his guides and porters. Most of the English in those days spoke French. Russell spoke and wrote both languages, though his writing in French is more elegant, his English prosaic.

Henry Russell's idyllic existence in the mountains was interrupted by the inevitable, school, first in France and then in Ireland. He was sent first to the Jesuit college of Pons near Saintes, and then to Pontlevoy in the Loire valley, an eleventh-century abbey which had long been a college for minor nobility, and was a royal military school until 1793. He learned to play the violoncello and wrote letters to his mother about his plans for forthcoming holidays in the Pyrenees. When he was fifteen he returned to Pau and a tutor. He climbed and dreamed in the Pyrenees, passing entire days in the mountains, inspired in his wanderings by the popular romantic poets and writers of the time, Walter Scott, Tennyson, Lord Byron and Chateaubriand. He asked himself why he was so happy to be alone, why he was so different from others of his age. It was the eternal cry of the adolescent: why am I different? Except that he really was, with a background and childhood experiences that had already set him on a highly original path.

His romantic inclinations were further inflamed by several years as a youth in Ireland, where he revelled in the wild western Irish coast. Tennyson went there too in 1848 to see Atlantic waves, and wrote of shimmering waterfalls, huge moons, terrific sunsets and forests full of wild deer. A peasant dogged the poet's steps in the extreme west, demanding, 'Be you from France?' It is nice to think of these two lovers of wild nature striding along the same Irish cliffs.

By 1848 when there were revolutions all over Europe, France was again no place for Catholic Royalists. After thirty-three years of monarchy France was ripe for revolution again, and the king, Louis-Philippe, was over-thrown and fled to Surrey. The Second Republic was declared, and, in a wave of nostalgia, the newly franchised population voted overwhelmingly for Napoleon's nephew, who only three years later declared himself Emperor Napoleon III, Le Petit Napoléon as Victor Hugo christened him.

The Russells scuttled back to Ireland. There Henry would have met his Irish grandfather, Patrick Henry, and other members of the family. He would perhaps have visited the ancestral lands in County Down and possibly been shown the ruins of the family pile, Killough Castle, long since lost to them.

Henry Russell's father always went to considerable effort to prove his noble ancestry. This was traced back to Robert de Rozel, who came to England with the forces of William the Conqueror in 1066. In England the Russell family became members of the peerage, the Dukes of

Bedford, and included Lord John Russell, prime minister under Queen Victoria, and later philosopher Sir Bertrand Russell. These Russells hung on to their fortune by turning Protestant.

The Irish Russells had helped Henry II invade Ireland in the eleventh century and were granted lands and given the title of Barons of Ulster. These invaders defended their territory against what they termed 'the Irish swarms' until the seventeenth century when Cromwell systematically colonized the entire country with English Protestants, stripping the Catholics of their lands and rights. The Russells hung on to the last vestiges of their territory in Ballystrew and Quoniamstown in County Down until the end of the nineteenth century.

The Russells went to live in Dublin. The children were sent to school, Christine to be educated at New Hall (Saint-Sepulchre, near to London, a convent school that seems to have specialized in foreign Catholic girls, since it was also where Adèle Domecq, John Ruskin's first unrequited love and the daughter of his father's partner in his sherry import business, had been sent from Spain ten years earlier). Henry and his brother Frank were sent, like their father, to Clongowes college, set up by the Jesuits in 1814. It remains one of the most famous Catholic schools in Ireland, and was also attended by James Joyce, until his parents could not afford it any more. Joyce mentioned it often in *Portrait of the Artist as a Young Man*, and remembered 'the troubling odour' of the corridors long after. The building, to the south-east of Dublin, is a proper castle with castellated turrets, approached by a long avenue of limes, and bears a distinct resemblance to Killough Castle. This was as close as Henry would get to a traditional public school education, playing cricket and rugby, and with strict discipline enforced. The Rules, covering every aspect of life and duties, were read every day.

It was very religious, with 6.30 a.m. mass daily in the boys' chapel, before breakfast at long refectory tables in the dining room with its tall stained glass windows. The boys slept in dormitories with curtained iron beds, each with its own washstand, and every move was overseen by strict Jesuit priests in black gowns and three-cornered red hats. Still, they cannot have been too harsh, since ever after Henry retained a special affection for their colleagues, delighted to find seminaries of French missionaries in his travels through Asia.

However, Ireland at that time was hardly a peaceful retreat. It was the height of the Irish famine, now considered the most appalling disaster of nineteenth-century Europe: the Irish holocaust. Between 1846 and 1850 as many as one million died from hunger and disease, and Ireland's population dropped from eight million before the famine to five million.

It is hard to believe that the suffering could have escaped the notice of the Russell family, even if their own workers were not starving to death in miserable hovels. There were skeletal hungry people everywhere, and food riots in Dublin itself. No doubt the Russells were merely typical of their class and period, believing that some people were ordained poor and their betters had only a duty of charitable relief. The only surviving evidence of Henry in Dublin is a photograph of him as a youth dressed in Elizabethan costume for a fancy dress ball.

After Clongowes Henry was sent for a year to Dublin University where he studied chemistry. The family spent their holidays on the west coast of Ireland. Here Henry went completely native. He fell in love with the sea, going out with the local fishermen in their tiny coracles, bathing at dawn in winter and summer, even breaking the ice and diving into frozen water. The image of his father's bathing habits in Pau somehow seems quite credible. Blasted by waves and sea, wet to the bone, the young Henry stayed out for hours. He strode along the cliff tops with the pounding seas below him, in an ecstasy of nature worship, his head full of romantic poetry. Fortunately he did not have the delicate health of a poet. He was never ill, and seems to have had the most amazingly robust constitution. Already he was desperate to travel the world, and as he looked west across the Atlantic Ocean his thoughts turned increasingly towards distant lands.

The family often returned to the Pyrenees, where Henry walked and climbed with extraordinary energy. In those early days he often went on expeditions with his family, and of course his mother. In 1851, when he was seventeen, they walked from Luchon to Gavarnie via Aragnouet, over the Col de Campbieil. It was early spring with the fresh scent of broom floating down from the hillside. I like to imagine the two together, the tall robust woman in her skirt and bonnet, and her gangling teenage son, with their hob-nailed boots, gourds and alpenstocks, striding over the snowy col together.

The same route was followed by the Pedestrian, in *A Peek at the Pyrenees*, sometime in late spring in the 1860s. Aragnouet, in the gloomy narrow gorge at the foot of the col, was a customs post and the *douaniers* (customs officers) immediately tried to discourage the Pedestrian's attempt on the col, insisting the snow was too deep. 'All the *douaniers* of the station, to the number of four or five, called to see us: and they stood around, admiring our light alpaca coats, our flannel shirts and flasks, examining them closely, and deliberating with one another as to their value, without taking much notice of their owners.' In fact most of the village turned out to see the pedestrians walking for pleasure.

The Pedestrian conceded the necessity of a guide, since there was no beaten track, and the snow during the last 600 metres was so deep they were sometimes floundering up to their hips. The col itself is about 2800 metres and according to their guide was always covered in snow. It took them three and a half hours to ascend to the top. Their guide, who was only wearing simple canvas snow shoes, prodded the snow with a stick before encouraging them on.

There was a splendid view. 'From the top there is a fine view of the Mont Perdu and other snow-mountains, which seem almost within a stone's throw; but the bright glare of the sun was so strong that we could only remove our veils for a short time to enjoy the prospect.' Hats with veils were very popular as sun screens in the days before sunglasses, but with better eye protection they would also have been able to see the Vignemale to the west, its double cones rising above the other summits and separated from each other by the enormous glacier shining in the sun. No doubt when Henry and his mother reached the top of the col they would have enjoyed such a splendid view of Vignemale, and perhaps recalled the storm they saw together.

Walking in snow is extremely difficult as I discovered after we had a tremendous fall of snow one night. Icicles hung a metre long from the roof and the car was a foot deep in snow. Even the donkeys in the field had icicles hanging from them. The world was quiet and monochrome, the trees black lattices against the whiteness, a faint hue of brown on the hills caught by the setting sun. Only the newly budding mimosa showed a touch of colour, and the blue windcheater of the sole human I could see, a farmer trudging across his terrace to feed his chickens before nightfall. As an experiment I tried walking in deep snow, sinking beyond my knees into the softness. It is very hard work even for ten minutes or so. I cannot imagine trudging for hours in leather boots, however well greased, or tweed coats, however thick. The peasant with his snow shoes had the right idea.

7

Le Far West

'My native country is for me the country that I love, that is, the one that makes me dream.'

Gustave Flaubert

Henry Russell had gazed at the Atlantic Ocean from the coasts of France and Ireland and dreamed of crossing it all his childhood. The Pyrenees were not enough. Not yet. He was determined to travel, and most of all he dreamed of the sea. *Moby Dick* was published in Britain in 1851 and there are enough echoes of Melville in Russell's own writing to suggest he was almost certainly inspired by that dramatic tale of adventure at sea. He was also affected by the idea of the Anglo-French alliance, a recent *rapprochement* between former enemies which for someone who was half French and half British was deeply gratifying. France and Britain were fighting together against the Russians in the Crimea, trying to limit their access to the Mediterranean. Despite being a flimsy excuse for a war and a military debacle it was the first war to be reported by journalists, and reports of heroic battles, including the Charge of the Light Brigade, were followed avidly by the British public, including impressionable young men like Henry Russell.

He had wanted to join the French navy, but could not enter French naval school because he was of British nationality through his father. So as soon as he was twenty-one he declared himself French in the Paris arrondissement where he was staying with his brother Frank. Then he signed on as a voluntary merchant marine, an alternative path into the navy. He engaged for eighteen months as a navigator on the sailing ship *Brave-Lourmel*, bound for Peru and the far shores of South America, via Cape Horn. The ship set sail in May 1856, the crew allotted the traditional two-tier bunks, with their few possessions in sea chests lashed to a ring on the deck. Their diet consisted of the livestock aboard, sea birds if they could shoot them, and the usual grim fare of salted pork, beef, pickled vegetables, molasses and dried biscuit.

The voyage did not go well. Henry loved the wild grandeur of the ocean, but he felt trapped, his liberty severely curtailed. Henry the free spirit did not submit easily to naval discipline and was horrified by the harsh treatment and floggings meted out to the sailors. He quarrelled with the captain, who despised him as an amateur and clapped him in irons for insubordination. Happily for Henry he had good contacts; his mother's brother was by this time chamberlain to Napoleon III and arranged for the French Consul in Lima to rescue Henry from the ship. Henry had only a few days in Lima, but it was enough to give him an overwhelming impression of the Andes, where the high snows reminded him of Vignemale.

Then he was shipped home again. He had a memorably terrifying experience rounding Cape Horn in a hurricane, with huge waves towering over the ship, cataracts of water pouring over the decks, and hailstones the size of gulls' eggs. But most of his time was spent perched high up in the rigging, reading and dreamily contemplating the sea.

He stayed only briefly in Paris, and then in June 1857

took off for North America with an Irish school friend, Francis Cruise. He declared himself a *touriste*, then a fashionable new word recently coined by Stendhal, with none of the pejorative implications it has since acquired. Henry defends the idea with some passion, writing in his introduction to *Souvenirs d'un Montagnard*, 'It is a mission as philosophical and noble as any other', insisting on the need for travellers who simply explore without particular purpose, paving the way for others, viewing nature for its beauty, interpreting it like musicians.

Russell and Cruise boarded a steam ship from Le Havre on 17 June 1857, wanting 'to see the country, its lakes, forests, its inhabitants and to explore "le Far West".' They made a voyage of 12,000 kilometres from Saint Laurent to Mississippi, Niagara, Chicago and New York, travelling on the great new railways and the huge steamboats which plied the rivers. Henry loved the river boats, delighting in their vast size, their tiers of decks, and the huge salons, magnificently decorated, where balls were held every night. He was astonished by the dining rooms, 'invaded, ravaged and abandoned in less than twenty minutes by hundreds of determined guests'. He marvelled that 'the stomachs of the New World have a capacity that in Europe no-one would ever understand'. This was good news for Henry, who was known all his life for his enormous appetite. On the very first page of his account of the voyage, in the middle of evoking the sea view in true romantic style – 'the spectral icebergs and livid rays of the setting sun' – he slips happily into a description of the ship's dining room, deserted by seasick passengers, where the tables were replenished four times a day – 'excellent good fortune for the survivors', wrote Henry.

When he and Cruise arrived in St Paul, Minnesota they were ready for adventure, challenged by forests 'full of assassins and wild beasts'. American exploration was still in its early days, with huge expanses of untamed country teeming with buffalo, and wagon trains heading west across the prairies into the sunset: a culture of romantic wanderers which must have influenced the young Henry Russell.

There is a genre of paintings, the American Sublime, produced during the early nineteenth century, that captures the romantic idealism of those early pioneers: huge horizons with virgin forests and green valleys with arching rainbows, fluorescent sunsets casting a golden glow over a land of promise and plenty. Vast prairies with only the tiniest of human figures to mar their emptiness promised space and freedom to Europeans fleeing oppression and poverty. The potential of such a vast wilderness, its combination of beauty and danger, proved irresistible to the young Henry Russell.

Russell and Cruise equipped themselves with shotguns, mules and a cart, provisions of salt pork, sardines and biscuits, and plunged into the forest, hacking their way through with an axe, and plagued by mosquitoes and flies. At night as they sat huddled round their campfire they heard the calls of wild geese and worried about bears. There was evidence of Indians, including Indian tombs covered in tree bark. Occasionally they glimpsed the native inhabitants canoeing silently down the river.

For Henry, Indians represented the noble savage of Rousseau and he expressed appreciation of their native culture: 'Poor Indians, infants of nature, disinherited race, retreating daily from white civilization, like sand-dunes before the sea, their degradation and brutalization is a terrible stain on the young and powerful republic of the United States.' Eventually he succeeded in meeting them and he observed their strength and suppleness, the long aquiline noses, and most of all the long hair which no-one is allowed to touch. Henry's effort seems to have been quickly rebuffed.

He was deeply impressed by their powers of endurance and their intimate knowledge of the land. 'You must observe everything,' he wrote later. 'American Indians are much better observers than we are. They can find north by looking at a tree, measuring the thickness of the bark, which is generally stronger to the north than to the south.'

But the cities, too, astonished him. He loved New York, which seduced him with its power and vitality. This lover of remote mountain tops had another side, which enjoyed the world, and he adored walking along Broadway, 'where all the citizens of the world circulate, shop, and bump into each other in a universal cacophony, a line of enormous omnibuses threatens to crush us all and street performers cry in all languages'. He observed it all closely, the architecture, the theatre, and read all the newspapers he could find. The people he found of inexhaustible energy, enterprising and determined. The most famous painting of the period, *Niagara Falls* by Frederic Church, was first shown with great pomp in New York in 1857, when Henry Russell was there; such an exhibition was a major event and since Niagara Falls had been on his list of essential sights to see when he set off on his travels to America, I like to think he would have revelled in the drama and power of Church's painting.

Russell's account of his American travels is the one place

he expresses his political opinions, those of a young European aristocrat on the most democratic society the nineteenth century had yet produced. He was astonished by the sense of equality everywhere. 'You are at the same time the servant and the equal of all. You are in the United States.' This was only three years before the American Civil War was fought over the issue of slavery, a question which caused intense debate in Europe as well. Henry at least was against it, though he argued that servants in Europe were often even worse treated than slaves.

The entire journey to the Americas was a hugely important experience, like his failed attempt to be a mariner. He wrote about it all as soon as he returned and his account was first published in July 1858 in the newspaper, *Le Mémorial des Pyrénées*. It was well written, the romantic hyperbole of his descriptions of nature and landscape balanced by acute observations of people and places with a fresh eye, more journalistic than poetic.

Back in Paris *la vie bohème* was in full swing. Henry stayed with his brother Frank, who was studying law, at the Hôtel de Bourbonne, on rue Jacob. This was the heart of the Latin Quarter, then full of young romantic poets and artists who had rejected conventional life and financial security in favour of art, a first wave of Bohemianism that must have further encouraged Henry in his personal odyssey of exploration. Happily for him family funds and the labours of their Irish tenants meant he had no need to starve in a garret.

Frank and Henry revelled in the pleasures of Paris, the theatre, the balls, the elegant salons. They indulged their passion for music at the opera and concerts. Henry adored dancing: 'Nobody loves the waltz more than I do,' he exclaimed more than once. He went to the gymnasium, enthusiastically embracing the new fashion for physical activity, boxing and gymnastics.

But he was still restless, and walked for hours all over Paris, from the grand boulevards to remote *quartiers*. He strolled through magnificent parks, but found them absurd, dismissing the miniature forests and lakes as feeble imitations of nature. He still sought adventure and inspiration. He had bought the new two-volume edition of Chausenque's writing on the Pyrenees, *Voyages Pédestres*, and his thoughts had already returned to the mountains of his youth. Vincent de Chausenque was a young army officer, inspired by the primitive, unknown territory of the Pyrenees, which he wrote about in all its aspects, the nature and landscape, the people and their customs. He and Russell corresponded for many years.

Then, epiphany. Russell writes, 'One day, a Sunday evening, I was struck by a sudden sadness, and took refuge in La Madeleine, far from the noise of the streets, just at the moment of benediction.' The huge new church had been started in 1764 but sidelined by intervening events– it was almost turned into a Temple of Glory to Napoleon's army, and was only consecrated in 1845. It was an awesome baroque edifice surrounded by a colonnade of Corinthian columns with huge carved bronze doors. The dim interior glinted with marble, gilt and sculpture, and it appealed to Henry's melancholy mood. 'The incense ascended in aromatic clouds, and the building was full of a saintly harmony . . .' His deeply religious spirit, nurtured by his devout mother, was touched. 'I left consoled, knowing the Pyrenees would heal me.'

He returned to Pau, where he arranged the printing of his account of his American travels and devoured Chausenque, inspired by his descriptions of remote valleys and cerulean lakes, and nights far from the noise of the world. He had been away for six years but was not disappointed. 'After having seen so much grand nature, I expected to find the Pyrenees small. But on the contrary they seemed truly monstrous in height.'

It was a very hot summer and Henry set off from Pau to walk to Eaux-Bonnes, starting at midday (he was never an early riser). His attenuated silhouette was a distinctive sight. He had the same wild Irish look as Samuel Beckett; very tall at 1.82 metres, lean and upright, with piercing blue eyes and fine cheekbones. Henry had wavy chestnut hair and a wispy goatee beard which seemed to float ahead of him. His shoulders sloped, as he put it, like a champagne bottle, and seemed to accentuate his height still further. He walked fast, his chest forward, his long legs striding steadily, ascending, one contemporary observed, with the inevitability of a hot air balloon. On that hot summer's day he walked for eight hours: 'Result, a sunburned nose that became more red than ever.'

The family were spending their summer high in the mountains in the Villa des Roses in Luz-Saint-Sauveur, a small spa not far from Barèges, at the foot of the valley of Gavarnie. We stopped there during our Pyrenean explorations and though we never found the Villa des Roses there were several of the period, chalet-style with candy-coloured eaves and shutters, pretty gardens shaded by pine trees, and wooden balconies looking out to the mountains. We stopped for lunch at the Hôtel de Londres, with its terrace overlooking the river, and a dining room with silver and napery that seemed hardly changed since the nineteenth century. While I ate trout and a green salad, Theo had developed a mountain appetite, Henry Russell style, and ate his way through a full menu, including a huge steak which he ordered bloody, much to the approval of the waiter, and only looked daunted when he was offered the fruit bowl for dessert, assuming he was expected to eat its entire contents as well.

Until then Henry had made only relatively easy excursions but now he began to explore unknown territory and set his sights on the summits. 'In all the valleys around Luz, Gavarnie and Cauterets there was not an inhabitant who had not shown me to his neighbour as a marvel or a phantom from another world.' He had never suspected the wonders he found hidden. 'All the glaciers carried my imprint, glaciers that ridiculous little tourists denied even existed.' The Pic du Midi was easy, an afternoon stroll, 'montagne de demoiselle'. The weather plagued him, however; there were always mists. 'Since I was almost always alone, I must have nearly lost my life twenty times.' Sometimes he would take a gun and join the hunters, chasing isards, the Pyrenean chamois, sought for meat and fur, on the high slopes. He spent time with his family, and if it was cloudy he would hire horses and go riding with his sister Christine. Of course most people could ride in those days; it was an essential form of transport, but one that demanded a much greater level of fitness and strength than we have today.

My friend Gerard has always explored the mountains on horseback, and I remember when I first came to Mosset the stories of this romantic figure descending from the hills on his horse like a Wild West cowboy. He had grown up in

South Africa and was used to wide open spaces. Like Russell he liked his nature grand. He once showed me on the map the route he had followed from the Cerdagne to Mosset, a journey over hill and vale which took no account of the roads which for most of us are the inevitable template of travel. 'On a horse you see so much more,' he explained. 'Of course you are higher up, but you don't have to look at your feet all the time. And you can go so much further.' And travelling with horses gives the terrain different meaning. 'You are always looking for meadows where they can graze, or sources of water.' When he ran a horse trekking enterprise for a while he was always getting lost. 'But it didn't really matter,' he assured me. 'You are always secure with horses. Even if the mist descends and you don't know where you are. We always had a pack animal, sleeping bags, provisions. You always have protection.'

As much as he could, Russell climbed, following in the footsteps of Chausenque. Several times he attempted Ardiden, the mountain to the west of Luz. He was unable to find Chausenque's path in the desolate massif of granite, until he discovered that the summit he sought was not a continuation of a chain but separated by a deep, wild valley full of lakes. When he finally made it to the top, although the view was magnificent, he decided it was not worth the trouble it took to get there, especially over the great chaos of snow and blocks of granite which threatened to tumble him down with them. He reckoned it would be better climbed in the middle of winter when snow would cushion the disagreeable rocks.

He successfully climbed Néouvielle, the high peak to

the east of Luz, which Chausenque was the first to bag. The entire trip, with a guide, leaving Barèges at 2 a.m., took seventeen hours. They struggled hard to get to the summit over steep rocky terraces. Once achieved, Henry admired the view while his guide made lunch of cold roast meat, cheese, bread and a goatskin gourd of wine.

In those early days there were few experienced guides and no accurate maps. For expeditions to new territory (which was still most of the High Pyrenees) there were only the local shepherds, but they were usually unwilling to risk going far from their known pastures. Russell found the hunters of isards and bears to be the most knowledgeable and they soon became his frequent companions. As exploring and climbing became more popular a whole new profession of guide emerged, men who were as skilled and courageous as their employers.

These days guides are hardly necessary and those that there are tend to be highly qualified and thus expensive to hire; there is much less wilderness in the Pyrenees, since now there are conveniently marked footpaths, indicated on carefully drawn accurate maps. Mosset still has a guide, though, Thérèse Caron, with whom I have made several expeditions. The most memorable was the day of the total eclipse of the sun in August 1999 when our entire group was outfitted with sungazing spectacles. Since this is after all France we had another objective that day, which was to see the cows which produce the excellent local beef, *rosé des Pyrénées*.

We set off from the tiny village of Prats-Balaguer, clinging to the steep side of the valley, the pointed steeple of its little stone church punctuating a clear blue sky, the sun still shining with full force. A motley group included Theo, two

Belgian friends, Marie-Josée and Joris, a university professor who grumbled about his blisters and muttered imprecations about 'Darkness at Noon' as the sky grew blacker, and Claudine, a middle-aged lady from Campôme, the neighbouring village to Mosset, who always plays the piano at the Mosset Christmas nativity play. She was properly equipped with shorts, boots and an alpenstock, which rather put my hastily composed outfit to shame; Theo's bright red and yellow school backpack and my husband's Keith Haring sunhat.

We climbed up the Orry valley for two hours or so, with Thérèse leading the way. She is as lithe as a mountain goat; her bobbed brown hair and fresh scrubbed face, trousers and rolled shirtsleeves make her look more like a teenage boy than a fifty-year-old grandmother. She is a devoted steward of the natural heritage and seems to know every rock and stone and tree. She explained that this was an old path, still used for the *transhumance*, and pointed out the Château d'Orry on the hillside above us. Now only one ruined tower remains, but once it played its part in relaying fire signals from the sea up to the Cerdagne; as the straw fires were lit one after another, a message could be sent in half an hour from one end of Roussillon to the other. We stopped for refreshment at a small lake and tried out our eclipse spectacles as a crescent of darkness began to eat into the surface of the sun.

Thérèse was seated on a rock drinking from a water-bottle, and as we watched two buzzards circling and calling in the sky above us, she described the vultures she had once seen nearby: 'We were on the plateau above Mantet, having lunch, when ten vultures appeared. We just lay on our backs and watched them circling round us. It was amazing!'

I asked her how long she had lived here, and she explained that although she grew up in Perpignan she had been visiting Campôme since she was two years old. 'We were just outside all the time, all summer long,' she recalled. 'We all loved walking. It was a family ritual to walk to Saint Christophe, a little chapel on the plateau above the village, about an hour's walk, when we were only three or four years old.' She was widowed young and brought up two daughters, working as a teacher of handi-capped children until she was thirty-six. Then the chance to start a tourist office in Campôme arose and she jumped at it. Now she runs the tourist office in Mosset and leads organized walks in the area several times a week.

'I need to see mountains,' she said, gesturing widely. 'I love the way they change all the time – there is always something new to look at. For me in a flat horizon, even by the sea, there is always something missing.' She described another memorable climb she made to the Pic des Sept Hommes between the valleys of the Conflent and Vallespir. 'When we reached the top there was a sea of cloud on one side and the other was completely clear. It was so weird, the strong wind just holding the clouds back on one side of the ridge.'

We continued up the path through a shady forest; since we were ascending anyway it was hard to tell if the increas-ing chill of the air was caused by the sun or the altitude, but by the time we arrived at the pasture the eclipse was almost complete. It was not completely dark, only strangely dim and cold, a weird premonition of a world without sun.

We were glad when the sun returned and we could head further up the plateau where the famous cows were grazing, cross the shallow river and bathe our feet and look for mushrooms. There was a small *cabane* there, a single-storey shack which served as a refuge on the GR10, the famous footpath stretching from one end of the Pyrenees to the other. The *gardien* of the *cabane*, who apart from vestigial denim shorts and a pair of boots was as naked and long haired as if he had just walked out of a Stone Age cave, was tending a fire surrounded by flat stones. He told us he spent all the summer months up here without electricity, taking water from the stream, sleeping under the stars, guarding the cows and occasionally providing meals for campers.

The next event was lunch since we had come not just to look at the *rosé des Pyrénées* but to eat them. Slabs of rosy meat were placed on grills over the fire, and greedily consumed with fresh bread, rice and salad. It was delicious, declared Theo, who had seated himself nonchalantly on the back of a huge glossy chestnut horse which was conveniently recumbent on the grass.

8

Mont Perdu and the Petit Prince
of the Pyrenees

'Those who wish to have the finest views in Europe, of mingled plain and mountain scenery, of river and of sea, must stand upon the summit of the Canigou. Those again who delight to view nature in her more lonely solitudes, and to find themselves in those regions so far above the world that the pleasures which they enjoy are no longer of earth; where loftier thoughts and imaginations take their place, where their own significance as human beings appears in strong reality, and where feelings of omnipotence and eternity dislodge all others, may be gratified upon the pinnacle of Mont Perdu.'

James Erskine Murray, 1836

I went up to the village one day to buy bread, and found a small group gathered in the *place* in front of the church. They were looking at a painting erected on a large easel and its creator, Gerard, was watching their reactions with amusement. His painting depicted a future Mosset, a village in ruins, the land abandoned to waste and scrub. Above the shattered houses and broken walls covered in ivy, the hillside looked just the same. It was as if the mountain had reclaimed its space. M. Oliva, the retired village mason, was scratching his head in wonder. 'Imagine!' he said. 'It could be like that.' Slowly more and more of the villagers came to shake their heads over Gerard's strange vision. Sometimes when we discuss the need to maintain these small villages and preserve the rural life of the mountains my husband remarks that he sees no reason why it should not all return to nature. Twice in recent years a wolf has been sighted in the Eastern Pyrenees, within only a few miles of our valley. Perhaps nature will triumph after all.

For determined Pyrenean travellers of the nineteenth century, most of the Pyrenees was still a great unexplored wilderness. Mont Perdu was the great mystery, a legendary peak that held out the promise of lofty thoughts and lonely solitude. As it is in Spain, it is more correctly labelled Monte Perdido, or it would be if it was actually 'lost' to the Spanish, which it isn't. (Actually, the true Spanish name, or, even more correctly, Aragonese name, is Las Tres Sorellas, The Three Sisters, which refers to the entire ensemble of peaks, Pic du Marboré, the Cylindre and Mont Perdu.)

From the north the view is blocked by the frontier peaks and can only be seen from a few points, one of which is the Pic du Midi, from where Ramond first glimpsed the mysterious mountain. From the south it dominates the view, but since early exploration was from France the name has stuck. Its very obscurity made it especially tanta-lizing, the paths were virtually unknown and anyone who succeeded in getting to the summit was regarded with awe. Just the kind of expedition Henry Russell had in mind.

Ramond claimed the first *ascension* in 1802 after two failed attempts. (Guides and locals didn't count, as if anyway they would do anything as outlandish as climbing for no good reason.) During the summer of 1858 Henry Russell made his first three *ascensions* of Mont Perdu within a few weeks of each other, though each time he was frustrated by terrible weather and storms. The first time he climbed with two guides from Luz, via a circuitous route, then the only one believed possible, through the Brèche de Roland, a doorway 40 metres wide, framed by the 100-metre high rock walls which effectively form the frontier. The name comes from the French epic poem *The Song of Roland*, which recounts the legend of Roland and the rearguard of Charlemagne's army pursued and defeated by the Saracens. In despair Roland attempted to break his magic sword against the rock but instead he cleaved the rock itself in two.

Another young man was also on his way to climb Mont Perdu: Alfred Tonnellé, who was later to be regarded along with Russell as one of the great writers on the Pyrenees. Indeed he wrote about the Pyrenees before Russell but was sadly destined for a very much shorter career. He was from Tours, born in 1831, the son of a doctor. He was highly educated and spoke several languages, including English, like a native. He adored music, poetry, art and archaeology. But he was melancholy and deeply religious, and spent entire evenings alone playing the piano. He arrived in the Pyrenees to write and explore the beauty of the unknown high mountains. Certainly a kindred spirit for Russell.

Tonnellé arrived at the *auberge* of Héas near Gavarnie from Luchon with a guide, and hearing there were other messieurs (Russell and a companion only known as Monsieur S.) also planning to climb Mont Perdu, he decided to await them at the Brèche de Roland. French smugglers helped to guide him there, and while he waited he observed their vain efforts to attract attention from their

Spanish counterparts; they whistled, shot off their guns, lit firebrands, all to no avail. Finally the owner of the contraband despaired and the smugglers abandoned their packs and fled.

Eventually, 'M. Henri Russell, homme distingué' arrived and they made each other's acquaintance and set off together. After negotiating their way down from the Brèche and around the desolate southern slopes of Marboré and the Cylindre they camped at Gaulis (Goriz) at the foot of Mont Perdu, ready for the climb the next day. The young mountain philosophers sat on a rock contemplating the view, and talked of their travels. Russell recounted his journeys in America, in 'le Far West', and his encounters with the American Indians. The shepherds gave them their cabin, which Russell ungratefully described as 'the most miserable I have ever known', and they shared the shepherds' soup, eaten with a wooden spoon. They gave their hosts some chocolate wrapped in silver paper. 'Great astonishment,' wrote Tonnellé; 'they attached the paper to their jackets as an ornament. Nuit originale.'

Russell described the weather, with typical understatement, as unsettled, and they set off before dawn to have plenty of time for the final ascent. Tonnellé: 'We woke at 3.30. General sluggishness. Began walking after eating dry bread and chocolate. Departed at 5 a.m. Ascension up a series of steep terraces like a giant staircase, not dangerous but hard. We were followed by clouds, great white rolls, climbing up behind us, covering all of Spain.'

They arrived at the summit at 9 a.m. It was Tuesday, 10 August 1858, fifty-six years to the day since Ramond had first climbed Mont Perdu. On the summit they found the bottle containing all the names of previous climbers, secured under a pile of stones. They broke it as was the custom, read the names over, and added their own, replacing them all in a new bottle.

This practice was not always observed. In 1875 a Parisian woman climbed to the summit with four guides; in a crevice she found a bottle in which all the preceding climbers had left their cards and fragile notes of their observations, thoughts and hopes. Madame threw them all to the winds, so she could declare in the salons of Paris, 'You will find the name of only one woman on the summit of Mont Perdu!' Not long after, however, a young stranger, now nameless, heard about this puerile act and, after climbing to the summit himself, sent Madame's card back to her in Paris.

Tonnellé recorded a veritable forest of peaks to be seen, and to the north the lake of Mont Perdu in the snow. 'The best view was that of the Vignemale and its glacier to the west.' Russell, however, was disappointed by the storms and icy fog they had encountered, and resolved to attempt it again. Russell and Tonnellé exchanged guides, and Russell returned to Gavarnie. The other descended into Aragon where perhaps he should not have been surprised to find, as he wrote, 'The inhabitants of the valleys take me for an Englishman, they know no other foreigners.'

Tonnellé's account of his Pyrenean adventure and his meeting with Russell, *Trois mois aux Pyrénées et dans le Midi en 1858*, was first published in 1859. He was thus the first to mention Russell in print. But his literary skills did not come to general notice until Henri Beraldi published his delightful and exhaustive account of nineteenth-century Pyreneism, *Cent Ans aux Pyrénées*. The section on

Tonnellé was published in 1899 and only then did Russell discover the identity of the 'pale pensive stranger I saw only once', with whom he had first climbed Mont Perdu: the Petit Prince of the Pyrenees.

Tonnellé continued his journey, writing feverishly, heading east to Andorra and the Roussillon, tantalized by views of Canigou, which refused to unveil itself of clouds. Ahead he could see the dark blue line of the sea, and after two months of burning mountain sun he exulted at the promise of the Mediterranean. He meditated on the inhabitants of the different climes regarding each other with envy: 'Those who live in the harsh mountains must imagine those regions more fortunate, the sun more gentle, communication easier, a sweeter life. But then the inhabitants of the plains look up and dream of a life more fresh, more free, more pure, happier on these serene summits, lost in the sky. This is the illusion of distance and a different life.' He watched the sunset over the Pyrenees from Cap de Creus in Spain, the easternmost point of the chain, where the mountains sink down into the Mediterranean, celebrating 'the splendour of sky, sea and mountains together'. But then, after travelling along the Mediterranean coast, he returned to Tours where he died of typhoid fever on 14 October 1858.

Russell himself made another frustrating attempt on Mont Perdu ten days later with guides and with the same result. He descended having seen nothing, 'not just in a bad mood, but furious,' he wrote. His pride was pricked. Deciding that the cost of guides was too expensive, and savouring the challenge, he returned alone. It was his first solitary climb and gave him a taste for solitude that never left him; indeed, he said, always made him happy. But this attempt too, in September 1858, was a disaster, recalled ever after as 'that fatal night, terrible, without provisions, lost, exhausted and frozen'.

He was lucky to escape with his life, but it was another of those experiences which forged his strength and the confidence in himself which was the key to surviving so many dangers. After the first two ascents of Mont Perdu he was determined to try again alone, and complete it in twenty-four hours. He set off on horseback up the valley of Gavarnie at midnight, to get an early start to the climb the next morning, with the melancholy bells of Luz tolling behind him. Even this part of the journey was not easy. It was recommended to follow the narrow winding path skirting the gorge, 'with a firm spirit and assured eye', difficult in pitch darkness, one would have thought. The pony was so terrified it threatened to throw its rider over the precipice of the Gorge d'Echelle (there was no bridge then), so Russell dismounted and led his horse. As he walked he savoured the quiet of the night, 'the autumn wind caressing the dying leaves, moaning like a spirit of the forest'.

He arrived at Gavarnie at five in the morning, stabled the horse, and had coffee at the Hôtel des Voyageurs, a place for which he sustained a lifetime loyalty. Moving at his usual speed he made it to the Brèche by 10 a.m. and stopped for lunch, regarding 'with great joy the arid limestone landscape and burning peaks of Aragon, and the firs in the deep valley of Arras (Ara), bathed in a trembling vapour, announcing a storm'. But on the Brèche itself it was cold and clear. Seeing 'the snowy silhouette of the slopes above against the limpid blue of the sky, one could not believe such a beautiful day could end badly'.

To the east long and undulating terraces covered in snow sparkled in the sun. Advancing a little through the windy Brèche he could see Mont Perdu, and the view alone made his blood rise. 'These passions are unknown to the man of the plain, who will never understand the magnetism of snowy peaks white against a sky of blue or black. On these hot days when all is sleeping it seems as if the trees, a precipice and a waterfall are sufficient for happiness.'

Happy 'as a child' he descended the grassy slopes of Millaris and climbed back up to the former 'miserable cabin' of Gaulis, which the shepherds had already left. (This particular cabin never seemed to get a good press, usually described as 'a filthy nest'. Poor Erskine Murray had discovered the body of a Spanish shepherd when he stopped to eat there. Poor shepherd too.)

Russell climbed as fast as he could, followed by huge clouds rising at speed from the gorges of Spain. He scrambled over the stony scree south of Mont Perdu, climbing the final rocky terraces like a chamois. At 3 p.m. he arrived at the *pic*. 'No view. Again! And menacing weather, the *pic* encircled by an icy sombre fog.'

He realized he was afraid and began a rapid vertiginous flight down the mountain surrounded by dark clouds, bolts of lightning and thunder. The gale passed his ears 'like the wind of a bullet'. Snow spiralled round him ferociously, blowing with fury, and he shuddered. 'The slopes of Mont Perdu which had been so brilliant that morning had a spectral, sepulchral air.'

Though anxious, he felt sure of his powers. 'I ran as if I had wings, without being able to see twenty steps in front, with nothing to guide me, because the snow had effaced everything.' Following his instincts he traversed the plateau of Millaris in a tempest of hail, and arrived at the Brèche de Roland 'alive, but that was all' a few moments before nightfall, ready to fall to his knees in gratitude. Undaunted, he still had enough enthusiasm to take pleasure in his terrifying battle against the elements and to appreciate the sunset. 'Just before night, in a sea of clouds full of thunder and lightning, I saw a hundred kilometres of red peaks in the setting sun.'

He suffered a terrible night; twelve hours of freezing hurricanes. 'I was wet, frozen, without provisions, not even a drop of wine, without covering, and alone. Surrounded by bears, precipices and glaciers.' He marched back and forth, clapping his arms to warm himself. 'Neither awake nor asleep, with strange illusions, believing I saw tombs, and taking the clouds for rocks.'

When day finally returned, the snow stopped and the wind dropped. He descended in the mist, without a map or compass, in the midst of snow that masked every familiar sign. 'It was the worst descent of my life.' But still he found the experience stimulating. 'How the senses are excited by danger, how one uses them, how far one can see, how well one can hear.'

He sounded as high as a kite. I asked another Dutch friend, Karel, a psychologist who was a keen mountaineer in his youth, how it felt. 'Yes,' he said, 'you do feel high sometimes, that feeling of being totally alone, and self-sufficient. I remember walking along a narrow ridge in deep mist, with only a few feet on either side. But it felt amazing. I never felt fear, at least not until I had children.'

In *Touching the Void*, mountaineer Joe Simpson's account of his terrible experience in the Andes, when he was abandoned at the bottom of a crevasse with a broken leg, he echoed the same feeling. 'I had never been so entirely alone, and although this alarmed me it also gave me strength.' Strength enough to drag himself out and back across the glaciers to safety, a story which was made into a very successful film.

Russell had got completely lost, and only just stopped in time on the edge of a deep abyss when he heard the sound of the great waterfall of Gavarnie. He calculated that he must be near the middle of the Cirque, and knew he had missed the path if he could hear the waterfall so loudly. Thus he veered to the left, and finally escaped the snow. Half an hour later, half dead with fatigue, cold and hunger, he arrived back at the hotel in Gavarnie. They had already organized a rescue expedition. He had gone forty-four hours without sleep.

Gerard described a similar experience, when he found himself trapped by a storm on the top of Madres. He had been travelling by horse, with a packhorse for supplies, for three days and found he had miscalculated the time it would take to return to Mosset. 'I realized I would have to camp on the top of Madres. There were only small pine trees to tether the horses, and I had no tent. Then the sky turned black and it began to rain! Really, torrents of rain.' He was hit by an almighty storm, which no doubt Russell would have enjoyed. 'I was surrounded by thunder and lightning; there were fireballs rolling down the mountainside. It was the worst natural phenomenon I have ever experienced!'

He was worried about the horses because they had iron shoes, and might be struck by the lightning. 'I didn't know what to do, let them go and then they would get lost, or keep them tethered. That was the worst part, not knowing what to do.' In the end he sat in the rain in his soaking sleeping bag and sang to them, old Dutch songs in a low voice, which kept them calm.

The morning dawned finally, with blue sky and sunshine. 'I just stripped off everything, spread out all the clothes and lay naked in the sun to dry.' He let the horses loose and they all romped about together in the grass. It sounded like a scene from Beethoven's Pastoral Symphony in *Fantasia*. Somehow I feel Henry Russell would have done the same.

The young Russell was still not satisfied; his adventurous spirit demanded more. He was determined to go further, and test himself to the limits of endurance. He was inspired by the Anglo-French campaign in China (which included the complete sack of Peking) and determined to go there, via Siberia. His departure may also have been stimulated by emotional crisis. In Paris he had already hinted at forbidden love, 'How beautiful it is, how seductive, this divine dream of two beings chained one to the other,' and dismissed it as an illusion. 'Unfortunately this love is often no more than a dream, a mirage; ideal love is rare on earth, one finishes believing it is impossible, and resigns oneself to live without it.'

Glimpses of family letters reveal that he had fallen in love and wanted to marry the daughter of a pastor. His father forbade it, because she was a Protestant. Russell wrote about this in an unpublished work called *The Story of a Heart*. This he later tried to destroy, though apparently copies still exist, hidden away in a family vault. His brother Ferdinand also had marriage plans that were frustrated by his father, who suggested another woman of 'the right religion and good family'. In the event, the two sons left home, Henry to pursue his lengthy travels in the Far East, and Ferdinand to join the British army. Neither ever married. And although Henry was always a great hit with the ladies, who fluttered round him, he never appears to have evinced any further romantic interest in a woman.

Who knows what their sister Christine wanted? She declared her intention of becoming a nun at about the same time, and although at her parents' request she waited a year, eventually she entered the convent of the Visitation in Toulouse where she spent the rest of her life. Frank at this time was still in the papal army.

24 September 1858, Bagnères-de-Bigorre: a small sad family group sat and watched the sun setting over the green Adour valley. Father, mother, brother and sister were awaiting Henry's departure the next day, the beginning of his great tour of the Old World. Russell savoured the melancholy parting amidst the falling leaves of autumn.

There is no sense of his parents' trying to hold him back; perhaps they had travelled enough themselves to understand their son's desire. But it must have been hard to say goodbye in those days; you never knew if you would see the traveller again. It took six months before Russell received the letters they sent him. Now that gap year progeny can e-mail or text their parents from all over the world such separation is hard to imagine.

I remember once watching the stars with Miles and Theo at Corbiac on an exceptionally clear night. One dark wisp of cloud passed across the moon, which was glowing luminescent and almost full. It had rained earlier and there was a smell of damp earth rising from the ground.

There was only a faint breeze delicately lifting the blossoms on the cherry tree and through the still air we could hear church bells tolling midnight.

The Milky Way was visible, a rich speckled band of a million stars, and Mars had appeared to the east. The distance is always hard to comprehend, the fact that the light we can see is so old that the star itself may be long dead. Miles and Theo began talking about the possibility of travel to the Red Planet. I realized both of them would go to Mars tomorrow given the chance. Perhaps I will wave goodbye to Theo one day as he sets out on a long space journey, like mothers of pioneers of old, not knowing if we will ever see them again, but waving them off on a great adventure.

9

Around the world in 1000 days

'I have a wild spirit, and what I love most in nature is the desert. I constantly thirst for it. I search for it everywhere.'

Henry Russell

Our Pyrenean postal service can be erratic, though it is remarkable how determinedly the post lady battles through wind, rain and snow to reach us. I sometimes think – most especially when the Tour de France and Lance Armstrong's US Postal team whizzes by our door and over the Col de Jau - that their motto would suit her very well: 'Neither snow nor rain nor heat nor gloom of night stays these couriers from the swift completion of their appointed rounds' (actually a quotation from Herodotus in the fifth century BC).

Her little yellow van was just pulling off as I arrived at our battered post box, and I shivered, pulling my coat more closely round me before I turned the key. There was a first fall of snow on Canigou, defining it again more clearly than ever in the summer, confirming the power of nature over creeping humanity below. In the post I received a copy of *2002 Bulletin Pyrénées* from Paul Mirat in Pau, in which appeared an article suggesting that Henry Russell may have been the inspiration for the character of Phileas Fogg in Jules Verne's classic, *Around the World in Eighty Days*. This was published eight years after Russell's account of his travels, *Seize Mille lieues à travers l'Asie et l'Océanie*, appeared in two large volumes in 1864. Fogg's travels and adventures echo those of Russell: his multiple means of transport – steamboats, railways, carriages, sailing boats, sledges, camels, horses and elephants – his crossing of India, sailing across the South China Sea from Shanghai, his railway journey across America and his encounters with American Indians. Russell's breathless evocation of the final stages of his return journey – five days in Hungary, ten hours at the Turkish port of Kustenje, two days on the river Danube and a week in Budapest – may have planted the idea for Fogg's record-breaking journey. In a later novel, *Michel Strogoff*, Verne cites Russell directly – 'le voyageur Henry Russell-Killough' – in his description of Siberia and draws directly on his experiences.

I had already tracked down a series of articles Russell had written in 1860 on his epic round the world journey, for *The Englishman*, the Calcutta newspaper. The Oriental and India Office of the British Library had yielded several boxes of microfilm, of newspapers 150 years old. Now I drew out the photocopies I had made, and struggled to read the faded fine print. Alongside Russell's articles were a translation of George Sand's latest novel, *The Black Town*, a review of a Life of Goethe, articles on elephant races at Benares, rains and smallpox in Delhi, news from the war in Turkey and whether the French were likely to invade Ireland in defence of the Irish Catholics. (Not in their interest, so no, concludes the writer.)

The advertisements on the front page told me more: sailings for London; supplies received (sardines, Wiltshire Breakfast ham, Oxford sausages, cocoa); dinner service for sale (used only twice) by W. J. Allen Esq. returning to

England; also for sale: grand pianos, English mares, turkeys for Christmas, remedies for cholera, chandeliers and billiard lights, kid gloves, guns and cricket bats. There was a grim warning about fake Worcestershire sauce.

Henry had set off for his journey in 1859 aged twenty-five, travelling across Siberia in winter, to China and Japan, New Zealand and Australia, returning via India, where he wandered for a year, then Egypt, the Middle East and home. It took him three years. When he arrived in Calcutta in 1860 he was broke, and money sent by his family had been lost, so with admirable enterprise he earned money writing articles on his travels, calling himself on this occasion Henri Russell (this was before his father was made a papal count). It is his best writing in English: fresh, direct, unadorned, and a world away from his ornate, over-worked French. It is as if he is a different person in English. His eye for detail from the horsemanship of the Mongols to the flavour of Chinese tea, his acute observations of people and of landscape, not to mention the hardships he sometimes underwent, are leavened by a deliciously dry humour. He was a great travel journalist.

He travelled for the pleasure of discovery and new experiences, a proto-hippie on the trail to the east. But at a time when geography was in its infancy and political information often sketchy, he felt a responsibility to make careful observations as he travelled: the disputed size of Peking, the climate, geology and crops of Siberia and China, the precise boundaries of Russian territory, the ecclesiastical practices of the Catholic church abroad and the whereabouts of various disappeared French missionaries.

He set off alone and travelled either alone or with local

companions. He was almost fearless, only reduced finally to terror by the prospect of almost certain death after several nights lost without food or shelter in the wild interior of New Zealand. He was still very young – and mischievous too; in China he got so fed up with street urchins poking holes in his parchment windows he took to spitting at them. In Peking he peered through the windows of a school and made 'hideous grimaces' at a class full of little boys, 'to ascertain if the effect produced by the human face expressing passions, was the same in all countries'. There are echoes of Rimbaud's insouciant wanderings across the globe.

Russell was not alone in his desire to explore. The mid-nineteenth century in Europe was a time of exotic travel as the Victorian British tried to escape the increasingly suffocating nature of nineteenth-century society and the French looked for Romantic escape from their own brutal political realities. The Orient offered an exotic alternative, typified by Victor Hugo's Oriental poems, Coleridge's 'Kubla Khan', Richard Burton's translation of *Arabian Nights*, the Oriental novels of Walter Scott and Byron's poetry.

The impressionable young Henry Russell, growing up in Ireland and France, devoured everything he could lay his hands on. He describes the pictures of China which had inspired him since he was at school; how he always longed to see Peking, Australia and the Himalayas. The French missionary, Abbé Huc, published his famous account of his travels in China and Tibet, *High Road to Tartary*, in 1853. When he followed in his footsteps ten years later Russell was asked for news of Abbé Huc by the Mongolians.

It was a journey that had been made forty years previously by the great German naturalist explorer, Alexander von Humboldt (who also preceded Russell to the Andes). Humboldt went to Siberia aged sixty in 1829, and died in May 1859 only a few months before Russell departed. Humboldt's findings in botany, geology and geography during his explorations in South America (a great influence on Darwin) were still being published in Paris when he died and Russell would surely have known his work.

The Royal Geographical Society was founded in 1830 and created a fashion for exploration which sent many young men abroad. The newspapers were full of the adventures of travellers. Missionary David Livingstone had returned from his explorations of Africa in 1856, Richard Burton came back from Mecca in 1853, and Sir John Franklin departed in search of the North-west Passage in 1845, never to return, the final fate of his frozen ship and starving crew for ever uncertain.

There were French travellers too, of course, though they seemed on the whole more inclined towards writing than adventure. Montaigne made a record of his journeys in Europe, though parts of it were written in the third person by his servant. François-René de Chateaubriand made many long voyages, travelling by horse day and night, peppering his accounts with biblical, classical and mythological references. He wrote of a journey to America in 1791 – which some reckoned he had embroidered if he did it at all.

Still, I know of no other Frenchman as adventurous as Henry Russell, with the possible exception of poet Arthur Rimbaud. Henry is portrayed in a photo from around this time, with eyes of deep intensity, thick dark hair and bushy eyebrows, jutting goatee beard and full moustache, clad in a heavy riding coat. He set off in 1859, travelling to Paris from Bagnères-de-Bigorre, then to Dieppe and across the channel to London. There he measured his course from the globe in Leicester Square – 'Six thousand statute miles to Peking', his ultimate destination – and climbed the dome of St Paul's cathedral, which from the whispering gallery offered the best view of London, a Victorian London of smoke and hansom cabs. He travelled by steamship to Moscow, where he equipped himself with provisions and furs and set off for Siberia in the company of two Siberians. It was November and winter was just beginning to bite.

Though it was already very cold, it was not yet fully winter, so there was not enough snow to travel by sledge, and the travellers did the first 800 kilometres in a five-day journey to Kazan in an open carriage in temperatures of minus 15 to minus 30 centigrade. At Kazan there was thick snow so they could switch to a sledge. 'We left for Asia at a gallop, drawn by four wild Tartar horses,' Henry wrote with a flourish of satisfaction. They barely slept for twenty days, carried like the wind across the snow, though frequently overturned. The cold, however, was, 'indescribable torture, impossible to sleep, difficult to eat. A bottle of *eau de vie* wrapped in furs at the centre of the sledge had frozen solid . . .' Finally they reached the Urals, 'the infinite steppes of Asia'.

Russell writes ever after of this period as the happiest of his life, and of Siberia in winter as the greatest beauty he had ever known. At night by the light of the moon, all was white, with wolves howling on all sides. A forest of cedars towered over them, 'like a diaphanous basilica'. Finally a great spectacle greeted their eyes. From the top of a slope unrolled a sparkling ocean of firs at the centre of which burnt a fire, the brilliance of Irkutsk, 'like a crystal city, its domes glittering like diamonds in the bright sunlight'. Beyond, the peaks of the Altai, 'whiter than the immaculate monarch of the Alps', separated the two empires of Russia and China. Henry thought of how very distant he was from the Pyrenees.

He was told it was impossible for him to go to Peking, that even the Russians were not tolerated there. But finally he arranged to travel across the Gobi desert, disguised as the secretary of a Russian officer. It is hard not to allow a thought for Peter Sellers at this point. 'I had to pass myself off as Russian, calling myself Russelloff, but I would have called myself Confucius if necessary.'

They travelled by sledge escorted by a fierce Cossack warrior, crossing Lake Baikal, one of the largest in the world, where Henry marvelled at sunrise over the immense desert of glazed ice, bare of snow which had been swept away by the wind. But even for Henry this was the limit: '. . . there was too much silence and too much solitude. It was as gloomy as the tomb,' he shivered. They crossed the lake at its narrowest point, threading through great obelisks of ice. After an hour the sun departed and they lost sight of land. Below them the ice murmured and cracked, 'with a voice I have never heard on land or sea'. It took four hours to cross, on a night so dark he could not even see the horses pulling the sledge, but only the reflections of constellations of stars on the ice. Finally after three more days the snows of Mongolia appeared and they arrived in Kiakhta, the gate guarded by a huge Cossack with a drawn sword at the ready. China at last. 'Here we beheld for the first time in our lives the beautiful curves of Chinese roofs, with which pictures had made us familiar from our earliest childhood.'

A bizarre vehicle had been prepared for Lieutenant Lavroff, the Russian officer, a narrow blue covered carriage containing a bed, which was immediately dubbed the coffin. The officer's obsequious 'Russian secretary' was regarded with considerable suspicion but they were finally granted permission to cross the Gobi desert. They supplied themselves with camels, horses and food, 'thirty pounds of soukhari, small pieces of dried bread, a great number of rabeliks, birds resembling in flavour the partridge which can be had in every part of Siberia for a few kopeks, some fried beefsteaks, salt, tea, sugar and rum'.

Here was Henry's true desert, ' the silent and dreaded solitude'. Never had he felt so alone, as they crossed the waste of sand and snow and forests of fir trees with great snowy peaks in the far distance. 'Everything seemed crystallized and shone like steel; the air itself had a metallic taste, and every particle of vapour fell slowly down in a shower of diamonds.' After one cold night, 'a solid mass of ice imprisoned our beards and paralysed our lips and eyelids'. They travelled with the Mongols, who rode their wild little horses with consummate skill, their graceful conical hats streaming with many-coloured ribbons. Accommodation was in Mongol yurts, trellised domes of wood covered in felt with a central pole that could be ingeniously lifted to create a sloping roof in case of rain or snow.

Henry visited the colossal golden lamaserie in Urga (now Ulan Bator), then a centre of the Buddhist religion second only to Lhasa in Tibet, and the only town in the Gobi desert. It was full of thousands of shaved monks in yellow gowns banging on drums suspended from the vaults. Henry sniffed at the 'wrinkled and dirty priests of Buddha lying on the floor, perfect images of misery and sorrow'. To Henry the good Catholic it was an 'infernal scene' and he had little time for a religion 'which not only brings no consolation to a dying man, but suffers his remains to be exposed on the top of the hills to become the prey of famished dogs'. He exhibited all the unquestioned European superiority of his time, especially when they finally persuaded their hosts to allow them to go to Peking. They summoned the Mongol general to their uncomfortable smoky yurt and showed him one of their canvas globes, explaining to him the power of western nations. They described 'the final conquest of India by the British', and warned him that the same fate might well befall China.

The journey to Peking by the authorized roundabout route was endless and excruciating and the main words Henry exchanged with the Mongols were 'near' and 'far'. Mostly, 'far'. At one low point a sandstorm eclipsed all, obscuring the sun with red sand, with a wind so merciless that Mongols riding camels in the opposite direction were facing backwards and protecting their eyes with spectacles of rock crystal. Henry finally collapsed on the sand with fever and dysentery and was welcomed into 'the perfect paradise' of the cramped blue coffin.

They came at last to the Great Wall of China, 'snaking across the landscape like a tapeworm', as Henry so charmingly put it. They climbed to the top, shot off a revolver in triumph and collected stones as souvenirs for museums back home. Beyond unfolded an immense country of cities and pastures: China. 'Behind us we left a nomadic and pastoral people in all its simplicity and honesty, and before us crowded the most sedentary, cunning and refined of all races.' Henry does later admit that he may have been a bit hard on the Chinese. The convoy of travellers were met at the great city of Kalgan by the sight of decapitated heads hung from the walls in cages.

He savoured his first Chinese meal – having drawn a picture of a sheep in his notebook, he was offered both mutton and an entire sucking pig. 'But in the sauces there was such a mixture of aromas, pickles and oils of all sorts.' He favoured the Chinese 'yellow tea', however, taken without milk or sugar and considered 'very soothing'.

Their struggles were eventually rewarded with the first sight of Peking across the plain. The road became crowded with carriages, mules, and gaily dressed women. They dined in a vast Chinese restaurant which Henry compared to the suburban restaurants of Paris on a Sunday, though the fare was very different: pickles in little saucepans with porcelain spoons, dried mutton and pork, little smoking loaves of bread, and worms and leeches, according to our gourmet correspondent.

They entered the walled city of Peking through a huge gate and by a zigzag route. Henry described the sight for readers for whom Peking was an unknown and wildly exotic place: the houses of wood and brick, gilded in gold, and fluttering with coloured flags; the sidewalk booths of jugglers, barbers, fortune tellers, cooks and orators, people playing shuttlecock and flying kites, and the heavily loaded camel trains swaying through the streets. The travellers were unspeakably relieved amongst all this paganism to glimpse the silver cross of the Russian mission. They were

warmly welcomed by Russians gone native in pigtails and
Chinese robes, eager for year-old news. They bathed, ate
hothouse pears and grapes and even drank champagne.
Henry described the beauties of the city, its gardens and
artificial lakes, and the Imperial city itself, forbidden along
with the Emperor to the sight of mortal eyes. He spent his
time buying curiosities, silks, snuff boxes and red lacquer
boxes, playing billiards, listening to music, and bemoaning
the lack of cigars.

He wandered unharmed in European dress but finally
adopted Chinese robes to avoid the intense scrutiny to
which he was subjected wherever he went. But he had
roused suspicions, not least by speaking French, and giving
lessons in English to the missionaries. He was ordered to
leave, and despite wild schemes to escape dressed as a lama
along the Great Wall of China to the sea, or driving himself alone to Shanghai, he finally had to accept the
appalling necessity of recrossing the Gobi desert, back to
Mongolia. He packed up his Peking curiosities, the lacquer
boxes, silks and two large Chinese jars with which he had
been presented, and sent them back to Moscow.

After an agonizing journey back across the Gobi desert, he
travelled on to Japan and Shanghai, caught on the way in a
Pacific typhoon. Henry stayed on deck, typically determined to experience it all, hanging on doggedly as the day
went black and the waves howled over the vessel. He
reached Australia after a journey of two months, via
Sumatra and Java, dropping anchor in dusky bays
surrounded by jungle, listening to the howling tigers in the
night. 'How would I ever rest tranquil again after such a
nomadic life?' he mused. They spent several days becalmed

at the foot of Krakatoa, which twenty years later was to erupt with legendary force.

In Australia he was struck by the most extreme heat he had ever suffered, and the drunkenness of the people – '... nine out of ten people were carrying bottles,' he observed. 'What drinkers they are!' He embarked for New Zealand, hoping for a reminder of his beloved Pyrenees in the mountains, and determined to climb the Kaikoras, two 3000m summits 200 kilometres south of Nelson. He departed alone on foot, without a bag, filling his pockets with essentials. He counted on finding *auberges* for sustenance. He was a bit worried since there was still war between English and Maoris. 'What if I met hostile savages in the wilderness? Would they strangle me and eat me?' He decided he was too thin to be of interest and set off. There were few lodgings, fewer bridges to cross the rivers, and he often came close to drowning. He met a Maori, fierce and colossal – 'Imagine a lion standing up' – who offered in English to take him to the top of a mountain where they could sleep snug in the ferns. Russell was tempted, imagining the tales he might tell in Paris of sleeping under the stars with a real savage.

Later, alone, he sat down to eat on a fallen trunk. Suddenly he was surrounded by a cloud of birds who landed on his head, shoulders and knees, ate his crumbs, looked him in the eye, and gave him a concert. Perhaps they had never seen a man before, they were so unafraid. Henry was deeply touched. 'The friendship of birds and savages – how unknown in Europe!'

He found the farm of a Scotsman, Mr Anderson, a little white house in the forest which seemed at the end of the world, and was given directions to the mysterious

Kaikoras. There was another farm only three hours away. No problem, thought Henry, and did not even take any food with him. 'Fatal omission, in a country where so many Europeans had already been lost, and died of exhaustion or famine.' Climbing over a rise he saw the two mountains for the first time, snowy, arid, and splendid, surrounded by dense forests.

But almost as soon as he entered the trees he was enveloped in thick mist, and without a map or compass he was soon hopelessly lost. It was raining heavily and by nightfall he was completely exhausted, soaked to the skin, torn by rocks and spiky branches. He had nothing to eat and was so thirsty he had to lick the leaves of the trees. For two days he was lost in rain and mist. 'I passed the worst, most desolate time of my life.'

But a new dawn brought hope, with a clear sky, and mountains illuminated by the sun: 'Even the river had changed its voice and sounded like the torrents of the Pyrenees.' Somehow he found the strength to return to Anderson's farm, sometimes on all fours, he was so weak. Back in the valley he remembered his British sangfroid and plunged into the icy waters of the river to galvanize his forces one last time. Finally he staggered to Anderson's door, more dead than alive, after sixty hours without food.

Once recovered, he embarked for India, stopping off at Ceylon, 'a true terrestrial Paradise' of coconut palms and exotic flowers and equally beautiful inhabitants. At Calcutta, then the British capital of India, he found the letters and money he hoped for had not arrived so he sat down and wrote about his experiences in Mongolia and China for the local paper, *The Englishman*. It took the entire month of July, and he noted at the end that he had written it all without journals, entirely from memory. (He didn't say what happened to his travel journals.) It was published in thirty chapters, two a week, from October 1860 to January 1861.

Henry's real goal in India was the Himalaya, of which he had dreamed since he was in school. He set out for the summer station of Darjeeling at 2300 metres, perched like an observatory on the summit of a mountain and facing the most gigantic inaccessible peaks on earth. He travelled up the Ganges, tall grasses on its banks shielding tigers and snakes, the river itself full of human corpses half eaten by birds of prey. He went to Purnah by ox cart and then a palanquin carried by four Hindu porters, brandishing flaming torches and issuing demonic cries to keep the tigers at bay when they travelled at night.

As they climbed it grew colder and the vegetation changed, palms giving way to rhododendrons, gaudy splashes of red against the great white snowy peaks beyond. He never forgot his first view of the Himalaya suspended in the sky like clouds, enflamed gold and red by the rising sun. 'The names had made me shudder since I was a child; Chamalari, and the famous Everest, the highest point of the globe.' He saw Kangchenjunga at sunset, 'draped in glaciers, as red as if it had appeared from a field of blood, against a sky already black'. He never forgot Kangchenjunga, and in later years always had a photograph of it on his wall in Pau.

Henry revelled in the view from Darjeeling, 'the great masterpiece of nature, a reflection of God himself, too sublime to describe'. Imagine, he wrote, 'the highest peaks of the Pyrenees perched on top of Mont Blanc, they would still not arrive at the level of Kangchenjunga. It is like Siberia sitting on top of India.' It was a feast for the eyes and soul he was to seek ever after. He was determined to see Everest – to climb it was not even considered possible then. It was not visible from Darjeeling, so he climbed Sinchal to the south-west in order to glimpse the 'monarch of mountains, whiter than sugar', far away in Nepal.

On his return journey he was obliged to walk, traversing the jungle at dead of night in fear of his life. To keep the tigers and wild beasts away as he walked, he sang in a deep loud bass, the most stirring powerful airs he could summon, accompanied by his cigar with which he made red circles and zigzags in the air. 'A memorable night,' he conceded, surviving unscathed.

During the following winter and spring he explored India, with a Hindu servant and a bullock cart for his luggage. Mostly he walked under the sun without a parasol. 'After a few days you get used to it,' he observed, though he added that he never drank alcohol, and was admirably sustained by weak cold tea.

He celebrated Easter at an English Catholic church in Shimouga, along with his faithful servant; and was astonished by the cacophany of the singing. 'On the left were men singing one hymn, "Come all you faithful", on the other side the women were singing quite a different hymn, and at the same time in the tribune I heard an explosion which turned out to be "God Save the Queen", played on every instrument available, the trumpet prevailing. All at the same time. We fled before the bears and tigers joined in too.'

Russell adored India, and ever after sported gaudy silk scarves, cherishing a love of colour which never left him.

'India enchanted me, the memory still electrifies my heart like a youthful romance.' But he had had enough, after three years of travel alone. When he reached Bombay he finally fell victim to fever and was laid low for a month. It is testament to his extraordinary constitution that he did not get sick before.

He left his faithful servant weeping on the shore, and embarked from Bombay for Suez in June 1861. 'Adieu Asia, and the most beautiful countries in the world.' He returned to Europe via Egypt, Smyrna, Constantinople, through Hungary, Austria, Venice, Genoa and finally Marseille, whence he took a slow *diligence* to Toulouse and Tarbes. 'With what emotion I approached Bagnères-de-Bigorre. There was my family. This was worth more than all the splendours of nature. It was the most beautiful moment of my journey, the purest happiness of my life, and in the arms of my parents, I asked myself in truth, if I had been dreaming for three years!'

After his travels he went home for ever. He never really travelled again, apart from visits to England and Ireland, trips to Paris and one excursion to the Alps. The Pyrenees seem to fulfil all his desires, and like Darwin and the Galapagos Islands, he spent the rest of his life digesting the experience. It was as if he had walked himself into some kind of harmony with the world, and expiated his wanderlust. His travels always remained a reference point, the palm-fringed beaches, the jungle, the Himalaya, the desperate lost nights in New Zealand, most of all his dazzling winter journey across Siberia. They provided him with a rich source of metaphors for his descriptions of the Pyrenees. Charles Darwin eventually came up with the *Origin of Species*; for Russell it was a simple passion for a mountain.

10

The rover's return and Gentleman Jack

'When I arrive I believe they recognize me.'

Henry Russell on the Pyrenees

Whenever I return to the Pyrenees after only a few weeks' absence my heart leaps to see the mountains again. Canigou is visible as the plane lands at Perpignan, rising beyond the vineyards, palms and fruit trees of the plain, and remains a constant motif as we drive up the valley of the Têt, the air becoming cooler and fresher as we head higher up. Sometimes it is as if nature has planned a special greeting, when rays of sunshine filter through the clouds like a heavenly blessing. I always like the fact that they are called 'glories'.

Once I came back after several weeks in London, and the very next day went for a walk with my friend Monique, the blonde northerner who lives in Mosset. We had begun talking walks together to practise our French and English, sometimes having to pause in the middle of the path for several minutes to wrestle with a complicated translation. Like the time Monique said she would 'go for a pee behind a broom', or when I wanted to *supprimer* (suppress) children instead of support them. That time it was early spring, one of the first sunny days after lots of rain. For me it was like re-entering another world, as if I had walked onto a film set, a dreamy landscape of budding greens in a thousand different shades, punctuated by white cherry blossoms and the pink and white flowers on the apple branches. Swallows, newly returned from warmer climes, swooped gracefully, and innumerable small birds twittered excitedly in the trees. Spring was commencing quietly, inevitably.

The air was so clear and pure, it was almost too rich. I had lost the capacity to breathe it all at once. We walked along the path uphill from the village, past the narrow canal of water that is channelled to all the gardens and fields in the valley, pounding along with full force after so much rain. Ahead was an elderly lady in her flowery pinafore, her back bent, face lined and craggy, bearing a huge cabbage in hands deeply ingrained with earth. She wished us '*Bonne promenade*' and said she had been getting her potatoes in; rain followed by sun was good for planting. She loved her garden and went every day she could for an hour or so. The little *potagers* which surround the village have always provided refuge for the women, somewhere they can retreat from the demands of house and family for a while, albeit working still.

Through the bare branches of trees yet to leaf, we could see the valley clearly. Houses that were normally hidden behind foliage were apparent, smoke rising from the chimneys, each little garden with its vegetables staked out and fruit trees flowering. Beyond were the old terraces on the hillside, once planted with vines and olives, long since abandoned.

The path opened out to soft green pasture, where an old shepherd in blue overalls and trilby hat sat on a large stone watching his sheep, tiny newborn lambs tottering beside their mothers. 'Better than staying at home and watching television,' he remarked cheerfully as we passed.

We headed up the wooded hillside spotting violets between the boulders, new yellow broom beginning to blossom, the ground a carpet of dry leaves and acorns, little runnels of water making new channels between the stones. We stopped to visit Monique's brother, Nénes, who keeps his dairy cows there, and supplies the milk and yogurt we buy from his wife, Isabelle, our beautiful milkmaid. He offered us tea in the tiny wood and stone lean-to where he often spends the night in preference to the village. From the side poked the chimney of a woodstove. Inside was a table and three chairs, a gas burner, water piped up from the stream, and a narrow shelf of a bed. I felt a bit like Goldilocks visiting the three bears. A big brown horse waited patiently outside the door.

For Nénes his little shelter also provides a retreat from the world, where he can sit and contemplate the massif of Canigou framed at the end of the valley. At night he can lie under the stars and hear nothing but the call of owls and tinkling of cowbells. He showed us the morels he had just found. 'Marie saw them first,' he said, proud of the country ways that his eight-year-old daughter had already absorbed from her parents. Hanging from a convenient tree branch was the swing he had made for her.

Nénes has a face deeply lined from years exposed to the elements, long tangled blond hair and an enormous smile exposing crooked teeth. I always think he looks like a cross between Jungle Boy and Keith Richards. He came to the Pyrenees from the Vosges to be a shepherd in the Vallespir, the valley to the south of Canigou, and still found it hard to live in a village all the time. He and Monique laughed over his life then, how he used to play Chopin to the sheep.

'They would all gather round and listen.' Nénes grinned. 'It kept them calm, helped them to eat better.' It was an image of this other, magical world that I will always treasure.

Russell returned to the Pyrenees of which he had dreamed for so long at the end of August 1861. In the *diligence* from Toulouse to Tarbes on his way to his family in Bagnères, he watched the mountains slowly appear as dawn lightened the sky and gilded the peaks. He was close to tears at the sight, calling them: 'Mountains I believe almost capable of loving me.' There was the distinct silhouette of the Pic du Midi rising above the plain, at its feet the valley of Campan: 'That bucolic valley where even the greatest saint would not want to die and leave without a tear.' From then on the Pyrenees were all he desired. '*Oui, c'est bien là ma patrie!*'

He was much changed by his travels, a man of twenty-five, strong, tanned and bearded. His blue eyes had that distant look of all travellers, as if they can see further than ordinary mortals. When his brother asked if he would like to go to the Bagnères casino to dance that evening, Henry burst out laughing.

He settled back into life with his family in Pau and Bagnères-de-Bigorre, and wrote about his travels, two enormous volumes which were published in 1864 to great acclaim and were eventually translated into Russian. He was made a member of the Royal Geographical Society and of the French Société Nationale de Géographie. But he turned his back on it all and focused his gaze on the Pyrenees, beginning a campaign that was to occupy the rest of his life.

Climbing was by then an increasingly popular sport, pioneered by the British in the Alps. Few had visited the Pyrenees, and there were still many peaks to conquer and many miles of unknown territory to explore. Almost immediately on his return Russell made his first ascent of the Vignemale, at 3298 metres the highest mountain on the French side of the chain. It was as if it had been lurking in his unconscious. Vignemale was the mountain that had made such a deep impression when he saw it in a storm as a child at Lac de Gaube, and though he seems to have written little about this first expedition, Vignemale was to become his obsession, the beginning of an eternal passion. According to Henri Beraldi, historian of the Pyrenees, 'From then on Henry Russell would want no other spouse than the mountain.'

But Russell was not the first to climb Vignemale. He makes a brief reference in his guide, *Les Grandes Ascensions des Pyrénées*, published in 1866, to the first ascent of Vignemale by Prince Moskowa. He seems to have accepted this version of events at that time, as did everybody else, though he concedes in later writing and without rancour that the first person to climb Vignemale had in fact been a woman. An English woman at that. And as it turns out a rather famous lesbian, Miss Anne Lister, from Halifax in Yorkshire.

I too was born in Halifax, and it became clear that I was in a veritable tradition of middle-aged ladies from Yorkshire turning up in the Pyrenees to research the ascents of Vignemale. Anne Lister's conquest of the mountain had been largely ignored until another Yorkshirewoman, Vivien Ingham, discovered her Journals in the Halifax library. She went to Gavarnie in 1967, hoping to find out more about Lister's achievement, and eventually published her findings in the *Halifax Antiquarian Journal*. Since then the true story of the first ascent, the Yorkshire lesbian versus the imperial prince, has been painstakingly unravelled.

Anne Lister was born in 1791 and inherited Shibden Hall near Halifax from her uncle. She ran the estate herself, developing new coal mines, and supervising workmen. She loved the masculine pursuits of walking, riding and shooting, and realized as a young woman that she was a lesbian. 'I love and only love the fairer sex,' she wrote firmly. Her portrait reveals sensuality and pride: dark eyes, full lips and a very determined chin. Her unfeminine behaviour and the mannish clothes she adopted, the long black coat and stout leather boots, did not pass without comment. Yorkshire folk called her Gentleman Jack.

She kept a detailed journal all her life, recording her domestic life, her work and her travels. But she also kept a secret record in a numerical code of her own devising of her sexual feelings and relationships, even the women she seduced, nearly all of whom were her married neighbours. This has recently been deciphered and Lister has become celebrated as a pioneering lesbian, the intimate details of her sex life and gynaecological problems minutely scrutinized. Unfortunately, becoming a lesbian icon has completely eclipsed her major achievements as a traveller and mountaineer, which I suspect would have annoyed her very much.

She travelled a lot, and was always intensely curious and observant, visiting coal mines, saltworks, factories, even the battlefield of Waterloo. She made two trips to the

Pyrenees, the first in 1830 when she travelled with the wife of the British ambassador in Paris, Lady Stuart de Rothesay, in three carriages, changing horses and drivers at each staging post. They stayed in Pau, Eaux-Bonnes, Saint Sauveur and Bagnères-de-Bigorre, and on several occasions Miss Lister managed to escape the suffocating companionship of her fellow travellers to explore the mountains. Despite disapproval (Lady Stuart thought she should take a carriage and a maid) she found a guide, Jean-Pierre Charles, who had guided the writer Chausenque in his explorations. Then she disappeared for four days in order to climb Mont Perdu (then still believed to be the highest mountain in the Pyrenees), sharing the famously primitive hut of Gaulis, overlooking the gorge of Ordesa, with the shepherds. She confided her experiences to Lady Stuart on her return but was otherwise discreet, saying 'I did not mean to say much about it to people in general, for it was not quite a lady's expedition'.

As an encore she did a gruelling fifteen-hour walk over the high cols of Aspin and Peyresourde to Luchon. From there she crossed the frontier again into Spain, where she stayed in peasants' houses and joined in dancing, singing and wine drinking at a local fete. 'I never in my life ate such fine, large, delicious grapes or drank such rich, strong wine,' she noted with eminent satisfaction in her tiny handwriting. She did get into trouble, however, and, suspected of spying, was escorted back to the frontier by Spanish soldiers.

She returned to the Pyrenees in 1838 with her female companion Ann Walker, somewhat less sturdy than Lister. They arranged spa treatments for Ann Walker's health and explored the mountains and valleys around Gavarnie.

Lister's journal recorded all their experiences, sleeping with the guides in rough shepherds' shelters and begging milk from passing cowherds. She noted every detail: the temperature of their rooms, the clothes she mended, the state of her boots, the number of fleas they discovered in Walker's linen, exactly what they ate and drank, the quality of the wine, the number of trout they ate one night, even the eggs they shared (Lister ate the white, and her friend ate the yolk). She always noted her reading matter, Chausenque for the mountains, and *Galignani's Messenger*, an English language newspaper published in Paris, for gossip about the British on the Continent.

Lister again hired Charles, her guide from her previous visit, and planned an ambitious excursion into Spain. She was very curious about Vignemale, which Chausenque had deemed impossible to climb, and immediately intrigued when Charles told her that a potential southerly route had been discovered.

Vignemale, on account of its impressive position, was then still believed to be the second highest mountain in the Pyrenees, but the great glacier on the eastern side had always frustrated previous attempts on the summit. A guide from Gèdre in the Gavarnie valley, Henri Cazaux, had found a route up from the southern side. Lister decided she would attempt it, and merrily planned two ascents, one of the nearby Piméné, to be followed the next day by Vignemale. She and her companion, Ann Walker, accompanied by guides and porters, climbed Piméné on 27 July, staying in a shepherds' hut on the way, 'about four feet high within and long enough and broad enough for one of the *bergers* to sit and churn in (shake their sheepskin bags with milk in them till the butter forms)'. The ladies ate the new butter with shepherds' bread and fresh milk.

The climb, however, was exhausting, and Walker was too ill to make it to the top. Once she got down again even Lister confessed she had no idea how she had climbed so steep a slope. Climbing Vignemale the day after was clearly impossible, especially since the weather was very unpredictable, and Lister reluctantly postponed her plan. Instead they returned to the Hôtel des Voyageurs at Gavarnie. Gloomily Lister watched the weather, praying for the low fog to lift. Then she heard she had competition. Napoleon Ney, Prince of Moskowa, the son of one of Napoleon's marshals, had also hired the guide Cazaux, to take him up to make a first ascension of Vignemale that very Thursday. Lister then decided to make her climb on the Monday before, 6 August.

She breakfasted on strawberries, raspberries and figs and set off from Gèdre for Gavarnie at 6.30 a.m. Charles equipped them both with alpenstocks and crampons, and porters and provisions were assembled. Anne itemized each garment she wore, which took layering to extreme proportions: flannel underwear, chemise, stays, petticoat, muslin fichu, black merino dress with a thick crape shawl crossed over everything. 'I had had tape loops put round the bottom of my dress and strings at the top and just before setting off, had my dress tied up all round me just about or above the knee.' (Apart from the inconvenience, long skirts were also a hazard because they dragged and scattered stones on anyone unfortunate enough to be following behind.)

She also wore white cotton socks, silk leggings, strong leather nailed boots, and black satin gaiters. She added a heavy cape, and a Maclean tartan cloak. In her pack she took extra stockings, *eau de vie* and a white nightcap, along with a pocket knife, notebook and passport.

They left Gavarnie at 6.45, still in fog, and ascended the valley of Ossoue, where they met up with guide Henri Cazaux and Charles's brother-in-law at the *cabane* Saoussats-Debats. 'We had scarcely entered the *cabane* before fire was made and pâte set on. It might be about an hour before all huddled round the pâte-pan, ten of us, five *bergers* and our five selves . . .' She declined the pâte – a porridge of meal and milk – but ate bread and milk. 'I lay in my tartan cloak, wrapped in my cape, upon a couple of *bergers*'s capes, and my jacket stuffed between me and the big granite stone forming one end of the *cabane*. My *sac de nuit* was my pillow, aided by one of the *bergers*'s goat-skin bags in which they keep their provisions of bread and meal.'

She slept little in the crowded smelly hut and they set off before dawn. The party ascended slowly from the south – where there is now a *corredor Anne Lister* labelled on the map – resting frequently and using their crampons on the snow. After several hours' hard climb, at one o'clock they finally succeeded in reaching the summit. They could see the glacier to the east and Mont Perdu in the distance but clouds hid much of the view: 'The French mountains seen but in a mistiness, clouds sitting over them. South – the Spanish valleys a sea of clouds.'

They inserted their names triumphantly in a bottle and hid it under a pile of stones on the summit, and began the descent just after 2 p.m. After a night in the *cabane* they returned to Gavarnie, where Anne Lister calmly drank a glass of water, brushed her clothes, washed her feet and got into bed. Then she and Ann Walker made a trip to Spain.

In the meantime, however, Cazaux had taken the Prince of Moskowa to the top of Vignemale on 11 August. He told the prince that the Englishwoman had been taken ill and failed to make it to the summit, so that he was therefore the first. Although Lister said she did not make the climb for glory, when she heard this version of events she was very cross. 'Annoyed. Either I had gone to the top or not,' she noted tersely. Eventually Lister had to go to a lawyer and have Cazaux sign a certificate that she had indeed climbed to the top of Vignemale. This he finally did, asserting: '. . . the 7th day of August this year I acted as a guide for Miss Anne Lister of Shibden Hall for the ascent she made to the highest peak of Vignemale on that day . . . we all reached the highest point of Vignemale together and that to my knowledge no person had previously climbed so high.'

The prince cursed Cazaux (who had hoped to gain two payments for first ascents) but said he accepted this version of events. However, on 25 August *Galignani's Messenger* published the news that the Prince of Moskowa had made the first ascent of Vignemale. Lister sent in a correction. 'We find that an English lady had, four days before, ascended with three guides to the same summit.' But still the credit remained with Moskowa, whose expedition had been a much more professional affair and produced scientific information which he subsequently published, along with a highly coloured account of his climb.

Lister continued her travels, but died not long after at the age of forty-nine on a journey to Sweden, Finland and Russia, where she caught fever at the foot of the Caucasus mountains. Poor Ann Walker had to travel back overland, by way of Constantinople, with her coffin. The *Halifax*

Guardian paid the following tribute in their obituary of 31 October 1840: 'In mental energy she resembled Lady Mary Wortley Montagu and Lady Hester Stanhope; and like those celebrated women, after exploring Europe, she extended her researches to those Oriental regions, where her career has been so prematurely terminated.' The full account of Lister's ascent of Vignemale was finally published in France in the year 2000.

There is a curious resemblance between Lister and Henry Russell in their individuality and eccentricity, their determined walking and extraordinary capacity for endurance. The word sublimation comes irresistibly to mind. However, unlike the solitary wanderer of romantic tradition Russell seems to have been an admirably well-balanced fellow. When he was not communing with nature on the heights he enjoyed *le High Life* of Pau, which he described as 'a perfect storm of unending pleasure' with balls, soirées and concerts almost every day of the week. Russell loved it all and even in summer would sometimes leave Gavarnie in the climbing season to return to Bagnères or Pau for a social event (on foot, *naturellement*). He adored dancing and the ladies of Pau could never agree whether he or his brother Ferdinand was the best waltzer in town. The brothers attended all the French salons, English masked balls, American receptions, *les garden parties*, charity galas and sometimes several afternoon teas a day. Events ranged from the Chinese lantern festival given by Lady Buxton and the costumed balls of Lady Campbell (nursery rhyme characters were in vogue, and Little Bo Peep was a particular favourite) to the garden parties of Mrs Church and Mrs Acton, and the Monday receptions of the snobbish American, Mrs Lawrence, anxious to marry off her offspring.

Count Henry Russell quickly became a social fixture, a big fish in a small pond, crafting the image of eccentric explorer. He had an aristocratic but affable demeanour, and was much sought after by the hostesses of Pau. He was an accomplished cello player and a great raconteur in the Irish tradition, recounting his voyages with droll humour, or grumbling about the terrible trials inflicted on poor Irish landlords by English politicians. Though he spoke perfect French and English he seems at some point to have added a slight English accent to his French. He would not have had one naturally, having spoken French from infancy. But several acquaintances noted the hint of an English accent, a certain charming hesitation. One can just hear the slight quaver, the affected 'well, my dear . . .' Sadly there is no record of anyone commenting on the accent with which he spoke English. Perhaps he inherited an Irish one from his father. Limited media and communication in those days meant accents were much less homogeneous than they are today. Tennyson kept his Lincolnshire accent all his life.

For women he seems to have been an elusive quarry. He was after all an English aristocrat, albeit with a dodgy title (England does not have counts; the equivalent title would be earl). He was comfortably off if not fabulously rich, elegant, amusing, well travelled and a good dancer. No doubt his lofty detachment gave him further allure. But he always escaped them. He enjoyed their attentions and returned their affection but never appears to have been tempted. His taste for solitude and his independence always asserted themselves and he withdrew. Since his childhood he had always said that only one love had truly possessed him. The mountains awaited him.

He was utterly enthralled by the mountains, enslaved like a lover, his greatest desire to find himself once again on top of a snowy windswept peak with all the Pyrenees below him. He often walked along the terrace of the Place Royale, from where he could see the snowy peaks glinting tantalizingly under the winter sun. Or he would stroll on the bridge over the Gave, the only place where the wind ruffled the still calm air.

Russell's early climbs are like a speeded up film. He wanted to go everywhere and climb as many peaks as fast as possible, leaping from summit to summit like some aerial deity. By June it was time to go, and often just as a taster he would set off on foot to Gabat, about fifty kilometres from Pau, or to Gavarnie, eighty kilometres away, or even Luchon. He never needed to get in training, and his youthful family hikes as well as his walk around the world meant he was always prepared to walk formidable distances. He was an extraordinary athlete, and could climb for hours, bound over rocks, slide over ice, battle with the forests, ford rivers and sleep outside at an altitude of 3000 metres without suffering any fatigue.

Watching the Tour de France passing through Mosset one year, on its way up the gruelling slope to the Col de Jau, I was struck by the sheer stamina of the cyclists, their exceptional levels of endurance. Like Lance Armstrong, Russell seems to have had exceptional cardiovascular strength. Tests on Armstrong show that he is a physical prodigy, with a heart a third larger than average. In tests for aerobic ability, which measure the maximum amount of oxygen the lungs can consume during exercise,

Armstrong's levels were the highest ever recorded. Russell's performance indicates a similar level of strength. He could climb 400 metres in an hour, not by hurrying but by regular walking without stopping. He never suffered from breathlessness or vertigo, and recorded the experience of mountain sickness only once, in the Alps. He would walk for ten or twelve hours at a stretch, and sometimes if necessary as much as fifteen.

Once he was within reach of a summit nothing could stop him, and only rarely did terrible weather force him to turn back defeated. He would clamber over sharp *crêtes*, scramble on hands and knees up rock faces, leap crevasses. Often his guide found it difficult to follow him. And once he arrived at his goal, he wanted to stay there, not tick it off and descend again. He was there to savour the spectacle. If the view was clear he checked all the surrounding peaks, selecting another for the next day.

Russell explored the entire range from the modest la Rhune in the west, the mountain of the Basques, with its magnificent view over the Atlantic ocean, to Canigou in the east, with its sweeping perspective of the Mediterranean. 'La Rhune and Canigou stand sentinel at each end of the chain, both are visible from the shore, tantalizing the dwellers of the sunbaked plain and shore with the pure cool sublime heights.'

In the region closest to Pau, he could tick off all the peaks that could be distinguished on the horizon. The most distinctive, from Pau, is the Pic du Midi d'Ossau, a volcanic chimney that is the highest peak to the west of the chain (not to be confused with the Pic du Midi de Bigorre further east). It was much admired by visitors strolling in the *parc* of the chateau. Mrs Ellis was entranced by 'the noble vista, through which it is seen from the Parc at Pau'. Green hills open out to a 'majestic range of hills of dark rock' beyond which extends the Vallée d'Ossau (the valley of the bears, as she explains with a suitable shudder).

Russell's own portrait of the Pic du Midi d'Ossau is equally romantic: '. . . fantastic, solitary, emaciated, its profile full of majesty dominates this group of mountains with melancholic dignity'. He added briskly, 'It is easier than it looks, lots of women have climbed it,' but he also admitted that his own first attempt to climb it in one day in early spring was a complete fiasco.

It was March 1863 and he was accompanied by a young English officer 'of Herculean force', Congreve, with whom he had dined at Eaux-Chaudes the previous day. Eaux-Chaudes, only twenty-seven miles from Pau, was very popular with the English, most of whom stayed at Hôtel Baudot. Russell's own name appears several times in the visitors' book. Murray's guidebook recommended it: 'H. Baudot. Dinner at 5, table d'hôte 3 fr, breakfast with eggs, 1 fr, tea 1 fr, beds 2 fr.'d Eaux-Chaudes lay wedged deep into the valley, with hotels and houses jammed into the confined space, the Etablissement des Bains almost overhanging the torrent. For visitors wanting to do more than walk about with tumblers of evil-tasting spa water, it was recommended as a base for exploring the wild and beautiful environs, as Henry Blackburn recommended in his *Spas of the Pyrenees*, 'to sketch the valley from different points, to examine the extraordinary stratifications of granite and limestone, to mark the traces of extinct glaciers, to collect fossils or wild flowers, to fish in the gave, or to hunt the isard'.

A few even attempted to climb the neighbouring peaks.

It was early in the year to be climbing and Russell and Congreve set off with two guides and a porter in the snow. 'But what snow! It was like sand, in the forest we were up to our knees, even hips.' Russell added a word of advice: 'As a general rule for snow in spring and winter it is best to stretch out as much as possible over firm ground.'

At the base of the Pic things got difficult, and then formidable. There were 800 metres to climb of vertical corridors of soft snow. 'How did we avoid an avalanche? Now it seems like a miracle, a suspension of the laws of nature. But we were young then.' They were already getting nervous about the descent, but since the snow was not shifting they continued to climb up a second chimney. By the third and steepest, confronted by a sheer wall of snow, they capitulated unanimously. 'To continue would have been suicide,' Russell conceded. 'We had to descend, without *piolets* or ropes, just simple metal batons. Then we disdained the minute precautions taken today, but we were wrong, it was naive ignorance more than courage.' He nevertheless always remained disdainful of the iron stanchions that were later installed to assist climbers.

It was only a short distance from Eaux-Chaudes to Eaux-Bonnes, the next spa, either by road, or over the Col de Gourzy, but it could be dangerous. A group of Americans got lost in the fog in 1881, and the Reverend Merton Smith, vicar of Plympton St Mary in Devon, came to a very sticky end there. He was in the Pyrenees for a month's holiday in August 1883, and left Eaux-Bonnes to walk over the col to Eaux-Chaudes. He never returned. Search parties were organized but he was nowhere to be found. The bishop of Exeter was greatly perplexed since he could not give Reverend Smith's job to anyone else without knowing if the vicar was dead or alive. There was gossip; some said he had fallen victim to the charms of a Pyrenean shepherdess, and 'was picking edelweiss and playing a flute on some high Alp to the delectation of the damsel'. Even worse, some suggested he had been captured by Roman Catholics and interned in a monastery. Others said he had been murdered for his money. It was eighteen months before a woodcutter found his body, wedged among thick bushes of box on the mountainside. He seemed to have fallen while picking a flower, and been killed immediately. His watch and purse were still intact.

Eaux-Bonnes was regarded as the more cheerful of the two spas, often compared by the English to Matlock or Buxton, a fashionable little village surrounded by mountains and tumbling waterfalls, a miniature town of promenades and courtyards, bustling with gaily dressed visitors of all nationalities. Around the town a level promenade had been cut into the mountainside, lined with shops and peep shows, and seats at intervals to gaze on the view. Here and there were *cafés chantants*, no more than little holes cut in the rock, where customers called for cognac or *sirops*.

Every day was regulated, as Henry Blackburn described. 'There is the particular promenade for the early morning facing to the east, the exact spot where you are to walk (and no further) between the time of taking each glass of water, the morning cascade, the noon siesta, the ride at three, another cascade and more water, or a bath, at four, promenade at five, dinner at six, *promenade horizontale* until eight, then the Casino, dancing, *société*, cards, or more moonlight walks.'

These days Eaux-Bonnes is the beginning of one of the

most astonishing drives in the Pyrenees if you have the stomach for it and a head for heights. The Route des Thermes follows a winding vertiginous course over several of the highest cols all the way to Luchon. The views of the mountains to east and west are magnificent: the Pic de Ger, the Pic du Midi de Bigorre, and the forbidding white granite pyramid of Balaitous, one of the great 3000m peaks of the Pyrenees.

The road itself is terrifying. I made a memorable drive along the eastern end in late October with Paul Mirat from Pau, ever keen to reveal the beauties of his beloved Béarn. But he was a valley dweller at heart, and soon regretted leaving the tranquil confines of Pau. I had suggested we might even walk, but he responded in horror. 'Gordon Bennett! You want me to walk for three hours plus . . . I only love my mountains from the boulevard. I don't want to be surrounded by ferocious owls and bears, wild grasshoppers and crazy *marmottes*. I'm not English!'

So we drove. He was as astonished as I was by the biting cold and wind on the heights, and when I enquired the names of the peaks we could see, tried to call a mountaineering friend on his mobile phone to identify them for us. Then a dense clammy cloud descended and we had to drive precariously along a road on the edge of a precipice. It might have been even more hair-raising could we have seen where we were going.

It is a desolate road and I tried to imagine anyone rattling along it in a carriage and four with only wobbly lanterns for lights, but that is what was commissioned by Napoleon III for the Empress Eugénie so she could travel easily from spa to spa with some nice scenery along the way.

11

The Golden Age

To sit on rocks, to muse o'er flood and fell,
To slowly trace the forest's shady scene,
Where things that own not man's dominion dwell,
And mortal foot hath ne'er or rarely been;
To climb the trackless mountain all unseen,
With the wild flock that never needs a fold;
Alone o'er steeps and foaming falls to lean;
This is not solitude, 'tis but to hold
Converse with Nature's charms, and view her
    stores unrolled.

George Gordon, Lord Byron, *Solitude*

Most of us are not often really alone. Solitude was something I sought in escaping to the Pyrenees. But my own solitude is usually restricted to a few hours uninterrupted at my desk, with no Catalan farmers bellowing my name from the garden, or a siesta in the hammock with only the birds for company. Occasionally I have stayed a night or two alone in the monastery. The first time I found myself in a fierce storm, and tried to make a drama of it, playing Keith Jarrett loudly, and watching the spectacle. Then I spent a few days trying to write completely alone, and woke one morning to find it had snowed. Everything was quiet, all sound muffled by the snow. There were no cars passing by, no tractors grinding up the hillside to feed the cows.

The birds were all tucked up. The cat slept soundly by the lingering cinders of the woodstove. It was as if I was the last person in the world.

I rarely walk far alone, being timid, afraid of dogs let alone the wild boar, which are numerous and haunt my imagination. (I am always assured that they rarely attack humans, which somehow does not comfort me in the slightest.) But once I went to visit a ruined village up on the hills above Prades. There was no tarmac road so I walked the kilometre or so over a grassy track which dipped down out of sight into the valley and I found myself unexpectedly alone with nature. I sat down on a mossy rock to savour the solitude. There were no houses to see though I knew the ruined village was only half a kilometre or so further on. Here the only evidence of humanity were the remains of the terraces hacked into the hillside at a time when the needs of the peasants meant every spare inch of land was requisitioned and even the steepest gradients were cultivated, planted with olives or vines or grazed by goats. The sky was white, so white that it was almost the colour of the snow which still tipped the mountains. Sky and snow blended so that the dark hills looked like photographic negatives.

The hillside was covered in low scrubby bushes, cistus, wild lavender and thyme. Even on a cool spring day the scents were strong, and mixed with a fresh smell of spoor, tiny black pellets scattered over the path. Rabbits, I guessed, and thought of *Watership Down*. At least I wasn't afraid of rabbits. I could hear an occasional rustle in the undergrowth, the call of a high bird, but that was it. For once there was no wind, so any sound was easily heard.

I think I expected to feel a bit afraid in all that space with no-one. But as I sat there listening, smelling, trying to tune my senses, making no movement, I felt simply part of it. Instead of fear or aloneness I felt something akin to comfort, solace. I knew there was nothing to fear. There were no humans and no human habitation so there was no need to fear dogs. Any hunters' dogs I would hear a mile off. Bears and wolves used to be a threat, especially at night, when Russell was exploring these mountains but they had all been killed off long ago.

Henry Russell loved to be alone, sure that it was the only way to fully savour the wilderness. He shared this conviction most profoundly with his dearest friend, Charles Packe, the other great British mountain explorer of the period, which is known as the Golden Age of British mountaineering in the Pyrenees.

Packe and Russell met late in the summer of 1863 at Lac Bleu near Barèges. It was a key encounter, resulting in a friendship which would endure to the end. Neither records any details of the meeting but a few years earlier Mrs Ellis wrote an evocative description of her visit to the lake, which she made on horseback with her husband in 1840. Lac Bleu is a deep tarn in a mountain hollow west of the Pic du Midi, surrounded by craggy peaks. 'I can never forget the strangeness and stillness of this place,' she wrote. 'It is a solitary spot, with no house or tree, or living thing to be seen in its vicinity, a stillness almost death-like reigning around. It might be dreary but for the rich warm colouring of the rocks, the depth and stillness of the water, and its intense blue. The surface is like an emerald sea; and there is neither ripple, nor oar, nor shelving shore where boat could be stranded, except in one particular spot . . .'

Both Packe and Russell were passionate about the

Pyrenees. Both were writers inspired by the mountains and adventurous travel. Russell's account of his travels in Asia and Australasia had recently been published, in two enormous volumes, and enthusiastically received by the critics. Packe was preparing a second edition of his *Guide to the Pyrenees, especially intended for the use of mountaineers*, the first ever to include the high peaks. They were kindred spirits and glad to find each other. Both despised the idea of climbing as a simple sport, what Russell called, 'the deplorable transformation of alpinism into mere athletics and gymnastics'. Their romantic appreciation of the mountains was a key factor in steering climbing in the Pyrenees away from the butch emphasis of the British Alpine Club, to become less of a sport and more of a philosophy.

They cannot both have been alone that day; they were probably introduced by a member of the Frossard family from Bagnères. Still, there weren't many Englishmen with a taste for solitary adventure exploring the Pyrenees at that time. Perhaps they sat on the soft turf beside the still blue lake and shared their provisions, gazing at the distant peaks, and indulging in one of those tentative conversations where new acquaintances share mutual references and touch base with one another, quoting their favourite writers, Byron on solitude, and Ruskin, who believed that mountain scenery was conducive to religious feeling. 'The mountains of the earth are its natural cathedrals,' as he put it. Both agreed that walking alone was the best way to appreciate picturesque scenery and experience the spiritual epiphanies they sought. Both were also convinced the English were better at solitude than the French. Packe wrote a little book, *The Spirit of Travel*, a youthful work published after his first visit to the Alps, naive and pompous, sprinkled with Latin and French quotations, and larded with pretentious advice. (Essentials for the solitary traveller were a map, a small Horace, Lucretius or Virgil plus a flask of brandy and biscuits in one's pocket.) In it he observed:

> One more often meets an Englishman travelling by himself than a native of any other country; foreigners indeed generally and the French in particular, seem to have no idea of enjoyment under any circumstances without society. The Englishman who has travelled in the Pyrenees must have been disgusted beyond measure by the frivolity and childishness of French tourists, who with cracking whips and idle shouts come galloping down the pass, and disturb the contemplation of those magnificent scenes which are best appreciated in silence and solitude.

The French did not always share the same taste for rustic beauty as the English – happily for one Englishman, who, finding his hotel room in Saint-Sauveur gave out onto the noisy street, found a Frenchman all too happy to exchange, since he was bored 'always seeing the view of mountains and rivers'.

Packe and Russell had narrowly missed meeting only two years before in Gavarnie at the Hôtel des Voyageurs. Packe had stayed there on 7 September 1861. 'Stayed four days and quite satisfied with the quarters,' he wrote briskly in the visitors' book. A week later Russell had noted in his elegant spidery handwriting his first ascent of Vignemale. When I later saw the book for myself I found the relevant pages had long since been torn out by souvenir hunters so it is unclear which route Russell took that first time. But since Packe later claimed the first ascent from the east, in 1862, presumably Russell had followed the same route from the south as Anne Lister. By the time they met they could compare notes on Vignemale too.

Charles Packe was a lean, intense Englishman, fine-featured, with aquiline nose, deep-set eyes and, later, a full biblical black beard. He researched his guidebook entirely by himself and mostly alone, and as the first real guide to the high mountains of the Pyrenees it remained a key text for the next fifty years or so. It is a handbook to the entire chain but concentrates particularly on the mountains around Luchon, which Packe considered the most important.

He was an early member of the famous Alpine Club (the Alpine Club, founded in Britain in 1858, was the first climbing club, and thereafter always insisted it was *the* Alpine Club, no national qualifier required.) Packe put up Russell for membership and he joined in 1864, the year after they met.

A few members of the Alpine Club had previously passed through the Pyrenees, climbed a notable peak or two and gone back to Switzerland, but it was over-whelmingly Packe and Russell who dominated the first epoch of climbing in the Pyrenees, when three-quarters of the chain remained to be discovered.

Packe was the kind of Englishman for whom Russell had profound respect, embodying the manliness and honour of the British Empire at its height. The kind of Englishman, indeed, he wanted to be himself. Russell wrote of Packe, 'He was sincere, almost too transparent, for he could no more disguise his antipathies than his sympathies. One read through him at once, he flattered nobody, and would have been a bad diplomatist. Indeed if plain speaking can ever be called a failing, it was the only one he had.'

For Packe, Russell must have seemed exotic, after his years of far-flung travel, his nautical adventures and his wild sojourns off the Irish coast. His combination of French and Irish blood gave him a poetic quality that the blunt-speaking public school educated Englishman found deeply engaging. Packe loved France and spoke French well, and liked to quote from Montaigne and Pascal. His affection for France endeared him to Russell who shared with him a deep commitment to Anglo-French understanding.

They complemented each other. While Henry waxed on about the effects of the dawn on the mountain peaks, and the sublimity of snow, Charles studied the rock formations and expounded the botanical details of the rare flower specimens he diligently searched for on his expeditions. Russell always respected his knowledge. 'He is the professional, I am only an amateur. I climb the peaks, he studies their structure, their measurements, their flora.'

Packe was born in 1826, eight years before Russell. He was the eldest son of a captain of the Horse Guards, and had a traditional upper class education at Eton and Christ Church College, Oxford. Though he qualified as a barrister in 1852 he never practised. He became owner of Stretton Hall in Leicestershire on the death of his uncle in 1867, and settled into life as a paternalistic landowner and English squire, a respected pillar of the local church and community. But he was above all a mountaineer. By the time he met Russell he had already explored much of Britain, climbing peaks in the Scottish Highlands and the Lake District, and sleeping out in all weathers. Botany was his particular passion and he discovered several rare species of flora in the Pyrenees, and his herbarium and rock garden at Stretton Hall were well stocked with rare Pyrenean plants. He also studied geology, fossils, weather systems and electrical activity and wrote several learned papers for the Alpine Club journal on these matters. (His papers on flowers were among the few ever to appear in that macho publication.)

He had visited the Pyrenees briefly in 1853, following a predictable 'quest for the picturesque' to the Lac de Gaube, taking the waters at Cauterets and climbing the Pic du Midi, followed by a few days in Biarritz. But he found these well-worn paths too touristy, 'too cockney' as he put it. Spa bathing was not for him, and much to the astonishment of his guides, he preferred swimming in the rivers. Nor did he enjoy city life as Russell did. 'The life of people in Pau is more artificial and effeminate and much more frivolous than in London. In London you can take advantage of scientific meetings and the society of scholars, but at Pau there is nothing of the sort . . .'

After Packe made the first traveller's ascent of Vignemale from the east, he wrote about it for the *Alpine Journal*, one of a handful of articles it ever published on the Pyrenees. His account bears out his reputation for generosity and sympathy with his guides. Packe, like everyone else at the time, attributed the first ascent to the Prince de Moskowa in 1838, and made no mention of Gentleman Jack. He had talked to Laurent Passet, a favourite guide from Gavarnie, about the possibility of climbing from the east over the glacier. Laurent had checked it out several times himself before Packe appeared to do it officially in September. The weather was poor and there had been fresh snow, and there was cloud cover for ten days. Packe gave up one attempt with Laurent and his brother Hippolyte, driven back by intense cold and blinding snow on the glacier.

Then the weather changed and they resolved to climb the following Monday, avoiding Sunday since Laurent was already unpopular with the curé for missing mass the week before when he went to Mont Perdu with Packe. 'On the Sunday, by way of making amends to the curé, I accompanied Laurent to mass, and in the afternoon assisted him in getting in his hay, the curé having permitted this necessary work to his parishioners, in consequence of the continued bad weather, which threatened to spoil the hay.' They set off on Monday before sunrise. When they reached the summit of Vignemale they were rewarded with clear weather and a magnificent view, and Packe set about industriously taking measurements with his compass and thermometer.

Despite their fondness for solitude both Russell and Packe used local guides and porters to carry the substantial provisions they always needed. The guides had often already recced the path in advance for their employers, though it was accepted that only the gentlemen climbers would receive the accolade. These men of the mountains were more than guides; explorers themselves, men of courage, prudent, but curious and great mountain lovers. With several of them, notably the Passet family of Gavarnie, Packe and Russell became firm friends, cherishing a companionship forged in harsh and difficult conditions which transcended their awareness of class.

When Packe travelled alone, he was helped by his beloved Pyrenean mountain dogs. They are huge beasts, so tall you don't have to bend to stroke them, with fine soft white fur marked with grey or tan, and friendly teddy bear faces. They look perfectly designed to adorn a fireside but were bred for guarding the flocks in all weathers on the steep mountain slopes of the Pyrenees. I am no dog lover but if I ever had a dog this is the one I would want.

With his dogs Packe could safely cross snowy cols and unknown glaciers, and once he roped himself to a pair to cross a frozen lake, knowing they could pull him out if the ice broke. He introduced the dog to Britain, bringing back five, named Wolf, Ossou, Patou, Néthou and Carlitte to Stretton Hall, where they were kept in an iron-railed grass enclosure in front of the house, a sort of self-styled dog park. There they made so much racket that the police often had to be summoned. (Before he died Packe expressed a wish to be buried with his dogs in the dog park, but after his death the family decided it was more fitting that he should be buried in the local cemetery instead.) It is not recorded what the family did with the life-size Pyrenean dog made of Dresden china that Packe had ordered at enormous expense.

The following summer, 1864, Russell and Packe met for an extended tour together. Before then, however, Russell limbered up with a seventeen-day zigzag tour on foot from Pau through the Pyrenees via Spain and Andorra. Throughout his journey Russell mostly slept in the open air, and his appearance clearly deteriorated. He no longer resembled 'un gentleman' but rather 'un Robinson', as he put it. He re-entered France and the Ariège, from Spain, by the Port de Salau and immediately sought an *auberge* for food and lodging. Two refused to allow him in at all. In the third place, in the village of Couflens, he was just polishing off 'a delicious leg of lamb' when the customs officers arrived to arrest him. Discovering he had no passport they threw him in jail in Saint Lizier. A notorious murderer had just been guillotined in Foix, and they took some convincing that Russell too was not of the same ilk. He concedes that his wanderings could easily have been interpreted as those of a man evading justice. (Ever after Russell remained leery of the Ariège, and always warned people not to go there without their passports.)

He formed a low opinion of the region, grumbling about the rackety old *diligences* which went more slowly than he did walking, the changes of horses, which were even worse than the ones they had been riding, the state of the roads churned up by traffic from the iron mines, and the poor slate-roofed villages so grim they looked like cemeteries.

I would never describe the Ariège as grim – there are too many sweet secret green valleys, clear lakes and rushing rivers – but of all areas of the Pyrenees I have visited Ariège always strikes me as the most louche, the most likely place to be a hideout for dangerous desperadoes. Though its peaks are not as high as in other parts of the Pyrenees it has deep valleys without exit, where the *soixante-huitards* (as old French hippies are called, after the 1968 *événements*) live in primitive tepees, keep goats and make cheese, and weave baskets that they sell every week at the market in Foix.

Visiting the Ariège a few years ago, we drove up to the high pass of Ascou-Paillères. The road was so steep and the hairpin bends so tight I had to scream halfway up to release the tension, much to Theo's amusement. We were in serious need of lunch and when we got to the bare windswept moorland at the top we were happy if astonished to see a hand-drawn sign for pizzas. The sign pointed to a simple wooden cabin, which obviously served skiers in the wintertime. Now it was still only early autumn and deserted. We were the only guests and warmly welcomed. Inside was a snug roaring log fire, beside it a baby in a rocking cradle. *Le patron* was eager to talk, as he served us homemade pâté with roughly cut slices of home-made bread, a freshly killed rabbit, and their own cheese and jam. He had come from the north and married a local girl, and the family lived there on the mountain top year-round, so far from the nearest town the children had to be educated by correspondence course.

Russell attacked the mountains of the Ariège, scaling Pic Collat, where the view extended over the entire Monts Maudits to the south. It was only mid-June, and there was still considerable snow, but despite warnings from the locals that climbing was '*Impossible!*' he succeeded in ascending both Montcalm and Pique d'Estats. He remarked that the terror of the locals for snow was akin to hydrophobia: 'A sailor on a horse or a Parisian by the sea has less fear than a shepherd of the snow.' For Russell snow added to the fun; as he approached Montcalm 'it was striped with snow like a tiger'. He ascended, without difficulty, to find the broadest summit in the Pyrenees, big enough for a regiment, he noted. Leaving his guide asleep on one mountain top he ascended the next, Pique d'Estats, from which he could see all of Catalonia, Andorra and the

Cerdagne as far as the Mediterranean, while below clouds covered the entire plain of Garonne. How often, he observed, it is clearer in the mountains than on the plain.

He wanted to climb Carlit, the highest peak in the eastern Pyrenees at 2920 metres and as yet unbagged, and took lodgings at the Hôtel Sicre in Ax-les-Thermes, not one of the most salubrious spas of the Pyrenees; visitors complained that the baths were used mainly for blanching pork and plucking fowl. When we passed through a century and a half later the sulphurous warm water of the open baths seemed to be mainly used for the old folks to soak their feet in.

Russell walked from Ax to Mérens, where he dined, and 'sustained by a massive omelette and venison' found a young man to accompany him on his climb of Carlit. He followed the Route d'Espagne towards l'Hospitalet and the border with Andorra, heading off left to follow a gorge full of pines and rhododendrons. Soon they were climbing, and reached Lac Lanous, one of the biggest lakes in the Pyrenees, where they spent the night in a fisherman's cabin beside the lake. It was bitterly cold, and the landscape bare and treeless, but finally they clambered over the rocks to the top, the first to make the summit, and Russell constructed a memorial cairn of stones to mark his ascent. The view was dramatic, but as bleak and desolate as any Russell had seen in France, despite the numerous lakes below. The descent was difficult and dangerous and he fell into a snow hole in a deep depression south of the peak, saved only by his trusty alpenstock.

He returned to Ax, via the Col de Puymorens (now with a road tunnelled through it) and the hamlet 'derisively named Hospitalet', as he put it. Whom should he meet at the Hôtel Sicre but the 'lamentable' Miss Eyre. After the success of her first book on the south of France she had been commissioned (for her sins, as she makes very clear, deeply regretting the Hampstead cottage from which she had been ejected) to write another about the Spanish side of the Pyrenees.*

She was ill and, dreading her journey into Andorra and Spain, had sought sanctuary in the little hotel, with its garden and fountains, and marble thermal baths. She wrote her journal daily while she convalesced, hymning 'the snow-wreathed Ariège that foamed over the huge boulders, and the wild, craggy, deep-shadowed, picturesque blue mountains, closing in the scene'.

Her concern about her travel prospects and particularly the weather was not helped by Russell's lurid account of his snowy plunge. 'I met at the hotel at Ax, a Mr Russell, a member of the Alpine Club, who had just returned from an expedition into Andorra, whither he went to make a more correct guide than has yet been published of this chain of the Pyrenees, and he told me that the day before, descending one of the mountains, he slipped and fell into

* It seems very likely that Mary Eyre was the sister of Governor Edward Eyre, who after an early career exploring Australia became notorious as Governor of Jamaica for his suppression of the Morant Bay Rebellion in 1865. His brutal actions, including the massacre of hundreds of blacks, divided Britain. A letter from his sister to the *Morning Star* is written in the same tones of asperity as those of the authoress on the Pyrenees, and she was roundly condemned for defending 'her bloody murderous brother . . . The curse of the nation and the world will ever rest upon your family for these bloody crimes. Bloody cries for vengeance on you all . . .' Edward did have a sister named Mary, but no biographies say anything about her, let alone that she may have been a writer. But the dates fit, since Mary was travelling in the late 1860s, and it may be that the controversy surrounding her brother obliged her to leave London in disgrace.

one of these deep beds of snow; luckily he escaped without injury. I believe he is the second Englishman who has visited Andorra; the Honourable Erskine Murray was the first, and for above twenty years had no follower. I, so far as I know, am the first Englishwoman who has ever dared to invade the privacy of that pocket republic. I recommend no single unprotected woman to follow in my track.'

Finally she set off on her mountain journey, grumbling mightily. 'What a figure I should have cut to eyes polite could they have seen me at 5 a.m. following my guide up the dirty little streets of l'Hospitalet in my cloak and flapping Leghorn hat, and by the aid of a chair mounting a lean sorry beast, accoutred with an old leathern bridle fastened beneath the animal's head with rope, and eked out with whipcord to lengthen it; a cumbrous man's saddle, over which was an old woollen rug; a sack with my shawl, containing my guide-books &c at one end, and a small tin bonnet-box in the other; while behind me was strapped my carpet-bag of clothes, and my small travelling bag, and in my hand, instead of a whip, I flourished the well-known "Mrs Gamp".' Her umbrella was to come in very useful for berating her long-suffering muleteer when he threatened to abandon her.

A week later Russell, who unlike poor Miss Eyre, was young, fit, male and wealthy, had met up with Packe again. Charles had been busily botanizing in the Cerdagne, in the Pyrénées Orientales, and he and Russell planned to explore more of the eastern regions of the Ariège, Andorra and the Mediterranean Pyrenees.

Russell observed that in those distant times, Pyrenean climbing was in its infancy: '. . . it entailed all sorts of privations, hardships and even risks, unknown to the present generation. Ice-axes had never been heard of, and when we crossed or scaled steep slopes of blue ice or frozen snow, we had to cut our steps either with a microscopic pocket axe, which was often dropped and lost, or with sharp stones and slates. Speed was impossible. The rope had only just made its appearance; it was scarcely ever used, and in crevassed glaciers we trusted almost entirely to sounding with alpenstocks.'

In the Ariège, they climbed Pic Carlit together, Russell for the second time in a week. Then they headed across the flat plateau of the Cerdagne. This is still one of the great unspoilt wildernesses of France, deep in snow in winter, and famous for its sheets of yellow jonquils in spring. Our favourite way to see it is by the Little Yellow Train, the narrow gauge railway nicknamed the 'metro of the Pyrenees', which takes you from the fortified town of Villefranche-de-Conflent in the Têt valley up to Latour-de-Carol (where you can change trains for Barcelona) via Font-Romeu, and Bolquère-Eyne, the highest rail station in France at 1593 metres. The little train was an extraordinary achievement when it was built in 1927, with the intention of opening up access to the high valleys; it is still a vital connection for the inhabitants of the Cerdagne if the road is closed, either by snow, or most recently a dramatic landslide which blocked it for several days. *Le petit tran jaune* remains a potent local symbol and there was a tremendous outcry when it was threatened with closure in the 1970s. It makes an amazing journey through vertiginous gorges and over towering viaducts, especially if you find a seat in the open carriage and can tolerate the excited screams of children as the train whistles through the tunnels.

It is an endearing little train, like something out of *Thomas the Tank Engine*; the cars it passes on the road always hoot, even villagers who must see it pass four times a day unbend from their vegetable gardens and wave as it goes by. Sometimes we take visitors in summer to see the world's biggest solar furnace, at Font-Romeu, its giant convex mirrors stepped across the valley. But my favourite trip was in winter, the brave little train snaking its way through silent forests, pines and chestnuts weighed down with snow.

In the Cerdagne Packe was delighted to find an example of the Pyrenean gentian, which he recognized from the dried specimen he had been sent by John Stuart Mill. Russell and Packe explored the Eyne valley, which even Russell concedes was 'an Eden of flowers', grudgingly noting in parenthesis *Ranunculus parnassifolius* and 'various charming ferns . . .etc'. His observation of flowers is considerably more diligent when he is travelling with Packe. He did once observe a rare red Pyrenean poppy blooming alone on the summit of Cotiella in Spain, and Packe later grumbled that he forgot to take a specimen. But I rather like the fact Russell simply enjoyed it in situ and left it to grow. According to Packe's subsequent paper for the *Alpine Journal* the Vallée d'Eyne offered almost every known species of Pyrenean flora, but especially the red Alpine poppy (*Papaver pyrenaicum*), the silver-leaved senecio (*S. leucophyllum*), the large purple primrose (*Primula latifolia*), and the yellow adonis (*Adonis pyrenaica*) and the umbellifer (*Xatardia scabra*).

Russell was not greatly enamoured of the sunburnt landscape of Catalonia. 'It was like Africa and Russia under the same sky,' he observed, 'beautiful but sad. Not Pyrenean enough for me.' He approved, however, of the lakes and the waterfalls (he is credited with discovering the Cascade d'Arse in the Ariège, though I don't know if he named it too). He conceded that the mountains of the Mediterranean Pyrenees were more graceful and less fear-inspiring than those in the west. But as far as he was concerned there were not enough glaciers and too many flowers. Nor was he impressed by the accommodation, though he did have a good word for Vernet-les-Bains, where he found a decent hotel on the way to climb Canigou.

Later the little spa town became known as Vernet of the English, who flocked there at the turn of the century. Rudyard Kipling in particular was fond of Vernet and visited three times between 1911 and 1914, seeking treatment for his wife. Canigou he described as a magician among mountains, and said it reminded him of the Himalaya. Anthony Trollope liked Vernet and Canigou too: 'No-one can pooh-pooh the stern old Canigou, standing high and solitary, solemn and grand, between the two roads which run from Perpignan into Spain, the one by Prades and the other by le Boulou. Under the Canigou, towards the west, lie the hot baths of Vernet, in a close secluded valley, which, as I have said before, is, as far as I know, the sweetest spot in these Eastern Pyrenees.'

Vernet of the English had however been and gone by the time I got there, and today there is little evidence of their passing. All the grand hotels were washed away in a great flood in 1940. The only one remaining is the Hôtel du Portugal, which boasts Kipling's entry in its visitors' book, but is now used as a holiday home for retired miners. Next door is a shabby casino, whose fine art deco tilework has been ripped off in favour of Sixties copper ceilings. We rescued one lovely old tile from a pile of broken ones.

There used to be an Anglican church in Vernet founded by the Colonial and Continental Church Society in 1889, but it has been closed for some time due to unspecified disagreements between the local worshippers and the Bishop of Gibraltar. The Rotary Club still exists, though the membership is almost entirely French. It has two women members, though the one elderly Englishman who does occasionally turn up at meetings grumbles about that.

There is most evidence of the English in the cemetery, where a few graves remain, their stone slabs broken and crumbling into the ground. Here lie Robert and Mary Snow under a grey polished marble slab, Philip Robert Pigott (died 17 March 1910), his gravestone inscribed 'Love is strong as death' in English, stiff upper lip to the grave, and Constance Marsden, 'Pray for her soul.' It has a wonderful view for a cemetery, Canigou rising protectively above it, puffy white clouds in a serene sky.

With Packe, Russell climbed Canigou for the second time, an ascent he reckoned tiring since it was necessary to start from such a low altitude. They took the route via the little village of Casteil, passing the Romanesque abbey of Saint Martin-du-Canigou, still in ruins then, on its rocky outcrop among the beech and chestnut woods. They crossed the plateau of Cady, covered in flowers and tinkling with the noise of a thousand springs. An hour and a half later they were on the summit. Russell was never privileged to enjoy the view, however. 'My conscience forbids me to speak of the view,' he wrote, 'because each time, I climbed in clouds. One might have believed one was in Manchester. But it ought to be marvellous, because to the east the horizon of the sea stretches for two hundred kilometres.' Russell wished he could sleep on the summit and see the sunrise from Canigou. 'It must be one of the most beautiful spectacles of nature.'

Later that summer Russell and Packe suffered a night of perdition together, which presumably cemented their friendship since it did not break it. Packe planned to spend a few days botanizing around Lac de Cailaouas in the Central Pyrenees, filled by the waters of the glaciers of the Gourgs Blancs, and Russell accompanied him. The weather was fine, and they left on foot from Luchon, sending two guides on ahead by a different route, arranging to meet them that evening by the lake (no doubt with the trout and bacon already sizzling over the fire).

'We were so sure we did not equip ourselves with provisions or covers, imprudence we would pay dearly for,' Russell wrote ominously. 'Never should one venture into high mountains without provisions. Always assume you might get lost, even with the best weather in the world.'

They headed west to the Esquierry valley, seeking the Porte d'Enfer, which would take them over to Lac de Cailaouas. As they started to climb the long slopes the landscape became more wild and savage. Then a clammy mist descended, and despite their maps and compasses they realized they were lost. They clambered through a breach but it was the wrong one and suddenly they found themselves on the edge of a precipice, with only darkness and glacial fog around them.

It was already late in the day, they were exhausted, hungry (especially Russell), wet and thoroughly demoralized. But to do nothing seemed out of the question so they struggled to descend a vertiginous ravine, praying the slopes would be gentler below, and they would be able to find some sort of shelter where they could await daylight without freezing or rolling into the yawning abyss. On the contrary, the further down they went the steeper the incline became until it was almost vertical and very slippery. Finally they were halted completely by a long overhang as smooth as polished marble. 'It would have made an isard afraid,' shuddered Russell.

'Then night came, and sad, pale and silent, we bedded down a few steps from a mass of snow, in a sort of natural bowl, to pass the night at a height of 2500 metres without a morsel of bread, without wine, without covers, without even knowing where we were, not only at the mercy of the weather, which was very menacing, but exposed to falls of stone from above. It was impossible to move, because we were clinging to the flanks of a precipice.'

They huddled together and finally fatigue overcame them and they slept fitfully for a few hours. 'Well before the day, a glacial rain woke me, and worries came with insomnia. What would become of us if a tempest chained us there?' The two friends clinging to the precipice in a howling tempest would have made a fine subject for a romantic painting. He remembered his terrible experience in New Zealand, 'lost, alone and without food in the mountains, struggling night and day, with all the furies of nature. The memory haunted me like a spectre.'

He asked himself why he was fascinated by such cruel cold desolation, and remembered the seductive charms of the tropics, the red horizons of seas and savannah, the long colonnades of palms, the fiery rays of the sun and the sublime calm and majesty of Indian evenings. 'When one thinks of these enchanted places how can ice and emptiness still charm the spirit? Nature deprived of everything, water, forests, grass, widowed of all colours and reduced to silence. The greatest painter in the world would be embarrassed if one asked for a landscape with nothing more than rocks and snow.' Yet it was in this terror that he found most beauty. 'Only nature can achieve such sublime effects, creating beauty out of horror.'

Finally nature relented and granted them a magnificent dawn. The sky lightened and the sun returned at last. The two friends climbed wearily back up the steep ravine they had stumbled down the night before and found the true Porte d'Enfer and the path to the lake and their anxious guides.

Russell was blithely undeterred by this experience, and set off the following day to conquer the tempting virgin peak of Gourgs Blancs, which towered above them. Packe, more circumspect, stayed behind to look for flowers around the icy lake. From the peak Russell found 'a Sahara of ice and snow, where the glare of the sun was unbearable'. But he loved it, his favourite combination of extremes, the brilliance of the sun and the painful whiteness of the snow. 'The view needed a volume in itself, and as for the snow, it cannot be described, I leave the page blank.' A rare modernist moment for a man of so many words.

I was reading his descriptions of snow and ice during the winter at Mosset. It had snowed a lot that year, and outside my window it was white with only the dark green of the pine tree giving relief to the monotone. The whiteness hurt my eyes and I could easily imagine snow blindness. A low mist was drifting down the valley and it too was white, a white veil over white snow. I could understand why Russell resorted to comparing it to the whiteness of a blank page. That morning, after a heavy fall of snow in the night, I went and rescued some of the trees, releasing lower branches from the snow which had pinned them to the ground, shaking the higher ones to loosen their burden and allow the branches to spring back. The weight had broken many boughs of the big pine tree and smashed several of the branches of the rosemary hedge. The sharp medicinal fragrance of the herb rose in the still cold air as I attempted to rescue it. Snow is powerful. I could understand why an avalanche could carry away entire forests.

Later Theo tried to give me a lesson in cross-country skiing. He had learned to ski in Mosset at the little ski station on the Col de Jau, which boasts of being the smallest ski station in the world. It consists of one rackety old ski lift which spends more time being mended than functioning properly, a snow blower with a broken window held together with sticking tape, and a wooden chalet, where half the village gathers on a snowy day, dogs and all.

Sausages are grilled on an outside barbecue and mothers and babies settle themselves on hay bales to gossip and watch the younger children sledge down the piste. Theo adored it and loved to demonstrate his prowess, and begged me to try. Finally I agreed and we set off together along the forest trail with me shuffling along on the unfamiliar skis. It was beautiful, a magic kingdom of our own. 'Perhaps we'll meet Mr Tumnus,' said Theo, who was immersed in *The Lion, the Witch and the Wardrobe*, and we imagined we could hear the bells of the sleigh of the White Witch or, better still, Father Christmas.

In truth I was no skier, and spent more time falling over and crashing into bushes than I did upright. But when I found myself occasionally gliding through the forest I could appreciate the stillness that Russell loved, the quiet, intense peace. The snow muffles everything. There are no harsh human angles, all is organic and smoothed out. The air is like crystal, cleansing. Biblical analogies rise up as they must have done for him. Russell writes so much about snow and whiteness, the purity of ice, it is as if he has an almost pathological desire for cleanness, the devout Catholic yearning to wash away his sins.

12

The music of the air

'Who saw the narrow sunbeam that came out of the south, and smote upon their summits until they melted and mouldered away in a dust of blue rain? Who saw the dance of the dead clouds when the sunlight left them last night, and the west wind blew them before it like withered leaves?'

John Ruskin

It is hard to imagine when one sees the elaborate kit required by walkers and climbers today – precision fitted shock absorbent boots, neoprene jackets with welded seams and magnetic stormflaps, thermal underwear, Gore-tex socks, fleeces, flares and torches, avalanche transceivers, probes, personal locator beacons, advanced trekking poles – that until quite recently no-one wore any particular outfit for climbing. Alfred Wills climbed the Wetterhorn in elastic-sided boots and cricketing flannels, and Albert Smith's companion went up Mont Blanc in a Cambridge boating outfit.

Russell's usual garb was a classic countryman's tweed Norfolk jacket, single breasted, belted at the waist and pleated back and front, over thick tweed trousers. He wore thick woollen socks to the knee, leather gaiters and nailed boots, made in the workshop of the cobbler of Luz. A soft fedora gave some protection from the sun (though he often bemoans the state of his sunburnt nose) and he invariably carried an iron-tipped alpenstock, which he always preferred to an ice-axe. Maps, if there were any, a compass, and a thermometer were also indispensable items in his pack. He had a habit of taking the temperature wherever he was, be it a mountain summit or a hotel room.

Good supplies were essential to long treks, and Russell's great appetite meant he could not survive long without substantial provisions, so he usually needed a porter. A 20-kilo bag would suffice for several days, packed with conserves, cold chicken, bread, cigars, and some fresh linen.

The need for supplies restricted expeditions, and even more the need for shelter. Unlike in the Alps there were no comfortable hotels at high altitudes and refuges were unheard of. The only resort for a night's shelter were the *bergers'* cabins, which were basic to put it mildly; an early photo shows five or six men squeezed together into a rudimentary shack of stone and slate, snoring round a smoky fire, all their pots and pans suspended from a tree outside.

Then Russell discovered the sleeping bag. There seems to be some doubt as to who was the first to spot the cosy bag made of lamb skins used by French soldiers stationed on the frontier on the lookout for Spanish smugglers. But I think there is little doubt the discovery should be attributed to Sir Francis Galton. He was a scholar and freelance scientist, a cousin of Charles Darwin and grandson of Samuel Galton, a member of the famous Lunar Society, whose members, the Lunaticks, met every full moon to discuss scientific matters. (The moon helped light their way home.)

Francis Galton wrote on subjects as various as finger-prints, eugenics, dog whistles, criminality, twins, visionaries and hereditary genius. His enquiry into people's ability to visualize mental images latterly attracted the attention of Oliver Sacks, the equally irrepressible author of *The Man Who Mistook His Wife for a Hat*, and other philosophical and psychological investigations. Galton described the sleeping bag in the fourth edition of his book *The Art of Travel. Or, Shifts and Contrivances Available in Wild Countries*, published in 1867. Galton's book became a key component of any self-respecting explorer's equipment from the 1850s on, packed out with advice for travellers gleaned from most of the wild bits of the world from Tibet to the Isle of Man; advice on diet and clothing, especially hats, to the management of savages and how to tie up a prisoner. Tips include how to secrete jewels in extreme circumstances (insert under skin and allow to heal over).

Galton and Charles Packe had visited Spain in 1860 to see the eclipse of the sun from Bilbao and it was then that Galton spotted the cunning sleeping bags. His book includes two detailed diagrams of the bags, unfolded ready for use and folded up with straps so they could be carried as backpacks. (He loved diagrams; he even includes a mathematical formula for regaining a lost road.) He gave lectures about the sleeping bag, and caused prolific corres-pondence in the *Alpine Journal*, and was toasted as the great bagman of Europe at an Alpine Club dinner. It seems that Packe subsequently introduced the bag to Russell, who became as enthusiastic a proselytizer as Galton.

To Russell it was a revelation; with such a bag, warm and waterproof, he could sleep anywhere, under a tree or a rock or on top of a mountain. He speedily found someone to make him a similar bag of six lamb skins, with the wool inside (otherwise a wolf might take him for a sheep, he explained). It weighed three kilos. He exulted like a child over his new acquisition, talked of it incessantly, and recommended it at every opportunity. It remained one of his proudest possessions for the next forty years of his life, during which it preserved him admirably from cold, rain and snow. The sleeping bag still exists and is now in the Musée Pyrénéen in Lourdes along with his compass, water bottle and alpenstock. It was top of my list of sights to see when I went there, and I was very disappointed to be told that it was so fragile that it could no longer be exhibited. There was something poignant about the thought of the trusty, sturdy bag of sheepskin now so worn and delicate.

There is also an echo of the mendicant monks of old, for whom a monastic cloak made of sheepskin was often their only possession, used as a blanket to sleep in and to carry their few possessions. With the sleeping bag Russell could escape the shepherds' huts: 'I prefer to sleep under the stars, without fire or shelter, at whatever height, than in the miserable huts of the *bergers*, which are often dirtier and more fetid than Mongol yurts.' Best of all he liked to sleep on the summit, to feel truly connected to the mountain. For Russell it was pure joy to see the sunrise from a mountain top. He liked his nature wild and magnificent, and though he sometimes mused poetically over the gentle green slopes of the valleys of the Béarn it was always the peaks in all their detached grandeur that seduced him. His body and spirit seemed to be in perfect synergy with the mountains.

With his sleeping bag there was no limit to his

explorations. He took notes assiduously and detailed each of his climbs in his journal. He noted the hours it took, and the movement of glaciers and rivers; made observations on clouds, altitude, winds and temperature. He scrupulously noted directions and frequently found mistakes in the few maps that did exist. He had profound respect for science and firmly believed his own explorations were useful to pave the way for the geologists, naturalists and engineers who would follow. But in the end stones, fossils, geology, botany all left him cold, and he was more interested in the sensation of the experience, simply enjoying the poetry and majesty of nature. Though he often noted with delight the solitary hardy flowers which shivered in the snow, he never studied them. If he did find something interesting he took it to M. Bordère, the teacher in Gèdre, who was an enthusiastic botanist. (He was well known to English visitors, who often purchased plants from him to take back to their gardens in England.) Russell would ask the name of the plant, but he always forgot it afterwards. He occasionally dots his writing with the Latin classifications but it is oddly unconvincing, as if he has simply decorated the margin with dried specimens.

There was no particular order to his exploration – he followed his fantasy and whim. He inspired many imitators who headed for the hills with only Russell's guide, *Les Grands Ascensions*, in their pocket. The little book, which cost 2F50, described an entire tour of the high peaks of the Pyrenees, with detailed descriptions of all the slopes, *couloirs*, crevasses, slides and chimneys, identifying many of them for the first time; times and distances were also included though most readers soon learnt that Russell's capacity far exceeded that of most people. There are also several maps, hand drawn and labelled by Russell himself. His practical instructions are terse, even brusque, as was the style of the time, rather as if he were giving instructions to a town pedestrian: climb here, press to the south, ridge, slope, pause for breath! His advice is succinct and detached: 'Here with an axe and lots of time one could descend to the waterfall, but a slip or the least accident will throw you into a 1000m abyss.'

But as well as the brief, practical guidebooks he first wrote, he also recorded his personal experiences, combining detailed accounts of climbs and routes with dramatic and highly coloured descriptions of the beauties of the landscape, the palette of dawns and sunsets, struggling to express in words the wonder and awe he felt.

I thought of Russell's endeavours to describe his experiences one night just after sunset as we watched a stormy amethyst sky, with clouds rolling so low over the hills they looked like a tidal wave. The sky was a wash of watercolours, lavender and pale blue and lemon, with wisps of black cloud like fine feathery brush strokes. Sometimes I wish I could paint, and think of Turner capturing the nuances of clouds and sky, trying to express the sublime on canvas. I feel sure Russell must have seen Turner's work. He was a fan of Ruskin, Turner's great promoter. Sometimes it is as if Russell is trying to write as Turner was painting, trying to put into words his response to nature. He writes with the romantic intensity of Byron combined with the humble patient observation of nature of Wordsworth or Ruskin, but adds a personal quality of total immersion that is all his own, like Turner tying himself to a mast to fully experience the storm he wanted to paint.

It is a perfect romantic image, the man on a mountain

top, alone with nature. He captured particular moments of joy, and you can feel him savouring the memory still as he is writing years later: the moment a tiny cloud settled on his shoulder at the same time as a butterfly alighted on his head; finding an unknown lake high in the mountains, pure and tranquil, with one solitary iceberg floating in the cold blue water, where it was so quiet 'you could have heard the flight of a butterfly'. He describes dawn on the Col des Crabioules, 'the aromatic pines, the immaculate azure of the sky, cows waking up and shaking their bells, the sound of waterfalls'. He once devoted an entire article to the colour blue in nature: the sea, the sky, the snows of Siberia, 'l'heure bleue' at dusk when all nature deepens into blue and violet.

There is a wonderful description of the glacier as he climbed Petit Vignemale one autumn evening in 1868. 'From Lac du Gaube I climbed diagonally across the glacier de Gaube, spiked with white cones like a sea of sugar covered in purple and gold by the declining sun. The glacier was still running with fast blue rivulets, but once the nocturnal cold had frozen their sources silence returned, though you could still hear strange cries deep in the glacier crevasses.'

A night on the slopes of Mont Perdu 'was so splendid, so suave, so blue, embalmed there in the fragrance of pines and flowers, that its magnificence prevented me from sleep'. Often his pleasures come after days of struggle and tempestuous nights, as if his Celtic spirit recalls something of the Irish monks and their capacity for asceticism, of endurance for the sake of inspiration. Or as if like St Francis he is willing to wait long enough, to sit still long enough, for birds to settle on his shoulders.

Unlike most of his contemporaries, from the great white hunters to contemplative fishermen, he had no interest in fishing or the chase, but he loved seeing the wildlife in remote valleys, the isards leaping over high rocks, a bear emerging from a forest grove, the flight of an eagle in a clear sky, trout leaping in high cold lakes. He had no desire to chase or kill them. For Russell it was enough to simply slip quietly through their domain. In his respect for nature and the environment he was a man ahead of his time.

He loved the wind, which he called 'the music of the air . . . the orchestra of nature. It electrifies and rejuvenates. One feels more.' He liked to recall all the winds he had experienced in his travels, the winds of the desert, the howling snows of high mountains, the typhoons of the China seas, dreamy calm oceans with the wind sighing in the sails. He said he could hear the mystique of Chopin in the storms of India or Africa, the power of Wagner in the forest.

'It chases the clouds, cleans the sky and purifies the air. It tempers the tropical heat, perhaps guides migratory birds across the Ocean. It is the wind that has covered the world in flowers.' The wind he loved best was the wind of the Midi, the Sirocco, 'which comes often in winter, with long lamentations, full of the fire of the Sahara, a sad dreamy wind that seems to cry of the desert'.

Russell continued his campaign, setting out every year with a new itinerary of peaks to conquer or old favourites to revisit. Once the railways were established he became a familiar figure with his water gourd and alpenstock, sitting in a corner of the compartment, reading a newspaper and smoking a cigar. He climbed more mountains more often by more different routes than anyone else in the Pyrenees. He climbed the Pic du Midi thirty times, twice more than Ramond himself. He made countless visits to the Brèche de Roland, a five-hour round trip from Gavarnie, which he did just when he felt like a stroll. But it was the high summits of 3000 metres which most attracted him, and in all he made thirty first ascents of the highest peaks. Peaks that were quite well known before he came along, such as Néthou, Mont Perdu, or Vignemale, he approached from different angles, or at different seasons, most spectacularly when he climbed Vignemale in winter.

He was rarely afraid, even when he was lost in freezing fog, occasionally obliged to crawl on hands and knees through snow and stones. Though he often heard bears and wolves he was never attacked. 'I always hid my provisions well,' he remarks nonchalantly. Even when he was in danger he preserved an extraordinary sangfroid. Occasionally having hired as a porter a *berger* who turned out to be very timid away from his known pastures, he would send him home and go on alone.

Provisions for extended tours continued to be a challenge, even with a porter to carry them. He always liked to stock up in France, because in Spain 'you have to live on air, bread and resignation'. Occasionally he struck lucky and found more supplies along the way. When he was looking for a new route to Posets, a 3375m peak on the Spanish side of the border, in 1875, he extended his exploration to nine days out in the open after a fortuitous meeting with a *berger*, who had a lamb which had fallen off a precipice. He cooked two of its legs and bestowed them on the hungry Russell. Nor were supplies always modest;

when he climbed Posets he had a bottle of excellent vintage white Bordeaux, presented to him by the vineyard proprietor, to open when he got to the top. No doubt someone else was carrying it.

There were sometimes disasters. He got completely lost on a climb to Pic d'Enfer, and spent the night in an impenetrable fog, in a storm of hail and wind, with his trusty sleeping bag full of water. Another time he lost his bag containing his map and all his provisions, apart from some sugar and a piece of bread.

Worst of all was the loss of his beloved alpenstock, while climbing alone to the summit of Maladetta. He leapt across a yawning crevasse between the glacier and the rocks, to find himself sinking deep into new snow on the other side. Having climbed out, he then dropped the alpenstock down the crevasse. 'The faithful friend I have never been without, that has often saved my life,' he moaned. 'I believed I loved it when I saw it descend without me, leaving me at the moment I needed it most.' It was indeed a fatal crevasse, and he notes sombrely that it was the place where the Luchon guide Pierre Barrau had been killed in August 1824, whose remains had never been found.

Unlike the ascetic Packe, Russell did not disdain the spas, and after a particularly gruelling walk would sometimes spend several days taking the waters. He favoured rustic remote baths over the social whirl of Luchon or Eaux-Bonnes, and recalled in *Souvenirs* five or six days he spent at Vénasque, high in the Spanish Pyrenees, 'the most peaceful and healthy sojourn, far from the bustle and enervating luxury of the Villes d'Eaux'. He spent his time bathing, or relaxed in a dressing gown, learning Spanish as he chatted to the other *curistes*, who included several sombre-faced priests, 'giving the dim corridors of the Baths the aspect of a monastery'.

Lounging in hot baths is at least as attractive to me as climbing mountains and I was therefore very pleased to find that our region of the Eastern Pyrenees remained rich in spas, seething hot sulphurous waters bubbling up from cracks in the earth, used for bathing since Roman times. Visitors come for a week or so to take a cure (as often as not recommended by their doctor so their treatment is subsidized by the French health service), wandering about in towelling robes as they drink and bathe in the waters, a calming, healthy alternative to a vacation. Just down the road from us is Molitg-les-Bains, a grand Thirties building on the side of a deep river gorge. It is surrounded by a romantic park of palm trees, shrubs and artificial grottoes and paths that wander round a lake and across a plunging waterfall. There is a Michelin-starred restaurant in a crenellated neo-Gothic chateau where the food arrives under silver domes, and a spa with carved marble columns and tinkling fountains. I sampled it one day with my friend from *Vogue*, and we tried all the treatments, from steam room to water massage. The atmosphere was calm, as hushed as a church, as if the hooded *curistes* were shuffling off to confession. It reminded me of a spa I had once visited in Tuscany where the steam rooms were deep in the bowels of the earth and you descended down steep rocky stairs to green-tinged caves full of people huddled in white gowns and hoods, breathing hot natural steam. We tried to drink the Molitg water too, dispensed from a great marble fountain in a salon which was domed and colonnaded like a Roman basilica, but we found its sulphurous taste unbelievably nauseating.

No wonder they needed barley sugar in Cauterets.

We were issued with soft pink robes by sternly solicitous attendants in white coats and ushered down dim echoing corridors off which opened a series of bathrooms, each of them a different coloured marble: black marble veined with orange or pure Carrara white; another the local rosy pink stone, another a yellowy quartz. Our own was a tasteful grey threaded with white and yellow. It really was all marble, the two wide baths which were being filled with water for us, the big pedestal basin, the wall and floor tiles, even the lavatory, as if the entire room had been carved from one vast block of stone. We lay in our twin baths up to our necks in the warm water as instructed, hoping to benefit from its particular properties, here recommended especially for the skin. It was so peaceful, with the window framed by trailing red hibiscus flowers opening onto the craggy green hillside, it would be hard not to derive some benefit. It was certainly relaxing, so enervating indeed that I could hardly lift my hands onto the steering wheel to drive home.

I preferred Saint-Thomas-les-Bains, tucked into another valley about an hour away, though this required a rather demanding drive up a narrow road hacked from the valley side, in winter made narrower still by snow drifts. Saint Thomas is also deep in a gorge, located where the hot mineral water bursts up through rocky fissures from the bowels of the earth, but there the baths are open to the sky. The best time to go is a winter's day with blue sky and full sun, when you scuttle from the changing rooms in a dressing gown or towel, into the chilly air and plunge into steaming deep pools of really hot water. The water comes out of the ground at 58 degrees and has to be cooled to 38.

The contrast is astonishing, floating in the deep hot mineral water and feeling a cold breeze playing across your face, as warm as in a bathtub at home, but surrounded by trees and mountains. Once Theo and I climbed out of the pool to rub snow all over ourselves, Theo laughing gleefully as I shrieked and shivered. Then we leapt back into the hot water, skin tingling like after an electric shock. As we played, an old lady with grey hair tied up in a bun floated by, spread-eagled on the water. 'You should come at night,' she told us, 'and lie here under the stars. *C'est magique!*'

13

The spirit of Gavarnie

'It is impossible to believe one's eyes, one looks in vain for comparisons. It is as if one world has ended and another begun. Another world regulated by different laws of existence.'

Ramond de Carbonnières

Gavarnie has always been the key place for connoisseurs of the Pyrenees, for tourists one of the finest destinations and for mountaineers the closest they can get to the heights. The great *cirque* and its stupendous waterfall is still the most popular sight in the Pyrenees. Gavarnie at 1375 metres above sea level remains the most remote and highest village in the chain, with only about 150 permanent inhabitants. Half a million visitors a year make quite an impact.

We made our first visit one autumn day *en famille*, setting out from Luz-Saint-Sauveur, whose magnificent situation satisfied every requirement of the traveller in search of the sublime and beautiful, as Erskine Murray described in 1837: 'Encircled by lofty mountains, its sole entrances are through the most profound gorges, and along roads scooped out of their rocky sides, hundreds of feet above the torrents which boil beneath.'

The route to Gavarnie is as stunning now as it was for early travellers, and we felt some trepidation at the descriptions of the horrors of the road. Early visitors were deliciously frightened. 'A black and hideous road,' Victor Hugo had shuddered. At the entrance to the wild gorges beyond Luz we stopped to admire the Pont Napoléon, along with a coachload of Polish pilgrims on a day trip from Lourdes. The building of the bridge was decreed by Napoleon III, who required better access to the Pyrenees for himself and the Empress Eugénie. It was opened in 1864.

It was constructed at Pas d'Echelle, where Russell's horse understandably took fright in 1858, and crosses the torrent of the Gave in a single magnificent arch at a height of 66 metres. It was a great feat of engineering for the time, and greatly impressed contemporary travellers. The lamentable Miss Eyre, a great fan of Napoleon, was deeply moved. 'It is indeed an imperial work ... how mortal hands could ever build that arch across that immense width – as it were in the very air. It is worth while to come from England to the Pyrenees, only to see this wonderful work of human skill and intrepidity.' She liked it best by moonlight, with moonbeans shining on the water below, and the moon itself sailing above the clouds. 'It was a sight to *feel*, not to talk of,' she sighed. Poor Miss Eyre, it should be added, was enduring her travels in a way that put my own timorousness to shame. She had terrible lumbago, triggered by slipping on a step: 'I could not put on my own boots, and our driver was fairly obliged to lift me into the carriage.' But she was determined none the less on an expedition planned to the Cirque. 'How on earth was I to ride to Gavarnie?' she wondered.

As we continued along the narrow rocky gorge beyond the Pont Napoléon, we stopped to read a marble plaque, a chilling reminder of an accident in 1923 in which twenty-one Dutch tourists and their French driver all died when their carriage plunged into the gorge. The locals still call it the Dutch Leap. The road widened out into the little village of Gèdre, nestling in a gentle valley at the foot of the mountains 'like an oasis in the desert, embosomed among stern and rocky scenery', as Murray put it better than I.

We too glimpsed the first peaks of the Cirque above us as the road narrowed again for the final approach and we were confronted by the gloomy prospect of the Chaos de Coumély, a deep harsh gorge, with the river pounding through it, scattered with a confusion of huge rocks which looked as if they had just rolled down the mountainside. 'A mass of colossal blocks of gneiss, the ruins of half a mountain,' as Russell described it. 'The original chaos, a hell,' wrote George Sand.

We discussed with some anxiety the statistical likelihood of more rocks rolling down on top of us and whether it would be safer to go faster or slower. This was no pastoral idyll – I was reminded of the Gustave Doré engravings of the Pyrenees, all gloomy vales, looming crags and thundering torrents, and began to better understand the Romantic delight in this combination of beauty and horror.

Miss Eyre, having been lifted rigidly onto her horse, the first time she had ridden in twenty years, had a very hair-raising time indeed. 'The rocky mountain road was worse than usual, because several gangs of men were employed in making it better against the expected visit of the Emperor and Empress who, it is reported, are to visit the Pyrenees this summer.' (In the event they did not come, and indeed the Pyrenees saw no more Napoleons, though most of the natives still speak of them with reverence and gratitude for the road blasting they did.) The road then was so narrow there was only room for one horse to pass between the cliffs at a time. Sometimes the path was simply a shelf of rock, paved with loose stones, which slipped under the horses' feet, with the river roaring below.

We arrived in Gavarnie in the infinitely greater comfort of a big Renault on a tarmac road, albeit within a few feet of the same deep precipice and torrential river waters. To the west was a brief glimpse of the Massif de Vignemale. Above us on a rocky outcrop stood the statue of Notre-Dame-des-Neiges, facing east and watching over all the travellers who arrived.

At the entrance to the village is a bronze statue of Henry Russell, who was called 'the spirit of Gavarnie'. It was solemnly inaugurated in 1911. Next to it is a bronze plaque in memory of Henri Beraldi, author of the classic seven-volume history of *pyrénéisme*, published at the end of the nineteenth century. Russell looked at home, dignified and secure in his grassy bank, his gaze directed westwards towards his beloved Vignemale.

Gavarnie lies at the foot of a mountainous barrier which creates the great cul de sac of the Cirque. It is a vast amphitheatre, gouged out by a glacier, with giant steps of limestone capped with snow and ice, above which tower five snow-clad mountains. The arena below is heaped with rubble brought down by the cascades which pour over the walls.

The great waterfall is the longest in Europe, and drops an astonishing 423 metres (the falls at Niagara are 47 metres). In spring, fed by melting glacier waters, it falls in one tremendous chute, and in winter it freezes into columns of ice. It is the source of the Gave de Pau, flowing down to the north and then west into the Atlantic Ocean. Gave simply means river and Gavarnie, therefore, means Riverborn, so I suppose Gave de Gavarnie is Riverborn river, which sounds like something out of *The Hobbit*.

There was always a small settlement of shepherds at Gavarnie who rejoiced in the rich high pastureland, living in simple huts of stone or wood and thatch. By the time Russell made Gavarnie his centre of operations in the 1860s tourism was growing apace. The population of the village itself had peaked, rising from 213 in 1350 to 350 in 1851, and falling back to 169 in 1984. In Russell's day, there would have been a few slate-roofed houses of stone or wood huddled around the church, and beyond the village the *bergers*' cabins. Though tourism was already beginning to affect the local economy with the demand for accommodation and guides, the village was still largely agricultural. There were cows, horses, mules, donkeys and pigs, producing butter, cheese and wool.

Despite the great *cirque* blocking the end of the valley, there was still traffic over the high frontier, smugglers from Spain, and pilgrims en route for Santiago de Compostela. The little church of Gavarnie still has vestiges of its history as a pilgrim refuge, with the fourteenth-century statue of Notre-Dame-du-Bon-Port, holding in her right hand a water gourd, symbol of the protection of travellers.

Throughout the eighteenth and nineteenth centuries Gavarnie became increasingly popular, especially with the English, who recounted their adventures in great detail and painted the waterfall assiduously. Poet Henry Swinburne was one of the earliest, visiting in August 1776, when he and his party invited the local curé to dine with them. The table, however, had to be taken outdoors since the clergy were not permitted to eat or drink inside an *auberge*.

Ramond himself came in 1788 and 1792 and for a while Gavarnie was *à la mode* for the French. They came, by foot or mule, an epic journey along the vertiginous river gorge, to gaze at the Cirque, the cascade and the snow bridges. Gavarnie was famous for its summer storms and it was particularly fashionable to go to Gavarnie to hear the thunder. The great architect Viollet-le-Duc (responsible later for the restoration of Carcassonne), writing letters home to his father on a youthful visit to the Pyrenees, sniffed at a grand cavalcade visiting Gavarnie dressed in silk dresses, fine costumes and, in his eyes most absurd of all, white gloves.

In 1807 Hortense de Beauharnais, sister-in-law of Napoleon, arrived. She always said the night she spent in the Hôtel des Voyageurs in Gavarnie was one of the happiest of her life. Nine months later she gave birth to a son, who was to become Napoleon III. Even now Gavarnie gossip suggests his father was a lusty local. In 1859 Napoleon III was in Luz–Saint–Sauveur with his wife, who was taking the waters (recommended for gynaecological complaints). He himself set off for Gavarnie, driving his own carriage with a modest escort of twenty guides on horses. But a thick fog descended and he abandoned the journey, never to see the legendary Hôtel des Voyageurs.

Nor did he ever see the Cirque itself. It would be foolish to attempt to compete with the likes of Victor Hugo in describing the first sight of the vast amphitheatre of the Cirque of Gavarnie, its 180-degree curve, and its un-believable waterfall, which from ground level seems to spring from the horizon. But even my husband, a dyed in the wool townie, said it was the most amazing thing he had seen in his life. Poets and artists exclaimed in awe at the sight, and a tribute to Gavarnie became *de rigueur* for any self-respecting Romantic. Victor Hugo called it 'the Colosseum of nature'. 'Horrible and beautiful, imposing and sad,' summarized one poet in 1785. The sculptor David d'Angers reported: '. . . tears flowed from my eyes. I was no longer on the earth.'

Tennyson went there in 1831 and in *The Lotos-Eaters* he was inspired by the waterfalls he saw, especially the great cascade of Gavarnie:

A land of streams! some, like a downward smoke,
Slow-dropping veils of thinnest lawn, did go:
And some through wavering lights and shadows broke,
Rolling a slumbrous sheet of foam below.

Apart from its ravishing beauty, the other main characteristic of Gavarnie is the unpredictability of the weather. After a day of clear blue sky and sunshine which afforded us clear views, it began to pour with rain, obscuring all in deep cloud. The cafés and ice cream parlours, the trinket shop selling souvenirs of Gavarnie, dripped miserably. The donkeys which have traditionally taken visitors up to view the Cirque stood forlornly in the rain, and we abandoned the possibility of walking there ourselves. (This was before I was awarded my blue shepherd's umbrella.)

I had read that when Reverend and Mrs Ellis visited Gavarnie in bad weather, they had left a boy outside while they dined to tell them if the veil of clouds had lifted. It seemed a pity we could not do the same. Instead we took refuge in the Hôtel de Marboré, with its roaring log fire, tartan blankets, and walls full of prints and photos of mountains and mountaineers. There had been enough of an English influence to even produce a good cup of tea.

When it stopped raining I went in search of the Hôtel des Voyageurs, famous as the refuge for Pyrenean *montagnards* for almost two hundred and fifty years, and for Russell a home from home. But it was late in the season and it was closed. Still, it was there, a long low slate-roofed building with creamy stucco walls, dark green shutters and a hand-painted sign swinging from an iron rail. I peered over the lace curtains hung across the windows and could see a reassuringly homely scene of dark low beams and simple wooden tables and a piano against the wall, all just waiting for the familiar sound of hobnailed boots tramping down the wooden stairs.

'There is no station in the Pyrenees to compete with the little inn at Gavarnie,' wrote Charles Packe, 'in combining good accommodation with proximity to the higher mountains. The fare is first-rate, the landlord civil, and the beds very tolerable.' Before we left the following day I telephoned to arrange to visit. This time the green shutters were open and I was greeted by Mme Henriette Laterrade, descendant of the Vergez-Bellou family, proprietors of the hotel since the eighteenth century. A petite woman with faded brown hair and large glasses, she smiled sadly when asked when the hotel would reopen. 'Never,' she said, to my dismay. 'It breaks my heart.' Finally the family had given up the hotel, and it was to be converted into apartments. These days Gavarnie is treated as a half-day tourist trip from Lourdes and people rarely stay long. Only the winter ski station keeps the village alive.

Mme Laterrade shook her head sadly, unlocking the door, 'When it took a day to get here people stayed *en famille* for two weeks; now it takes an hour or so they only stay an hour and a half.' I was glad to have the chance to see the hotel as it had been, but sad at the poignancy of its end. In the gloomy light within, I could see one large room, with low wooden rafters, bare stone walls and tiled floor, a huge fireplace still full of half-burnt logs, an upright piano with a stuffed bird on top. A glass cabinet was full of mementos, cups and plaques of the Club Alpin. Pictures and drawings adorned the walls, Victorian engravings of travellers and bear hunts, photographs of mountaineers, and several shots of Henry Russell, one of him standing outside the hotel, with a small crowd of villagers who look rather as if they have put on their Sunday best to welcome him. 'My grandmother was here from 1850 to 1914,' explained Mme Laterrade, 'when *le grand Russell* came every summer.' A sturdy wooden staircase with hand-turned banisters led to two upper floors added in the 1880s when the popularity of Gavarnie was at its height.

'This was Russell's room, number 23,' she said, crossing the floor to open the shutters so I could see better. A shaft of sunlight illuminated the dust motes. It was very simple, a fireplace, an armoire, a single wooden bed, and a plain wooden table and chair by the window where he would write. Beyond, the mountains.

Downstairs she showed me the hotel's *livre d'or*, a large leather-bound book, full of signatures and memories of great *pyrénéistes* and a host of unknown walkers and climbers. The interior was too dark to see properly so Mme Laterrade sat me outside on a chair to look through it. Several of the pages were loose, and many had been stolen over the years – and the wind threatened to blow even more away. As I tried to hold down the fragile pages, I was relieved to hear there was a microfiche copy in the archives of Tarbes.

The writing was still clear, the ink brown but still distinct. Entries were sometimes brief, just a name and a date, sometimes long and discursive. Often the margin was decorated with pictures and sketches, in 1882 a scribbled line of music from one Pablo Bizet, perhaps a distant cousin of the composer. The names unrolled before me: Brulle, Bazillac, Swan, Frossard, English names, French, Russian and German ('too many Boches' grumbled a French entry in 1870 during the Franco-Prussian War). In 1865 somebody had written out their last will and testament over two foolscap pages – what on earth were they attempting the next day?

The London Bicycling Club expressed their satisfaction. Miss Florence Swan, sister of Henry's young friend Charles Swan, made several entries. The first complained petulantly of the absence of the billiard table she was promised the previous year; in the second, August 1893, she wrote with great pride, claiming to be the only woman to have ascended Vignemale in a single day. Perhaps by this time Miss Lister's two-day marathon from the south had been conceded, at least in Gavarnie.

Mme Laterrade pointed out Russell's frequent entries over several decades. 'Sometimes he signs himself Henri and sometimes Henry,' she said. Some of his entries are in French, some in English. There were the early entries of Russell and Packe (closely followed on 4 September 1862 by Count Bismarck, the future chancellor of Germany, still welcome then). A brief note asked for Russell's letters and newspapers to be sent on to his house in rue Marca, Pau. 'Here is another, in French,' she said, running her finger down the page. '31 août 1880. After passing a glacial night on the summit of Grand Vignemale (3298m) with Brioul and Haurine, I leave with great regret this excellent hotel, where I have stayed for three weeks.' Then he cannot resist noting, 'Temperature at 2 a.m. on the peak of Vignemale *at least* (underlined twice) minus 3 degrees.' Signed, for variety, Cte H. Russell.

'That must have been the occasion he was buried all night on the summit,' I observed.

'*Il était très particulier*' (which could mean special or peculiar in French), replied Madame Laterrade with a respectful nod.

In the very early days staying at the Hôtel de Voyageurs was an intimate affair. Originally the accommodation, like that of most *auberges*, consisted merely of beds curtained off in green serge, in the corners of one large room heated by a huge log fire. Meals were rustic and merry. One visitor recorded being presented with an entire roast sheep, isard, *truite au beurre*, the best Spanish wine served from a goatskin, and dessert of sheeps' whey perfumed with vanilla and scattered with brown sugar. After dinner there was dancing, with music from guitars and castanets.

On 19 August 1864 a memorable dinner took place at the Hôtel des Voyageurs, though sadly the relevant pages of the *livre d'or* have long been missing. Russell and Charles Packe found themselves staying at the hotel along with Emilien Frossard, the anglophile Protestant pastor of Bagnères and a keen mountaineer, and his two sons, Charles and Emilien, all deeply interested in the new sciences of geology and mineralogy. There was also another Englishman, Farnham Maxwell Lyte, the photographer. Lyte was the son of the Reverend Henry Francis Lyte, the vicar of Brixham in Devon, author of the famous hymn 'Abide with Me'. Henry Lyte spent his winters abroad to try to cure his tuberculosis and died in 1847 at the Hôtel d'Angleterre in Nice. He is buried in the English cemetery of Nice's Holy Trinity Church.

Farnham Maxwell Lyte was born in 1828, and was nineteen when his father died. He also travelled for his health, perhaps having contracted his father's illness, and spent most of his life in Pau and Bagnères-de-Bigorre, where though not a clergyman himself he was very much involved in establishing an Anglican church.

Most of all, though, he was a photographer, and perfectly named. He is often called the father of Pyrenean photography, and was the first thus to popularize the sights of the Pyrenees, sending an album of forty-eight views to Napoleon III, at the Emperor's request. He was the first to photograph an eclipse of the sun, in 1860 from the slopes of the Pic du Midi, eighteen years before the Observatoire was built. He – or his porters, anyway – struggled with his equipment to some very inaccessible places, capturing the play of light and clouds, sunrise and sunset on the high summits. He photographed the heights of Gavarnie, the Lac d'Oô above Luchon, and even the Brèche de Roland, where tiny figures in the *brèche* are dwarfed by the monumental shapes of the cliffs of snow and clouds above. His photographs have a simple, modern sensibility on a par with Edward Weston's Arizona pictures, strong images superbly framed. He helped to found the Société Française de Photographie and was a member of the Photographic Society of

Great Britain, exhibiting frequently in the 1850s and 60s, and receiving several international medals and awards for his work.

He was a scientist, an eccentric Jules Verne character, a mad professor constantly tinkering with chemistry and optics. As an astronomer and metereologist, he was deeply involved in the creation of the Pic du Midi Observatory. He was always inventing: a new method of photographic development using honey, or equipment to preserve the purity of the resin extracted from the pine trees of the Landes to make turpentine.

Henry Russell recalled him in Pau towards the end of the Franco-Prussian war of 1870. 'I met him in the street in Pau radiant with joy, as if he had discovered a new continent or a star, and armed with a formidable gun which he had invented, and he was firmly convinced there would be no more hope for the Prussians if the French army adopted this weapon.'

As these gentlemen settled down to the Hôtel des Voyageurs's repast of mutton, duck and trout, all talked of their day's explorations and particular interests; Packe showed them the rare plants he had collected and talked about his plans for mapping the Monts Maudits in Aragon, Frossard showed them some of the handsome drawings he had done, and his sons described their geological investigations. Maxwell Lyte talked of his efforts to photograph cloud formations and the effects of light on the mountains. Russell described his recent attempt to find the source of the Grande Cascade de Gavarnie.

Packe and Russell probably recalled the events of the previous year, their terrible night together looking for the Porte d'Enfer, and their recent separate climbs of

Balaitous. It was a mysterious peak, reputedly climbed only once before by two army officers in 1825, but no-one had any idea how they got there. Indeed, it had not even been named, and although it was visible to the north-west of Vignemale from Tarbes, once one approached closer it disappeared from view and was quite invisible to anyone in Cauterets or Gavarnie.

Russell had been greatly impressed by Packe's effort, climbing from the west, and the difficulties surmounted. 'He wandered for seven days on and almost all round the mountain before setting his foot at last on its real summit!' Packe at the time had believed he was the first, though when he got there he found tent poles and empty sardine tins as evidence of the earlier triumph.

Russell followed by the same western route ten days later, with the guide, Gaspard, and supplies for several days. After sleeping under a rock and crossing a crevasse, using Gaspard as a bridge, they quite suddenly found themselves on the summit. Russell diligently noted down the contrast in temperature, 3 in the shade and 35 in the sun. They could see the Atlantic ocean in the distance. Gaspard, Russell recalled, was astonished, since he had never seen the sea before. On the Spanish side, looming to the east, were the mountains of Aragon, Posets, Nethou and Perdiguère, looking, said Russell, 'like enormous crocodiles sleeping in the sun'.

Each of these mountain lovers brought their treasures, stones, plants, photographs, emotions and memories to that particular evening. All were inspired by the same spirit, the love of science and of the beauty of nature. By the time they had got to the hot wine punch, they had decided that they should form an association devoted to the Pyrenees, to better understand the mountains and make them more widely known and appreciated by others. Though Frossard and Lyte were not as ambitious climbers as Packe or Russell, their devotion to the Pyrenees was equally valued. No attempt was made to separate conquest of the mountains from purely scientific research.

This took place only nine years after the Alpine Club was founded, for which actual conquests had to be declared and proved before membership was permitted. It was a full eight years before the Club Alpin Français was started. Other members, both French and English, were recruited: lecturers, botanists and engineers as well as mountaineers. A name was chosen after much deliberation: the Société Ramond, after the first great explorer of the Pyrenees. Chausenque, now eighty-five years old, was made honorary president. Frossard was made president, Packe became secretary and Russell treasurer. Astonishingly for a French society, of the founders two of them were English, one was half French and half English, and Frossard was married to an Englishwoman, and many of the early members were also English, including the Reverend Wentworth Webster, the Anglican chaplain of Saint-Jean-de-Luz, and the librarian of the English colony of Pau.

A review was founded, the *Bulletin de la Société Ramond* (which still exists) and in the early years was a very English-dominated publication. The very first article was in English, and in the early years there were often articles in English.

One experimental expedition they discussed did not quite work out as planned, as Russell later recounted. Frossard and Packe had been discussing a climb of Mont

Perdu, and Russell was tempted by the Cylindre de Marboré, two adjacent peaks. 'We would be able to climb together to the open col between the two peaks; we could even talk across the kilometres from one to the other!' Could the human voice travel so far in such clear air, they speculated. They asked Laurent Passet, honoured guide and a particular favourite of Russell and Packe, who was considered something of an oracle in these matters, what he thought of their plan. His laconic reply after a few minutes of reflection, was cherished ever after. 'Messieurs, I believe you will be able to talk, but as for hearing I have no idea!' Sadly, after a foggy night the climb to Mont Perdu was abandoned so the experiment never took place. Passet died only a month or so later.

Opposite the Hôtel des Voyageurs I spotted a small white house with Maison Passet still hand-painted across it. The Passet family had been farmers, but also experienced shepherds and hunters with an intimate knowledge of the mountains around them. It was natural they should take on the role of guides to the messieurs who arrived, full of enthusiasm for the mountain air they had breathed all their lives, demanding to be taken to the peaks and glaciers for no apparent reason. After Laurent died, his son Henri replaced him in Russell's service, along with his cousin Célestin, the son of Hippolyte, Laurent's brother. Both were destined to become guides of legendary ability. Célestin was described as lean, lithe and dashing, and a photo of him in his *montagnard* beret with a rope across his chest reveals high cheekbones, hooded eyelids and a firm cleft chin. He was renowned as a hunter and climber, and once climbed Mont Perdu and Vignemale in a single day.

Henri was more solid, round-faced and good-natured. He was intelligent, a mine of information on botany, geology, animals, the origin of place names and the philosophy of human life. He was shrewd, with great skill and foresight, always finding a solution to any difficulty, and able to deal tactfully with the most querulous client. He had one major fault which was that he snored a lot, and would sleep outside, even in great cold, so as not to disturb the clients.

Both Henri and Célestin did well for themselves, travelling the world with clients like Sir Victor Brooke, Edward North Buxton and Edward Whymper. The Passet cousins owned houses and fields and both opened hotels in Gavarnie. Their skills have been belatedly acknowledged but while they were alive their prowess was taken for granted, and their achievements as often as not were attributed to their employers.

Bastien Passet, who died only a few years ago, was the grandson of Henri, and the last porter and guide in Gavarnie. He still managed to make a living, keeping sheep, and horses and donkeys for the trip to the *cirque*, and teaching skiing in winter, but it was difficult. No longer were people prepared to pay guides properly; it was a profession that had come and gone. In an interview with *Pyrénées* magazine not long before he died, he was bitter. 'All the glory went to lords and rich clients.' The famous Couloir Swan, a steep cleft in the Cirque of Gavarnie, had been climbed by Henri Passet in 1885. 'My grandfather Henri Passet cut 700 steps in that corridor of ice. He took with him an Englishman named Swan. And now the couloir is named Swan. His cousin, Célestin Passet, cut the Couloir de Gaube at the top of Vignemale. But the path does not carry his name. The guide was like a servant for these *messieurs-dames*. I had to walk in wool socks on the rocks to save my nailed boots.'

I knocked tentatively at the door of the house, hoping to find a Passet at home. There was an old lady sitting behind the lace curtains, but when I enquired the reception was frosty. 'Nobody wants to know about all that any more,' she said. 'It is all over.'

It is true that nobody asks for guides any more. Sadly, the people of Gavarnie have been forced to abandon their traditional livelihood in favour of shops selling Gavarnie snow globes, and cafés serving overpriced ice creams for the visitors who pass through so rapidly. They have no knowledge of their history and no museum of past glories. It is as if the great *cirque* which blocks the end of the valley has blocked them too. As if they could not see its beauty for themselves.

Theo and I paid a further visit to Gavarnie the following year, this time in summer, a warm blue day with no wind that augured well. We had spent the night in the Hôtel du Compostella just next to the church and before nightfall I had paid a brief visit to the cemetery to pay my respects to the graves of the *montagnards* buried there, and the skulls of the Templars, thirteen of whom were massacred here. Then as dusk fell we watched the cloud drop over the Cirque like a curtain at the end of a play. We hoped it would draw back again the next day.

Over our croissants and apricot jam next morning we looked anxiously through the lace curtains. The sky looked dark and threatening, and someone muttered something about a storm. Sylvie, the hotel proprietor, on her way out to the garden with her arms full of sheets, stopped to ask anxiously if we were planning to walk just to the Cirque or as far as the cascade. I said I wasn't sure, it depended on the weather. 'Well, watch out for the snow bridges, even avalanches,' she warned, and advised, 'When you get to the Hôtel de Cirque, ask for Pierre Vergez. He will tell you if it is safe.'

We were determined to get there this time, and after some discussion decided against the donkeys that were waiting patiently in a line, along with small horses and larger steeds, for the first tourists of the day. The path up the valley to the base of the Cirque lay alongside the wide river bed, its water a pale glacier blue pounding over the boulders and stones it had brought down with it.

Ahead of us lay the Cirque, the mist lifting and evaporating as we approached so we could see its great carved limestone terraces still iced with snow. I could easily understand why people used to believe they had been made by the waters receding from the Flood.

Russell had warned in his guidebook, 'The gigantic amphitheatre of Gavarnie is on such a scale, that distances are most deceptive. It seems half an hour's walk to the Cirque, and yet is over four miles.'

Soon we turned from the wide path which even at this early stage – it was not yet 9 a.m.– had begun to fill up with a steady posse of animals bearing small children, with fathers gripping the reins tightly. I was glad I was not responsible for a donkey, however docile. We left the main track for the signposted old route up towards the Cirque, winding through trees and fording small rivulets that crossed the path, jumping from stone to stone, equipped with our new sticks and an unaccustomed backpack (for me) of bottled water and waterproof clothes. As we walked together I talked about *The Pilgrim's Progress* and Chaucer's *Canterbury Tales* and Theo responded with the quest of *The Hobbit*, and *The Lord of the Rings*. I thought again of Henry and his mother, who would have been so familiar with the Christian symbolism of the path.

In a little over an hour we caught a glimpse of a large grey stone building through the tall pines, with Hostellerie du Cirque written in bold white Thirties lettering across the middle. Beyond rose the austere, treeless grey mass of the Cirque, blockading any further progress south. It was still in shadow except for the topmost peaks, where the sun had just alighted from the east. Beyond the high forbidding ridges lay Spain.

After the last of the pines, we arrived at the hotel, the final habitation before the Cirque, 'apparently at the end of the world', says Russell. 'From here the great black limestone precipices seem stupendous, there is nothing beyond but rocks, glaciers, eagles and isards. Marine fossils have been found at 10,000 feet on the Cirque.'

At the *hostellerie* the horses and donkeys were tethered because they could go no further. I got out the map and between us we identified the mountain peaks we could see, all of which echoed with Russell's name by now: the Marboré, the Brèche de Roland, the Taillon, striated with lines of snow. I liked the idea that Russell had climbed all around the top terrace of the Cirque itself, and even tried to find a way to the waterfall for us.

The Cirque, he wrote, is 'a semi-circle of alpine summits, mostly square and horizontal at the top, which forms a broken terrace about five miles long, and averaging 9000 feet in height. The loftiest part is the rounded and snow-capped Marboré (10,574 feet) from the top of which a stone may fall 5500 feet into the Cirque.' No doubt he had tried it.

'The stupendous waterfall (1380 feet in height) is frozen all the winter, when it dies, as it were, in its cradle; it begins to flow in the middle of May, and is then most imposing; less so in summer. Spring is also the best time for seeing avalanches tumbling down the Cirque, like cataracts of foam, as if there was a sea behind, and the waves had broken over', wrote Russell. We could see the cascade now quite clearly, making its great leap, and several smaller ones tumbling from the terraces. The vegetation dwindled to nothing and ahead were shale, stones, several icy rivers and still great thick slabs of snow.

'After the Baraque you enter the Cirque proper, covered with millions of rocks fallen from above. It gradually becomes colder, until you reach the base of a mud-hill like a moraine at the foot of the grand waterfall. Beware of its artillery of stones and ice, and do not go too near.' There was no question about whether we should go further. Theo was determined.

'Come on, Mum.' I drank some water and shouldered my pack again. Once within the bowl of the Cirque there was a glacier river to cross, and a snow bridge to negotiate. A whole shelf of snow overhung the water, which had eroded a deep dark tunnel below it. Theo leapt ahead, prodding boulders and melting snow, advising me where to put my feet, 'Stand on that stone, Mum ... Be careful there. Now you will have to jump . . .' The worst moment was negotiating my way underneath the overhanging ledge of snow that looked like a thick layer of royal icing on a Christmas cake, hoping not to dislodge it with my back pack. 'Don't talk so loud,' warned Theo. 'You'll start an avalanche.'

I shivered and dipped my hand in the icy water. We were still in shadow and it was cold, and we stopped to put on our jackets. There was a final hard climb over the snow field, now already melting, up the shale and scree almost to the waterfall itself, but we stopped within a hundred yards or so, already feeling the chill spray as it smashed onto the ground, and poured itself forth into several new rivers.

It was unbelievably high, tumbling almost from the top of the Cirque, pouring abundantly, in two great leaps. Seeing its endless flow I began to understand better a favourite quote from Annie Dillard: 'Experiencing the present purely is being empty and hollow; you catch grace as a man fills his cup under a waterfall.'

The sun had lit half the bowl by now, and as we finally turned reluctantly to clamber back down again, we were soon perspiring and had to put our caps back on as protection against the sun. The contrast was brutal.

We were glad to find lunch at the hotel. There are no longer rooms to be had, but the dining room has an authentic flavour with its old marble bar and stuffed *bouquetin* (the ibex of the Pyrenees) and isard on the walls. We lined up for a choice of hearty *garbure* soup of cabbage and bacon, local *mouton* and bilberry tart.

Pierre Vergez was not there, but his wife Mme Vergez, a trim, blonde woman, who was overseeing the lunch service with an eagle eye, was delighted to talk. She explained that the family running the hotel was the same family that had run the Hôtel des Voyageurs. So there was some continuity after all. She hoped it would go on. 'We do have three sons,' she said with great pride. Would I like to see the

Salle des Guides, she enquired, and showed me to the room where traditionally the guides had eaten together while their clients dined above. The walls were scrawled with signatures, comments and drawings of peaks and paths, and hung with ropes, old crampons and ancient hand-made wooden skis. In the corner were several venerable old alpenstocks, including that of another of Russell's favourite guides, François Bernat-Salles, his name inscribed on a metal plate nailed on the shaft. I looked through a book of old photographs and postcards, and the register which only dated back to 1926, so sadly there was no record of Russell there.

There was still a hint of a storm, and although I was tempted to stay and hear the legendary thunder, we set off back again, retracing the pilgrim's path.

14

Luchon and the Accursed Mountains

'This not a land of men but of mountains.'
Hippolyte Taine

Bagnères–de–Luchon, Luchon as it is always known, is a spa town nestling in a fertile hollow of wooded hills and pastures almost in the centre of the Pyrenees. It was one of the main centres for nineteenth-century visitors to the Pyrenees, and like Gavarnie provided a good base for climbing the surrounding peaks. Beyond lay the mysterious and unexplored Monts Maudits, the Accursed Mountains (Maladetta in Spanish), a massif of granite and glaciers in the Spanish region of Aragon at the very heart of the chain. Then it was the least known region in Europe, and full of tantalizingly high peaks including Nethou (Aneto in Spanish), the highest peak of the Pyrenees.

We followed the route to Luchon recommended by Russell in *A Fortnight in the Pyrenees*, a tiny book of admirable clarity and precision that would fit in a vest pocket. That little had changed was hardly surprising given his emphasis on mountains, but it was gratifying to discover that even some of the hotels he recommended were still in business.

We took the Route Thermale, the road made in the 1860s for Empress Eugénie, still the most spectacular way to drive through the Pyrenees. We began from the Vallée de

Campan south of Bagnères-de-Bigorre and climbed the famous Col d'Aspin, a favourite excursion from Bagnères, particularly recommended for the sunset.

I hauled the Renault round the hairpin bends of the winding road to the wild desolate col. There we saw the whole chain of the Pyrenees spread out before us, and caught our first glimpse of the mysterious Monts Maudits far away in Spain, and saw, as Russell promised, 'the Clarabide, Oô, Crabioules and Maladetta appear in the south-east like a continuous chain of glaciers, covering several degrees of the horizon.'

We also followed his recommendation to Arreau, far below us in the Vallée d'Aure, a little village of stone houses clustered each side of the wide rushing river. The Hôtel d'Angleterre, Russell's favourite lodging, is still in business, and run by the same family. Though the stables have now been converted into bedrooms, the heart of the hotel, its fireplace, stone walls, low beamed ceilings and solid wooden furniture, are unchanged. From the French windows of our bedroom we could look down the street of stone and criss-crossed half-timbering, with the pointed slate spire of the church at the end and the great wooden doors of the old forge opposite. We could imagine Russell arriving after a long walk, and demanding to know what was on the menu. He said how hard he found it to leave, and savoured the memory of the succulent lamb they served. Dinner that evening was thus not hard to order and I am delighted to report that Russell's recommendation of a hundred and fifty years earlier held good and led to one of the best meals I ever ate in the Pyrenees: a marinated trout stuffed with a cucumber coulis, and, *naturellement*, the *carré d'agneau* in a crust of herbs, in its own juice, followed by apricot clafouti. My twelve-year-old companion declared himself satisfied with a confit of duck with the crispiest skin he had ever tasted. I felt sure Russell would have approved.

We made a detour for another classic excursion to the Lac d'Oô. The path starts where the road ends at les Granges d'Astau. At first it was gentle, a soft green valley scattered with boulders with a silver stream below, but it rapidly became extremely steep. Marianne Colston did it on horseback in 1821, and reckoned it worse than any other she had ever seen. 'A staircase of four or five hundred steps would be smoother, more gradual, and of easier ascent for a horse, than this mountain passage . . . The ascent is often very nearly perpendicular, and to complete the whole, the horses must frequently place their feet at the very edge of a tremendous precipice.' She felt safer on the horse than her own feet, however; 'had I tried the latter, I think I should have precipitated myself into the abyss'. Our path on foot over rocks and stones was certainly arduous but it was flanked by dense woodland and hardly dangerous. Moreover it was Sunday afternoon and we had plenty of company, Spanish, French, Irish, dogs, babies in backpacks, and one determined fellow who was trying to cycle up to the Lac. We said *bonjour* many times as our paths crossed his, and he panted for breath before the next rough scramble.

It was a great relief to see the still, smooth lake, a clear green basin, half a mile across, with a magnificent cascade thundering at its southern extremity and mountains all around. Russell judged it 'one of the most exquisite spots in the Pyrenees – a capital starting point for glacier exploration or isard-hunting'. We decided against either, and where Colston had stopped to make sketches, we sat on the rough scree by the lake, took photos and ate our lunch of baguette and cheese before returning, our way downhill immeasurably easier, with frequent stops to cool our hands and faces in the little streams that crossed the path.

After that we drove over another lofty pass, the Col de Peyresourde, from which the descent is so steep and long that spectators for the Tour de France hand out newspapers to the cyclists to tuck in their shirts and insulate them against the freezing ride down. Finally we arrived in Luchon, recommended for walking above all others, says Russell, 'being within a few hours' walk of the largest glacier-fields and highest peaks in the Pyrenees'. Murray's Guide concurred: 'No place in the Pyrenees equals in beauty of situation, in variety and interest of excursions, and in luxury and gaiety, Bagnères-de-Luchon.' (Arthur Young, the English eighteenth-century agricultural writer whose observations of France on the eve of revolution remain a key text to this day, had been less enthusiastic about Luchon: 'The baths are horrible holes; the patients lie up to their chins in hot sulphurous water, which, with the beastly dens they are placed in, one would think sufficient to cause as many distempers as they cure.')

As well as a gateway to the mountains Luchon was also a very fashionable spa with a rich source of sulphur springs, popular since the days of the Romans. It is still a gracious town of long avenues lined with elegant mansions and hotels, shaded by trees, and surrounded by snowy peaks. At the end of the Allée d'Etigny are the baths, a magnificent establishment with a grand colonnade of marble pillars and a vast marble hall within, where the *curistes* drink, inhale and bathe in the waters. Beyond are the inevitable Jardins Anglais, all manicured lawns and artificial cascades.

In the nineteenth century Luchon combined natural beauty with good shopping, the social and cultural distractions of balls and grand opera throughout the summer season. There were sports of all kinds available, from golf to croquet, and churches for all denominations, including Protestant temples for the English, with seasonal incumbents who preached sermons suitably adapted to their delicate clientele.

Excursions were all the rage, even if they were done by sedan chair, or in mounted cavalcades. The guides of Luchon played their part to perfection. They were organized into companies, and adopted a special costume: white trousers, black velvet jacket, blue cravat, red waistcoat, and a dark blue beret, with a white pompom for walking guides and red for the horse guides. Baring Gould, the prolific writer of hymns and travel books, sniffed at them for 'adopting an imaginary Pyrenean costume . . . and taking people to spots they could perfectly easily find without them'.

Luchon had long been popular with the French, who called it the Queen of the Pyrenees, and it was easily accessible from Paris once the railway arrived in 1873. From 1890 there was a Pyrenees Express from Paris to Luchon. Being further from Pau, Luchon was less visited by the English, but for anyone who really wanted to complete a tour of the Pyrenees it was essential, and for the British Luchon came closest to the popular Alpine mountain resorts like Chamonix or Interlaken. Henry Blackburn, in *The Pyrenees. A Description of Summer Life at*

French Watering Places, describes the mixture of visitors, taking the waters, dozing and eating ices and listening to the brass band in front of the *thermes*, the señoritas with mantillas and red camellias in their hair, Parisiennes with little hats and peacock feathers, Spanish dons in white jackets and chimney pot hats, dogs carried in baskets, middle-aged men killing time, old and faded dandies preserved like Quentin Crisp, and French families, the women industriously knitting and children playing with the pet poodle.

For the luchonnais their guests were of two sorts, either Parisians – the name they gave to all who paid the full tariff, whether they were Russians or Brazilians – or *volaille* ('game'): economical people who came for the reduced prices at the end of the season.

Stephen Liégeard was a typical 'Parisian' visitor: a royalist Burgundian aristocrat, politician and poet, now most famous for coining the name Côte d'Azur for the Riviera. A faded photo shows a smooth face over a high stock collar and cravat, with carefully groomed whiskers and a moustache as gratuitously curled as an art nouveau railing. He adored Luchon, and after a brief visit in 1872 wrote his own guide to the Pyrenees. His style of *pyrénéisme* was leisurely; his Pyrenean day consisted of dining at the renowned Arnative restaurant, at 10 a.m. (the usual hour for *déjeuner* then, with *dîner* at 6 p.m.), where he enjoyed fresh salmon trout or *cèpes à la bordelaise*, followed by watching the excited departure of riders and carriages for excursions and promenades. He strolled under the trees, listened to music from the little bands in the pavilions on the promenades, and looked out for imperial princes and Grande Horizontales, like la Belle Otero (whose breasts were the models for the cupolas of the Carlton Hotel in Cannes).

He did actually make several *ascensions* but disliked nailed boots and flea-ridden *cabanes*, and when he climbed Nethou, he dramatized it out of all proportion, describing dangers at every step. Liégeard went well equipped, taking his own vintage Burgundy as well as supplies from the Arnative, including 'several chickens, two hams, a sausage, gigot of mutton, fillet of beef, eight cutlets, a good slice of veal, a dozen loaves of bread, a few bottles of Bordeaux, two flagons of Frontignan, not forgetting coffee, fine champagne, and a big gourdful of anisette Brizard, to temper the water'. Russell was highly amused by his account. Liégeard was obsessed with Russell, *le noble comte, Sir Russel*, as he calls him. He wrote a poem about him and pursued him everywhere, but was for ever frustrated; wherever he went the noble Count had already left. He should perhaps have invited him to dine.

For Henry Russell Luchon was a happy combination of his favourite activities, waltzing his way through parties and balls one day and striding off for punishing solitary climbs in high mountains the next. In the high season he liked to stay at the fashionable Hôtel des Bains; in the hotel register for 19 June 1878 he registered with a flourish as Comte Russell de la Maladetta, along with such personalities as Princesse Amelia de Schleswig-Holstein, Lord Bolton and the Duke and Duchess of Abercorn.

Luchon is not as sumptuous as it was, but nor is it as down-at-heel and faded as many of the Pyrenean spas today. The grand hotels and houses can still be seen, with their elegant balconies, only partly obscured by a street-level excrescence of shops selling sheepskin slippers and walking sticks, and coach tours of the Monts Maudits. The *thermes* establishment is still magnificent, the marble hall full of *curistes* stretched out on chaises longues in white towelling robes.

The museum is the kind I like, old and dusty and full of un-PC stuffed animals – owls, herons, squirrels, even eagles and one poor baby bear – and geological samples with hand-written labels and unidentified Roman fragments. A whole room is devoted to the *pyrénéistes*, the nineteenth-century *montagnards* of Luchon; there is a splendid relief map of the Monts Maudits massif, a sedan chair and a glorious medley of ancient hobnailed boots, old iron crampons, several iron-tipped alpenstocks, even a little tin lantern attributed to Russell himself. There is the summit register for Nethou, and the *carnet* of a guide full of testimonials to his prowess and honesty from long dead clients.

Theo and I bought ourselves the iron-tipped walking sticks that seemed to be *de rigueur* (especially for a woman of nearly fifty with a dodgy hip), although they were hardly necessary for our first ascent to Superbagnères, the high plateau above Luchon which promised fine views of the surrounding mountains including a glimpse of the Monts Maudits.

The cheat's way to get there is by *télécabine*, rising silently and dramatically above the roofs of the town and over the trees to the cool, windswept plateau above. *Parapentes* of red and yellow floated gently down beside us. At Superbagnères there is a magnificent Belle Epoque Grand Hôtel built for skiers at the turn of the century, and looking like a marooned ship with its Thirties white railings high on the plateau.

It has since fallen on hard times, and we found we were almost the only guests, marooned in the echoing elegance of former years. Faded black and white photos and 1930s posters recalled skiing parties and balls of long ago. It was significantly colder than Luchon and shrouded in cloud, to our great disappointment. Happily, the next morning, when we descended to the empty salon, there were blue peaks etched with white framed in the tall arched windows. The mist cleared further as we walked along the ridge at the edge of the plateau to see the distant crests of the Monts Maudits, the Nethou, and its neighbouring peak the Maladetta, to the south. Below us lay the deep green Vallée du Lys, with its snowy Cirque and famous waterfall, the Cascade d'Enfer.

This used to be a favourite excursion from Luchon, and later we drove along the lovely valley, its gentle wooded slopes thrown into dramatic relief by the snowy peaks and glaciers of the Cirque de Crabioules which tower over it. By the time we had walked up to the cascade we were alone. Just ahead was a narrow slate fissure through which a long torrent of water was rushing fiercely, dashing down to the rocky bed of the stream below, a perfect waterfall. I think it was special because we could get so close to it, sit on a large smooth stone and simply revel in the refreshing negative ions of the spray. Theo held my hand and said it was the most beautiful thing he had ever seen. There is something special about sharing a waterfall. The cooling spray makes it more physical than a view, and you know your companion is feeling the same response as you.

The adjacent electricity generating station is an appropriate reminder of the critical importance of these abundant water sources to the local economy. As we sat in awed silence, trying to follow a single drop of water down its tumultuous course, a very nice young man with an rucksack emblazoned with the logo of the EDF (Electricité de France) appeared, and warned us not to climb down to the stream at the bottom of the cascade, since a sudden surge of water would carry us away. He was like a guardian angel appearing out of nowhere to warn us of tidal waves and floods.

From the Vallée du Lys we turned up another steep and winding road through a forest of pine and beech, to the Hospice de France, nestling in a wooded valley basin surrounded by steep barren slopes. The Hospice is a large stone mountain *auberge* with a venerable history, sheltering pilgrims, smugglers, bandits, mountaineers and tourists since it was founded by the Knights of St John in the fourteenth century. It was famous as the last habitation in France before the Spanish frontier, and for Russell and the *montagnards* of the nineteenth century it was the first stop on the steep path to the Port de Vénasque and beyond to the Monts Maudits. Everybody stayed at the Hospice de France, from Ramond, Flaubert and Viollet-le-Duc, to the intrepid Marianne Colston and Lady Chatterton. None seemed to find it a particularly salubrious experience; contemporary descriptions have the flavour of a Caravaggio painting: the flickering fire and huge blackened fireplace burning entire trunks of wood, the long wooden tables and benches, dancing shepherds with skinfuls of Spanish wine, smugglers loaded down with oil, saffron and dried fish, elegant Paris ladies in silk gowns, and a bemused Englishman waxing his boots in the corner. All slept on hay or benches and took pot luck with the food, which might include freshly killed isard, or even sorbet made from mountain snow.

I was disappointed to find it abandoned, after the road was closed following a landslide in 1977. Local efforts at rehabilitation are under way to reopen it, but there was little sign of progress. Shutters flapped dismally, corrugated iron blocked the old doorway, and there were even signs of graffiti on the walls. Why anyone would come this far to spray graffiti baffled me completely.

Above was the famous Port de Vénasque, the gateway to the Accursed Mountains. It sounded a punishing climb, to an altitude of 2400 metres past frozen tarns and windswept ice and snow. Even Russell says, '. . . a hard climb begins, in a chilly solitude with abrupt precipices on both sides. A few melancholy pines are seen here and there, like a funeral decoration, and after passing the perpendicular rock called Culet, where many deaths have occurred from avalanches, you enter the kingdom of rocks, desolation and snow.' We walked partway up the path zigzagging up to the pass, beyond the Trou des Chaudronniers (the Tinkers' Hole, where an entire company of tinkers died in the snow), and stopped to bathe our feet in the icy clear water of the stream like so many pilgrims before us. Sadly low cloud prevented us climbing very far, but we could imagine the caravans of laden donkeys and mules, trudging up and over to Spain, or descending to the warmth of the hospice, its glowing lights at dusk a welcome sight to the weary traveller. I was chagrined later to find a Victorian postcard showing a proud family having reached the Port, sturdy-looking women in long skirts and huge flowery hats, clutching their alpenstocks, the men sporting white shoes and straw boaters.

Russell's description of the view of the other side leaves little to the imagination. 'You have at once before you the entire Maladetta, a livid and ghastly mass of granite and glaciers, forming a dazzling semicircle six miles in length. The valley which separates you from it has a look almost infernal, being only decorated with thousands of frost-bitten pines, broken by avalanches, lightning and wind, their trunks in ruins, and twisted as if in pain.'

Russell first began exploring Aragon in 1863, investigating unknown valleys and peaks at astonishing speed in the most torrid heat, sometimes alone and sometimes with Charles Packe. The area then was totally unmapped, and until quite late climbers based their knowledge of the area on the experiences of the accident-prone Cambridge don, Thomas Clifton Paris, in 1843. Russell refers to his explorations, though it is hard to believe he can have gleaned much from the progress of his hapless compatriot.

Still, Clifton Paris's account remains a gem, as I discovered when I found his *Letters to the Pyrenees* in the Rare Manuscripts room of the British Library. Inspired to travel to the Pyrenees by romantic texts like *The Song of Roland* and *The Mysteries of Udolpho*, Clifton Paris set out. 'My heart beat quick and a joyous tide ran through my veins, as I hailed for the first time the wild and solitary regions so famous in song and story.'

He wanted to explore the unknown region of Aragon to the south of Vignemale, where even today there are few roads or towns. He and his companion, Mr O., had only the haziest idea of a route, no guide and no Spanish maps. The French maps stopped abruptly at the frontier. They had no walking sticks, no walking boots and wore light-weight city clothes and top hats. Nor did they speak Spanish. Having crossed the frontier at Port de Gavarnie they settled down to some sketching, but their drawing pads immediately aroused the suspicions of local farmers. Two armed men arrested them, examined their passports, and turned out their bags. They refused to believe the foreigners did not speak Spanish and took them off to a fine lunch of the best bread they had eaten since England, meat and dried fish. The guards kept their glasses filled and offered them cigars before taking them to Torla, three hours' march down the stupefying gorge of the Ara valley.

They were released after a night in a flea-ridden *auberge* with inedible food and high prices, where they consoled themselves singing English songs in response to the Aragonese chants of the other guests. Next day they got lost again and were caught in a storm. Happily when they staggered into Biescas they found a good *auberge* and celebrated with the Cambridge Boat Song from their balcony.

Finally the intrepid pair made it to Panticosa, top hats intact, and were delighted to encounter *le grand Michel*, chef of Hôtel de France in Pau, who was doing the summer season at the spa, fully equipped with his dazzling *batterie de cuisine*. It was raining so they stayed for four days, enjoying the cooking and discussing possible itineraries with the chef, who suggested two different routes back to the Port de Gavarnie. Boldly the two Englishmen decided to attempt both routes and make a round trip back to Panticosa. But as soon as they set off climbing towards the Col de Brazato, an icy fog descended and they found themselves deep in snow and a violent wind, shivering in their light clothing. Clifton Paris suggested they return to Panticosa but Mr O. was tantalized by glimpses of a soft green mountain tinkling with cowbells on the other side of a deep river gorge. They wandered about to find a way down, but could see only steep drops below them, until finally Mr O. got stuck overhanging a precipice of several hundred feet, with a torrent fuming below.

Eventually they slid their way down to the valley. It was almost nightfall and they spent two hours constructing a rudimentary shelter of river stones. 'The labour kept us warm and passed the time,' Clifton Paris remarked philosophically. But more clouds brought rain from the least expected direction and their shelter was soaked. They were miserable. 'We then crouched down close to each other, buttoning up our coats of brown holland as tightly as possible, and I hung a letter before my face as some protection from the cold wind, whilst my companion threw his handkerchief over his head and face.' They huddled up with hats pulled down and knees pulled up, shivering together. Their only supplies were two cigars, which they postponed smoking as long as possible. 'They were food and drink to us.' They tried singing through chattering teeth, 'but our ghastly mirth died away and we sat shivering and suffering in silence the rest of the night'. In the morning they managed to find a shepherd to guide them and staggered back to Panticosa in a pitiful state, having fasted for twenty-seven hours.

Many attempts had been made on Nethou itself, the highest peak of the Pyrenees, but it had only finally been conquered in 1842. The death of the guide, Pierre Barrau, who fell into a crevasse of the Nethou glacier in 1824, rather put everyone off. His companions heard him cry, 'I am sinking. I am sinking, I am lost!' and then nothing more. The glacier yielded his remains 117 years later, a scrap of scarf, a crampon, a horn-handled knife, part of a shoe, a fragment of bone. You can see them in the Luchon museum.

Russell first climbed Nethou with a French friend and two guides. He trained himself, as he puts it, by walking in one day from Bagnères-de-Bigorre to Luchon, a journey of seventy kilometres. By the time Russell arrived the summit register had a considerable list, including French climbers, many English, geologists, a palaeontologist, an engineer, magistrates, *notaires*, and several army officers. Then there were the determined techies observing their barometers and thermometers; the Burgundians who opened a bottle of Chambertin 1846 on the summit; twenty women; a Greek; and a fireman from Toulouse. The first woman registered there was English, Miss Marshall, who had climbed in July 1848 with her father, the Reverend A. Marshall and two guides from Luchon. They left their names and that is all. Nethou was always an ascent to boast of and a late nineteenth-century postcard, sent from the Dordogne, shows a proud fellow posed on the summit, leaning on one knee, with beret, alpenstock and monocle. English, of course.

Their comments were sometimes as banal as holiday postcards: observations of the temperature, the view, the guides. 'Excellent snow, magnificent weather, admirable view.' Sometimes they were more tense – 'forced to our knees, difficult snow, wind to take the horns off bulls, intense fog' – and always, 'Prudent guides, guides good companions.'

Then a familiar insouciant voice. Russell wrote, 'What a sky, not a cloud. I have never seen a more desolate and grandiose panorama. I can see Canigou to the east, and Balaitous to the west.' After which Russell had sat down and calmly smoked a cigar on the summit.

He climbed Nethou another four times, but the most memorable occasion was the ascent he made in 1866. In Luchon Russell had met one Captain Hoskins of the Royal Navy (later to become a distinguished admiral, toughened up no doubt by his night out with the Count). He suggested he and Russell climb Nethou together. Russell had consented but, feeling bored with a climb he had already made twice before, decided to make it more exciting. They would sleep on the summit! 'A night passed at such a height, on a narrow *crête*, at the mercy of the wind and the thunder, what could be more splendid and moving?' They would be able to see the sunset and sunrise from the highest point of the Pyrenees!

They asked twelve guides to go with them before one finally accepted such conditions. They walked all the way from Luchon, over the Nethou glacier, and at sunset arrived at the final granite ridge, the Pont de Mahomet, a narrow *crête* with an abyss on either side (Russell remarks casually that this is the only difficult bit) which led to the summit. After the sun had gone, things got a little strange; Russell writes of the violet tones of the sky, the wind and the cold, the livid snow invaded by menacing shadows. From the east enormous black clouds appeared full of lightning. 'We did not talk any more.' Then a spectral moon appeared, and there was an apocalyptic storm. Even Russell was anxious in case the wild winds would whip them off the narrow ridge, so they secured themselves with rope to one of the cairns of stones erected by earlier visitors. One thinks of Odysseus tied to the mast to resist the songs of the sirens.

Finally the storm ceased and the night became as quiet and still 'as a cemetery at midnight'. After that Russell slept well, cosily buried in his warm sleeping bag. Poor Hoskins, however, had only blankets and froze; his teeth chattered, he turned blue, and in the end wrapped himself around his snug chum. Thus they awaited the dawn. As for their guide, he snored happily through the drama, though when the dawn rose, the snow glowing scarlet with the new sun, even he was so awed by its magnificence that he fell to his knees. For Russell it was a 'sublime night' he would always remember.

It was with his English friend Charles Packe that Russell really explored the Monts Maudits, climbing the heights in their hobnailed boots and Norfolk jackets, equipped with nothing but a compass, their sheepskin sleeping bags and a rucksack packed with provisions. Packe had set out to map the entire Monts Maudits, and had already spent several years exploring the region, mostly alone or with his Pyrenean Mountain dogs. Russell called him the Christopher Columbus of Aragon. It was Packe's Vignemale, the region to which he always remained most attached. He planned to spend the year of 1865 pursuing his investigations, with three weeks' camping south of the massif around Nethou, equipped with compasses, barometers and other measuring equipment, arranging for corresponding observations to be made in Luchon.

The two friends spent August 1865 climbing together, camping by the lakes of the Maladetta: twenty-six fresh clear lakes full of trout, surrounded by virgin pine forests and plenty of 3000-plus metre peaks. Just Russell's idea of a summer vacation. As usual Packe and Russell pursued different interests. (Often even when they follow the same route their accounts are quite different.)

'When the sun rose, we shook hands and parted for the day, but always met in the evening, the very best of friends, though we had not the same pursuits or tastes. Whilst I indulged in eccentric, solitary ascents of untrodden and snowy peaks, which swarmed in those days in Aragon, where I never met a human being, Packe did more useful things. He mapped those peaks, he measured and named them, botanized in their valleys, and read their history in their rocks and fossils.'

Russell set off alone to climb what he thought was the Vallibierna, which Packe had already climbed, but he ascended the wrong peak by mistake, a first ascent by default. 'It was far from easy,' he recalled. He had to climb with his hands to get to the top, 'not to say my teeth.' There he found himself on a peak adjoining the great Nethou linked only by a narrow ridge. He named it le petit Nethou (it was only 200 metres lower than Nethou itself) but since Packe was drawing the maps, he honoured his friend by naming it Pic Russell (3201m) instead. In return Russell named one of the lakes they found after Packe. (Its Spanish name is Lago la Vall.) Next day Russell bagged the Vallibierna (3067m) after all, leaving his friend to fish and work on his map undisturbed. In the end both men preferred to go alone. Russell said finally, 'It is happiness to be two, but it is a lesson to be alone.'

They shared the nights, however. 'Many a romantic night have I spent with him on the desolate shores of the Rio Bueno lakes, buried in sheepskin bags, under the stars and moon, happier than children or monarchs. We never had a tent. And yet it was terribly cold.' But they both loved to sleep in the open air, even above the snow line, now they had their trusty sleeping bags. I imagine them sitting round the fire, flames flickering on their faces, boots off, wearing espadrilles (as good as slippers for climbing rocks, said Russell), damp clothes hanging from a makeshift line between the trees, cooking up mutton or fish with wild spinach they had gathered, followed by any wild fruit, like *fraises des bois*, they might have found. In his guide Packe recommended 'a good supply of fat bacon stowed in tin boxes . . . It always contributes to the meal, whether eaten as rashers or used for frying fish or making soup.' (An Andorra speciality to this day is trout with bacon, cooked on a slate over an open fire.) Their romantic nights were somewhat marred by the limited fuel for fires and cooking, and by the shepherds who once stole all the trout that Packe had caught in the lake.

It seems they did not carry guns, which was unusual in those days. It is hard to know at such a distance how Packe and Russell really felt about hunting. Neither really seems to have approved; Russell said he would hate to kill any animals, and Packe records spotting several isards one day, and how glad he was not to have a gun, since he would have been regarded as faint-hearted by his companions not to have shot them. Still, both were men of their time and seem to have accepted the inevitability of hunting as an integral part of the male character. Russell was great friends with Sir Victor Brooke, and in a second edition of the *Souvenirs* asked him to contribute a chapter on hunting in the Pyrenees. Despite his own distaste for animal sports, Russell clearly accepted that hunting was an inevitable part of mountain life.

It still is, as I learnt from Henri, my Catalan friend in Mosset, whose great passion is *la chasse* (hunting), along with quite a few of the men in the village. You can hear their guns sometimes early in the morning, or see them later in the day with their kill. Theo once went to eat his school lunch as usual in the village café, and the little crocodile of children passed a jeep laden with a huge stag and a wild boar, trophies of the day, killed by the chef, though I don't think they were served venison for lunch. Since we are rather fond of venison, it is hard to object to the hunting.

We shared a riverside picnic with Henri and Monique one day, since I was determined to eat trout the traditional way and we had been given a bag full of the small silvery fish by our neighbour. It was nearly Christmas but as so often in the Pyrenees in December it was warm, and we could set off down to the river in T-shirts, with our basket of loaves and fishes. The leafless trees made dramatic patterns against an astonishingly blue sky and the white-tipped peak of Canigou. A rich mulchy fragrance rose as we crunched over late autumn leaves in a spectrum of reds, oranges and golds and we picked up fallen walnuts that had escaped our harvesting, and now blackened our fingers as if in reproach at the waste. We watched the river flowing fierce and full after heavy rains, full of the logs and branches it had torn along with it, and felt thankful that our valley with its natural drainage had escaped the floods that had devastated the plain below.

Henri constructed a fireplace from a circle of stones, and we collected dry sticks of wood to make a fire. Then sausages were skewered on twigs and the trout were cooked with bacon on a slate over the flames. For dessert we ate blackberries we had gathered on the way.

As we shared a bottle of wine beside the embers of the fire, I asked Henri about hunting, and he laughed richly, his face furrowed by a huge smile. 'I came to Mosset as a child, and that was when I learnt to hunt,' he explained in his earthy Catalan accent. According to season he hunts deer, wild boar and birds. 'Nothing else comes close to the feeling, the emotion I feel, while waiting, sometimes a whole morning, listening with all my senses for an animal to arrive.'

I was reminded of another friend, a South African who lives in Provence, who once described running with the bulls at Pamplona, and said that nothing else made him feel more alive. I really wonder about this hunting instinct in men. Is it really an instinct to kill, or more an instinct to provide food by killing animals?

Henri grumbled about the anti-hunting lobby, admittedly rather muted in France, where hunting is seen more as a right gained by the peasants than an aristocratic pastime. 'These *écolos*,' he said, 'they don't understand the land. We look after it, we know it.' There is increasing tension between the farmers and hunters who manage the land, and the growing numbers of visitors and walkers who see access to the countryside as a natural right. Henri saves his worst ire for the mushroom hunters, who arrive in droves from the towns and take everything, not under-standing that in order to grow again, some must be left for nature. 'They think nature belongs to everyone, but it doesn't,' said Henri firmly, as he covered the ashes with stones to ensure there was no danger of fire.

15

Sunset and sunrise on the Pic du Midi

'It was the first time I found my self in the presence of such grand mountains. I received a profound impression which has affected me all my life.'

John Stuart Mill

It was, according to the Alpine Club, unusual to see both sunrise and sunset from the summit of a mountain. I was privileged to experience both on the Pic du Midi, and finally understood what Henry Russell was getting at. I read his instructions first.

You cannot be too strongly advised to send on your carriage as far as Gripp, where it will wait for you, and to ascend the Pic du Midi on your way. It is the finest view in the Pyrenees, and horses easily go to the top. But much snow will be found before the end of May. Half an hour will take you to the Lac d'Oncet, a deep and dismal sheet of water, on the eastern side of which, at an elevation of 7709 feet, stands the Hostellerie du Pic du Midi, not open nor clear of snow before the middle of June. The lake is frozen for eight months, and contains no trout; but ham, eggs, fowl, wine, tea and coffee are generally to be had at the *hostellerie*, where it is customary to sleep, so as to go up and see the sunrise from the top of the Pic, only one hour distant. North of the inn rises the solitary and shadeless cone of the Pic. An hour's zigzags from the inn (say three hours from Barèges) will place you on the summit of the Pic du Midi (9439 feet).

I was certainly tempted by the menu of the Hostellerie du Pic du Midi, not to mention the sunrise. Alas, the menu was a hundred and fifty years out of date. The hotel had first opened in 1852, built on the Col de Sencours beside the Lac d'Oncet halfway up the Pic du Midi, a basic two-storey structure of stone with stables and a veranda. All the building material and equipment had to be brought up the mountain on the backs of mules. A grand opening was held on 13 September 1852 at 11 a.m., with a banquet, music played by the orchestra from the casino in Bagnères, a hymn and mountain songs. Guests had assembled at 4 a.m. in Bagnères.

Sadly, the following year an avalanche swept it all away, and a new building with a stronger vaulted roof was erected. It was here that Maxwell Lyte took the first photographs of a solar eclipse in 1860. The building later provided accommodation while the Observatory was built on the summit, and on one grand occasion welcomed a hundred members of the Club Alpin Français in 1902. (Russell, as far as I know, declined.) It continued to be used, by road workers and construction workers for the observatory, up until the Second World War, when it was finally abandoned. It was used again during the construction work for the new observatory museum which opened in 2000.

The tariff for the hotel in Russell's day was as follows: To sleep in the communal dormitory 1F, separate bed 2F, faggot of wood 50 centimes; *déjeuner* of two dishes (wine not included) 2F50; a litre of best quality wine 3F; a bowl of milk with sugar, 50 centimes, without sugar 30 cm; a glass of punch 50 cm; eau de toilette 10 cm (presumably a substitute for washing); un *bain de pieds* – a hot footbath, necessary after the climb – 25 cm.

I had been invited to spend the night in the Observatoire, where there are rooms available for permanent staff and a few visitors. Sadly, though there is a shop and a restaurant as well as an astronomy museum, there is no longer accommodation for simple sunrise watchers. Russell had recorded a memorable night spent on the Pic in 1882, and I wanted to follow in his footsteps. The chance of my sleeping in vertiginous caves on a pile of hay, or even equipped with a sleeping bag more sophisticated than Russell's antique sheepskin, was beyond unlikely.

Happily, the observatory on the Pic du Midi is still functioning. It was threatened with closure in 1983, a victim of scientific progress, the development of satellite observation and budget restrictions in France, so has relaunched itself with a new role. While still pursuing scientific observation, both astronomical and meteorological, it is now also a museum and tourist experience. For a long time it was the highest observatory in Europe and even now is only exceeded by three others, one in the Sierra Nevada in Spain, and two in the Canaries, at Tenerife and Las Palmas. It has always played a key part in the life of the surrounding valleys; everyone knows someone who works at the Pic du Midi.

One mild though rainy October day I set out from the gentle haven of the green valleys of Béarn to reach the top. I had assumed the names Pic du Midi de Bigorre and Pic du Midi d'Ossau signified that they were in the middle of these regions. Not so. In fact Midi refers to midday, and the mountains were thus named by the local shepherds, who used them like a sundial. The sun was directly above the peak at midday. Time for lunch. Each mountain had its time; there was also a four o'clock mountain, a five o'clock mountain, and so on.

There was always great rivalry between the Bigourdans (the inhabitants of the Bigorre) and the Roussillonnais as to who had the highest mountain, the Pic du Midi or Canigou. These mountains simply looked taller than the others behind them because they stood out from the plain rather than forming part of the rest of the chain. It was not until 1787, when Ramond himself climbed the Pic du Midi and saw to the south the great peaks and glaciers above the Cirque de Gavarnie, that he realized that the Pic du Midi was in fact lower in altitude.

It was a critical moment in Pyrenean exploration; he considered it to be the best observation point in the Pyrenees. It was possible to see from Mont Vallier in the Ariège to the Pic du Midi d'Ossau in the Pyrenees Atlantiques and sometimes as far as the Atlantic itself, a distance of nearly a hundred miles. The Pic du Midi de Bigorre was always one of the great challenges for tourists to the Pyrenees. The English philosopher John Stuart Mill said the experience had changed his life.

My climb involved driving up to the ski station of la Mongie at the base of the Pic, and a fifteen-minute cable car up the mountainside. I consoled myself for this indulgence with Tennyson, who once joked to Wordsworth (his predecessor as Poet Laureate, whom he called 'Old

Wordie') that hot air balloons ought to be available at the foot of every tall mountain so that no-one need climb. Wordsworth was not amused but it struck me as a good idea.

It was chilly and raining when I arrived in Bagnères-de-Bigorre and the first thing I did was buy a cherry-red fleece to keep me warm. When I told the shopkeeper I was going up to the Pic du Midi he reacted like a medieval peasant who still believed dragons lurked on the mountain tops.

'*C'est terrible là!*' he warned. 'It will be much colder up there.' He looked at me as if I was mad. 'There's nobody up there,' he insisted, 'just wind and rain.' Wherever you went I discovered people always warned you it would be worse higher up, as if they never went any further themselves. Even in Prades people shake their heads dubiously when you say you live in Mosset, a few hundred metres higher up.

I sat happily in Bagnères, eating a hearty lunch as the rain poured down, not even hearing my newly acquired mobile phone in the depths of my many-pocketed bag. So it was not until two hours later that I listened to the message from the Pic: 'You must get here as soon as possible. There is a storm threatening, and the cable car will close.' Suddenly the drive about which I was slightly apprehensive anyway became urgent. In good weather the valley of Campan is broad and green and sweet, but now black clouds made it menacing. I took the road to la Mongie, the ski station 1800 feet below the Pic, from where the cable car departs. Beyond la Mongie is the infamous Col du Tourmalet, at 2115 metres the highest pass accessible by car, and one of the most brutal of the steep cols on the Tour de France route. All along the increasingly tortuous road the names of the cyclists, painted by fans, were still visible. I was glad I wasn't on a bike. A red sign flashed that the Pic du Midi was still open with the time of the last departure of the cable car, but I missed it as I flew past. I wasn't going to turn back now anyway. There were signs for falling rocks, followed by several signs for *verglas fréquent*, frequent skids, soon followed by the village of Gripp, which seemed an appropriate name. I gripped. I could see clouds above and had no idea how thick they would be, and then the first wisp of white floated across the road between the trees. The first avalanche shelter appeared, a simple corrugated roof to deflect the snow from the road. At least there was no snow. Yet. Another road sign for cows reminded me that there were animals at liberty, and I fervently hoped it was only cows. (Not bears, wild boar, wolves or whatever else they are trying to re-introduce to the Pyrenees.) Then I entered the cloud, a soft white blanket which grew increasingly dense. The cows inevitably loomed in front of me and I decided not to stop but just keep going slowly and they moved. They always do.

For a mile or two of hairpin bends the cloud was so thick I crept along slowly in second gear; the car lights made almost no difference and then to my great relief I was through. Above the clouds the sky was clear and the ugly ski resort buildings of la Mongie appeared. There was already snow on the higher flanks of the surrounding peaks. I was late. The last official public cabin had already left, but finally I persuaded them to take me up, despite the solid cloud enveloping the windows of the cable car, and thick flakes of snow like drops of milk on the surface of a glass. I was thankful we had been up the year before in clear weather, otherwise I would have been plunging entirely into the unknown.

Meteorological observations were first made on the Pic du Midi in the 1730s by François de Plantade, a lawyer who devoted himself to astronomy. He described his sightings of the aurora borealis, the planet Mercury and the solar eclipse. He died in August 1741 after climbing the Pic for the final time, collapsing 500 metres below the summit, sextant in hand, declaring 'How beautiful it all is!' Over a century later the first building was constructed, brainchild of the Société Ramond and two determined members: Charles Xavier Vaussenat, an engineer from Grenoble, and General Nansouty, nephew of one of Napoleon's generals. A faded photograph shows them posed on a ladder in front of the stone wall protecting the meteorological instruments on the windy Col de Sencours; Nansouty with his long white moustache and little Indian skullcap, pipe in hand, has his arm round the shoulder of his friend, Vaussenat, a full-bearded man in a coat so dusty he looks as if he has been building the wall himself.

From 1873 Nansouty installed himself in the Hostellerie de Sencours, fully supplied with red wine, biscuits, meat and vegetable conserves, sugar, coffee, tea, milk, rum, candles, five cubic metres of coke and a complete pharmacy. He made observations day and night and climbed right up to the peak, a further one and a half hours, daily, winter and summer, to make observations. In December 1874 a terrible tempest heaped twelve feet of snow on the roof of the refuge, one of the windows was broken by a flying block of frozen snow and the door gave way. They had to leave, a gruelling journey down the mountain. Nansouty's diligence was vindicated when he warned of floods in 1875 so that the valley was alerted in time and the population evacuated.

Plans were then made to build on the summit itself, at 2877 metres, which would at least be free from avalanches. Apart from stone which was extracted in situ, and water for the mortar, which was obtained from melted snow, all the materials – sand, tiles and schist for the roof – had to be carried up on the backs of men and mules, a strenuous climb of at least eight kilometres. Weather conditions made it even more difficult; they encountered lightning, hail, storms and freezing temperatures (in winter as low as minus 37) and faced the extreme difficulty of getting help in case of accident. Three porters died on one occasion, swept away by an avalanche.

After the observatory was completed it was kept going by porters and mules who trudged up and down with supplies all summer; most famous was Jean de Gripp, who from the age of sixteen made more than 5000 *ascensions* in his traditional clogs and beret, including three in one day. All the stores had to be in place before winter, when only the most determined climber could get there over a firm cover of snow.

Even the cable car up the Pic du Midi today is not for the faint-hearted. Two separate systems are required to reach the top, both with full-length glass windows so you feel as if you are suspended in mid-air like a bird or a butterfly. The first cabin arrives at a bleak ridge in the middle of nowhere, the second swings you dramatically across the valley below, the lake tiny in the distance, the stone refuge like a doll's house. The cable ascends so far you can't even see the end. When it strains up the final slope to the summit it is buffeted by the wind, which is particularly fierce around the Pic du Midi, because it stands aloof from the rest of the chain.

As the doors of the cabin opened, it was suddenly very cold, and through the cloud and snowflakes I could see drifts of fresh snow. Once inside the observatory it was warm and still, like entering a space station. I was welcomed by Gerard Coupinot, head of the scientific team, an avuncular man in a woolly jumper with a dark beard and hair curling over his collar. He led me through a labyrinth of passages (there are three kilometres of corridors) to a small room full of laptop computers with screens swirling with stars and galaxies, where I met *les amateurs*, Michel and Sylvain, members of a year-round team of volunteers who help keep the observatory functioning. Marie-Hélène, a young teacher from the town of Barèges, the other side of the Col de Tourmalet, was there on a training course in star watching for local teachers, part of an initiative to intro-duce the work of the observatory to more local people, and especially children. A children's fresco of the planets adorned one of the walls. Marie-Hélène was getting rather concerned about her prospects of leaving the Pic that day. The wind was getting up, and beyond 60 kph it was too dangerous to operate the cable car. (In 2000, 130 tourists were obliged to spend the night on the Pic when a storm made it too dangerous for the cable car to operate.)

About twenty centimetres of snow had fallen the previous night, the first significant fall of the year. This was nothing, though. Often during the winter there might be as much as three metres of snow on the terraces and then it is impossible to go outside at all. The doors won't open and they have to poke holes through the snow outside the windows to see anything.

The original buildings of the observatory remain, tucked just below the summit. Old postcards show the summit itself with visitors standing round the observation table. Over the following years the complex grew, additional accommodation and platforms were added and the edifice blossomed with dramatic white domes, the first of which was the Baillaud Coupole in 1906. Finally the actual summit itself yielded to progress, sliced off in 1957 in order to erect a 105-metre television antenna.

The observatory still functions as a meteorological station, supplying Météo France with data, but it is equally important as a stellar observatory, with an impressive variety of domes and telescopes. I was shown the oldest telescope. 'This Newton telescope, fifteen centimetres in diameter, was the largest they had when Russell came here in 1882,' said Gerard. Then there were no domes, and all observation was done outside on a windy platform right on the Pic. My guide explained that the desire to observe at such heights was not, as I assumed, to be nearer the stars (three thousand metres makes little difference when measurements are usually in light years) but because dust particle pollution is reduced and the skies are clearer.

Les amateurs took me on a rapid tour of the observatory and its equipment, though the thick cloud meant there was nothing to observe out there. The observatory is particularly known for its studies of the surface of the sun and solar spots, and Michel and Sylvain demonstrated how the picture of the sun gets refracted so that the image can be seen without looking directly at that dangerous star. Then we retired to their lair, a room with tall windows onto the terrace on three sides, a magnificent view were it not for the thick pillowy duvet of cloud that still obscured everything. Among the photos of stars, galaxies and sun spots taped to the wall were two clocks, one for earth time and one for sidereal time: star time, that is, based upon the movement of the earth relative to a particular star other than the sun. I thought star time sounded like earth shine and could not imagine if they were real, academic or simply poetic concepts. *Les amateurs* offered tea, explaining that it might taste a bit different since water does not reach boiling point at that altitude. They explained that the temperature water boiled at depended on air pressure, and would reach only 98 degrees not 100 at that altitude. This was why early researchers had laboured up mountains equipped with kettles, attempting to establish altitude by measuring the length of time it took water to boil at different heights. The tea was fine.

Both young men clearly lived for their time on the Pic, clad permanently in big red weatherproof jackets, hanging open, ready to rush outside as soon as the opportunity arose. Sylvain, with angular features and short cropped hair, was also an enthusiastic climber, happiest on his own. 'I like to be alone with nature,' he said, with a frank gaze that belied any pretension. He had just qualified in engineering.

'Why not work in astronomy?' I asked.

'There are no jobs in astronomy,' he said sadly. 'Star gazing does not produce anything.'

Michel, sallow-skinned with dark Spanish eyes, told me about his day job as a fire protection officer with the SNCF, French railways, from which he escapes to spend weeks at a time as a volunteer for the observatory. He showed me a computer image of the swirling surface of the sun, explaining that each granule lasts only a few seconds. 'Each of them is the size of France,' he said with awe.

On days like these there is not much sun or star watching to be done. The staff are totally dependent on the weather, which can change very quickly, so they need to be prepared for long periods of inactivity, and then a sudden response. A bit like fishing. So they read, or do some *bricolage* on the observatory building. (DIY repairs have included using the rubber parts of a German Panzer tank in the rim of one of the domes.) They have to be ready for the violent storms that sometimes rage round the Pic, when everything electrical must be switched off. 'Then we all watch the lightning strike the radio mast. It attracts lots of lightning,' Michel explained with satisfaction.

It clearly takes a certain type to spend days and weeks at a time marooned up here among the stars. In the museum I saw photos of the hermetic existence of the early days when they might have been trapped here for months. It was like a monastery, with everybody there committed to the worship of the heavens. They found their own amusements; there was even a photo of someone on a swing, a swing on a mountain top!

I was struck by the gaze of the men who had founded and directed the observatory. All had eyes of such depth, used to looking unfathomable distances. Russell's eyes were like that too. Here were Vaussenat and Nansouty, and Jean Rosch, director from 1947 to 1997; when he arrived in 1947 you could still only get to the observatory by vehicle between July and October. Otherwise the journey had to be done on skis. Even then they needed to ensure they had supplies for up to three months.

I retired to my own monastic cell, fully equipped with a single bed, washbasin, table and wardrobe, and peered gloomily through the double-glazed windows at thick impenetrable cloud. I could see nothing and consoled myself with Russell's own account of his visit to the observatory in 1882. General Nansouty had only taken possession of the summit a few weeks before, and Russell found a little colony of four: the General himself, an observer, a cook and a valet. They had a vast store of provisions, coke, medicines and drinking water obtained from the snow. There was even a telegraph wire, partly underground, which connected them with the plain. 'Without this means of connection with humanity, the exile would be too complete and too frightening,' Russell observed, though he never seems to have been tempted to install anything similar on Vignemale. 'To climb in November, to the summit of a mountain of 2877 metres on a resplendent day, to find an imposing two-storey house, to be received in the most affable and generous manner, to have a marvellous dinner, and sleep in an excellent room heated to 16 degrees, it seems like a dream. Only eight days before snow had come as far as the plain, General Nansouty had recorded deathly cold of minus 22 degrees on the summit of the Pic.'

Russell was astonished by the luxury, the fine wines on the table, new furniture, a stove, books, a soft bed. 'One would never have thought we were 3000 metres above sea level.' At 6 p.m. he dined with General Nansouty, who looked like a Gaul out of *Asterix* with his long blond curling moustache and intense blue eyes. He smoked a pipe incessantly and liked nothing better than to show off his collection of snails and insects. Dinner was very satisfactory, and they no doubt discussed the trials of the observatory construction as they sat snugly in the new low stone building high in the clouds, safe from the elements. 'I expected the meal of a hermit,' Henry wrote, 'but an exquisite soup was succeeded by a regiment of steaming plates, beef, veal, a majestic chicken, potatoes, salad, dessert, marsala wine, coffee and liqueurs. Cigars ended the feast, then around 9 p.m. I strolled, in a relatively gentle temperature, on the terrace constructed to the south of the house with a view, perhaps the most beautiful and extended in Europe.'

I peered again through my own snow-framed window and saw that a jagged break in the cloud had revealed a tiny fragment of blue sky. There seemed a miraculous chance of the sky clearing in time for sunset. I hurried to join my new sun-worshipping friends, who equipped me with one of their weatherproof red jackets to go out on the terrace. The clouds had simply floated away, fluffy golden-hued puffs dissolving into the firmament, revealing a panorama of the earth and the sky and everything that moved. The extent of the view was amazing. It was not like being on a plane, because you could stand quite still and take it all in. It was like looking at a giant relief map, with tiny towns, green valleys and snowfields below. Michel pointed out the distant masses of Toulouse, Tarbes and Pau. 'You used to see as far as the Massif Central in Russell's day, but now it is too polluted,' he said. He identified the range of mountains to the south, a sea of snowy peaks like forked icing on a giant cake. 'There, that's Vignemale, you can just see it, with the glacier between two peaks. And there's the Brèche du Roland.' I could see clearly the huge gap, like a missing tooth, in the serrated ridge of peaks to the right of the great curve of the Cirque de Gavarnie.

It seemed as if almost everyone left at the observatory that night – about fifteen people – emerged to watch the sunset. It really was like a moment of worship, a celestial sacrament. As the sun sank below the horizon of peaks, the sky reddened and streaked with ruby and gold, and almost the entire chain of the Pyrenees reflected the spectrum of colours. Finally only yellow and green tones were left, as the sky above darkened and wisps of black clouds rose like smoke beyond the vanishing white summits. Below, the cold black waters of Lac d'Oncet deepened even further. For perhaps twenty minutes everyone watching was silent, a shared communion. It was one of those moments of total focus, of never wanting it to end, of thinking of nothing else (except briefly loved ones to share it with, and especially my brother, who had a capacity to see further than most). It was the most beautiful thing I have ever seen in my life. I wept, happily. It was beyond beauty, impossible to fully comprehend. I began to understand a little more of what Henry Russell and my brother sought and found in their silent contemplation of the sublime in nature. It was the closest I got to understanding the beckoning silence, perhaps the closest I even wanted to get. When I spoke to the observatory nurse about it later he said of course he always watched the sunset. 'Why else work there, after all?'

So when we went for dinner after that with the small group of staff and visitors left for the night on the Pic it really had the feeling of a monastery, an enclosed community dedicated to one task. Observing rather than praying. It was easy to understand why so many Pyrenean voyagers resorted to spiritual metaphor to describe their experience.

Dinner was substantial, simple and very good, if not as sumptuous as that offered to Count Russell by General Nansouty. We helped ourselves from a large cauldron of traditional gascon *garbure*, a hearty soup complete with cabbage and chunks of bacon. Then the cook whipped up mushroom omelettes, served with macaroni cheese, and followed by slices of apple tart or compote. They maintain supplies for a week, in case of bad weather. It was a bit like a space station or an Antarctica base. Everyone looked after themselves and cleared dishes away afterwards. Each table had its jug of red wine and carafe of water, but no-one drank more than a glass of wine. Most were off to work, after all. Conversation was all shop, ranging from the recent discovery of another planet to the best place to see the aurora borealis.

There were other visitors, a lab inspector from Paris, and two English students. Sandra Jeffers was a Scottish astronomy PhD student, tall, confident, with a cap of smooth blond hair. Later she showed me the weather station she was checking on the Internet, the Dundee Receiving Station. Her passion for the stars had started at home with a telescope. 'When you first see Venus or the rings of Saturn through a telescope you don't forget it,' she said in a soft Scottish lilt.

James Silvester, a student of astrophysics from the University of Hertfordshire, agreed, and when I picked up his *Astronomy Now* magazine to look at the price of telescopes, advised me to start with a good pair of binoculars. 'A decent telescope will cost at least three hundred pounds,' he explained. I was intrigued by articles like 'Beat Bino hand tremble,' a picture gallery of planets and a cover story on 'How to see the Northern Lights'.

Now the sun gazers turned to star watching, as the sky, which had clouded over again, cleared briefly. We bundled up and went back outside, clambering round the cupola terraces, clinging to railings and crunching through thick pure snow. I have never seen such clean snow. It was very cold, minus 10 degrees, with a harsh wind whipping the snow up into the air. Icicles hung from the low roof of the observatory building, and clouds brushed past the tall antenna and across the moon. The stars appeared and the moon illuminated the peaks. It was like standing on the roof of the world. I saw the view just as Russell did: 'The moon came over the horizon, there was no cloud, and from the Atlantic to the Mediterranean, my eyes saw all the chain of the Pyrenees, all the snow and ice, separated from land by a zone of shadows. The moon rendered everything deathly pale, and the legions of silvery mountains seemed to be floating in the night.'

Les amateurs took me for a closer look at the moon, sliding open a segment of the roof of the cupola, beyond which I could see deep sky and stars and then the moon itself. Michel clambered about on a stepladder, manually adjusting two telescopes. Peering through one I could see the entire globe of the moon, hanging like a pale luminous Christmas tree bauble, through the other a closer view of the curve of the globe with the craters clearly visible. You would believe you could see a man on the moon.

Leaving them to their night shift I retired, taking a shower in water that had been pumped up from Lac d'Oncet. Sunrise was at 8.10 a.m., I was informed. They knew exactly, of course. I stealthily opened the window of my room onto the icy kingdom of snow beyond. No doors or windows seemed to be locked. If you want to open a window onto a world of nothing but ice and snow you can. I guess there is not much risk of burglary at 2877 metres. I remembered a story of one of the astronomes (I can't resist thinking of astrognomes) who always slept with the window wide open and no heating. By morning as much as five cubic metres of snow had sometimes drifted into his room.

Russell's night went as follows: 'Slept until 3 a.m. Suddenly awoken by the moon, passing in front of my window. What a spectacle prepared for me, almost super-natural, a thousand colossi of snow, not a breath of wind, not a cloud, not a noise, all the world slept. I woke before the dawn, to be sure to see the sunrise, what a morning, it was freezing, and as clear as Norway, the horizon limpid, the sun fired all the chain as it appeared and in one second three hundred kilometres of deathly-white frozen peaks were red as rubies. It was a morning to give the saints nostalgia for the earth. The General was as enthusiastic as me. He even let his pipe go out, a rare event!' Then Russell had two breakfasts ('one is so hungry at these heights') and descended.

I too spent most of the night in anticipation of the dawn and was rewarded with an experience to rival Russell's, from the first glimmer of light silhouetting the eastern horizon of peaks. If I were ever to enter for the Turner Prize it would be with a sunrise video, I thought. A work of complete originality that was different every time. Turner would have approved, and how after all could you paint a phenomenon of constantly shifting colours? This was a dawn of baroque splendour, beginning with a single strip of pure gold along the horizon of the hills, splitting the darkness like a ripe fruit, followed by purple and dove grey.

A weird antique jade came after and finally shades of rose and apricot heralded the sun itself. Full daylight seemed dull by comparison, even if it was my birthday.

The weather had remained unpredictable and a security man with a walkie-talkie was rounding up everyone who was hoping to leave that day, including me. Gerard too was about to descend to his life and family in Tarbes and was tumbling floppy discs into a briefcase with a distracted air as if he found it hard to return to earth. When I asked him if it was difficult to spend his life like this he said, 'It's like being a mariner or a fisherman. It goes with the job.' As we descended in the cable car he pointed out the steep winding path up to the Pic which Nansouty had climbed every day to take his measurements before the observatory was completed. Before the proud summit of the Pic du Midi was harnessed. As we looked at the buildings, the antennae, cables, all the essential engineering, Gerard confided, ' To be honest, I think Russell hated it all. It was one of the reasons he was determined he would never construct any building on Vignemale.'

16

Little Paris of the south

'Pau: the Hub of the Sporting World.'
New York Herald Tribune

Later that autumn, after the first snows had gilded the mountain tops, I found myself again in Pau, on the Pont du XIV Juillet, formerly the Pont du Jurançon, which spans the Gave de Pau just below the chateau. It was one of Russell's favourite places. Here he liked to stroll, especially when Pau was warm and still, to catch any breath of air the river could offer. A gentle breeze lifted the air just as Henry promised, and in the shallow clear water flowing below darted shadowy silvery trout. He liked an evening promenade to see the sunset, and I too was rewarded with a symphony of colour, layers of pink, copper, emerald, amethyst and silver. It needed Henry's words to do it justice or a Gauguin to paint it. The bridge was just a few steps down from his house. When he wasn't climbing mountains Henry Russell spent most of his time in Pau with his family, at number 14 rue Marca, with the chateau to the east and the horizon of the Pyrenees to the south.

The houses on rue Marca, which runs steeply down to the Gave de Pau, are classic French town houses with stables and an open courtyard on the ground floor, accessed by a large door into an arched passage. The main living accommodation is on the first floor, with tall salon windows and ornate ironwork balconies.

Number 14 has a plaque to Henry Russell, and I had visited it once before on my tour of Pau with the enterprising Paul Mirat. He had rung the doorbell of an acquaintance with an apartment on the third floor, in order for me to see Henry's view of the Pyrenees. His friend was entirely charming about this interruption and turned out to be Jean-Jacques Camarra, a bear specialist, engaged in the reintroduction of bears to the Pyrenees. 'If a bear kills a sheep they call me!' he explained brightly. He allowed me to climb right up to the roof terrace, from where I could see the chateau, the roofs of Pau, the chimney pots, and best of all Henry's splendid view of the Pyrenees.

The house is U-shaped with the middle of the U facing south towards the Pyrenees. The courtyard is shaded by a large palm tree reaching almost to the first floor, where there is a long sun-drenched balcony running the length of the building. Here Henry liked to sit and write at a little table, or simply stroll and smoke a cigar and contemplate his view.

This time I rang the bell of number 12, the apartment of Didier Lacaze, to whom everyone had referred me when I asked about Russell in Pau. He had been working on a biography for many years, the second biographer I had met. '*Il adore Russell*,' everybody said, 'he even looks like him.' Not only did he live in the house next door to Russell, he had also spent twenty-five summers on Vignemale, looking after the refuge there. He had published a number of articles about Russell and edited a collection of historical accounts of climbs of Vignemale (attributing the first *ascension* to Gentleman Jack, I was pleased to note).

Lacaze welcomed me into an apartment lined with wooden shelves and crammed with books. Engravings and paintings of the Pyrenees hung on the walls. On a highly polished round table were an inlaid box, a leather blotter, pens and letter openers. Opera played softly. Long French windows looked across to a newly planted park. Lacaze grumbled ruefully about his view. 'I bought the apartment partly because it looked out onto a park of mature planes but now they have all been cut down!'

He offered tea and sat me down on a low sofa in front of the fireplace. A large black labrador settled himself beside me, resting his head so firmly on my leg it was impossible to move. Lacaze brought tea in delicate white and gold porcelain English teacups, and folded his long legs into a chair beside the fire, a small portrait of Russell on the shelf beside him. Lacaze was also very tall, with a distinguished patrician air, accentuated when he lit his pipe and puffed thoughtfully. He smiled when I suggested he was in the perfect location to write about Russell. 'Well, I admire him very much, and I did buy this house because I knew he had lived next door. What I had not realized was that his brother Frank actually lived in this apartment, at number 12.'

The Russells, he explained, spent most of their life in Pau. 'But they only ever rented, and had no property of their own. They were nomads, a particular breed of aristocrat with connections and relations everywhere. They came to Pau because Mme Mère (as Russell's mother was always known) had relations here, and she was content to stay in the region, being well connected and of a respected family.'

They remained a close family and Henry seems to have

been a model son, devoted to Mme Mère, especially after his father died in 1875. He looked after her solicitously until she died in 1892, only fifteen years before Henry himself. After his father's death he became head of the family, and was a very benign paterfamilias by all accounts. Frank's son Maurice recalled the relationship between Henry and his mother for a centenary tribute to Russell. 'It was very harmonious. At family dinners after a serious conversation they would suddenly break into jokes and teasing, with Henry making faces, until everybody was laughing. It was hard to know who was the most childish.'

Russell had simple tastes. 'The family were not at all materialistic,' Lacaze observed. Russell's visitors describe a plain, almost austere room, 'like a monk's cell', adorned with photographs of mountains, including Everest and Kangchenjunga in the Himalaya, as well as the Pyrenees. There were a few cherished souvenirs from his travels in Asia: Chinese artefacts like the porcelain jars he had shipped back via Moscow, Mongolian trinkets, perhaps a long silver Mongol pipe and a quartz snuff bottle, or carved Indian boxes; certainly one of the stones he had taken from the great Wall of China. The most important object in the room was his violoncello, a Gagliano of particular grace, noted for its warm deep sound. (An example from 1760 was for sale recently at $200,000.) It stood always beside the music stand in the corner.

Music was the key to Russell's existence outside the mountains. He believed music to be superior to all other art forms, and was passionate about the work of Chopin and Rossini. 'No other art creates emotions as sweet or intense. Music alone is the most mysterious and divine of all the arts.' He was an accomplished cello player, and playing and listening to music gave him the same profound happiness, the same chance to experience the sublime, as climbing mountains. He wanted to tune himself into nature, tune into the vibrations of the world. Comparing climbs in winter and summer, he said, 'was like comparing a funeral march of Beethoven with the angelic melodies of Mozart'.

Among the many legends about him was that he liked to take his cello to the top of Vignemale to play to the spheres, but he always laughed when asked if this was true, explaining that the transport and the weather would ruin the instrument. 'I sometimes dreamed of taking it with me, but it is heavy and very fragile, and all in all, I always decide at the last moment to replace it with a leg of mutton. So much more practical.'

He was always surrounded by books, too, travel books and adventure stories as well as poetry. He wrote at a small wooden table, with a quill pen and a crystal ink pot with a gold stopper, and dried his writing with sand from the Maladetta kept in a porcelain container. A box of cards headed 'Count Russell' was always to hand. His correspondence was enormous, with both English and French friends. He also wrote notes on all his excursions, regular articles for a range of publications, including the bulletin of the Société Ramond, the Journal of the Club Alpin Français, the *Pau Gazette*, the *Journal des Etrangers*, and the *Alpine Journal*. 'He seems to have sometimes regretted his lack of career,' said Lacaze, when we discussed Henry's writing, 'but he was always occupied.'

He wrote books in both French and English. After the first publication of his travels to America in 1858, he had published his *Travels in the Far East* in 1864. In 1866 he published his *Grands Ascensions*, and then several small guides in English, *A Fortnight in the Pyrenees* (Pau, 1868), *Pau and the Pyrenees*, published in London in 1871, and *Biarritz and the Basque Countries*, published by Stanfords in 1873. The English guides are written in a good clear style, though he apologizes for his inadequate English, but they bear no comparison to the high-flown literary style of his masterpiece, *Souvenirs d'un Montagnard*. This was first published in 1878, but Russell was not satisfied with it. He hated the chronological order in which it was presented, and chucked all the copies he could find off the bridge in Pau. It is now very rare. A second edition was published ten years later and became bedside reading for a generation of Pyrenean mountaineers, but Russell never achieved the literary recognition he would have liked. Being in the provinces didn't help. 'He was too far from Paris to be part of a literary scene,' explained Lacaze. 'And he also had a tendency to overwrite, reworking material over again, adding details and adjectives.'

Russell, nicknamed 'Sir Henri Russell Killow-Mètre', was a familiar figure in Pau, striding across the Place Royale with his long legs and pointed beard, and pausing to gaze with limpid blue eyes on the Pyrenees. Andrée Martignon, the daughter of Czerniewski, the church organist with whom he often played music, recalled meeting le Grand Russell at her father's house when she was a little girl. 'I found him sitting in an armchair facing a large photo of Vignemale, which he had inscribed to my father "a cordial souvenir de l'Ermite du Vignemale". As he spoke his eyes followed the form of the glacier, and I was fascinated by his distant gaze, the gaze of the eternal traveller, and by his quiet voice, and his gentlemanly manners. He had a high buttoned jacket like an artist, black and white checked trousers, a red cravat, a handkerchief in his pocket. As he left he gently stroked my hair.' After Russell left she describes climbing on the sofa to look more closely at the photo of his mountain, and later when the evening coloured the distant peaks in a violet haze, she tried to imagine his life up there on the summit, 'the mysterious peaks where I knew he loved to live'.

I asked Lacaze about Russell's reputation. 'In Pau he was known as the one who walked around the world, and viewed right from the beginning as eccentric,' he said. 'He was already a legend, even before he began climbing mountains alone or building villas on the summits.' Letters addressed to l'Ermite de Vignemale, Pau, were always delivered by La Poste.

In his dress, even in the mountains, he was always fastidious. In Pau he favoured *le look country gent* of checked tweed trousers and jackets, topped off with a bowler hat. It is sad one can only look at black and white photos of him because his main eccentricity was a passion for flamboyant colours acquired on his travels in India, and he always sported a cravat and pocket handkerchief of brilliant blue, cerise or purple. He once presented his nephew Maurice, about to go to college, with three silk cravats, of red, pink and azure blue.

A preference for bright colours is hardly evidence of homosexuality, but for many reasons I had often wondered about Russell. He did not marry, though neither did his brother Ferdinand, after both were prevented by parental pressure from marrying when they were young. Russell had many intimate relationships with other men, but that was typical of the time, when women were for marrying, not friendship. Deep emotional commitment was often more likely to be found with male peers with shared interests and friendships forged through mutual experience of danger. But Russell writes with such candour of the pleasure of his nights out in the mountains with Packe, it is hard to believe they could have been anything but innocent. One could certainly argue with Freud, who was yet to come, that his mountain climbing was a sublimation of his sexuality. When I describe Russell to my psychoanalyst friends, however, his passion for the mountain, and the way he penetrated it with caves, they chuckle knowingly at the metaphors. It was not a subject easily broached with many Russell fans or family.

Tentatively I enquired if Lacaze thought Russell was homosexual. He shook his head. 'Any possible evidence has been destroyed,' he said sadly. 'After he died his brother Frank, who was a very conventional person, destroyed many letters and journals. They were thrown into the Gave or burnt in this fireplace.' We both looked rather regretfully at the fireplace, imagining a little heap of ashes which might have told us so much more about our quarry. Such destruction suggests there may have been something the family wished to hide. Lacaze added, 'The place they do believe he was homosexual is Gavarnie, from the stories of the guides.' Many mountaineers established intimate relationships with their guides, with whom they spent time in difficult circumstances, sharing cramped accommodation and dangers for days at a time. Physical intimacy would be hardly surprising, though it was never publicly spoken of.

If he was homosexual, does it matter? It was obviously not the most important thing about him, and he may have never or rarely expressed his sexual inclinations, but it is likely to have affected his character and his behaviour and thus is relevant. Being unmarried in such a society immediately marginalized someone. Lacaze pointed out, 'Because he was single, he was not in a position to receive guests formally. Perhaps that was one reason why he built the *grottes*, where he could be At Home for his friends.' It is highly unlikely that Russell would have pursued his mountain explorations to such an ultimate extent had he been conventionally married with children.

Before I took my leave of Didier Lacaze I asked him what interested him most about Russell. 'He is most intriguing to me seen within the historical context of the nineteenth century. The way he shifted from being French to English, reflects the shift of power and philosophy of the century.' It was a shift from French Enlightenment and Revolution to Victorian industrialization and power, a move from the idealistic to the pragmatic that of course eventually left romantics like Russell communing with nature on mountain tops, far behind.

I think it must have been a deliberate choice on Russell's part to embrace the English side of his dual nationality. For someone considered as eccentric as Russell, the English label gave him more freedom to indulge his eccentricity. The English were supposed to be eccentric, and any odd behaviour was thus legitimized, or at least permitted. Thus he could live as he wished, and escape the restraints and strictures of conventional, highly regulated French society.

Society in Pau was increasingly colonized by English and Americans. By the 1870s the attractions of Pau had shifted, and life was totally dominated by a sporting calendar in which Russell undoubtedly participated at least socially, a busy round of hunt balls and golf and polo events. Every possible kind of sport was pursued: hunting, polo, golf, cricket, tennis and pigeon shooting. A hippodrome was opened in 1842. (It is still there and twinned with the Cheltenham hippodrome.) Sydney Clarkson, proprietor of the London Pharmacy, even opened a skating rink.

'Pau was the hub of the sporting world,' exclaimed Paul Mirat, as he conducted me on another whistle-stop tour of his town in his battered little car with its incongruous 'Live free or die' sticker from New Hampshire. It felt like a ride on the dodgems as we narrowly avoided collisions and routinely abused other drivers. In between gesticulating fiercely at a driver with the temerity to overtake him, he explained, 'There was a column called that about the sporting life of Pau in the *New York Herald Tribune*. James Gordon Bennett started it.'

'*The* James Gordon Bennett?' I enquired. 'Who sent Stanley to Africa in search of Dr Livingstone? And bought a waiter in Monte Carlo a restaurant because he served him a decent mutton chop?'

'The very chap,' confirmed Mirat. 'Pau was full of Americans in those days.' The names were a roll call of highly respected American families from Boston, New York, Philadelphia and New Orleans: the Winthrops of aviation fame, the Lawrences of Sarah Lawrence college, the Huttons as in Barbara Hutton, the Woolworths heiress; the Ridgways and Monroes, Philadelphia bankers, the Peabodys, the Tiffanys, the Goulds, Kings, Johnstons and Princes.

Back in the mid-nineteenth century they were still little more than robber barons, grown rich from the railroads and Chicago stockyards. They headed to Europe in search of respectability and aristocratic titles to marry, seeking out enclaves, like Pau and the Riviera, already colonized by the British, hoping a bit of class might rub off as they mingled in a Belle Epoque world of Balkan monarchs, Russian princes, monocled English army officers and gold and diamond barons from South Africa.

If they could combine mama's search for noble titles for her daughters with pa's passion for sport, and horses in particular, all the better. Pau answered very well. Though their ignorance of correct behaviour caused a few sneers, their largesse compensated. They always entertained lavishly, with copious food and wine, and their extravagance was legendary. Most outrageous were the Hutton girls, Jenny and Annie, who hunted like Amazons during the day and partied as enthusiastically at night. (Indiscreet lady's maids told of white satin lingerie hiding a multitude of bruises.) The Huttons were bankers and railroad magnates who bought an enormous villa with twelve hectares of land, vast stables, forty horses and as many servants. Despite their wealth the house was chaotic; dinner was always late, because the servants were still in the vineyards, or the butler was dead drunk under the table. Their father, Major Hutton, was a great devotee of the baccarat table at the Cercle Anglais. When he was old he arrived in a wheelchair, but he always wore gloves to play since he had been told in his youth he was never to touch cards.

The Lawrence family, in business in Boston, were like characters in a Henry James novel, marrying off daughters and nieces to English peers – Lord Vernon, and Sir Gordon Cummings, a close friend of the Prince of Wales –

and a French nobleman, the Marquis de Breteuil. The marriages accomplished, Mrs Lawrence sold off the town house they owned in Pau (now the Banque de France on the Boulevard des Pyrénées) with all its contents. Antique dealers from Paris, London and New York descended to buy up the art, antiques, gold and jewellery which had served their purpose.

Others were more loyal to Pau. The father of the Phelps family loved the climate so much that in his will he decreed that his daughter would lose all her rights to his fortune if she ever returned to live in the terrible climate of New York. (A New York tribunal annulled his will as immoral.)

As we drove round the fancier quartiers of Pau, Trespoey and the Allées de Morlaas, we peered through the gates of a variety of villas, some still sumptuous like the Villa Nirvana, with its Oriental excrescences, and the Villa Jouvence, where the Brooke family had lived, a large mansion surrounded by a vast park, still strictly guarded. But many are now sadly dilapidated, with ivy growing over stately portals, and broken windows in once grand conservatories. One villa was about to be turned into a hotel and we were shown round by the proprietor, admiring the original woodwork and marquetry, the art nouveau staircase and marble bathrooms, and nodding nervously to the current incumbents, a family of squatters, camped out on old velvet sofas in a dusty salon.

We went to see the headquarters of the Pau Hunt, and were greeted by an enclosure of howling hunting dogs. The kennels had been bequeathed to the Hunt by the Torrance family, explained Mirat, 'in memory of their son who was killed in a steeplechase'. They are still used today, albeit by a Hunt that is entirely French, not least including Mirat himself. I dutifully admired photographs of red-coated horsemen leaping fences and triumphantly brandishing foxes' tails. The Hunt, which developed from Wellington's first forays, was one of the most popular sports in nineteenth-century Pau, and the runs were named nostalgically: Old England, and the Hill District, the Home Circuit, and even Haut and Bas Leicestershire.

Decent horses had to be brought from England, and the béarnais seemed to have little idea of how to hunt a fox; they had hunted stag and wild boar for centuries and were pleased to see a reduction of foxes, but could not understand breeding them deliberately to be hunted. Then in 1840 a proper hunt was established by Sir Henry Oxenden, who became the first Master of the Pau hounds.

Unfortunately he did not last long, because when his wife died he returned in grief to England, having ordered all the horses to be killed and fed to the hounds. But a wily Frenchman saved a few hounds and the hunt went on. 'If hunting is banned in England, you could invite Prince Charles to Pau,' I offered.

'So where did James Gordon Bennett fit in?' I enquired. Mirat told me the tale, which stemmed from a crisis with the Pau Hunt. In 1879 a problem arose when the Comte de Bari, brother of the last king of Naples, arrived in Pau with his own team of hounds and began to hunt on the same land as the Pau Hunt, wearing it out and annoying the peasants (who were used to being suitably compensated for damage to their land and crops). The British threatened to go to Biarritz to hunt instead and the very existence of the Pau Hunt was in jeopardy.

American members came up with an idea. Send for

James Gordon Bennett, famously rich proprietor of the *New York Herald Tribune*, then the most powerful newspaper in the United States and the only one with a European edition at that time. Gordon Bennett was the prototypical crazy American, excessive, extravagant and with no regard for conventions. He had come to France in 1877 after leaving the USA in disgrace – he had been engaged to a respectable beauty but at a family New Year party in Manhattan, with drinks served by an English butler, Bennett had got completely drunk and pissed in the fireplace. He was thrown out, horsewhipped by the lady's brother, then challenged to a duel. He left for Paris soon after, where he spent his fortune at Maxims and the Ritz, and bought himself property and a magnificent yacht on the Riviera complete with a Jacuzzi and a ship's cow. He was an enthusiastic horseman, given on occasion to tearing off his clothes and driving his coach and horses at high speed with only a cigar in his mouth. His scandalous reputation lives on in the incredulous expression, 'Gordon Bennett!'

He arrived in Pau by express train in November 1880, installed himself in the Hôtel de France and persuaded the Comte de Bari to amalgamate the two hunts. At a special meeting of the Cercle Anglais he had himself confirmed as Master of the Pau Hunt. He took upon himself all the expenses of the Hunt and celebrated with a magnificent meet of a hundred carriages and a hundred and fifty riders. He drove the coach of the vanquished Comte de Bari himself (clothed – one assumes. It was a foggy November day). Bennett returned to Pau the following year and thereafter the Hunt mastership was dominated by Americans. A riding school was established to improve standards, but the

English were not allowed to attend since it was intended for the improvement of foreigners.

The most prominent American to be Master of the Pau Hunt was Frederick Henry Prince, owner of the Chicago stockyards and several railroad companies. He spent a fortune on it. To be a member of the Pau Hunt in those days cost about 8000 francs a year. By comparison a teacher then was paid about 1800 francs a year. Prince was a keen sportsman, rarely out of the saddle – he even organized dinners on horseback, and was always brandishing a riding crop. He was once brought to court for banging his groom over the head with a polo mallet. His wife, daughter of the mayor of Boston, was a timid woman whom he never permitted to handle money in any form lest she become infected. She was so paranoid about germs that she never spent two nights running in the same bedroom, and slept in an oversized child's cradle, which was disinfected every evening. When she stayed at the Ritz in Paris she brought her own clean curtains to drape the walls.

Their villa in Pau was magnificent, with a table to seat fifty, lots of crystal chandeliers, and woodwork purchased from a chateau in Gascony which had belonged to an equerry of Louis XIII. Such munificence was to no avail when they came to entertain the Prince of Wales; they laid on a sumptuous banquet for the entire Pau colony, with the finest food and wine. The Prince of Wales, though, preferred beer, and a hasty sortie had to be made to a nearby bistro for the humble beverage.

Prince's son, Norman, went on to distinguish himself in the First World War, forming the Escadrille La Fayette, a American squadron of armed planes flown by volunteer Americans. He was killed in 1916. There is a statue of him in St Patrick's Cathedral, New York.

The apogee of American life in Pau was the visit of General Grant, hero of the American Civil War and former president of the United States, as part of his European tour in 1878. The extravagant menu for the banquet in his honour was typical of the time: shrimp soup, followed by hors d'oeuvres, turbot, *filet de boeuf béarnais* and mashed potatoes, Toulouse chicken and chestnuts, York ham with spinach, truffled pheasant, flambéed woodcock on toast, Russian salad. Desserts included Vicksburg ice pudding, ice rice, vanilla slices and baskets of fruit. Drinks included Pommery and Roederer champagne, Châteaux Margaux and Lafitte, amontillado sherry and Harvey's Bristol Milk for the English.

The grand event was completed by a toast to the President of the French Republic and a rousing chorus of 'God Save the Queen' followed by 'For He's a Jolly Good Fellow'. The only person not invited was Mary Todd Lincoln, the widow of Abraham Lincoln, who stayed in Pau for her health between the years 1876 and 1880 but had apparently rather disapproved of the way General Grant conducted the campaign during the American Civil War. She called him a butcher and a fool.

Americans thus began to dominate both the sporting world and the social life of Pau, rather to the disdain of the English, who by then were beginning to slip off to Biarritz and the Riviera. Pau's popularity with Americans was confirmed by Bostonian descendant of the Pilgrim Fathers, Edwin Asa Dix, who published *A Midsummer Drive Through the Pyrenees* in 1891, after a Grand Tour of Europe. He called the Pyrenees 'one of the most beautiful gardens of Europe', compared Pau to Menton and Nice, and eulogized the social life of Pau as 'the little Paris of the south', with its aristocrats, great fortunes, parties, balls, dinners, theatres and churches. He compared the view from Pau to the view of the Eternal City in *The Pilgrim's Progress* (and to the Adirondacks). The fact that he was staying at the Grand Hôtel Gassion, then one of Europe's most luxurious hotels, probably assisted his spiritual response.

To complete my visit to Pau I was honoured with an invitation to dine at the Cercle Anglais, once the most prestigious of the English clubs. It began life in the 1840s in the Hôtel de France as a reading room for English, French and Spanish papers and evolved into a literary salon which to begin with was open to all nationalities, even French. When the Hôtel de France expanded to accommodate the increasing number of visitors to Pau, a whole new clubhouse was built, with a grand courtyard for carriages to turn, and a wrought iron balcony the length of the west façade overlooking the Place Royale.

By the 1870s the Cercle, modelled on London gentlemen's clubs, had become much more exclusive, using the traditional system of voting by black and white balls, so that a number of black balls would exclude a candidate. There were only a hundred members and like the golf club it was restricted to English and Americans, typical of the increasing snobbishness of the social life of Pau.

The clubhouse was designed by an English architect and magnificently appointed, with much of the decoration imported from England: brass plates on the doors made by Archibald and Smith of Leicester Square and cut glass knobs on the banisters. There were twelve new gaming tables of wood and red and white marble, a wood-panelled bar with white marble top, tall-backed armchairs and red plush sofas, divans of black leather and green velvet, English beds, linen and pillows. There were Royal Worcester ewers and basins for the eight bedrooms, all with the names of peaks of the Pyrenees. In the entrance hall was a wall clock with a brass pendulum, a great brass lantern, and dominating all a white marble bust of Queen Victoria on a pedestal.

The Cercle also imported a barman, Peter Mackintosh, from Glasgow, who had started in London at the Travellers' Club as a boot black at age thirteen. He was famous for making the best sherry-cobblers in London, and was always called Mac by the English. When necessary he would escort a tipsy member to his carriage and give discreet instructions to his coachman. They even had an English housekeeper for a few weeks, Mrs Haines, who came armed with *Mrs Beeton's Book of Household Management*, but after criticizing Mac she was soon shown the door.

The bar, with its high-backed sofa, was where members liked to come direct from the chase for a pipe and a brandy and soda. The walls were soon covered with caricatures of the members of the Cercle and the Hunt. Less popular were the temperance rooms, as the reading and writing rooms were dubbed by a smoking and drinking guest who had never entered either. The reading room, with its log fires and Persian rugs, usually accommodated a few snoozing members, but the writing room with its Regency desks and headed stationery was very little used.

As the style of visitor to Pau changed, the number of invalids declined and the sportsmen increased, the club took on an increasingly sporty air, with antlers and fox heads festooning the walls, and a glass case with a stuffed salmon from the Gave. As more and more Americans came to Pau, bourbon made its appearance at the bar and gin rummy in the card room. The baccarat room was taken over for poker and blackjack, while the old colonels with their military moustaches muttered about brash new-comers in the smoking room.

After the Second World War, when most of the British and American colony had disappeared, the club moved for a while to a salon in the Hôtel Gassion, and finally admitted women members. And in 2002 they admitted me. They had found new accommodation in the Villa Lawrence at the heart of Pau, a small chateau with Dutch gables in a large park. It was originally built by Pierre Schlumberger, a Protestant minister from Alsace who came to take care of his sick daughter and to preach the gospel. He was joined there in 1850 by John Nelson Darby, the founder of the Plymouth Brethren, a Calvinistic Protestant sect who believed in the priesthood of all believers. They had quite an impact in Béarn, apart from the Vallée d'Aspe, where the local priest sat on the bridge and refused to let them pass.

The villa was subsequently bought in 1893 by the Lawrences to accommodate their mentally handicapped son. Despite the park surrounding the chateau, planted with oaks, cedars, magnolias and rhododendrons, his screams could still be heard, and until the 1930s he was occasionally to be seen walking with his nurse, wearing a panama hat and a flower in his buttonhole.

My invitation was a rare privilege since usually the dinners are reserved for men only. Sometimes it seemed Pau was taking its role of upholding English tradition a little too seriously. When I arrived the men were putting on a very creditable performance as English gentlemen, drinking whisky, sitting on old leather sofas, surrounded by decapitated animal heads on the walls. It was a pity none of them could actually speak English, except for the talented Paul Mirat, who explained to me that they had only recently moved to the building. Deers' antlers leaned against the walls waiting to be hung, and boxes of books stood half unpacked, spilling treasures, including works by Russell inscribed 'Aux membres du Cercle'. But already on the walls were engravings and cartoons of the Pau Hunt, along with portraits of the Queen and Prince Philip, and a marriage photo of the ill-fated Charles and Diana. A polished mahogany cabinet held the trophies of the Hunt, while the bust of poor Queen Victoria was still in a corner waiting to be allotted her place.

As we dined on cold *rosbif* I talked to one or two terrifyingly elegant French women with perfect coiffures and heavy gold jewellery, and a charming gynaecologist who expressed great interest in Russell, and offered to send me material from his own archives. The other guests seemed nonplussed at the presence of a real English person at the Cercle Anglais, so I was rather relieved to meet two other English couples also invited for the first time. Here was the new wave of English invaders to Pau. Both couples owned chateaux in the environs of the town.

Rory Constant, a tall gentle fellow with a dark beard, told me his great-grandfather had fought with Wellington in the Béarn. His wife, Mini, a delicate blonde who grew up in South Africa, was a Master of Wine and they planned to start offering wine courses in their fourteenth-century chateau.

The other couple were English furniture maker Edward Rich and his German wife, Angelika, a marquetry specialist. They invited me to lunch the next day in the huge eighteenth-century chateau where they have set up shop just outside Oloron-Sainte-Marie, a sweet little town with a splendid Romanesque church, close to the mountains. They bought the chateau in 1998 from the local council, who had tried to rescue it, fixed the roof and run out of money. 'It was in ruins,' said Edward. 'A shepherd lived in the barn and kept his sheep in the dining room.' Edward's woodwork skills have restored wooden panelling, added magnificent wooden doors and created workshops and modern bedrooms and bathrooms as settings for his original modern furniture. Some of their restoration decisions have been radical, such as installing plate glass in original stone window frames. 'There are over a hundred windows,' said Edward. 'Count 'em. And they were all broken.'

We ate lunch in a vast frescoed dining room, sampling the *foie gras* they had made themselves with French friends. 'When we were invited to join them – it was an annual event – ' said Angelika, 'we turned up in immaculate white aprons, and found them all in old ski suits, it was so messy.' The *foie gras* was divine, and seemed to me a very worthy occupation for newly imported Brits to Béarn, if as politically incorrect as fox hunting.

17

A man for all seasons

'The Alps were for athletes and warriors, the Pyrenees were more svelte and delicate. The Alps astonished, the Pyrenees seduced. The Pyrenees were for artists and poets. The Alps inspired terror, the Pyrenees tenderness. The Alps represent man, the Pyrenees woman. I love the woman best.'

Henry Russell

Russell felt both English and French and loved both countries with the same deep attachment, fervently hoping for their continuing friendship. Happily there were no further hostilities between France and England after Napoleon was vanquished at the battle of Waterloo in 1815. Russell was very conscious of the profound differences between them, however; English food was *le plum pudding* versus *omelette sucrée* and English conversation *rosbif* versus champagne. In a lengthy and tedious treatise on the benefits of having an aristocracy, published in 1871 when the French had just rid themselves of their last Emperor, Napoleon III (who went to live in Chislehurst), and launched the Third Republic, Russell wrote that the English were fundamentally conservative with a universal and profound respect for authority. In France, he opined, there was a complete absence of the same sentiment. As a youth he had opted for French nationality instead of

British in order to join the merchant marine; which meant he was called up in 1870 to spend a few fruitless days marching up and down with a bayonet in the army training ground of Pau.

He made regular visits to England, and to Ireland to visit his estates and troublesome tenants. He travelled around the country; several pieces in the *Souvenirs* have English datelines like Bournemouth and Penzance, where he may have visited the family of his good friend, Maxwell Lyte, who after Henry Lyte's death had stayed on in Berry Head House, high on the cliffs overlooking Torbay in South Devon. (It is now a country hotel.) He records a visit to Gloucester cathedral, and went climbing in the Malvern Hills. 'All England is green,' he exclaimed.

London in those days, however, was Sherlock Holmes's territory, all hansom cabs and pea-soupers. He describes arriving from Boulogne by packet steamer up the Thames, a river 'so dirty and powerful it seemed to carry all the treasures and mud in the universe. No-one who has not seen this spectacle, so desolate and so grand, can have the least idea of England.' He peered through a crepuscular yellow cloud to the banks of the river where 'a type of sun appeared vaguely through the mist', to see a forest of masts, and smoke escaping from tall grey chimneys. 'And this was the month of August!'

Sometimes, according to him, the fog even came indoors: 'I will never forget a concert in St James's Hall where the great pianist Von Bülow was playing. The room was invaded by intense fog. The great artist and his piano disappeared completely, and Liszt's Polonaise Héroique (one of his stormiest pieces) had no more effect than a sonnet. The fog completely killed the sound.' He compared it to the silence climbing to the Lac de Gaube in dense mist. After one four-month sojourn in 'the multi-coloured fog' of the capital he was heartily glad to return to the Pyrenees.

He was very proud of his membership of the Alpine Club, though, and despite the London weather attended the meetings when he was in town, then held in the club rooms in St Martin's Place, near the Garrick theatre. From the mid-1850s on, when the railways had reached Switzerland, the Alps were all the rage, and were swarming with English, both climbers and tourists. The highest peaks yielded rapidly to a new generation of explorers, most of them British, who called it the Golden Age of Mountaineering.

The Alpine Club was formed in 1857 and membership was originally restricted to those who had climbed a mountain 13,000 feet (4000 metres) high, but eventually broadened to include those who had contributed to a knowledge of mountains through art or literature. These included John Ruskin and also Matthew Arnold, who though he had only a passing interest declared, 'Everyone should see the Alps once, to know what they are.' Macho explorer Sir Richard Burton was another, his qualification being: 'General travel; mountain ranges in all parts of the world'; and Thomas Atkinson, a bricklayer's labourer and bigamist, who travelled across Central Asia for the Tsar.

Twice a year, winter and summer, they held Club dinners. At a typically jolly affair at The Castle, Richmond, novelist Anthony Trollope said that in Washington he had been asked whether it was true that there existed an Englishmen's club that held its meetings on the summits of the Alps. 'In my anxiety to support the credit of my country, I have transgressed the limits of veracity, but I told him what he heard was quite true.' Great cheers all round.

Russell's own philosophy of mountain climbing put him at the heart of the debate between the scientists and the aesthetes, between those who climbed for climbing's sake and those who did it for scientific purposes. Russell read and quoted Ruskin, the controversial and highly opinionated art critic. Ruskin's passion for the picturesque reached its apogee in his celebration of the Alps. Mountains for him were 'the beginning and end of all natural scenery'. He rarely climbed them himself, however, saying, 'All the best views of hills are at the bottom of them.' He preferred to look but not touch, rather like his peculiar unconsummated marriage; he once compared his wife's body to a mountain slope of dreadful ravines. 'You are like the bright-soft-swelling-lovely fields of a high glacier ... where men fall, and rise not again.' Freud understood, observing that the pyschical foundation of travelling was separation from the mother: 'All of these dark woods, narrow defiles, high grounds and deep penetrations are unconscious sexual imagery, and we are exploring a woman's body.'

I decided Ruskin may have had a point one dark early morning in winter after I had waited for the school bus with Theo. I went for a walk towards the dawn, a lemony streak just breaking on the horizon. As it grew lighter and the valley widened out my view of Canigou changed, and the craggy outline with which I was so familiar meta-morphosed into a larger mound, which, it seemed to me, resembled nothing more or less than a breast with the peak as a small but distinct pointed nipple. It was immensely comforting somehow, and I imagined the entire earth as the body beyond the breast, the earth mother of the American Indians. Perhaps it is part of the attraction of mountains that they could all resemble breasts and nipples of a variety of shapes and sizes. And then there are the deep dark secret valleys, that made poor Ruskin so anxious. What mountains do not have is any phallic symbolism whatsoever; they are far removed from the fast cars, rockets, guns and bullet trains of macho iconography. Climbing mountains is not necessarily a demonstration of power; despite all the talk of conquest perhaps it is really only a quest for the lost breast. I could love men who loved mountains.

Whatever his pyschosexual problems Ruskin's mountain worship was perfectly in tune with Russell. Ruskin's writings and drawings of the Alps had an enormous influence at the time, persuading many in that era of rapid technological and scientific development that nature, and mountains in particular, offered escape from the mundane and the key to the sublime. Though a keen geologist himself he despised those who took a predominantly scientific view of climbing, and recorded a typical encounter between the two tendencies:

'How beautiful,' I said to my companion, 'those peaks of rock rise into the heavens like promontories running out into the deep blue of some transparent ocean.'

'Ah – yes, brown, limestone – strata vertical, or nearly so, dip eight-five and a half,' replied the geologist.

The other great peak-promoter of the period was Albert Smith, who appealed to a different class of person with his travelling show in which he described his ascent of Mont Blanc, with the aid of lantern slides, songs and St Bernard dogs. It was peppered with salacious details, such as the overweight climber whose head blew off 'by reason of the rarefied air', or the possibility of seeing somewhere on the glacier 'an entire boys' school from Geneva, shut in the ice ... like strawberries in a mould of jelly'. For six years it was the most popular show in town, and a veritable Mont Blanc mania ensued; people danced the Mont Blanc Quadrille and the Chamonix Polka, and played a board game called The Ascent of Mont Blanc.

Mountaineers, like poets, were the celebrities of the period, and among them was Sir Leslie Stephen, writer and literary critic, editor of the *Dictionary of National Biography* and father of Virginia Woolf and Vanessa Bell. He was almost an exact contemporary of Russell (1832–1904), and from 1865 to 1868 was president of the Alpine Club, followed by several years as editor of the *Alpine Journal* (where he published Russell's sole contribution). More than anyone else Stephen's attitude to mountain climbing paralleled Russell's.

There were many similarities. Both were uncommonly tall; Stephen with a red straggly beard and long legs like a compass, usually clad in a long tweed coat stained yellow by ropes. He was another prodigious walker, with considerable powers of endurance. Stephen too was fond of a celebratory smoke when he had reached the summit, in his case a contemplative pipe (which Ruskin thought a sacrilege). Though he agreed with his philosophy of mountains, Stephen thought Ruskin silly, but he was as appalled as Russell by the scientists who toiled up the slopes laden with clinometers, barometers and prismatic compasses.

Like Russell, Stephen preferred to climb in contemplative silence. He liked to commune with nature, experiencing sunsets, identifying distant peaks and noting flowers and plants; his 'Sunset on Mont Blanc' Virginia Woolf considered his best piece of writing. He describes the dramatic moment when the shadow of Mont Blanc falls on the landscape: 'As we gazed we could see it move . . . for a time it seemed that there was a kind of anti-sun in the east, pouring out not light, but deep shadow as it rose . . . Would it never stop and was Mont Blanc capable of overshadowing not only the earth but the sky?'

Stephen too viewed with dismay the new generation of climbers, the growing chasm between the Alpinist of old to whom a climb meant at most a night on a mountain with the minimum of equipment and a return to a comfortable inn for dinner and conversation, and the new explorers in the Andes and Himalaya, who more nearly resembled army generals leading an army of porters in the assault on a peak.

Unlike the devout Russell, however, Stephen did not see the hand of the creator in a mountain landscape. He had been ordained as a clergyman, but rejected his Christian faith, declaring he could worship mountains if nothing else.

Stephen was at the centre of the intellectual aristocracy of Britain at that time, entertaining visitors like Henry James, Edward Burne-Jones, John Everett Millais, Robert Louis Stevenson, Rider Haggard and Sir Arthur Conan Doyle. He and Russell shared many friends in the Alpine Club, and no doubt Stephen's excellent command of French, as well as his philosophical approach to mountain climbing, would have endeared him to Russell.

It is nice to think that Russell may have visited Leslie Stephen at home at 22 Hyde Park Gate, to discuss his paper for the *Alpine Journal*, talking and smoking in the study with the three tall windows overlooking the roofs of Kensington, the groaning shelves of books, the rocking chair where Stephen wrote all his books, and the stack of rusty ice-axes and alpenstocks in the corner.

Stephen donated his old equipment to the Alpine Club, and his alpenstock is still hanging on the wall today, as is his portrait, along with other distinguished presidents of the Club. I had looked forward to spending days doing research in a wood-panelled library in Pall Mall or St James's but sadly the Alpine Club has fallen on hard times. It took several tube changes and consultations of the London A-Z to find the current premises in the back streets of Old Street, wedged between designer cafés, video art galleries and young architects who were yet to up and come.

Huge paintings of mountains were crammed into an office much too small for them and temporary shelves groaned with precious manuscripts, including several copies of Russell's books, signed to his esteemed colleagues. I leafed through the volumes of the *Alpine Journal* in its early years, finding accounts of climbs and new expeditions from the Andes to the Caucasus; from Norway and Greenland to the Rockies. Some were fascinating though by no means all – Ruskin called most mountain literature as interesting as coconut matting.

Among the obituaries, book reviews, proceedings of the Club and, chillingly, 'Accidents', there are hints on sketching in watercolours, India rubber versus paper as a material for Alpine maps, the observation of a circular rainbow and an ongoing discussion about giving names to newly discovered places: the Royal Geographical Society advised that people 'before putting forward any personal or fanciful name' should find out first if a local name existed, and 'no-one should commemorate <u>himself</u> in this manner'. Russell and Packe had clearly not observed these recommendations when they named Lac Packe and Pic Russell. Nor indeed did Captain Everest.

The Alps remained overwhelmingly the main preoccupation, the preferred place to learn the craft of mountaineering. Mont Blanc was the most popular ascent, the ur-Alp to climb, attracting such an assortment of aspirants, from hardy climbers, who brought their own ladders and ropes from England, to breezy day-trippers clad in cricketing flannels, that Murray's Guide of 1851 was led to observe: '. . . it is a somewhat remarkable fact that a large proportion of those who have made this ascent have been persons of unsound mind'. (Nothing seems to have changed; more than two hundred people die on Mont Blanc every year.)

Russell duly made one visit to the Alps, though only one. In 1867 he was invited to Switzerland by a childhood friend, another French count, and he climbed Mont Blanc, the Breithorn, and Col de l'Alpubel. He described the beautiful panorama from his villa, on the horizon 'the immense snowy curtain of the Alps, where every evening Mont Blanc was set on fire, reddening the shadows which engulfed it'.

He could not resist climbing the mountain and left Geneva by *diligence* for Chamonix, to find a hotel full of

English people, including several members of the Alpine Club, which was not at all to his taste. 'I like better to be alone, to take pleasure in nature in my own way.' After dinner he sat dreamily on his balcony with a view of Mont Blanc, 'the monarch of mountains, more livid and cold than a phantom'. Next morning he hired two guides ('at an exorbitant price') and departed for les Grands Mulets, the traditional base for approaching the summit. The heat was intense even in the shadow of the pine trees, and the path snaked up the slopes so fast that in two hours they had already climbed 1000 metres.

At Pierres Pointues (2049m) they found a chalet, beyond which the grass disappeared and only a few pines and rhododendrons remained. 'Soon stones and sterility invaded everything. We shivered and entered the ice for a day and a half . . . It is a solemn moment, even for those who are used to it, when one embarks on a glacier, to combat an element more perfidious than the waves of the sea, with a thousand abysses around you, where one false step could kill you.'

Here Russell began to feel the difference between Alpinism and Pyreneism. The glacier was like 'a capital city that an earthquake had reduced to ruins, all its palaces and columns and bridges mixed pell mell'. After a labyrinth of ice they arrived at a sinister black rock, the celebrated Grands Mulets, at over 3000 metres. Here to Russell's delight he found an *auberge*, with kitchen, beds, furniture and cosy stove, where they slept in order to make the ascent the next day. Russell's own sunset on Mont Blanc 'was strangely sad and splendid'.

He was woken by the guides at 3 a.m.; they drank warm wine, and murmured concerns about the weather, since there was a tempest raging on the summit. They donned great fur gloves and huge gaiters, and Russell was reminded of dressing for Siberia. Then they roped up, and began the climb in a line, stretched out diagonally across the snowfield, which was black and blue like metal in the dimness. 'I have never seen anything as arctic as the high gorges of the Alps,' he recalled, and when at 4 a.m. the sun rose, 'It was such a symbol of life and resurrection that you believed yourself warm.'

The weather was terrible, a cyclone of wind and hail, and at 4000 metres Henry's lungs began to suffer. Finally they were obliged to retreat in wild winds, hail and impenetrable fog. 'The cyclone of 19 July 1867 is something I'll never forget!'

They made a second attempt the next day, crawling across a crevasse on their stomachs like crocodiles. Russell found the altitude increasingly difficult. 'I felt asphyxiated and arrived at the summit like a somnambulist.' He for one was convinced of the reality of mountain sickness, and protested vehemently against those who denied its existence, who said it was simply a result of fatigue or lack of training, citing as proof the fact that as soon as one descended it rapidly disappeared. The first annual of the Club Alpin Français of 1874 confirmed his view. In an article on mountain sickness, M. Paul Bert asserted after experiments, 'The failure of oxygen in the air at high elevations is the cause of the discomfort suffered by human beings while in balloons or on high mountains.' Russell might have heeded M. Bert's advice: 'By carrying with us a bag of oxygen, instead of a bottle of champagne, we may defy our old enemy and arrive with comparative ease on the summit of Mount Everest.'

On the summit of Mont Blanc Russell was impressed. 'What a spectacle, Italy bathed in sun, when one is frozen!' What struck him more than the view, however, was the emptiness that surrounded them, a veritable desert, and he shuddered at the thought of being there on a winter night. It was as if he had found his limit, the edge beyond which he had no desire to go. He was disappointed not to see or feel the true geological summit, buried under centuries of snow. 'What is the real form of this mountain, we have no idea.' It was not a mountain he could get to know intimately.

Then Henry went on to Zermatt, to stay at the Hôtel Monte Rosa. It was a hotel with a recent and tragic history, since it was here Edward Whymper had stayed when he made his ill-fated first ascent of the Matterhorn only two years before. Zermatt was still reeling from the tragedy.

Whymper (1840–1911) was a young illustrator, who worked in his father's engraving firm in London, and had made several sketches for the first volume of *Peaks, Passes and Glaciers*, the forerunner of the *Alpine Journal*. In 1865 he was still only twenty-five; his photo shows him beardless, fresh faced, with huge eyes and deep cleft chin. On visiting the Alps to make sketches for his illustrations, he became captivated by the excitement of mountaineering. He was obsessed with the Matterhorn, which the locals were convinced was the highest mountain in the world, and believed it was impossible to climb. Whymper made several attempts during his summer holidays, competing for the prize with several others.

He did finally make it to the summit first, in June 1865, only to then suffer the greatest Alpine disaster ever known. On the descent, a rope snapped and, though Whymper survived, four of the party fell, sliding inexorably from precipice to precipice, 4000 feet to their deaths on the glacier below. One of them, a lord no less, was never found and all that remained was a shoe, a pair of gloves and a coat sleeve. (He was Lord Francis Douglas, heir to the Marquess of Queensberry.) It was the end of the Golden Age and there was a bitter media backlash against the new sport.

'Why is the best blood of England to waste itself in scaling hitherto inaccessible peaks,' thundered *The Times*, 'in staining the eternal snows and reaching the un-fathomable abyss never to return? But is it life? Is it duty? Is it common sense? Is it allowable? Is it not wrong?'

Despite the tragic associations, Russell found the Monte Rosa hotel in Zermatt excellent and particularly approved of the food. He makes no mention of the accident that was still the talk of Zermatt, not least of the landlord of the hotel who had seen the survivors return and tidied up the dead men's rooms. Perhaps Russell went to see their graves. But the story of Whymper and the Matterhorn must have endeared him less than ever to the Alps, or to climbing in search of danger.

Bad weather prevented much climbing and he contented himself with long walks accompanied by 'my good friend Hinchliff'. Hinchliff was a founder member of the Alpine Club – the first meetings were held in his chambers at Lincoln's Inn. He was a good friend of Packe and equally fond of botanizing. Russell may also have met up with Leslie Stephen, who was in the Alps that July on his honeymoon. Russell did climb the Breithorn, a respectable 4148 metres high, and was delighted to find a comfortable auberge at 3322 metres, 'with beds, provisions, and very good coffee'. Better still, only three hours later, 'I was smoking a cigar on the summit of Breithorn' (Stephen would have approved) and returned to the hotel before nightfall, 'having done the fastest climb of my life'. More than anything it was the memory of these high altitude refuges that Russell took back to the Pyrenees.

Since Saussure and Ramond it had been common practice to express a preference and Russell did so with typical hyperbole, deciding that the Pyrenees were more feminine, tender and delicate than the Alps. 'The Alps represent man, the Pyrenees woman. I love the woman best.' He was heartily glad to be back in the Pyrenees. 'They have a grace, a nobility of contours, of warm colours and sun I do not find in Switzerland.' He never returned to the Alps.

The Pyrenees were never as popular as the Alps. The English who came to the Pyrenees only rarely numbered among them the macho members of the Alpine Club. There were a few exceptions; the year before the Alpine Club was formed two Englishmen, known only as Halkett and Behrens, climbed Posets, though little is known of their ascent. John Ormsby climbed Mont Perdu in 1868, where he recorded an encounter with the Reverend Emilien Frossard. One-time president of the club Douglas Freshfield came in spring 1874 and climbed Vignemale. Edward Whymper made a tour, climbing Vignemale and Mont Perdu with Henri Passet, the guide from Gavarnie, who impressed him so much he asked him to go to the Andes. Passet said no.

In 1882 Francis Fox Tuckett, a devout Quaker with distinctive mutton chop whiskers, made a lightning tour of the major peaks over a period of ten days and despite his accident-prone reputation (he was always escaping avalanches) appears to have suffered no ill-effects. While he was there he apparently taught Henry Russell the use of the rucksack.

Russell occasionally climbed with his compatriots, among them the great white hunter Henry Halford, and James Bryce, an indefatigable traveller with a passion for mountains, later a Liberal government minister and ambassador in Washington. Bryce climbed Mount Ararat (where Noah's Ark was supposed to have landed) alone in 1876 and his research into the evidence for the Ark is now cited by creationists as evidence against evolution. Happily he has left a more positive legacy, being the first to introduce a bill into the British parliament to allow access to private moors and mountains, the Access to Mountains bill of 1884, which finally became law as the Countryside and Rights of Way act in 2004. I like to think Bryce's youthful climbing adventures in the Pyrenees may have influenced him, and Russell should get some credit for our hard-won Right to Roam.

Generally, though, the Pyrenees were dismissed by English mountaineers: '. . . the peaks are stumpy, the glaciers are few and far between, the valleys are hot, good guides are rare, there are no convenient climbing centres,' wrote an *Alpine Journal* correspondent. But most of all, 'In the Pyrenees the climber is nobody. There are no processional departures and returns at his hotel, no telescopes are fixed on him, no chief place is kept for him at tables d'hôte. No "Pyrenean Post" exists to glorify his high deeds. To climb unseen by men on peaks unknown even to geographers may be the fancy of a few; the reverse, despite their pretence, is the folly of the many.'

Climbing unseen in the Pyrenees was left largely to

Russell and Packe. Russell's own attempts to promote the Pyrenees probably backfired when he recounted a grisly tale of banditry in the one paper he delivered to the Alpine Club in London in 1871.

'It was in July, after the hottest days I have ever experienced in Europe, and a little after midnight ... The previous night we had slept on the summit of Cotiella, at about 10,000 feet, without fire or shelter so we were very tired.' There were four of them, Russell, his friend Albert Lequeutre, and two guides, Henri and Célestin Passet from Gavarnie. 'So after midnight, after admiring for hours the exquisite grandeur of the whole scenery, the lofty old pines which stood in thousands all round us, and the full moon which sent streams of silver on the glaciers of Mont Perdu in the distance', they settled for the night in an empty *cabane* with the two guides sleeping beside the fire outside. 'We had not slept for half an hour when I was seized convulsively by Célestin.' There outside the cabin, '... four hideous Spaniards were just before the door, armed to the teeth, with glittering daggers round their waists, an axe and a rifle'. One of the bandits levelled his gun and fired, grazing the ear of Lequeutre.

They all fled. 'I need not tell you that, since we were not there to fight for honour or country, and we had no weapons but alpenstocks, we ran away ... I, however, saving my knapsack, but leaving behind my boots, sleeping bag, alpenstock, etc.' Russell reached the shelter of the woods before their attackers had reloaded, 'running madly down, until at length my lungs gave way, and I had to stretch myself under a dark pine and rested there. Then I began to shudder, as I thought of my three companions, not knowing what direction they had taken, and having no doubt that they were all either murdered, or lost without hope in those immense pine forests where none of them had ever been before. No words could possibly express my anguish during that terrible night' – anguish made worse still when he heard the hideous yells of the brigands. 'Thinking the last moment had come, like eleven years ago on the New Zealand peaks, I recommended my soul to God.' But hidden in the darkness they did not see him, and 'the moment daylight came, hearing nothing, I most cautiously crept down to the little village of Plan, four miles below, where awaking almost everyone, I at once despatched to the fatal forest the strongest man I could get, being myself barely able to stand, after such emotions and two consecutive nights without sleep'. Finally his companions emerged from the forest, 'silent and ghastly, but thank God, alive'. Célestin had escaped but Lequeutre had suffered badly. 'Knocked down by seven bandits, with three huge blades upon his breast, and the muzzle of the gun in his face, he probably owed his life to his coolness, but lost his purse, his rings, his watch, etc.' They caught Henri Passet too as he climbed down too soon from a tree. 'He had to bow his neck under the axe, and felt the edge of it for several minutes at the root of his hair. But they did not kill him either, and Lequeutre, once sure of his life, and utterly overpowered by fatigue, not only smoked, but fell asleep while they were still there! They were even civil enough to give him back one of his shirts!' Finally they disappeared, having bombarded the *cabane* with stones, but Russell doubted if they were ever apprehended, adding drily, 'Justice in Spain is as slow as railways.'

Such a tale may have had the opposite effect from persuading members of the Club of the delights of the

Pyrenees, despite Russell's plea: 'I hope the Pyrenees will not suffer from it, as such an accident never happened before in any part of them, and they are just as safe as Regent Street, by night or by day.'

His article was accompanied by a drawing of the bandits, with their swords at the throat of their victim. It was drawn by Edward Whymper himself, whose own *Scrambles in the Alps* was hot off the press. He had asked for a picture of a bandit to copy, and since this was unavailable, Spanish bandits being singularly unwilling to pose for drawings or photos, Russell sent one of himself, dressed as a bandit for a ball.

In the same paper Russell expressed his theories about winter climbing, a minor vogue at the time of which he had experience. He reckoned that winter was often the safest time to climb: 'in midwinter both snow and air appear to fall asleep . . . the sky is clear, spotless and calm. Never have I seen weather more cheerful and lovely, on the whole, than in Siberia in the heart of winter. Winter is the proper season for travelling in high latitudes, and, for my part, I have no doubt that if ever the poles are reached, it will be in winter, on the ice and in sledges – never by navigation.' He was right about that, as the expeditions of Amundsen and Captain Scott were later to prove.

Russell no doubt wished to take the opportunity to stress his own achievement to the members of the Alpine Club, his own winter climb of Vignemale in the winter of 1869. It was the first ascent of a major European peak in winter, and Russell wrote a letter to *The Times*, published on 27 February 1869, noting his achievement. It appeared on the second page of the paper, which on those days still devoted the front page to small ads:

The French Pyrenees
To the Editor of The Times
Sir,

Perhaps it may interest some of your countless readers to learn that the Grand Vignemale (10,820 feet), the highest peak in the French Pyrenees, was successfully ascended on the 11th of February by myself and two guides, with much fatigue, but without accident or danger, all the crevasses being hidden and the rope unnecessary. Warned by sad experience in the Alps, I had taken extraordinary precautions against the cold; but strange to say, they were worse than useless, for the heat was overpowering, and at 9000 feet, on the white and dazzling glaciers, it became almost unbearable. Higher up it gradaully grew colder; still, on the very summit, in an atmosphere of equatorial stillness, the thermometer marked 50 degrees in the shade and 85 degrees in the sun, at 3 p.m., a far greater heat than I have ever experienced at such a height in midsummer.

In clear and calm weather winter ascents are more fatiguing than perilous, avalanches being then very rare, and I believe Mont Blanc might be ascended on certain days in midwinter.

As for the heat we experienced, I leave it to meteorologists to explain such a paradox, which I think is no exception, for I have seldom climbed mountains in winter without finding the heat greater than in the plains.

I have the honour to remain, Sir, yours very truly,

Count Henry Russell

Gavarnie, Hautes Pyrénées, 12 Feb 1869

His climb was never subsequently acknowledged, however. The accolade for the pioneer of winter climbing goes to the eccentric American, W. A. B. Coolidge, who at the time Russell climbed Vignemale in 1869 was only nineteen. For the record, however, Coolidge did not make any winter ascents until 1873 when he and his aunt climbed the Wetterhorn and the Jungfrau in January, along with his long-suffering dog, Tschingel, who became famous for climbing thirty-six peaks and making the first canine ascent (on foot) of Mont Blanc. He was often thrown across crevasses and his paws bled on the glaciers, but he did not complain.

Vignemale had long been waiting in the background for Russell, and after many flirtatious glances he had climbed it for the second time the previous year, the autumn of 1868, accompanied by Hippolyte Passet. When they arrived at the grand crevasse of the glacier they found it was split right across, with no snow bridges to cross, so they were obliged to climb down into the 100-foot abyss by cutting steps with the ice-axe (Hippolyte cut the steps) right to the heart of the chasm, and then make their way along it like a street, to climb out higher up where there was less of a slope.

It was then Russell had resolved to climb Vignemale in winter. He arrived in Gavarnie on a superb February day and his account of the climb in French is considerably more poetic than his brisk English summary for the Alpine Club and *The Times*. The English gentleman he aspired to be was much more prosaic. Only in French does he reach such heights of hyperbole. It is as if his very experience is more profound and poetic when he does it in French: 'The

Cirque was covered in ice and shone like a breastplate, all the waterfalls were frozen, and there was no sound.' Before dinner he climbed part of the way up the Ossoue valley to take a look at his quarry, returning to the hotel full of enthusiasm. 'What a magical picture, nothing there but sun, silence, snow and blue.' He left next morning, departing before 6 a.m. with Hippolyte and his nephew Henri, carrying lanterns because it was still dark. 'When the sky lightened behind Piméné, there was a glacial light breeze but it woke us up. In front of us to the west, the great glacier of Ossoue was purple as if it was running with blood. By sunrise we were already at 1800 metres on snow we would not leave again for twelve hours. We had no trouble until the ravine where the cascade of Oulettes thundered under the snow.'

In summer they always climbed the waterfall on the right, but the snow made it dangerous, so they had to climb up the other side. 'We advanced silently as phantoms, in absolute silence, nothing in the world is as mute as a solitude of snow. The heat, bizarrely, was extraordinary. Where the rays of the sun hit the snow the air seemed full of flaming sequins, the snow seemed to be sending out as much light as the sun. The great heat on the mountains in winter is because of the extreme whiteness of the new snow; in summer the snow is dirty and does not reflect the solar rays.

'At three we were on the summit of Grand Vignemale. I will never forget those few minutes we passed up there in the heart of winter, with the certainty that not one man in Europe breathed at our level. From the height of this celestial cathedral I saw under my feet the chain of the Pyrenees frozen from one end to the other. I was at the centre of a paradise of snow.'

The sun was already reddening the snow as it set, and they had to leave quickly, before the temperature fell. 'At these heights it freezes almost immediately the sun goes. On the ice the descent was going to be perilous and after eight hours of sun, we sank up to a metre in the soft snow. There was no moon, and it was frighteningly black.'

But they were back in Gavarnie again with lanterns in hand, a bit before 10 p.m., after sixteen hours of forced march. 'Next day two feet of snow fell, even on the plain. Though it was too late to punish us for violating the winter sanctuary, it rapidly effaced any trace of our passing.'

He loved winter, which reminded him of his time in Siberia, 'the most brilliant and sweetest time of my life, my voyage in Siberia in full winter, my little Tartar horses flying like the tempest across the forests of giant pines and infinite steppes, the carillon of their bells mingling with the howls of the wolves, crossing enormous rivers at triple gallop as if terror-struck by the whiteness and the eternity of the most resplendent and vast horizons in the world'. He recalled 'the clarity of the moon and the stars over the Gobi desert in 50 degrees of cold, as my camel brought me to Peking, led by a young Mongolian girl on horseback in a red tunic, singing nocturnes at midnight, the wind carried to the sky'.

For Russell the Pyrenean winter offered the same splendours. 'People imagine a sort of polar night, eternal whiteness, villages cut off and no sun appearing for six months, constant snow and eternal tempests. The truth is that on the summits, around 3000 metres, it is generally more clear in all seasons than on the plain.' As a general rule, he reckoned, 'the colder it is, the clearer it is. The limpidity of the sky in winter is one of the principal characteristics of high mountains. Winter is the season with the most sun. In climbing we rediscover azure sky and sun. How many times have we received from the observatory of the Pic du Midi telegrams announcing, "Clear sky. Fog at 2000 m!" It could even be easier to climb in winter, because all the crevasses and waterfalls and huge rocks are buried under so much snow, so that you can go anywhere without a rope. Avalanches are rare.'

18

The philosophy of exercise

'The limits of bad feeling can be expressed in metres. One is a better person at 3000 metres than at sea level.'

Henry Russell

Not long after the *foie gras* I ate in a béarnais chateau, I was eating wild spinach and dandelion leaves at a rustic wooden table outside the refuge of le Caillau at 1537 metres in the Pyrénées Orientales. I had been curious to know what real *montagnards* might have gleaned from nature, and had spent the morning investigating edible wild plants with an enthusiastic food-for-free botanist. The setting was bucolic; intermittent sunshine pierced the canopy of beech and pine trees, illuminating boulders silvery green with moss and tiny purple autumn crocuses. Here and there a fat white toadstool with lurid red spots thrust through the mulch. Cows grazed on the nearby mountain pasture, their bells clanging sonorously.

The food was less to my taste, and as I struggled to chew the tough fibres of the various leaves we had gathered I reflected that this was why they had been left in the wild. All the good ones had been cultivated. Still, I listened dutifully when Armelle plucked ripe red rose hips from a branch, and informed me that just four provided a daily dosage of Vitamin C. Armelle, a tall, strong-boned woman with a tangle of unruly red hair, runs the refuge, welcoming travellers in the mountains to simple, basic accommodation. She spends several months here in the summer and visits intermittently in the winter, when supplies sometimes have to be dragged through the snow by sledge. Like so many of the guardians of the refuges in the mountains, she is often alone. I asked how she felt about it. 'I feel rooted here now. I don't like society very much. I was once here for eight months without going down once.' She smiled, pensively chewing rose hips. 'I think it gives me a different perspective on life down there.'

It was growing chilly outside, and we went into the building, a low stone structure that was originally accommodation for miners in the nearby talc mine, and later provided sanctuary for the Resistance. There were solid wooden tables and two large dormitories, the austerity tempered by Armelle's delicate constructions of bark, pebbles and dried flowers. Wet clothes were drying on an ingenious frame of sticks and rope. Armelle piled a bunch of kindling into the big fireplace and lit a blaze. It was cosy and we huddled close, holding our hands to the flames. 'It must be hard sometimes?' I asked.

'If I get the blues I just have to climb above two thousand metres and look at Canigou.' She smiled. 'That makes me feel better.'

'What kind of people come here?' I asked.

'All sorts – sometimes they stay for several days, just walking, collecting wild strawberries, looking for mushrooms. The important thing is they can sleep up here, wake to the sunrise, stay in the mountains.'

There are now about a hundred refuges all over the Pyrenees, some large and comfortable, others little more than shacks, providing beds and meals for walkers and climbers, enabling them to spend extended sojourns in the mountains. It had been Henry Russell's fervent wish that people could find a way to spend time at high altitudes, without the constant need to descend for shelter and supplies. His initiation of the building of refuges was his most practical contribution to the enjoyment of the Pyrenees.

When the Club Alpin Français was formed in 1874 it advocated mountaineering as good for the soul. As befitted the Third Republic it was a far more egalitarian set-up than the stuffy old English Alpine Club, which permitted membership only on the basis of achievement. Indeed, to join the CAF there was no need to be a mountaineer at all and it soon had several thousand members. The conditions of entry were merely, according to a contemporary, 'not to have assassinated anyone and . . . the power to contribute twenty francs a year'. They even permitted women to join. The members were divided into *alpinistes de pics* (the men of the summits), *alpinistes de cols et demi-sommets* (more gentle promenades) and *alpinistes de banquets*. Soon the veteran *pyrénéistes* like Russell, despite their initial proselytizing, were grimacing at the invasion of the crowd who had never seen a mountain peak.

The new president of the CAF, Ernest Cézanne, proclaimed, echoing Ramond, that young people did not get enough exercise, and advocated mountain exertions as good for body and soul. 'In contemplating the solemn beauties of nature, this astonishing vision of the infinite, who would not feel closer to God?' At that moment this was a remarkable reflection of the philosophy of Henry Russell, though as time went on sport triumphed over

God, and the Pyrenean philosophers were left to sniff at 'acrobatics' and pursue their contemplative worship of mountains in peace.

Russell's approach to mountain climbing was best expressed in his first publication on the Pyrenees, a slim volume published in 1865, *Ascensions and the Philosophy of Exercise*. He believed firmly that climbing mountains was good for you, both body and soul. 'The limits of bad feeling can be expressed in metres; one is better at 3000 metres than at sea level.' He truly believed that mountain climbing made you a better person. 'The worship of mountains has a profound effect on the spirit. They offer a sublime perspective of the material world. What is gas, electric light and fireworks when one has seen the moon rise resplendent, on a beautiful summer night on the austere glaciers of the Maladetta.'

A new generation of mountaineers appeared in the Pyrenees, many of whom became friends, even disciples, of Russell, though by no means all subscribed to his romantic philosophy. Every year *le clan Russell* gathered round him at Gavarnie, the spiritual centre of Pyrenean climbing. Never a year went by without Russell's going to Gavarnie. He was venerated in the little village and well cared for by several generations of the Vergez-Bellou family at the Hôtel des Voyageurs, where he would take his usual room. His arrival in July announced the beginning of the season and though in his younger days he sometimes walked all the way, later he would often arrive with a flourish in a landau drawn by four white horses, with tinkling bells, like royalty.

He shook hands with everyone, embraced his guides, particularly the Passet family who lived opposite the hotel, and heard everyone's stories. He drank in the view of the Cirque crowned by his favourite summits, Taillon, Astazou, Marboré and Mont Perdu, anticipated seeing again his beloved glaciers and waterfalls, and glimpsed the tantalizing view of Vignemale before he arrived in the village. Then no doubt he immediately demanded to know the day's menu.

His days at Gavarnie followed a certain routine, the morning always given over to correspondence, until the moment when a snowy shower of torn paper was tossed from the window, and he announced he was done. The morning meal, that is lunch at 10 a.m., was eaten before the crowds arrived, the tourists who came for the day, many of them by now pilgrims from Lourdes, to visit the Cirque by mule, and depart. Sometimes a major excursion was planned for the day, or Russell would provision himself and his guides for a longer adventure.

Even if he was not intending to go far he would go out every afternoon laden with food and drink. He was always immaculately turned out, his Norfolk jacket neatly buttoned, on his head a small hat to guard against the sun, and always a scarf of red or blue cascading from his pocket. He would stroll in the pastures around Gavarnie or wander in the forest of Pailla, and always returned as astonished and refreshed as if he had seen it all for the first time.

Dinner was always important and he could get very petulant if he found a menu not to his taste, and would beg and plead for isard or trout. There was a Russell family legend about an uncle in a high position at the royal court, who after a sumptuous dinner had expressed himself still hungry and polished off an entire rabbit in a few mouthfuls. A similar story was told of Russell at Gavarnie. He had his own table, where he could stretch out his long legs and eat as much as he liked. On one occasion when there were several other mountaineers present, Pierre Vergez, the landlord, said he was going to test M. le Comte, and see how much he could eat. Russell was thus served a prodigiously large meal, but he became suspicious and took good care to leave nothing he was served. When he had finished M. Vergez came and complimented M. le Comte on his appetite and received compliments in return. But then said Russell, turning the tables, 'I could still eat something more.' Nonplussed, Vergez returned from the kitchen with a roast duck, which Russell rapidly despatched.

After dinner the faithful assembled in the empty dining room, sitting round the flames of the log fire if it was cold, or poring over maps spread on the table, and talked mountains and adventure and listened to Russell's tales of his travels in Siberia and Japan. All bemoaned the increasing invasions of *pyrénéistes de weekend*, excursionists who travelled in large noisy groups, invading their sanctuary. Russell called his friends the Tilleul Club after his favourite limeflower tea, a soothing tisane which he liked to drink after dinner and had persuaded everyone to try.

At nightfall, when the last carriages had left and peace descended again, he liked to smoke his cigar on the Pont du Gave, listen to the rumbling of the torrent, bask in the moonlight as the white globe rose like a lamp over the summit of Marboré, or wait in anticipation for a summer storm, watching the first flash of lightning in the deep shadows of the Ossoue valley, accompanied by his chosen companions, *le happy few* as they described themselves.

Among them were men like Wallon and Schrader, who

were soon busily mapping properly for the first time the most remote regions of the Pyrenees, particularly the Spanish side. Franz Schrader, born in Bordeaux in 1844, ten years after Russell, was a descendant of Huguenots from the Cévennes. His father was a great follower of Rousseau, and ran a small school inspired by radical principles of education. He did not believe in academic qualifications, and instead taught his son carpentry, stressing the importance of creating real things. Though Schrader never did get any official diplomas, he became a great scholar, learnt English, German, Spanish, and taught himself Greek and Latin, geography and mathematics. He began drawing, both technical and scientific, and painted watercolours. He had never seen mountains until 1866 when, at the age of twenty-two, he went to visit a friend in Pau, who lived at number 16 rue Marca, the house adjoining Russell's at number 14. He arrived at night so it was not till he opened his window the next morning and looked to the end of the street that he saw the Pyrenees. It was love at first sight. He ran straight to the terrace of the chateau, utterly bewitched by the mountains that would transform his life.

He was a scientist, more in the mould of Ramond than of Russell, and in 1873 invented a device for measuring summits, an *orographe*, which he had first read about in a fictional work as a child. He decided to map the Pyrenees. He gave himself ten days to get to know the geography of Mont Perdu, but ten years later he was still not finished. 'It is a long geological poem, it is enough to have read part of the first line,' he remarked philosophically. Exploring scientifically and methodically he mapped all the Pyrénées Centrales between 1882 and 1900. He became president of the French Alpine Club from 1900 to 1903 and is buried in the little churchyard at Gavarnie.

He divided the territory with Edouard Wallon, who was determined to map both the French and Spanish side of the Pyrenees and establish mathematically the precise altitudes of the highest peaks. He was a lawyer from Montauban, with grizzly hair, a long droopy moustache and a strong Midi accent, who was always folding strips of paper into profiles of mountains. He sometimes accompanied Russell on his climbs, 'a valiant and practical' fellow who was always fully equipped, unlike the unburdened Russell, with pens, paper and scientific instruments.

Russell occasionally grumbled petulantly at their efforts, especially when their more accurate measurements reduced the heights of mountains he had climbed. He had always measured the peaks simply by eye, but then he even set his watch by the sun. Like Ruskin, as Fergus Fleming puts it in *Killing Dragons*, 'He did not want them to be mapped. He wanted them to be understood.'

But in conversation he was always tactful and avoided argument, skilfully deviating from irritating subjects. He seems only to have expressed himself with bitterness over political issues, what he saw as the loss of liberty in France (at least for the aristocrats), or the proposal for Home Rule and tenants' rights in Ireland. He always listened with the air of learning something new, and would simply lower his eyes in deference when the scientists diminished a summit or challenged the dimensions of a glacier.

The mountains were always his reference point. 'Sometimes there was just a word, a glance at the peaks, and you understood,' recalled his good friend Henri Brulle. He had become the Harold Acton of the Pyrenees, '*le père du pyrénéisme*' as Brulle called him, dispensing advice, discussing projects, and offering suggestions for new climbs and explorations.

Henri Brulle was a key member of Gavarnie society, a protégé thirty years younger than Russell, whom Russell sponsored to join the elite circle of the Alpine Club. At least to begin with Brulle subscribed fully to the master's 'poetical and picturesque school of mountaineering'. Brulle was another gascon, a lawyer from Libourne, near Bordeaux. He made his first mountain expedition to Vignemale at the age of twenty in 1874 via the Col de Cerbillona, the route taken by Ann Lister in 1838. He was dashing, handsome, broad-shouldered and clear-eyed, with a wonderful handlebar moustache.

He was very daring, and soon succumbed to the acrobatic school of climbing that Russell so disparaged, encouraged in his more daredevil exploits by his friend Bazillac, after they met in 1878. Bazillac, also gascon, born in Mirande, was a pale delicate-looking boy with a chestnut beard. His anaemic air and bookish, refined tastes disguised a wild spirit and a muscled vigorous body. He and Brulle shared a taste for danger, and soon became inseparable.

Between them they clocked up many exploits. 'We wandered capriciously from peak to peak,' as Brulle put it. These included a fourteen-day tour in 1881 of amazing rapidity during which they ascended two dozen great peaks, including every known one over 3000 metres. In 1882 they explored the Eastern Pyrenees and made a night climb of Canigou. He and Bazillac even tried to climb the treacherous Balaitous in winter. They also climbed in the Alps together, taking with them Célestin Passet, which rather affronted the Alpine guides, and there Brulle evolved into a more sporting *alpiniste*, learning the use of ropes and ice-axes, which Russell always disdained. In letters exchanged between the two after the trip to the Alps, Brulle had clearly experienced good weather and been dismissive of the dangers of Mont Blanc. Russell warned him how treacherous the storms and cold there could be. His warning was to prove prophetic. Saddened and bitter after the death of his son Roger in the First World War, Brulle gave up climbing for many years. But he returned to the Alps aged eighty to make one last climb and died after both feet were frozen on the Géant des Alpes.

But Brulle always remained faithful to Gavarnie and, as he wrote later in a paper for the Alpine Club, considered it the best of Pyrenean centres: '. . . towards evening when the crowd of vulgar tourists has disappeared, the village recovers its primitive and pastoral aspect,' he wrote. He recommended the rock climbing around Gavarnie, the challenges of climbing the waterfall and most of all the two noblest mountains in the neighbourhood, the Vignemale and Mont Perdu. 'They are near enough to Gavarnie – one on each side of it – to have enabled me to climb them both on the same day, without having missed any of the meals at the hotel.' This was a prodigious achievement typical of the new style of *alpiniste* climbing and Henry no doubt grumbled that he could have had little time to contemplate the view from either mountain.

A typical story about Brulle records him departing from Luchon at midnight and arriving in Gavarnie at 6 p.m. the next day. That evening he asserted to his assembled peers, 'I could have gone on to Cauterets if I had not had business in Gavarnie.' And to prove he was not in the least tired he lined up three chairs in the salon and jumped over each one.

The Club Alpin Français grew and more people came to the Pyrenees, which were given as much space as the Alps and the Massif Central in the journals and annual of the CAF. Russell contributed frequent articles (other contributors included Viollet-le-Duc and George Sand). He described his recent climbs, extolling the pleasures of a night spent out on the mountains, and his own attempts to carve caves out of the Vignemale.

Despite the growing preference among mountaineers for *pyrénéisme de difficulté*, Russell was still a firm believer in exploring the Pyrenees with the least pain possible, and after his visit to the Alps he realized that refuges were the answer, making it possible for people to spend more than a day on a climb and have more time to savour their surroundings. He became increasingly concerned about the lack of shelters, writing about it in one of his first papers for the CAF journal.

He began his first campaign for a refuge to be built on the route to Mont Perdu, because 'to climb it required a return journey from Gavarnie of twelve hours, or a night spent under the stars in a desert of snow'. In 1876 he started a subscription, raising funds from the Société Ramond, the Club Alpin Français and private friends including Charles Packe. He investigated the possibilities thoroughly. He was soon forced to abandon his initial idea of an artificial cave which would make minimal impact on the natural landscape, and eventually accepted the need for a hut. Finally he and Wallon selected a site to the west of Mont Perdu, tucked under a limestone outcrop, safe from avalanches and rockfalls. Although there was permanent snow around the cabin it was a sunny site: '. . . even the sick should come once to see the sunset,' Russell opined. 'It would make them better.' The Mont Perdu refuge was inaugurated in 1877 with a large party, including many of the new generation of *pyrénéistes*. By 1883 Russell was already scouting a site for another refuge at the Brèche de Roland.

Refuges thus became a familiar phenomenon of the Pyrenees, though they tend to have a mixed reputation, a melange of smelly socks and bonhomie that does not appeal to everyone. Indeed, Russell himself always preferred his own caves, and would probably not have appreciated the experience of one uncomfortable visitor to a Pyrenean refuge in 1899, who summarized his companions thus: 'The Parisians complain, the English snore, the Spanish all smuggle.'

Therein lay the rub. Russell was a victim of his own success. As more and more people arrived, he became increasingly dismayed by the invasion. Much as he wanted to share his own love of the mountains and encourage people to explore for themselves, he was horrified by the large excitable groups of climbers who arrived in increasing numbers, disturbing the peace and solitude he felt was key to experiencing the beauty of the Pyrenees. As far as he was concerned they were missing the point. In the *Souvenirs* he dismissed 'the Tourists who go to Port de Vénasque, have a good dinner in front of the Maladetta, looking more often at their chicken or their newspaper, and descend proudly to Luchon to discuss the Monts Maudits and compare them to the Alps, etc. Even those who have climbed Néthou do not know the Pyrenees. For that you have to spend three or four days in the valleys of snow to the south of the Monts Maudits, where Russia and Spain seem to meet.'

In 1880 a grand reunion of the Club Alpin Français was planned in the Pyrenees. It began with a long banquet at the hotel in Luz, with speeches, poetry, local dances and endless toasts, in particular to the elderly Reverend Emilien Frossard, who was to die the following year. Russell was offered the presidency but refused; despite his growing fame he had no desire, he said, to be a spectacle.

Next day the group left very late for Gavarnie and Mont Perdu and Russell grumbled at the sight of 'eighty tourists armed like soldiers', and muttered about the 'vulgarization of the mountains'. None seemed to have been very used to mountain climbing and they were soon lost, taking several hours over a difficult descent in order to regain their tracks.

On their return to Gavarnie there was yet another banquet (*filet à la Marboré*, *isard sauce Roland* and *plum pudding pyrénéen*). To his embarrassment Count Russell was seated in the place of honour, despite his disparagement of their activities. To his right sat Franz Schrader, president of the south-west section of the CAF, and to his left the guide Pierre Pujo, in his capacity as mayor of Gavarnie. Russell's proverbial courtesy prevailed and he conceded himself cured of his bad humour by the festivities and their generous hospitality.

Nevertheless, he was horrified by the invasion of tourists. The festivities were the last straw. The very next day he took off, feeling a desperate need to be alone, and get as far away as possible. It was the following night that he had himself buried on the summit of Vignemale. It sounds almost biblical, like the Last Supper before Jesus goes off alone to the Mount of Olives to meet his destiny.

19

The hermit king of Vignemale

'This is the human paradox of altitude: that it both exalts the individual mind and erases it. Those who travel to mountain tops are half in love with themselves, and half in love with oblivion.'

Robert Macfarlane, *Mountains of the Mind*

After his burial on the summit of Vignemale, Russell was resolved. For years he had preferred to spend as much time as possible on the heights of the mountains. Now what he wanted was a permanent refuge of his own. This was the key period of his life and he describes his growing passion for Vignemale in great detail in the *Souvenirs*. First he listed his priorities:

1   To establish myself on one of the highest mountains.
2   To select the best possible site for my future installation.
3   To find a way to live there.

The mountain was already found. The Vignemale, highest of the frontier mountains, first glimpsed at age six from the Lac de Gaube, and the first place he went on his return from Asia, 'my favourite peak since I was a   small child'. After years of loving and leaving so many peaks he was resolved to commit himself to one mountain alone. 'She will become my spouse.'

Vignemale is perhaps the most mythical, certainly one of the most romantic peaks of the Pyrenees, due largely to its discreet and elusive position. Apart from the view of the north face from the Lac de Gaube, a brief glimpse is afforded from Gavarnie, when just a few steps before the village the east face suddenly appears, the glacier flashing like a diamond exposed to the light.

It straddles the frontier between France and Spain, but is hard to reach from either side, as if not wishing to be claimed by either, and refusing to submit to anything as banal or terrestrial as a national boundary. Once climbed, however, Vignemale offers a stupendous view of the surrounding peaks and of both countries to north and south. Russell called the peak his throne, from where he could survey his entire glacial kingdom, and most of the peaks he had climbed.

It is only really accessible during a brief summer season when snow and ice have melted sufficiently to make walking or climbing safe. The section of the GR10 (the walking route which crosses the Pyrenees from the Mediterranean to the Atlantic) skirting Vignemale is considered the most difficult part of the route. Climbers need patience to wait for a propitious day without snow clouds or storms, and Russell and his contemporaries often had to wait days or weeks for the right moment. Often the snow did not clear sufficiently till mid-July, and by the end of September there was too much risk of winter weather returning to attempt it. Sometimes they had to come back the following year for another attempt. Didier Lacaze, Russell's biographer, never forgot the summer of 1995 when the snow never stopped and he was alone all summer in the refuge de Bayssellance, the highest guarded refuge in the Pyrenees.

The mountain's very inaccessibility must have heightened its appeal to Russell, now so desperate to escape the world. The most popular means of access, and that used most often by Russell, is from Gavarnie, about half a day's walk, along the stony path of Val d'Ossoue up to the Ossoue dam. From here the highest peak of the massif can be seen, the Grand Vignemale at 3298 metres. The entire massif consists of five pyramids of rock, separated by steep chimneys. To the right of Grand Vignemale can be seen the Petit Vignemale at 3030 metres, and to the left the pyramid of the Cerbillona, almost as high. Slung below the north face is the blinding white Ossoue glacier, at three kilometres long and 8000 metres wide the largest glacier in the Pyrenees.

The route from Cauterets, via the Lac de Gaube, is still more imposing. The route goes via the waterfalls of the Pont d'Espagne, up to Lac du Gaube, and round it to the north face of the massif. The least frequent means of access is from Spain, to the west, up to the Col de Cerbillona, which is the original route followed by Ann Lister and the Prince de Moskova. It avoids the glacier but is much steeper and more stony and difficult to climb. This route shows a quite different character, a Spanish mountain, typical of Aragon, its south face a harsh ochre, most dramatic, as Russell discovered, in the red light of dawn.

In planning his sanctuary Russell therefore decided that Gavarnie would be the best base for supplies. The site of the cave proved more difficult. He wanted to be as near as possible to the summit. The rocks which form the great black pyramid of the peak would have been perfect, since they faced south and even in full winter the snow never stayed long, but they were too hard to dig, being impregnated with iron. Packe's observations, made on his first ascent in 1862, were typically precise: although the mass of the mountain is limestone, he noted, 'the flanks of the mountain are of granite, and the summit of a dark clay schist, containing iron pyrites'.

Russell decided instead on the Col de Cerbillona, which rose majestically above the glacier, descended gradually to the south and was open from east to west. There the limestone would be easier to dig. 'This beautiful belvedere was nearly always dry and baked by the sun, and was perfect for meals, or for long gentle reveries at all hours of day and night. The view was unsurpassable. The immensity of the snows which unfurled to the east looked like a polar desert.'

By the following year, 1881, he had decided on the type of habitation he wanted. He was determined to avoid any kind of construction. Like Hilaire Belloc, who had said the buildings on the Pic du Midi made it look as if it was in harness, he too found the observatory too artificial. He loathed tents, finding them ugly and heavy to carry. Again he listed his reasons:

1 Human geometric structures look ridiculous and even profane, clinging to a giant palace of snow, marble and granite constructed by God. And piles of stones are too ephemeral, a blast of wind can annihilate them.

2 Nothing is more ugly, more hideous than a house in the middle of the sublime eternal chaos of mountains.

3 All edifices constructed at high altitudes would be freezing, even uninhabitable, without fuel for heating, and the wind creates the danger of asphyxiation by the fumes.

He concluded: 'I clearly needed a human work, but one that seemed natural, and that would be warm and dry all the time, without the need for a fire. It needed to be solid, invulnerable, something eternal. An artificial cave!'

This then became his dream. 'An eskimo would build with snow, the Swiss like wood, and I love rock. Nothing is so warm and solid.' But where was he to find workers willing and strong enough to mine rock at such an altitude? They would need to stay for several weeks and sleep outdoors without shelter, on a mountain famous for its terrible storms, where they would be more exposed to the fury of the elements than a sailor on a ship.

It was also very remote from habitation. Every time the workers needed supplies or equipment they would have to cross three kilometres of glacier, riddled with dangerous crevasses, often obscured by thick fog, followed by a descent of 2300 metres to Gavarnie and then to Gèdre, a journey of at least twenty kilometres carrying an enormous weight of mine rods, powder, charcoal and provisions. Even to Russell the problem seemed insoluble.

Eventually, however, he found in Gèdre a group of robust and resolute men who were both miners and mountaineers, including a stonemason prepared to finish off the cave with a wall and a stout door. Like the guides and porters, they did not consider their own frequent climbs of Vignemale in the same class as Russell's own carefully recorded ascents.

So on 5 August 1881 Russell ascended to his proposed site with guides Mathieu Haurine, who was almost as tall as he was, and Pierre Pujo, now the mayor of Gavarnie. 'We arrived as the sun set in scarlet clouds, and while the guides slept I walked on the glacier lit by the moon.' He could see the great Ossoue glacier falling away to the east and beyond it the snows of the Monts Maudits. To the west near Biarritz were the blue slopes of the Pays Basques. The moon was bright, the night calm, and they slept happily under the stars.

A few days later the workers made the perilous journey, taking with them a huge tarpaulin which they secured with large stones to create a primitive shelter. Then the mine blasting began, the noise reverberating round Vignemale, and the terrified isards fled.

But the work went badly. The drills soon became blunt or bent, and without a forge to hone them again had to be taken back down to Gèdre each time they needed sharpening. The workers were rapidly demoralized, not least by the tempests of snow which twice forced them to flee to Gavarnie in panic. But they persevered and on 6 September Russell went up to observe progress. When he saw the square metre hole they had managed to dig he was very disappointed. 'It looked like a niche for a saint. Two small children could not have got inside.' Worse still, the glacier had dropped by six metres over the summer so the door was on the level of a first-floor window.

'Then there was a night I will never forget! Never, even on Cape Horn, nor in Siberia in the dead of winter, have I passed a night like that. There were nine of us, six workers, two guides, Henri Passet and Haurine, and me. We had no tent, not even a rock to shelter us. Only the tarpaulin, under which the miners stretched out every night on the col, the only place not covered by the glacier.' Russell was so tall his feet stuck out at the side when he lay down. Then there was the mother of all storms, and they were engulfed by wild Atlantic winds, most furious at the approach of the equinox. 'The rocks vibrated like an earthquake, hail and stones sliced through the air like shells, the snow flew in spirals. We were frozen, blinded, asphyxiated, deafened, terrified, ready for death.' The tempest began about 8 p.m., and lasted all night. Around midnight, Russell decided to stretch his frozen legs.

'Vignemale trembled as if it was going to fall, the glacier boomed and fumed like an angry sea. I tried to get out from under the tarpaulin to walk, but it was impossible, I was thrown to the ground by the wind.' The tarpaulin was twisting convulsively, the ropes screaming, and it threatened to take off at any moment. Against all the odds it held and saved their lives. By morning they were completely buried under an enormous weight of snow, so frozen, blue and mute that no-one could eat. Henri Passet, the strongest of all, was so frost-bitten his fingers were transparent and he could not even cut his bread. Then, as dawn reddened the snow, the wind dropped, and they could attempt the descent to Gavarnie, plodding over the glacier in an icy fog. 'We marched without noise, like spectres, detouring round monstrous chasms, crossing snow bridges of almost transparent snow, peering into the depths below.'

Russell was mortified. 'Thus ended my sad and useless campaign of 1881. The Vignemale was profaned, and had made a heroic defence, its honour was safe. But the giant would soon capitulate. We just had to change our tactics.'

How many hours were spent that winter, round the fires of Gèdre and Gavarnie, as the workers discussed how best to fulfil the eccentric wishes of M. le Comte.

Russell meanwhile consoled himself by waltzing the winter away in the salons of Pau, and visiting his aristocratic friends, including the Comte de Toulouse-Lautrec, in Lavaur in the Tarn. 'The friend of all the muses. He provided such intellectual challenges, ascensions to make me forget Vignemale.' This was presumably the eccentric father of the artist Henri de Toulouse-Lautrec, a man most famous for his passion for hunting, his exotic pets and his wholesale neglect of his troubled son, who was by then twenty-three and training to be an artist in Paris, despite the disapproval of his Albi family. The Comte de Toulouse-Lautrec was also fond of fancy dress, anything from Circassian chain mail to a Scottish plaid with a dancer's tutu instead of a kilt, so perhaps they whiled away the hours in costumed balls.

Anyway, the fireside debates were fruitful, and the following summer of 1882 the heroic workers hauled a small forge up the mountainside, and improvised a stone anvil. But at the beginning of July there was a hurricane of snow lasting several days, which forced them to flee before they could do anything. On 10 July they returned in calm weather, and three weeks later they had completed Russell's first cave, measuring a creditable sixteen cubic metres.

Le Comte loved it. 'My heart thumped as I approached my door to open it for the first time,' he wrote, and he exclaimed with joy at the sight of 'the little marble room that I had despaired of ever seeing except in my dreams'. He stayed there for the first time at the beginning of

August, 'three days in the eternal snows without the least deprivation', as he characteristically put it. He was accompanied by a new young friend he had met in Pau, Francis Swan, eighteen years old, fresh out of Eton and in officer training at Sandhurst. 'Very affable and as lithe as an isard,' said Russell. A young Packe, perhaps. They were delighted with the accommodation.

'How lovely it is, how warm, how clean!' Henry enthused. 'Had the fair sex been represented doubtless we would have waltzed', and perhaps they did anyway. They made themselves at home, in the small stone cell closed with a door of sheet metal painted red. They had no furniture, but hung red hooks along the walls to hang hats and water gourds. The holes made by the drills were perfect for candles. With the door closed it was warm, at least by Russell's standards, with the temperature never less than 7 degrees. But outside it froze so much at night that water was a problem, and they had to wait till eight o'clock in the morning for the little rivulets of water on the glacier to defrost enough to make their breakfast chocolate.

They hurried to see the sunset from the summit, conveniently only twenty minutes away. 'Every evening we were magnetized by the sight, like an ocean of gold and fire.' To the north they could see France covered in clouds, to the south Spain still under the sun. Then they descended to the cave, lit candles, and a little spirit lamp to make punch and hot coffee, and settled back on their beds of hay enveloped in a cloud of pipe and cigar smoke. Henry opened the door, so he could watch the moon rise to the east, and sometimes went out to smoke and observe the glacier shining in the moonlight.

The first night they were awoken by a tremendous noise,

like a detonation but strangely regular, as if a man was hitting rocks with a great hammer. At first they thought it might be an enormous bear, but finally worked out that it was the subterranean defrosting of the glacier.

Russell was delighted with it all. Staying at such an altitude meant even the highest peaks could be climbed without difficulty. For hours at a time they strolled over the snow, in bright sunshine, and Swan even wrote letters. They liked to dine on the Col de Cerbillona, which was always hot in the sun. Flat stones served as a table. 'This became our restaurant, in view of four-fifths of the Pyrenees, from Biarritz to Andorra. We lived like princes.' The cave was christened Villa Russell. 'I had no hesitation in giving it my name since I had paid for it all.' Having achieved his preferred level of habitation, his sociable instincts reasserted themselves. He wanted to share the experience. 'Here I wished to receive all my Pyrenean friends, one after the other.' Finally the need for supplies obliged the two friends to descend and they held a gala evening before they left. 'We lit all the candles and made a colossal punch.'

They varied the descent, taking Anne Lister's route down the southern escarpment, via Spain. 'The danger of this path is not so much the extreme steepness of the slopes as the continual chutes of big stones which tumble down,' Russell observed. 'But what a superb descent. The gigantic surfaces, zebra striped with snow from top to bottom, well burnt by the torrid Aragon sun, made a splendid chasm which shone like a mirror.'

The following summer, 1883, Russell climbed Vignemale again; it was too early in the season but the mornings in

Gavarnie were so brilliant and sparkling clear that he could not resist. He made the ascent with his new young friend Francis Swan and Swan's younger sister Florence, aged seventeen, accompanied by guides Henri Passet, Mathieu Haurine and François Salles.

'Miss Swan was not at all concerned at the idea of sleeping outdoors at 3200 metres, should the cave be blocked by the glacier,' Russell commented approvingly. 'I have rarely seen so much courage and self-confidence in such a young person.' Swan had happily followed Russell's advice and equipped them both with sheepskin sleeping bags. How Miss Swan dressed is not recorded; perhaps like Anne Lister she too taped her dress round the hem so it could be pulled up over the snow, but several photos of women outside the caves with Count Russell indicate that at least for some trousers were permitted wear.

They set off from Gavarnie with three porters, and a horse loaded up like a dromedary. At Oulettes at the head of the valley they stopped for lunch, and the porters unloaded the horse and distributed the weight among themselves. Under a fine sun they set off to climb. But when they arrived the door of the cave had disappeared, the thin sheet of metal succumbing to the immense pressure of snow which had engulfed it. This time the capricious glacier had risen right above the cave. The intrepid Miss Swan climbed up and discovered a gap between the snow and the wall of the cave, so they could slide behind a wall of ice. Once they had left their bags and provisions they climbed to the peak, Miss Swan excitedly leading the way, just in time for the sunset.

After dinner Miss Swan permitted cigars and punch, but she remained too excited to sleep. Russell insisted it was warm enough, however. 'We were admirably protected by a strong wall of ice. It is singular to be warmed by means of a glacier, but we know that eskimos are never so warm as in their snow huts.' The next day, 25 July, Swan and his sister returned to Gavarnie, where Miss Swan proudly inscribed her achievement in the visitors' book at the Hôtel des Voyageurs.

Russell stayed on in the cave with Haurine and François Salles, who had carried up twenty kilos of dry grass to make beds. Salles, a big man with a curling moustache, was famous for the prodigious weight he could carry. And also for his ability to sleep; sometimes he fell asleep like a wax-work in the middle of rolling a cigarette. He was never ambitious and when not hired as a guide he continued his work as a shepherd. He never had any money. Once when he was threatened with eviction for non-payment of rent, his friends decided to help him build a house. One gave him some land, others brought stones they had cut and dressed for the walls, others nipped into the forest (at night, to avoid the *gardiens*) to cut some wood for the beams. There is a photo of him only six months before he died at age seventy-nine in 1934, still in Gavarnie guarding his sheep, in clogs and beret, holding his shepherd's crook.

Between them all they demolished the ice that obscured the view and the light. Finally they found the door buried under the snow and pierced with holes, probably from hail-stones. They reinstalled it, stopping up the holes with whatever they could find – hay, paper, even chicken bones. Henry was as pleased as ever with his accommodation.

He liked to watch the dawn from the mouth of the cave, lying in his sleeping bag, like Neanderthal man waking to the first warm rays of the sun. The sun rose straight in front of the door, over the horizon of snow. 'Never have I seen such dawns. Never so much glory and grandeur, the light so tropical, the snow so white, the sky so blue and limpid.' He began exploring the snowy deserts and peaks that surrounded him, revelling in the sun. 'So much sun makes you forget the earth and chases away black ideas. The spirit takes on the honesty of the snow.'

He found a little friend, spending hours watching a tiny snow chaffinch jumping about on the glacier in front of the cave door, eating proffered crumbs. 'He came with the sun every morning to say hello, having slept I know not where. Two months later he came right into the cave, feeling quite at home. The following year there were three, I was feeding an entire family!' Russell was reminded of his experience in New Zealand when birds, unused to humans, perched all over his head, shoulders and arms as if he were a tree or St Francis himself. 'I would never hurt them, they are sacred beings to me.' Compared to his hunting friends, happy to decimate the bird and animal species of the Pyrenees, his respect for animals was well ahead of his time. His love for nature and for his mountains sprang from a deeply religious source, and he often writes of feeling the presence of God from his lofty perch. Not surprising then that he devised a plan to celebrate mass on the summit itself.

This grand event was planned for the following year, 1884, and an initial expedition was made with guides Haurine and Salles in the middle of July to unblock the cave and 'render it as dignified as possible for the ceremony which would create the highest chapel in Europe'. Russell conceded that its state left a lot to be desired, being still full of snow on 20 July. En route they hid caches of supplies, as he had heard they did on Arctic expeditions, thinking of the forthcoming visitors.

The floor of the cavern was still covered in ice, so the first night was disastrous. 'The ice melted under us, and we slept in a river.' Still, it was warm, thanks to a new metal door. Dusk offered a dramatic spectacle: 'A bloody tropical redness came from the west, subtly lighting all the snows of Vignemale. The rocks very black, like reefs in a sea of blood. It was terrible, indescribable, like the volcano of Krakatoa, transforming all the colours of the sky with ashes and smoke. It was like a final adieu to the world.'

The next day they had to remove all the ice, dig away all the snow that blocked the sun and dry the hay from the previous year, still intact by being deep frozen in the ice. Then they cut a deep alley of snow in front of the cave, ready for ice steps to be made in the slope when the glacier receded. Russell reckoned it looked as grand and mysterious as an Oriental Buddhist sanctuary.

Finally, by covering the snow with large flat stones, they created a terrace in front of the door. There they could sit in the sun in front of a great plain of snow and feed the attentive little chaffinches. After they all returned to Gavarnie the indefatigable Haurine was sent up to cut as much grass as he could carry to cover the floor. Then for the twelfth time Russell himself climbed to Vignemale, where he would stay for nine days. It was a time of amazing contrasts, 'of violent wind and sun, of snow without end and equatorial light, of supreme calm and terrifying storms'.

The porters sometimes had to go down to Oulettes for provisions, and he was left alone all day. 'It was a bit like

Robinson Crusoe, a life of seven or eight hours a day with just the three little birds for company.' He went from days of total solitude to times when guests were arriving almost every night. The very first night there had been visitors even before he got there himself, Edouard Wallon, and Léonce Lourde-Rocheblave, another keen mapmaker who collaborated with Schrader on the map of Mont Perdu.

'I arrived at dusk and found them in my marble cell, floating gently on a sea of grass, and in an atmosphere of 15 degrees.' This was thanks to a radical innovation, a stove donated by Henri Bellou, the hotel proprietor of Gavarnie. The porter Gregoire Junte had carried up the entire contraption on his shoulders in half a day, stove, pipe, charcoal and all, a weight of thirty-five kilos.

At dawn Russell opened the cave door. 'At 5 a.m. as the red rays entered the cave, we went out to salute the sun. It was a solemn moment, below the darkness, above the enflamed glacier.' There was a cloudless sky and Wallon busied himself taking photos of glacier and snow. Poor M. Lourde-Rocheblave, however, was suffering from gum inflammation so the visitors were obliged to leave early so he could find a dentist. Russell watched them disappear behind the wall of ice which that year had formed about a hundred metres from the cave.

He was alone again, and Vignemale was racked by such storms he could not go outside. 'I was desolate, listening to the thunder, the hail, howling wind. At one point there were three storms at the same time surrounding me in a circle of lightning, each with its own particular voice.' It is as if he is at the whirling heart of a Turner painting. 'These things have much more effect if one is alone, and why one is never bored in the mountains. Once between two storms

I received a visit from a solitary pensive isard, strolling on the glacier.'

But he was not alone for long. 'My cave was like a kaleidoscope.' Again he became a victim of his own success as more and more people heard of his exotic eyrie. The astonishing number of eighty visitors made the long and arduous pilgrimage in the space of the next two weeks or so – it is hard to imagine how they could all have found accommodation in the cramped little cave. All came loaded with gifts; M. Lorenz Preller, proprietor of Excelsior, an emporium at Eaux-Bonnes, which fulfilled every possible need for sophisticated *montagnards*, brought madeira and port, excellent Bordeaux wines were sent up by Henri Brulle, and fine perfumed tea brought from Pau by M. Daniel, famous tricyclist and head of the Syndicat d'Initiatif.

Russell's guests often had idiosyncratic special subjects with which to entertain him. M. Regelsperger discursed knowledgeably on the subject of lightning; Emile Belloc was a specialist in Pyrenean lakes and a keen photographer, and spent hours photographing Russell on the glacier. Henri Brulle followed his wine up to pay a visit himself.

But they all forgot one thing: *l'esprit de vin*, of which Russell consumed prodigious quantities to warm food and boil liquids. 'Cooking well at such altitudes is difficult, because of the scarcity of fuel. I use *l'esprit de vin* for everything. It is cheap, simple and quick.' Ever the gourmet, Russell hated to eat and drink everything cold. 'It dries the mouth,' he opined, 'so much so that after a few days you can't swallow anything at all.'

Water was obtained from the snow, melting it in the sun if there was any, or by boiling it. This was a tedious business, but then one of the guides discovered a little stone hollow which collected a permanent pool of water. 'It was a goldmine. We could fill our bottles in a minute, and I could make soup, tea, chocolate, punch or coffee in less than five minutes.'

That year they built a tower on the top of Vignemale, adding two metres to its height. It was so tall it could be seen with the naked eye from Lac de Gaube. It was a favourite subject for postcards until it finally fell down in one of the mountain's apocalpytic storms.

The mass was due to be celebrated on 12 August. Russell was alone the day before. 'There were such storms I despaired of seeing anyone. My porters went down to Oulettes to meet the pilgrims in the afternoon, and hurried back rather than leave me alone all night.'

Meanwhile Vignemale staged once of its best storms. 'It was a beautiful but terrifying spectacle, wild gigantic clouds, confused metallic explosions of thunder, and flashes of lightning. The earth and the glacier trembled. And I was alone. Even the chaffinches had disappeared, taken by vertigo and terror. The lightning was so close that I closed the door of my shelter, and hid in the heart of Vignemale, sadly lighting one single candle.' It is a poignant image, this man alone in the dark with a single candle at the heart of his beloved mountain.

He feared for his friends in the storm. 'At last I heard voices far off, on the horizon of ice, and a half hour later, could see black marks on the white terrain. Then behind a great white wave of snow a human head appeared, then another, and another, at last an entire caravan, carried along with cries of joy, even British hurrahs.' A procession appeared of priests in cassocks and black birettas, carrying alpenstocks instead of holy sceptres, guides in their traditional silver-buttoned blue jackets and doughty Englishmen in tweeds and hobnailed boots.

All were white with snow, shivering and wet. 'But they were saved. They were at the door!' They all crammed into the tiny cave. 'Fraternity became a law of nature, and no longer a fiction. In a desert one loves someone very much or not at all. It is like being on a boat.' There were fifteen people altogether. They included Père Pascal Carrère, a solidly built man with a broad face, deep cleft chin, thick white hair and a ready smile. He remained an intimate confidant of Russell till the end. The other priests were Père Cassagnère and Abbé Pomes, the priest of Saint-Pé, who had just returned from Rome. There were four tourists, 'of which one, M. Clifford, represented one of the most illustrious families of Angleterre', M. Theil, the builder of the cavern, and five guides including young Victor Chapelle, son of Henri Chapelle, a favourite guide who had been killed in a hunting accident a few years before.

They lit the stove, Henry made tea and they dined one after the other while their clothes dried out. 'The exquisite wine sent up by M. Brulle was a great success, but even with water, we would all have been happy.' A toast was proposed to the admirable clergy of France (no anti-clerical sentiments here) followed by singing, dessert, coffee and cigars. 'The coffee was so hot it burnt the fingers even though boiling point is lower at such an altitude.'

After dinner they went to walk on the frontier of Col de Cerbillona (Russell had named it the rue d'Espagne) to see the sun shining like a river of gold on the glacier. Despite the precipices and storms that separated them from the civilized world, they could still see Bordeaux and Toulouse to the north and Saragossa in Spain to the south.

At 11 p.m. they returned for Henry's famous punch. The wind had dropped, and it was silent. 'The snow shone and Vignemale seemed like a cathedral in the moonlight.' Back in the shelter Abbé Pomes stood up and recited a prayer. Then everybody said goodnight and tried to lie down as best they could in the cramped space. Brave Haurine slept outside.

Unfortunately, by the next morning the wind had got up again, but it was still clear and beautiful. Even more people arrived, the young Comte de Champeaux, Henri Passet from Gavarnie, and a large caravan from Cauterets, with another priest, another photographer and several guides.

Russell had hoped that the mass could be offered on the summit itself, but the ferocious wind made it impossible. Instead the censers were lit and the sacrament of bread and wine was offered by the priests, their white surplices billowing in the wind, on the snowy bank in front of the cave. 'It was cold outside, but despite that, how to be there without being moved, to the depths of the spirit, by the grandeur and poetry of this spectacle at sunrise, on a wild sea of ice. It was more moving and eloquent than all the pomp of a basilica. Paris or Rome had never seen anything like it. One seemed closer to heaven than under the most splendid vaults of the world.'

As the host was lifted to heaven the sun rose, illuminating the ocean of peaks and burnishing the snows. Père Carrère raised his hands to the sky and solemnly blessed Russell's little shelter, transformed into a chapel. It was a great moment of theatre. No medieval hermit could have done it better. It lacked only the sudden appearance of stigmata for Henry's religious instinct to be completely satisfied. Most of the spectators shivering on the glacier were still frozen from the night, but despite the pitiless wind and cold most bared their heads, honoured to be there on that desolate peak, a frontier separating two nations, at 3200 metres above sea level.

Henry was fifty. Mother church had blessed his union with the mountain, his mystical marriage with nature. All that remained was to make it legal.

20

The troglodyte of the snows

For I would walk alone,
Under the quiet stars, and at that time
Have felt whate'er there is of power in sound
To breathe an elevated mood, by form
Or image unprofaned: and I would stand,
If the night blackened with a coming storm,
Beneath some rock, listening to notes that are
The ghostly language of the ancient earth,
Or make their dim abode in distant winds.

William Wordsworth, *The Prelude*

Though reluctant to seek out a rocky refuge of my own, I have come to cherish the eccentric loners I have met in the Pyrenees. Skall, the Austrian rainbow warrior, in his hut on the mountainside, digging his garden and channelling fresh water from the stream, in the company of several dogs and a goat, or Christiane, a woman of at least fifty with wild hair and clear piercing blue eyes, who guards a herd of several hundred cows high up on Madres. She lives alone for six months of the year in a stone house I first mistook for a ruin, simply furnished with a long wooden table, and a bed in the hayloft above. I had tea with her one day, and asked if she ever got bored. No, she said, and indicated a prodigious stack of *policiers* (detective novels). It was odd to think of this recluse lost in an imaginary world of urban crime.

Sometimes I go to visit Caty, our very own mountain hermit, the nearest I can get to a mountain sage. People in the village talk of her with the same mixture of awe and puzzlement that Henry Russell occasioned. They make pilgrimages to see her, taking gifts of wine, or food for her animals, just as Russell attracted a stream of determined acolytes to his remote mountain residence. Caty has lived alone on a mountain plateau at an altitude of 1200 metres for the past twenty years, returning to the village every week or two for supplies and a few drinks in the bar, but ultimately content to be solitary. She cares for a sanctuary of horses, stray dogs, numerous chickens and a very large pig. She saved an entire herd of horses, who until recently were bred locally and then sent to Italy to be turned into horsemeat.

I walked up through the woodland from Mosset to visit her one day with my friend Monique, taking it in turns to speak French and English as we walked. Neither of us is particularly fluent and we often struggle for the right words, but somehow walking together has created a special kind of intimacy. Caty greeted us with a wave and a shout as we appeared on the horizon, echoed by the neighing of horses and barking of numerous dogs.

Caty is tiny, wiry and strong, as brown as a South American Indian, with short springy silver-streaked brown hair, dressed in loose pants and a faded T-shirt, with dusty espadrilles on her tanned feet. A cow I had not previously noticed mooed plaintively, and she hurried off to attend to it. Her small hands with their narrow wrists stroked the animal's soft flanks with gentle confidence preparatory to removing stitches after a Caesarean birth. 'Her calf died, so she has been very unhappy,' Caty explained. Then she milked the goat, deftly massaging the teats as the milk spurted into a small saucepan. I was pressed to drink a warm cupful immediately. It was delicious.

We ate lunch together, eggs from her chickens, fresh goat's cheese she had made ('from a virgin goat,' she laughed gleefully), Monique's chocolate cake and a bag of cherries from my garden. There were chickens pecking at our boots, horses peering over the fence, and a tame cockerel which had jumped onto Caty's lap as soon as she sat down. The great Pyrenean sheep dog for which I had developed a secret passion nudged me to stroke it, which was not difficult given its head was on a level with my elbow. It was like something out of Doctor Dolittle. Even the cobwebs were left hanging from the rafters, Quentin Crisp style, so as not to disturb the spiders.

We were surrounded by mountains, with Canigou a blue haze in the distance across a plateau of soft grass scattered with huge rocks, with no sign of civilization except Caty's own ramshackle barn, divided into living space and animal accommodation in traditional peasant manner, without running water or electricity. It was hardly convenient; that winter we had a lot of heavy snow and she was completely cut off for weeks. One snowy day we were snowed in ourselves and heard a helicopter overhead. It landed at the horse farm two fields away and we watched anxiously as people hurried to and fro. We expected a stretcher at least but eventually a small figure appeared pushing several bales of hay, which were loaded into the side door of the helicopter. I guessed, correctly, it was hay for Caty's animals. We have a very sympathetic mayor who had organized bottled gas and animal fodder to be taken up to Caty. I think for everyone Caty is emblematic. Despite or because of her eccentricity she is cherished, as if people need someone like her to live on the edge, pushing the boundaries of what we consider to be normal life. Somehow we need her to be there.

I asked her why she chose to live the hermit life. 'I always wanted to live in nature with animals, ever since I was a child,' she said. After growing up in a wealthy family in Paris (her mother was chief model for Hermes) she escaped to the Pyrenees over twenty years ago, arriving with a boyfriend and a plan to raise goats. 'We came one day in January; it was cold with a bright blue sky and no wind. It was perfect.' Soon the boyfriend left but Caty stayed on. 'The local farmers were very sceptical. They called us *les Pink Floyds*,' Caty recalled, a French term for hippies then. 'And when I stayed on they were aghast. A *parisienne* is going to stay up there all winter, alone!' Defiant: 'I stayed eighteen years!' Looking at this tiny person in her vast landscape I decided that, given the chance, you can simply expand to fill the space.

I wondered if she was ever afraid. She threw back her head and laughed at me, as if this was the last place in the world she need feel afraid, and for answer took Monique and me to see her most special place. We walked for half a mile or so over the soft turf, carpeted with clouds of pale yellow narcissi, stopping to greet and nuzzle several horses on the way. We stopped at the spring where she bathed and collected drinking water pumped into an old bath tub. Next to it was a deposit of natural kaolin and at Caty's instigation we all smeared our faces and arms with the mud and lay on the soft grass in the sun until the clay was dry and cracking on our skin. It felt so smooth and soft when we washed it off in the spring water afterwards – a natural mud pack. For a little while we were all children of nature.

Then Caty showed us the plague stone. A huge slab of granite rock several feet taller than we were was inscribed with the date and an inscription in Catalan: '*Asi en lo cortal de Joan Loyga eses tat abaracat per la pesta*: Here at the cortal of Joan Loyga was erected a shelter from the plague. 1653.' It was here that a small colony of villagers had retreated to escape the plague in the seventeenth century, drinking this pure water to survive. This was their memorial. To Caty it represented security, a place of safety, anchored in the middle of the nature she found entirely benevolent.

Later when a film was made about Mosset, Caty became one of the stars and a memorable sequence features her, the outsider, the *étrangère*, with a local family, people who have lived there for generations. She is taking them to see the stone, which they have heard of but only she knows where to find, showing them their own secrets, showing them what is already there.

I think Russell fulfilled the same function. People thought him mad but held him in awe nevertheless. He was the holy fool, the visionary, the sage on a mountain top. And like Caty, like Skall, like the Egyptian desert fathers – the early Christian hermits – whose remote caves were sometimes surrounded by crowds of disciples, his very solitude attracted acolytes. The more he tried to escape the more he was sought out.

His passion for Vignemale did not abate. He often wrote about it as if he were a painter, describing the mountain in all its aspects, finding new angles and new lights, like Cézanne and Mont-Saint-Victoire, or Monet and his many paintings of Rouen cathedral. He depicted it at all hours, in all lights, and in all colours: Vignemale frozen, Vignemale radiant and burning, Vignemale white, blue, polar, lunar, Vignemale pink, yellow, red, Vignemale the ogre, ready to devour all who approached, an idyllic Vignemale gentle and seductive, Vignemale like the holy mountain of Moses, the Sinai, all fiery storms, lightning and thunderous voice. He wrote an entire essay on the clouds on Vignemale, which he often watched for hours at a time.

As soon as the snows started to melt, he would abandon Pau and its cosmopolitan pleasures and head for Gavarnie, ready to begin planning the first expedition to open the cave. After 1885 he did little more climbing in the rest of the Pyrenees. He records one expedition to Luchon and the Pico Gallinero, in Spain, south-west of Posets. From the summit he was rewarded with a gratifying sunset of purple and gold, and returning via an unknown valley he spent the night under the moon and stars. He writes in his characteristic voluptuous style of the dawn, the dewdrops glistening on the grass, the suave and splendid night and the spray of a waterfall in the moonlight.

But he felt he had been unfaithful to his true love when on his return to Vignemale he was almost decapitated by a huge stone rolling down the mountainside. 'It hit my hat and covered me in dust, brushed against Haurine, but killed no-one. The next year we found the huge hole it had dug in the ground.'

That year another cave was dug, this time for the guides, but the weather was terrible, and Russell spent a grim week in fog, hail and snow. There were still visitors, however, including a professor and his wife from Toulouse, M. Daniel, the tricyclist from Pau, and Lamazouère, a photographer from Bagnères-de-Bigorre, best known for the huge photographic panorama he took from the summit of the Pic du Midi. Russell, with several of his visitors, finally abandoned ship at the end of August, fleeing in a violent snowstorm. Haurine had declared that morning that it was impossible to leave, but since they had no more provisions they were obliged to descend despite the conditions.

'We were hammered by hailstones, the wind whipped us fiercely, and we were covered in frost and ice. We looked like polar shipwrecks,' Russell recalled. 'We were asphyxiated, swallowing so much snow it was impossible to breathe, and our fingers were blue with cold.' Fortunately they were equipped with a rope and a compass and managed to avoid the great crevasse without departing too far from the right path.

Undaunted, Russell planned a third cave, which was finished in 1886, the Grotte des Dames (the Ladies' Cave), dug four metres above the others, to escape the caprices of the glacier. This cave Russell considered the best of all though it was very small, only eight cubic metres. 'It was always warm, even in intense cold, and always dry, never a drop of water came through the ceiling. At least a dozen ladies passed the night there!'

That year, 1886, Russell recorded his fifteenth ascent of Vignemale, but conditions even at the end of August were difficult. A lot of new snow fell, making it hard to go outside. 'Each time we left our morose prison the snow crystallized on us in five minutes, great icicles formed in our hair straight away. We looked like marble statues and had to return immediately.' He spent one exciting hour in a total tempest on the col, but even for Russell it was too much. 'The noise and anger was like the end of the world, as if hell had opened up.'

Being incarcerated in the cave for days on end was grim; with the door always closed, it was too dark to read, and 'a sepulchral silence reigned'. There were four of them altogether, Russell and three of his favourite guides, Haurine, Salles and Célestin Passet, whom he considered as much friends as guides. They spoke little though Russell records an animated conversation about Irish Home Rule, a subject which was enough to stimulate him to talk even in such conditions.

But finally food was the only consolation. 'We became so sad we only opened our mouths to eat. That we did regularly: veal with tomato sauce, mutton, turkey, Scottish herrings, *boeuf à la mode*, all imaginable vegetables.' They had discovered the tinned food of Chollet et Prevet; 'admirable invention', remarked Russell. The plates steamed, the cave was full of vapour and they got through a litre of *esprit de vin* each day. Still the snow rose, and by the fourth night they began to believe they would be snowed in completely, and not even have any air. 'I slept little I was so worried. The thought of a morgue haunted me.'

But at last the snow stopped. '26 August: the sun rose with oriental pomp. It was like a resurrection, we opened the door again, we could leap on the snow, laugh and sing, run like escaped fools, I felt twenty years younger, electrified by light, air and liberty. I saluted the peaks as if they were my brothers.' Once outside they began to rummage for caches of provisions. 'I found lots of things hidden last year under the rocks, among them three bottles of Médoc, one in pieces, one full but open, but the other still intact. The wine was exquisite. The cigars less so.' Finally on the sixth day of their sojourn they could climb to the summit of Vignemale.

One night a familiar voice was heard at the door, and a figure in a priest's soutane and stout boots appeared. It was Abbé Pomes, one of the three priests who had celebrated mass in 1884. He had left from Lourdes at 6 a.m. and arrived twelve hours later. 'We passed a delicious evening, which would have been the envy of those who were poisoning their spirit and body in casinos and theatres,' opined Russell pompously, no doubt influenced by his clerical chum. The next morning they saluted a magnificent dawn. 'We made a poetic promenade on the snow, which was like a desert of diamonds. The surface was like marble and despite the sun we left no traces. The purely physical effect of the savannah of sparkling new snow, burnt by the sun, under a sky as black as the depths of the sea, is enchanting.' It was such joy to be warm at last. 'With closed eyes one could imagine oneself inside the sun. It was ecstasy.'

Vignemale and its eccentric inhabitant soon became famous. It was the mountain à la mode. In 1884 alone, nearly a hundred people had arrived to conquer the peak and visit its self-styled hermit. By 1888 Vignemale was almost a fashionable destination, part of a tour of the Pyrenees for the most intrepid, English, French, American and Russian as well. With the help of guides and porters they struggled determinedly, often through snow and ice and wind, to cross the glacier and reach the summit and its legendary incumbent.

Henri Brulle recalled Russell's hospitality. 'Invitations were always issued with impeccable tact, and etiquette followed, especially with women present.' There were certain obligatory rites: watching the sunrise was *de rigueur*, as was the punch served regularly at 11 p.m. Le Comte always liked to be complimented on his caves, and no-one was allowed to mention how damp or uncomfortable they were. 'Sometimes a drop of water ran down the neck or there were insects in the straw but it was not polite to mention it, and one simply dried or scratched discreetly. For all the Happy Few, they were the best nights of our lives,' recorded Brulle. The question of supplies was always of the greatest importance because Russell had a great appetite and liked to entertain. 'So much cooking equipment! for frying, and decoctions and infusions. For sleeping there were kilos and kilos of straw. And he was not insensible up there to little presents, most of all flagons of alcohol, which were used a lot for cooking.'

Russell spent one of his best weeks on Vignemale in 1887. 'The most brilliant I ever passed in the mountains, superb sun, intense light, barely a cloud, and no wind. I was truly happy in my immaculate kingdom of snow. On the glacier, the moon shone every night, and the sky was full of stars. During the day the plains of Spain were red as Africa. It was like seeing Siberia and India at the same time.' Russell sat content on a throne of snow on the summit.

'The King of Vignemale' as his guides had nicknamed him held court for many visitors that year, including, to his dismay, seventeen members of the Society of Excursionists of Béarn. He also had a visit from his old friend, Charles Packe, with one of his Pyrenean sheep dogs, Diana, who must have taken up a considerable amount of space in the cave.

'An acquaintance with Count Russell is almost a corollary of knowing the Pyrenees, more especially since he has made his three caves on the summit of Vignemale,' wrote Packe in his *Alpine Journal* review of Russell's revised 1888 edition of the *Souvenirs*, this time organized geographically by Russell, from east to west along the chain. 'A sketch of Count Russell in his cave on the Vignemale would be an interesting addition to "Celebrities at Home".'

What did they talk about, these two old friends, fast becoming the older generation? No doubt they discussed their own failing powers, and the changes in the Pyrenees, the increasing flood of weekend excursionists and the rise of *pyrénéisme de difficulté*, or acrobatism as they called it. What they would have made of today's climbing gyms with no mountains at all doesn't bear thinking about. Packe called Russell's book 'a protest against the increasing number of members who look solely to making a successful ascent, blind and deaf to all else concerning it'.

It may have been a while since they had met; Packe had inherited Stretton Hall, in Great Glen, in 1867 and married soon after – his wife, Selina, had several Pyrenean climbs to her credit – and had settled into his role of English squire and JP in Leicestershire. He alternated his visits to the Alps and Pyrenees every year, and had published little more after his esteemed guide, save a few articles in the *Alpine Journal*. But Russell often visited England, and may have visited Packe at home. Their correspondence is either destroyed or guarded by over-zealous families.

This is the only visit to the caves by Packe that Russell records; one suspects that Charles, the prosaic Englishman, may have been a little sceptical about his friend's obsession, though he too had always shared the same passion for sublime solitude. Perhaps Charles was reinvigorated by his visit to his old friend. Afterwards he paid at least two more visits to the Pyrenees, retracing his paths of old.

Perhaps they talked about Packe's return to the desecrated valley of Ordesa. He had long bemoaned the primitive Spanish habit of clearing the land for tillage by burning the forest, and now disastrous fires had severely damaged the valley in a way that would not have been permitted in France: '. . . but in these mountainous regions of Spain everyone seems to feel, and I believe really is, beyond the reach of law.'

This, however, applied especially to the British, who had helped to destroy most of the flora and fauna of the Ordesa valley by the end of the century. The Spanish created the Ordesa National Park in 1918 in an effort to protect it. In 1868 Sir Henry Halford began the great massacre of the *bouquetins* which was continued by Sir Victor Brooke, the number one sportsman of the Pau colony, who obtained from Torla the annual concession for hunting in Ordesa, and hunted there from 1878 to 1887 with his brothers and the American Arthur Post, another key figure in the sporting life of Pau. Another companion was Sir Edward North Buxton, whose wittily titled memoir *Short Stalks* recounts animal killing on an epic scale; he took over the Ordesa concession from Brooke, and was probably responsible for the death of the last *bouquetin* of the Pyrenees. To reduce the distance between Gavarnie and the Ordesa valley he had crampons installed on the sides of the gorge. The British even left litter. In 1876 a hunter chasing a bear in the wild reaches of the gorge spotted a white patch on the ground and discovered a page of *The Times*.

The Pyrenean flora fared little better in the hands of the British. While hunting, Buxton had noticed a certain kind of rare jonquil which he dug up and planted in England. When a drawing of the flower appeared in the *Gardeners' Chronicle* it was identified as the rare *Narcissus moschatus*, which had become all the rage in England after a Daffodil Congress held in April 1884, organized by horticulturalist Peter Barr, who had searched Europe for rare natural hybrids of the flower. In 1889 Barr turned up in the Ordesa valley and over the next few years it is estimated he dug up at least 10,000 bulbs, destroying acres of pasture land in the process. By the time Packe returned the Spanish were on guard, and he was almost arrested for digging up a dozen bulbs.

Russell and Packe probably discussed the guides. Packe remarks of Henri Passet in one of his papers that 'like others who have reached the head of their profession, he is rather disposed to rate his services at an exorbitant value'. They may have noted the progress of young Victor Chapelle and remembered with sadness his father, killed in 1873, 'the prince of Pyrenean guides'.

Henri Chapelle, named after the chapel in the tiny village of Héas, had been one of their favourite guides, an original character whose singular appearance – rounded chest, narrow nose, pale grey eyes, wrinkled skin, tangled blond hair and fringe of beard – distinguished him from the sallow, dark-haired local southerners. A cook in his youth, Chapelle could make a fine omelette, if he ever had any eggs, and his house, with a large ham generally hanging from the beams, was treated like an *auberge*. Russell was a regular customer. Chapelle was small and, though lame after a horse had thrown him, always quick and nervous, never walking if he could run or jump. He spoke an excited mixture of French, Spanish, patois and even scraps of English he had gleaned on a visit to England, invited by Charles Packe, who considered his guide such a gentleman he had presented him with a top hat. In return, esteeming Packe a *montagnard*, Chapelle had given him a beret. The guide had not enjoyed England, missing the Pyrenees so much he had climbed a tree to try to escape the fog.

Sadly, Chapelle had been killed in a hunting accident in 1874. He was wearing an animal skin and was mistaken for an isard and shot with twenty-six rounds of buckshot. He was brought back to Héas, where Russell saw him before he died, resigned and stoical. Packe wrote a Latin inscription for him, which was carved on a memorial stone at Troumouse.

One particular event in the social calendar of Vignemale has passed into legend: the grand banquet on the glacier planned by Brulle and his friends. As Henry put it, 'My amiable colleagues, Comte de Monts, M. Brulle and M. Bazillac, paid suitable homage.' A huge convoy of fifteen people arrived, the porters so loaded down with luxuries they added a metre to their height. As the long column of marchers appeared over the snow in the glow of the late sun, their huge shadows stretched across the glacier looked at least thirty metres long. Russell admitted that at first an invasion of so many people had troubled him: 'But they were friends, as enraptured by the Pyrenees as I was, and who rendered my life so pleasant and charming during their stay that I was sorry to see them go.'

A tent was erected on the snow facing the caves, and the company spent three days wining and dining in sumptuous comfort. ' Never in my little empire of snow had I seen so many good things,' Russell exclaimed, reconciled to the invasion by the appearance of so much good food. They were equipped with rugs, armchairs, bedding, Eskimo costumes, Oriental perfumes, lanterns and vaporizers – 'without counting the cigars, the fine wines, and a monumental ham that would have served as a cushion.' Rugs were spread out on the glacier, and fires kept going till midnight. Lanterns flickered over the snow like a lighthouse. The weather was perfect, with cloudless skies and not a zephyr of wind. Finally Mme Brulle herself arrived to stay for twenty-four hours, and in her honour a beautiful multicoloured carpet was laid out on the snow in front of the tent between columns of snow decorated with red lichen.

Russell remained unconvinced about the tent. 'I have never been a partisan of the tent,' he sniffed. 'Happily it was calm. But a few days earlier it would have been swept away in a few seconds. I don't think a tent on a glacier or snow, near the summit of a high mountain, is useful for long. You need firm earth, a dry solid floor. Even with a fire, with a floor of snow it is always cold.'

Sadly, the caves were doomed. By the following year the glacier had risen further and two of the caves were lost permanently under the snow. Over the next five years the only one to reappear was the Grotte des Dames. Reluctantly Russell decided to relocate, and over the next three years three more caves were dug lower down the mountainside, below the level of the glacier, at 2400 metres. It was a good site, still in full sun and sheltered from snow, with such a tremendous view that Russell called it Belle Vue. To the south-east was a view down the valley d'Ossoue as far as the Cirque and peaks of Gavarnie. It was much farther from the summit, of course, but Russell consoled himself that it still only took two and a half hours to get up there and he could easily get there and back in ten hours with two hours on the summit.

Conditions were not entirely satisfactory, however. 'At Belle Vue the big cave is very warm and very useful. It drips often near the door, up to a metre in but not farther, and since it is four metres long there is still at least six square metres which are always dry. I have slept there in all weathers, in appalling storms, and have never been wet. I cannot say as much for the middle cave. That is a complete fiasco; the vault is full of water and it drips in cascades. But the other cave, which is ten metres in depth, is a success and can lodge twelve people.'

There is an endearing picture of Henry, sitting on the ledge in front of the Grottes de Belle Vue, in a homburg hat (he seems to have possessed an extraordinary variety of hats) and a tweed jacket over a pristine white collar, his legs crossed, leaning over to read the book on his knee. Hanging on the wall is his water gourd and a large leather satchel, and next to him on the ledge a large leather Gladstone bag, a box of cigars and a bottle of wine.

*

After so much labour Russell decided it was time to regularize his liaison with Vignemale, and in 1888 he applied to the local commune to lease it. The exchange of correspondence over this bizarre request is a model of French bureaucracy. In December 1888 Russell wrote to the Préfet of the Hautes Pyrénées formally requesting a lease of ninety-nine years for the glacier and peak of Vignemale. He stressed that he was only interested in the rocks, ice and snow and not the lower pastures.

He argued that all the work he had done there, and the benefit to the public of the cave refuges he had created, entitled him to become proprietor. At a meeting of the commune of the valley of Barèges in February (which included Pujo, one of the local guides, and Russell's great friend M. Vergez-Bellou, proprietor of the Hôtel des Voyageurs in Gavarnie) it was unanimously decided to grant the concession for a nominal fee of one franc per annum. It was noted, pragmatically, that M. le Comte Russell's enterprise in constructing refuges had made the ascent of Vignemale easier and helped attract tourists to the region. The lease was signed and the territory solemnly outlined in pink on the commune map.

Russell was delighted. Now Vignemale was truly his. 'It is certainly the highest property in Europe,' he noted gleefully, 'and despite its sterility, I would not change it for the most beautiful domaine in France.'

It was more than mere property, however. It was a love affair. 'One adopts a mountain, one marries it, one adores it, one presents it proudly to one's friends, one finds in it so much virtue and beauty, one has eyes for nothing else. That is how it happened for me with Vignemale. Because of living there I fell in love with it.'

What he could not change, however, was the growing enthusiasm for *pyrénéisme de difficulté*, and of the acrobats he railed against the most enthusiastic of all was his own protégé, Henri Brulle. Brulle was determined to conquer the Couloir de Gaube, a steep vertical corridor rising 600 metres vertically almost to the peak of Vignemale. No-one had ever attempted to climb it. As far as Russell was concerned there were easier and more aesthetic ways to the top. But Brulle saw it as a challenge. 'It is from the extremity of the valley of Gaube that the Vignemale looks most defiant. A great ice couloir cleaves its dark and inaccessible ramparts but it is itself so fierce-looking and vertiginous that it had been haunting my dreams for a long time.' He made the attempt in August 1889 with his daredevil chum Bazillac, the Comte de Monts and the guides Célestin Passet and François Salles. Russell thoroughly disapproved, despising risk-taking for its own sake. Despite his protests he was unable to convince them to stop, so instead climbed up to the summit by an easier route, in order, as he put it, 'to watch them die'.

At first the climb went well, Brulle wrote in his account for the Alpine Club Journal. Then things got difficult. 'Little by little the slope increased alarmingly; ice succeeded snow, and the ascent became very severe. Very near the top of the couloir we came upon a really diabolical obstacle. It was a great boulder, hemmed in between the two rock walls, slightly overhanging, about five metres high, and covered with a thick coating of ice. We spent there two terrible hours, in an intense cold, and unable either to turn or force the passage.'

While they contemplated a long bitter night on the ice, Célestin Passet hacked away furiously with the ice-axe, cutting 1300 steps in the ice, and scattering great chunks of ice on the climbers below. Célestin said not a word, and before admitting defeat he rested and insisted on a last try. 'Against all hope he got his knee onto the top of the wall, could haul himself up and let down a rope to aid the others.' Still one of them slipped and was left dangling in space till the others could rescue him. After seven hours' further scrambling over stalactites of ice, they finally emerged on the ice plateau, and speedily scaled the summit. On the way down they stopped for tea with 'the hospitable troglodyte of the Belle Vue caves'. The troglodyte's comments on their prowess are not recorded, but in this instance at least, Célestin Passet, the guide, is justly credited with the first ascent of the Couloire de Gaube, rather than his employers. It was to be forty-four years before anybody did it again.

Although visitors were always received with Russell's characteristic courtesy, he was beginning to feel besieged, his solitude too frequently invaded. He began to dread the crowds of tourists even more. On one occasion when he had decided to spend the night alone, a large group arrived. He simply left, and was seen proudly crossing the plateau giving them a solemn salute of farewell.

A Russian resident of Pau, Michel de Chrouschoff, recalled trying to visit Russell, 'the celebrated *anglais*, known as *le Robinson des Pyrénées*'. He wrote that no self-respecting mountaineer should visit the Pyrenees without meeting Russell, whom he considered the true poet, the Homer of the Pyrenees. But M. le Comte often proved elusive. 'You may have to scale twenty peaks before locating him. They tell you he is in his Vignemale cave, 3000 metres up. You climb, you arrive at the celebrated cave. You open the door which protects the guests from the bears during the night. You enter, but there is no-one there. A note is fixed to the door with a nail, informing you that the Count has left for Luchon and the Maladetta. You go back down to Gavarnie, having drunk a few mouthfuls of the excellent rum that Robinson always leaves on the table for unexpected visitors. Then you make your way to Luchon, you climb the Maladetta, but a shepherd tells you that the terrible wandering Jew is in Spain, exploring unknown territory, playing at Christopher Columbus.'

By 1892 Russell was desperate to regain the summit, and decided to dig out his highest cave yet. 'I regretted my wild life in the high regions and my splendid desert of snow, where despite the tempests, the isolation and the cold, I had spent days so peaceful and sweet midway between heaven and earth.' Although conditions lower down were easier – the climate relatively gentle, Gavarnie much closer and communications better – and he had a good source of water instead of melted snow, he was nostalgic for the snows, 'the infinite whiteness, the mystical nights, the horizons without bounds. I had lost it all in descending 800 metres and I wept for my aerial cells, my dear disappeared caves. My heart always rose there, and 2400 metres seemed almost on the level of the plain!' He decided he had grown to love the snow as much as the sea. 'Perhaps,' he mused, 'one day there will be snow cures?' Perhaps.

So he sketched out a plan for another cavern, the seventh, a number of biblical significance for Henry no doubt, which would be only twenty metres from the summit of Vignemale, thus the most elevated of all. He became obsessed with the struggle to dig it. The rock there was very hard, which was why he had been dissuaded from digging the original caves there. In order to dig out just eight cubic metres it required four determined men working for six weeks, sleeping forty-two nights in a microscopic wooden cabin at 3280 metres, beside a summit which was constantly struck by lightning. One night there was a terrifying storm and their provisions were pulverized, so that nothing was left. 'Panic, famine and despair!' It became clear that despite their determination it was impossibly dangerous to spend very long up there without an invulnerable refuge, and that gunpowder was not enough. Then Russell had another idea. 'Dynamite!'

'So the following year, procuring some kilos of dynamite, I went back up with my four or five brave workers from Gèdre. All went well, complete revolution. With my new engine, the hardest rocks cracked, with stones projected fifty metres over the glacier. Instead of six weeks like the previous summer, twenty days were enough to dig eight more cubic metres and I had then the joy of possessing, five minutes from the summit, a very beautiful cave, of more than sixteen cubic metres, very dry, in full sun, and with an incommensurable view.' He named it le Paradis. The cave did not have a door, due to the risk of lightning, which would have burnt a wooden door and possibly been attracted by the metal version he had put on all the other caves. It was, apparently, the first recorded private use of dynamite, but there is something unsettling about Russell, in his frustration, blasting his way with such violence into his mountain.

Several years later, the cave was discovered by another Englishman, Harold Spender. Spender was a liberal journalist and politician, the son of Victorian novelist Mrs J. K. Spender and father of poet Stephen Spender. Henry Russell was an enigmatic name in English mountaineering circles, and Spender was keen to visit him in his mountain cave. He records his attempt, with his companion Hugh Llewellyn Smith, in his book *Through the High Pyrenees*, an account of two visits to the Pyrenees in 1896 and 1897.

The two friends climbed to the summit of Vignemale but found it covered in cloud and saw nothing. When they came upon Russell's highest cave, le Paradis, it was empty, but they were impressed by its snugness. 'The entrance is low and narrow – half closed with masonry – and you have to crawl to get in. But once within one is snugly housed, in a rock-bound chamber, secure from cold and wind, and even provided with its own water supply, which trickles through the rock and falls in great cold drops into your upturned mouth. It is a sumptuous lodging for the mountaineer, and no man within that rock chamber need fear to spend a night on the summit of the Vignemale.'

Spender called it 'one of the most remarkable assertions of man's power over the high mountains anywhere existing'. He compared it to the huts on the Matterhorn and Gross Glockner in the Alps, but pointed out that Russell's cave was more permanent. 'We ate and drank, and grew warm and cheerful for our return.' Once they had slid and scrambled down the glacier again they arrived at the lower caves of Belle Vue. 'They are slightly more roomy than the grotto above, but in all essentials are the same – just little holes in the rock, scarcely big enough for a man to stand upright, carpeted with hay, and as warm and snug as they are barbarous to view.' Russell's caves can still be seen today, according to the new *gardien* of the Bayssellance refuge, Stefan Gavard, though the retreat of the glacier has left three of them accessible only by climbing.

Spender and Llewellyn Smith were disappointed not to find Count Russell 'at home'. He had apparently come and gone for the summer, having experienced very bad weather. They talked about Russell to the guides, who 'spoke of Count Russell with a sort of awed respect, as of a great and mysterious individual whose purposes however strange, and however far beyond their divination, were necessarily wise. And this was the general view of him in the valley. There was no understanding of the meaning of the grottoes, and decided head shaking over the whole affair, many freely intimating that they would rather sleep out of doors. But there was a general agreement that Count Russell could not be far wrong, for his heart was in the right place – to wit, in the Pyrenees.'

Spender was touched by Russell's passion. 'It is the story of a romantic attachment, none the less noble because its object was a mountain. He himself, indeed, describes his feeling towards the mountain as resembling filial piety; but it is more like the passion of a lover for his mistress.'

21

Baron de Lassus and the Chambord of the Pyrenees

'There is nothing to look up to; all is below.'

Edward Whymper

I wanted to know more about Russell in later life and wrote to the family of Baron Bertrand de Lassus, who had been one of his great friends and admirers. I received a gracious reply from Baroness de Lassus, inviting us to lunch at the Château de Valmirande, built by the baron in 1899. Her late husband was Bertrand's nephew and the family cherished the memory of the relationship between the two mountain-lovers, Bertrand and Russell.

So, on our journey through the Pyrenees, Theo and I arrived at the Château de Valmirande in Montréjeau, a small town at the foot of the Pyrenees. We sounded our klaxon as instructed outside the great iron gates, which swung open to receive us. We drove in along a curving drive through a lovely park of mature trees, to the grand entrance of the chateau, flanked by picturesque parterres to the north and south.

It has been called the Chambord of the Pyrenees with good reason, as it bears a remarkable resemblance to the great sixteenth-century Renaissance chateau built by Francois I in the Loire valley. Like Chambord it is bristling with a cornucopia of turrets, spires, cupolas, terraces and fancy chimney pots, with at least a hundred windows, and almost merits the same description, 'the skyline of Constantinople on a single roof'.

Mme de Lassus appeared at the great carved entrance door, a spry and refined old lady as tiny as her chateau is large. She ushered us inside the magnificent lobby, sumptuously panelled in wood and marble, with a huge chimney-piece and monumental staircase elaborately carved with dragons and other mythical beasts. Large oil paintings adorned the walls and glittering chandeliers hung from the high coffered ceiling. In pride of place was a portrait of Baron Bertrand de Lassus himself, always known as Uncle Bertrand. We had arrived bang on time, after Theo negotiated a tricky short cut off the over-crowded Route Nationale, his first attempt at navigational map reading. ('We always dine at one,' Mme de Lassus had said firmly when we spoke on the phone.)

We had lunch in the dining room, the oval mahogany table laid with crystal glasses and crested tableware; a classic delicious meal of melon, grilled sole and perfect peaches, accompanied by a St Emilion grand cru we had all been to select from a magnificently cobwebbed wine cellar.

The Baroness spoke excellent English in a cut-glass accent like the Queen's, and explained she had been brought up by an English nanny and an English governess. She was not from the Pyrenees, but said 'I feel anchored here', which sounded subtly more upper class than putting down roots.

At this table Bertrand de Lassus and Henry Russell dined together many times, eulogizing their beloved Pyrenees, and admiring the view to the south, which combined the carefully managed picturesqueness of an

English park and the distant wilderness of the mountains. On a clear day they could see as far as Spain and the Monts Maudits.

'Oncle Bertrand chose the location of the chateau for this view,' explained Madame, 'buying up *parcelles* of land until he had enough to build on.' He employed one of the most fashionable architects of the day, Louis Garros, known for his Bordeaux chateaux, and the hundred-acre park was designed by Eugène Bühler of Bordeaux and planted by a botanist professor from Toulouse.

When the young Baron de Lassus met Henry Russell he was only twenty, a scion of southern French aristocracy and a fervent admirer of M. le Comte, thirty years his senior. There is a picture of them together, posing proudly on a flight of stone steps, both looking the epitome of late-nineteenth-century dandies. Russell is in bowler hat, his neatly trimmed goatee beard now white, staring coolly into the distance, eyebrows slightly quizzical. His jacket is buttoned high, over a white stock collar and cravat, watch chain and handkerchief dangling from his pocket, and one hand is resting on his cane. Baron de Lassus is marginally more casual, gazing directly at the camera, with hands in the pockets of his three-piece tweed suit, jacket open, waistcoat tightly buttoned over a growing paunch. He looks distinctly pleased with himself, sporting a jaunty fedora, and a perfectly curled dark moustache.

The Lassus family were important landowners in Montréjeau, on the plain of Lannemezan north of Bagnères-de-Luchon. They were newly created barons under the Second Empire in the nineteenth century. His mother came from a rich banking family and from an early age young Bertrand had a substantial fortune at his disposal.

After he finished his studies in Paris he decided to establish himself *au pays*, in the country. He loved the mountains and by age fifteen was already a keen climber. He rooted himself firmly in the locality, and loved playing gentry and dispensing largesse as a generous benefactor to the community. The Boulevard des Pyrénées in Montréjeau, a shady promenade with fine views of the mountains, is a legacy of the Baron, and a bronze statue of him in a characteristically lordly pose presides over it to this day.

As soon as he began climbing the peaks of the Pyrenees, Lassus kept a detailed record of all his triumphs, and a framed plaque listing his one hundred ascents of the Pyrenees, with a photograph of him surrounded by his guides, can be seen in the museum in Luchon. He and Russell first met on the Pic du Midi, at the Hostellerie de Sencours, where Russell was preparing to climb to the Observatoire on the summit. They had several long conversations and were clearly immediately engaged by each other; the young Lassus in awe of Russell and his reputation, and Russell himself at fifty-four basking in the attention of a new young acolyte. Lassus wrote to Russell, 'Reading your works has strengthened my passion for the mountains. I too want to know the grand ascents, great climbs, taste the feeling of life in these superb regions . . .'

Lassus climbed Vignemale for the first time in August 1890 at the invitation of Russell. Perhaps he was already familiar with Russell's preference for fine Bordeaux but he did not arrive empty-handed. Guides François Salles and Célestin Passet of Gavarnie were loaded down with provisions, including bottles of vintage Pauillac, Margaux, Champagne de Reims and Chartreuse.

They arrived in a tempest of snow at the Grottes de Belle Vue where Russell gave them a warm welcome and made them tea. Then followed what Russell described as 'a charming evening with my young and enthusiastic friend'. Dinner was followed by punch. They strolled and sat outside contemplating the view until 11 p.m., enjoying, said Russell, 'an unforgettable magical scene'. Their friendship was thus cemented over several bottles of good Bordeaux and henceforth they met frequently, both in Pau and later at the new chateau at Valmirande, where Bertrand entertained so many of his Pyrenean friends.

After lunch we had coffee with the Baroness in the *salon d'hiver*, with its comfortable cane furniture, gaily painted frescoes and huge mirrors, which magnified the light and sun in winter. She showed us the chapel, a neo–Gothic extravaganza of stained glass and frescoes. 'Both Bertrand and Henry Russell were profoundly religious,' she said, and told us the story of Cardinal Matthieu, archbishop of Toulouse, who came to dinner to bless the chateau when it was completed in 1899. The cleric complained that there was no chapel. '"You shall have your chapel," Bertrand declared, and so he did!'

'Now you must see the library.' The library held two floors of glass-fronted book cases, and Mme de Lassus showed me the many editions of Russell's works, all exquisitely bound in red leather, tooled in gold, and dedicated by Henry to Bertrand, 'Mon jeune ami'. She spread out albums of photos of the Pyrenees, several of Russell, and of Bertrand himself, a man carefully crafting his rustic image, posed with a cloak artfully draped over his arm, a flower in his buttonhole, plus fours and a long patterned cravat tucked into a wide waistband.

Bertrand de Lassus modelled himself on Russell, determined to emulate the master in his exploration of the mountains. He quite literally followed in Russell's footsteps, recruiting Henri Passet, one of Russell's most faithful guides, to lead his expeditions, hoping some of the magic would brush off. Passet obliged by regaling him with Russell's adventures on the same paths. On the glacier of Maladetta, he pointed out where Russell had fallen and lost his precious alpenstock, and while exploring the Monts Maudits they met a woodsman who recognized Henri Passet and remembered Russell's notorious adventure with the bandits. In the years that followed, Passet, a simple Gavarnie peasant, was often invited to Valmirande to help plan Bertrand's expeditions.

In August 1892 Lassus spent several days with Russell on Vignemale, an experience Lassus recorded in purple prose to rival Russell's 'Midnight and Dawn on the Summit of the Great Vignemale'. This time he needed three donkeys and five men to carry essential supplies. As it turned out this was just as well, since the next few days *chez* Russell were so busy with guests Russell for one could have compared it to Paddington Station.

After a night in the Belle Vue caves below the glacier, the entire company climbed to the summit. But it was enveloped in thick fog and they took refuge lower down in the Grotte des Dames, the only one of the three original caves to escape the rising glacier. It proved to be miraculously dry. At about six o'clock that evening several more shadows appeared out of the fog. They were Henri Brulle and guide Célestin Passet, followed by two priests, Père Carrère, who had said mass on the summit for Russell in 1884, and Abbé Heche, the curé of Gèdre, a plain simple country man known for wearing his clogs even in church. They had been invited by de Lassus to say mass again on the mountain summit. They were also accompanied by two porters, one of whom Bertrand observed with admirable solicitude was absolutely shattered.

Sadly for the newcomers the accommodation in the tiny Grotte des Dames was already overcrowded. One gets the feeling Bertrand had got rather carried away with his invitations. Brulle in particular must have felt like a displaced favourite from the king's court. As for the priests, they could only smile benignly and say their rosaries. The extra guests were all obliged to continue on to the summit before night fell. There they spent a bitterly cold night in a tempest of hailstones, huddled together in a half collapsed wooden shelter, all that remained of the *cabane* of the workers still in the process of blasting out the latest cave, le Paradis. Russell and his companions found them the next morning, half perished by their night in the open.

To Bertrand's disappointment at least, a violent icy wind meant they could not say mass on the summit itself, and all had to huddle into the unfinished Paradis cave. The frozen clerics obliged with two masses, their Latin invocations echoing round the interior. According to Lassus it was a touching ceremony: '. . . considering the sublime simplicity of the temple, it possessed a majesty which the pomp of our finest cathedral could not equal,' he wrote, echoing Russell.

All were glad to return to the Grotte des Dames for a cup of tea, and though Lassus pressed everyone else to stay with him, they all departed rapidly, and vanished in the fog. The weather grew worse, all attempts to climb to the summit again were rebuffed by the wind and hail, and

Lassus scuttled back to the cave. Passet meanwhile slept and snored for four hours in a shelter west of the col. The gale lasted twenty hours and they were obliged to stay another night. Lassus remained enchanted, revelling in the lurid green and pink of the sunset, the lightning striking the summit, and then the full moon with a double halo reigning over the chaos.

Despite the clammy fog the following day even more people turned up to climb Vignemale; two ladies arrived with guides from Luz and climbed up to the summit. Meanwhile Lassus gathered together his baggage and hurried back down over the glacier to Belle Vue, where he found the Count entertaining the husband of one of the intrepid ladies, who was feeling rather ill. The ladies returned, the rain continued, Lassus got a migraine. Then yet another group of six visitors appeared, on an excursion from Lyon. Russell's legendary hospitality failed him at this point, and he said it was impossible for them also to sleep in the Belle Vue caves, so they were despatched back up to the Grotte des Dames, a further two hours or so over the glacier.

The next day a gang of four customs officers dropped by for a couple of hours. After lunch the Lyon 'tourists' were spotted heading straight down to the Col d'Ossoue, carefully avoiding Russell's refuge. The experience apparently left a bitter memory of Russell in Lyon. Then another friend of Russell's, the Comte de Monts, arrived with two young ladies from Cauterets, stayed two hours and went on to Gavarnie, an incredibly long hike which reinforces the opinion that nineteenth-century ladies were made of stronger stuff than we are.

That evening Russell and Lassus watched the sunset

together, sitting on the terrace of the Belle Vue grotto, looking down to the vast amphitheatre of the Cirque of Gavarnie and the valley of Ossoue buried in fog. The moon rose slowly over the surrounding icy crests, shining on the wild gorges around them. The haze began to sink, leaving delicate spirals around the peaks, and finally vanished completely, with Vignemale shining like a beacon in the moonlight.

Lassus was seized with the desire to climb the mountain again. 'I am going to attempt a nocturnal ascent of the Great Vignemale,' he announced portentously to Russell, who was deep in thought. 'His only reply was a pressure of my hand and a smile. "A grand idea. Better start immediately. I rejoice already at the prospect of the wonders which await you on those heights . . . You will be the first to completely traverse the whole glacier at midnight."'

There were twenty minutes to go till midnight. 'Then we have time to prepare some punch to drink to the success of our splendid enterprise,' said Russell, calling Haurine, who acted as butler and cook on the Vignemale. The punch recipe has been preserved and is still followed by Lassus's descendants; it is unlikely to differ in the slightest detail from that of the Count himself: rum, grenadine, orange juice and demerara sugar. While the punch was steaming Lassus woke up the long-suffering Henri Passet, and told him excitedly of his brilliant new scheme. They assembled round the punch, shook hands, and at precisely midnight by his pocket watch Lassus set off with Passet and another porter.

His description of the climb is classic, as he became entranced by the weird beauty of the glacier at night, pale and spectral, its great blocks of ice illuminated by the ethereal light of the moon, 'like colossal spectres conceal-ing its skeleton beneath a winding sheet of ice'. They climbed carefully, crunching over a crisp new fall of snow, avoiding the treacherous glacial crevasses. They crossed yawning precipices over fragile snow bridges, occasionally halted by a deep fissure with vertical shining sides. Happily the imperturbable Passet was quite at home, and negotiated the dangers with his usual sang-froid. By 2 a.m. they had reached the Col de Cerbillona and the Grotte des Dames. But they pressed on to the summit and the Paradis cave, the only difficulty being their own shadows cast by the moon, obscuring the way in front of them. There they rested, the first to use the new shelter, still unfinished. 'The inside was perfectly dry,' wrote Bertrand, 'and although there was no door, I did not for a moment suffer from the cold.'

As they awaited the dawn, there was no wind and the silence was awesome. About 4 a.m. they got out the rum bottle and made more punch. As the stars paled and the sky lightened, Bertrand set off, and in five minutes he had climbed to the summit where he wrapped himself snugly in a plaid rug and settled down for the performance. He describes the dawn in extravagant imitation of Russell: 'Suddenly the horizon glowed with what looked like red blazes, the first touch of dawn gilding the entire chain of the Pyrenees, which stretched before me all the way from the Mediterranean to the Atlantic.'

After four hours on the summit, he descended, and it took another hour in the morning sun to warm up his frozen limbs. He and his guides descended again – no doubt Passet had slept through yet another sunrise – to find Russell eager to hear all the details. They had another banquet and promised to meet there again the following year.

In 1994 Mme de Lassus herself climbed Vignemale with a group of friends to mark the anniversary of Bertrand's midnight ascent, just over a century before. They toasted the venture with 1868 cognac at Valmirande the night before and set off for the Bayssellance refuge the next day. At 1 a.m. they set out from the refuge for the summit, reaching it just after sunrise, where they drank the celebrated hot punch in honour of Uncle Bertrand and his friend, Count Henry Russell. This inimitable lady was then seventy. 'And next year for my eightieth birthday,' she announced over lunch, 'I plan to climb the Maladetta.' I had no doubt she would make it.

In 1894, on 18 July, Russell celebrated what he called his silver wedding, his twenty-fifth ascent of Vignemale, with Lassus, who arrived at Belle Vue with Henri Passet and several porters as heavily burdened as usual. Lassus wanted to spend the night at the lofty new cave, le Paradis, but Russell at that moment declined, saying he had already climbed to the summit that year. His health was already failing, and he was finding it increasingly difficult to summon the strength he once had.

Once installed in the Paradis Lassus went up to the summit to pass the evening, though a little mist partly obscured the glacier. Then Passet came up to warn him there were three figures approaching across the glacier. Lassus was discomfited at the idea of a group of strangers invading his solitary night on Vignemale and despatched Passet to try to see them off. Henri returned a few minutes later.

'*C'est le Comte Russell!*' he announced.

When Henry arrived with two guides, Lassus demanded to know what had made him change his mind. 'The explanation is very simple,' said the Count. ' Two days ago I made my twenty-fourth ascent of Vignemale, and I did not expect to make another this year. But then knowing you were up here I decided to make my twenty-fifth ascent, therefore my silver wedding, and celebrate it with you!' Lassus felt suitably honoured and offered the habitual feast. Russell can almost be heard murmuring, 'One gets so hungry at these heights. Austerity is difficult . . .' According to the report in the local paper, *La Gazette d'Argèles-Gazost*, it was a 'Homeric fête', with sardines, cold chicken, bear ham and *vin de Pierre Vergez-Bellou*. They sat together by the light of the full moon, contemplating the eternal snows from le Paradis, smoking cigars, and singing songs in honour of the saints of Ireland and France.

A couple of weeks later that summer, on 30 July 1894, Russell wrote to his old friend Henri Brulle, describing the beautiful weather at Belle Vue and inviting him to visit, with friends if he wished, 'because there are twenty kilos of straw in the Paradis'. He was not to bring anything with him, instructed Russell, 'except a bit of Gruyère or jam, because we have plenty'. Then he carefully spelt out the menu he could offer:

> Soupe Riz Crécy-Oseille
> Julienne-Tapioca
> Poisson
> Filets de Sole
> Viandes

Fricandeau boeuf, veau, mouton
Vins
Bordeaux
Café, Thé Russe, Punch
Cigares
Poires

Over the next few years Russell continued to climb Vignemale at least once a year. In 1895 he recorded spending five superb days, with all seven caves accessible by the end of August. One night ten people stayed the night, including the Queen of Holland and her daughter, an intrepid Alpinist. Other visitors included Henri de Curzon, a Parisian music critic, and several photographers, Maurice Gourdon, Juan de Parada and Maurice Meys the celebrated reporter and photographer for *Illustration*, a huge man with white hair and long white beard, who took the famous photo of Russell stretched out in his sleeping bag. 'We had an enormous quantity of supplies, and lived in luxury, especially with the arrival of the generous Baron de Lassus. There was a bell three times a day for meals. All that was missing was a piano,' noted Russell.

Lassus paid his last visit to Russell on Vignemale in 1896. This seems to have been relatively uneventful though on the way from Gavarnie Bertrand lost his hat in the waterfall and despite strenuous efforts Henri Passet failed to retrieve it, though he did find Lassus's dark glasses wrapped around a rock. It is interesting to note that Lassus, ever a man of style, was wearing spectacles, a rare accessory until the 1930s; in another photograph he is shown with a white veil attached to his hat, which was a time-honoured way of attempting sun protection. The guides usually wore their traditional berets, which, drawn low over the eyes, offered some shade from the sun. Russell himself never seems to have worn any eye protection, relying on the brims of his various hats. He never referred to snow blindness though he did once complain of shooting lights in his eyes at night which must have been the effect of the sun and snow, and one visitor noted with concern the state of his nose after decades of sunburn.

For Russell 1896 sounded a sad note. Already he was bereft; his beloved mother had died in November 1892. 'My own life has been shipwrecked since the bitter day I lost my mother,' he wrote in a letter of condolence to a bereaved friend. He was already fifty-eight by then, and he and his mother had always continued to live in the same house on rue Marca.

Then in 1896 Charles Packe fell ill, and Russell went to England to be with him as he lay dying, to talk of the mountains and share last memories of their experiences together. Russell too was ill: 'The day will come when I cannot climb any more . . .' he wrote mournfully. In 1898 he climbed Vignemale for the thirtieth time and swore it would be the last. Still, he revelled in the voluptuous velvety blue sky of the Midi, 'the proud graceful snow pyramids like cathedrals of nature, the snow steaming in the sun with a golden vapour, sparkling like a tropical sea'.

In 1899 he had to go to Ireland, to deal with his land and his tenants. He did not return until September, and did not climb Vignemale that year. In a fit of nostalgia he wrote for the *Gazette de Cauterets*, 'Vignemale is my wife and my seven caves are our children.' In 1900 he climbed it again, and again made his final farewells. Plans were under way for a Club Alpin Français refuge below the glacier of

Vignemale, and Russell had strong opinions on the most suitable style of building. He wrote several letters advising on location and the critical factor of wind direction. He pointed out that in the summer there was little wind – he knew because he could only smoke his cigars without it. In winter he reckoned snow would protect the building. He thought back to his days travelling in some of the most exposed places on earth, staying in Mongol yurts and Tibetan lamaseries, and he recommended a low round tower as the most resistant to wind and snow.

The refuge, now named Bayssellance, was finally inaugurated in August 1900, but Russell's suggestions were ignored and it was constructed along conventional lines. The weather was so terrible for the ceremony that Russell stayed in Gavarnie with Lassus, dismissing the structure as neither cave nor palace. In 1902 two hundred people stayed in the refuge. Russell did not.

Lassus and Russell continued to meet, often at Valmirande, where Lassus liked to entertain his mountaineering friends. The guest book includes the names of Russell and Henri Beraldi, the historian of the Pyrenees, who had been visiting Luchon since his childhood, along with Henri Passet, enjoying his deserved elevation, and the Vergez hoteliers of Gavarnie.

Before we took our leave of Mme de Lassus she showed us the park, Bertrand's 'exotic Pyrenean forest', as Russell called it, the lake and its artificial grotto. We imagined the two friends strolling among the newly planted trees, pausing by the lake, and discussing further refinements of the chateau. While Russell created his simple caves from which to regard the Pyrenees, Bertrand had built an entire chateau, which Russell described as his 'quasi-royal palace', with the express purpose of getting the best possible view combined with the greatest possible luxury.

Despite Russell's personal disdain for the tent, Bertrand's next enterprise was camping. *Camping à la Lassus* was a grand affair, more akin to the base camps of the Himalaya than a rustic bivouac. Grandest of all was the camp in the gorge of Salarous, on the south side of the Cirque de Gavarnie, at an altitude of 2550 metres, between the peaks of Taillon and Gabietou.

They stayed for fifteen days in all, and Passet was required to spend the months of April and May at Valmirande in order to plan it. Seventeen donkeys and thirty-three guides and porters were required for transport, trudging over the mule path from Gavarnie to the col. Most of Gavarnie seemed to have been recruited for the expedition.

There were tents of green canvas with beechwood poles, including a bathroom tent, and a large dining tent. Henri Passet was even given his own accommodation (though no doubt that was on account of his snoring). They took folding teak tables, chairs, and washbasins, iron beds, wool mattresses, sheets and covers. The sight of the iron bedsteads on the backs of donkeys was never forgotten in Gavarnie. Equipment included photographic apparatus, guns and ammunition, a pharmacy, wine, conserves, and paints and canvases for the camp artist. By the time it was all unloaded it looked like an army encampment. Photographs show Bertrand at the centre of it all, looking as proud as Napoleon.

Gelibert the artist sat drawing all day under an ample hat, usually surrounded by a group of intrigued observers.

Juan de Parada, a Spanish photographer from Bordeaux, came along as usual to take photos of Bertrand. The ubiquitous Père Carrère appeared regularly to say mass, celebrating the sacrament on a makeshift altar decorated with flags and alpenstocks.

Two porters were despatched daily to Gavarnie to replenish supplies. Local shepherds came, full of curiosity, and the inquisitive *douaniers* from the frontier turned up to check all their papers. A daily itinerary was established, of sunrises, climbs, photos. Camp life was punctuated by meals, punch and English tea at five o'clock, followed by dinner with magic lantern slides and singing, and a champagne dinner on the last night.

As the nineteenth century drew to a close, the world was changing. In the mountains the tourists were arriving in greater and greater numbers, gymnastic sportsmen had almost vanquished the romantic Pyreneists and their search for beauty, British hunters had killed all the *bouquetins* and British gardeners had picked all the daffodils.

Pau too had changed, its fortunes declining as further aspersions were cast on the benefits of the climate. Many of the English had deserted Pau in favour of Biarritz, other Pyrenean spas such as Vernet-les-Bains, or headed for the Mediterranean Côte d'Azur. By the time the magnificent Boulevard des Pyrénées was finished in 1899 it was too late to call it Boulevard des Anglais.

The construction of the boulevard was only one of many changes to the Pau that Russell had known since his childhood. The Villa Beaumont, where he had lived as a child, had been bought by the town, and turned into a grand park, a winter garden and palmarium, linked by the Boulevard des Pyrénées to the Place Royale, creating a long promenade with grand views of the mountains. Here in 1901 a great banquet was held in honour of Russell, who had just received the Légion d'Honneur.

Car races began to take place between Pau and Bayonne in 1899. By 1901 there was a tram line running down rue Marca and in 1908 a funicular railway connected the station with the promenade above it. The Place Royale was dug up in a 'volcano of cement' to finish the work on the Boulevard des Pyrénées.

But Russell continued his life in Pau much as before, going to concerts in the new Palais d'Hiver and playing music, which consoled him more and more. In 1905 he wrote, 'I played so much music, a divine art to make me forget a winter more cold than Paris.' He played for two or three hours a day, alone and with others, including his friend the organist from the church of St Martin. Number 14 rue Marca was a house of music at that time. On the first floor Russell played his cello, on the second floor lived Dr Philippe Tissié whose daughter played the piano, and on the third floor was a professor of philosophy, who tootled away on a hunting horn.

Russell worked on his books, publishing *Pyrenaica*, a selection of his writing, in 1902, and reworking all his mountain memoirs into a new edition of *Souvenirs d'un Montagnard*. He maintained his voluminous correspondence with mountaineering friends, both English and French, sending letters and postcards headed Count Henry Russell. He took up the new English fashion of sending Christmas cards, such as the drawing of three Arabs with camels under the stars which he sent to Henri

Brulle in 1895. He signed himself variously, Le Solitaire du Vignemale, the Troglodyte of the Snows or the Dreamer of Vignemale, and sometime enclosed a photo of himself on the glacier. He seemed to enjoy his eccentric reputation.

He and Henri Brulle kept in close touch and Russell suggested Brulle wrote an article for the *Alpine Journal*, accompanied by his own photos. This became a piece about the joys of Gavarnie as a climbing centre, and Russell laboured to produce an accurate translation. 'I have taken only one liberty,' he said, 'in adjusting the heights of Mont Perdu and Vignemale' – a typical Russell obsession. He added that he rather liked the title of 'troglodyte', which suggests that Brulle coined it for him.

Brulle often sent him photographs of the Pyrenees, its peaks and glaciers, which Russell greatly admired; of Brulle's pictures of the northern glacier of Mont Perdu, he commented, 'so admirable, moving and dramatic, they give such a good idea of the glorious snows of the Pyrenees'. They were added to the growing collection of black and white photos of mountains on his walls. One of which he was particularly proud was of Kangchenjunga, the 8000m Himalayan peak, which brought back memories of his youth. 'A colossal mountain which is one of nature's masterpieces.' Later he added a big photo of Everest as well.

He loved photographs, and counted among his friends most of the early photographers of the Pyrenees, whose work from the 1850s on did much to popularize the region. Of early photographers of the School of Pau two of the three were British, Maxwell Lyte and John Stewart; the other, Jacques Heilmann, came from Alsace. Russell showed a modern eye when he observed the photographic possibilities in a landscape, the contrasts and shadows he could see. Although he never wielded a camera himself, he posed happily on glaciers and river banks, and most famously in his sheepskin sleeping bag. He had been firm friends for many years with Maxwell Lyte, one of the co-founders of the Société Ramond, and also knew Maurice Gourdon and Lucien Briet. 'How can anyone say photography is not an art?' he commented to Brulle. 'Yours combine the charm of art with reality. I am jealous, me who only takes bottles and boxes of conserves to the mountains.' He always regretted never taking photos himself, 'But I suspect I would never have had the patience.'

He was a mentor for a whole new generation of *pyrénéistes*, of which Louis Le Bondidier was typical. Le Bondidier had come to the Pyrenees from Lorraine to work in 1901 and reading Henry Russell gave him the desire to explore the high mountains, which he did with Russell's guidebooks in hand like an invisible companion. He and his wife wrote to Russell offering to describe their own climbs as a contribution to the book he was working on (the final edition of *Souvenirs*). Russell courteously invited them to Sunday lunch in April 1906 at 14 rue Marca, but had to explain that it was not that kind of book; it was not a guidebook but his personal memoirs, so it would be difficult to include other people's climbs.

It was the first time they met and Le Bondidier recalled the occasion in great detail: the little salon on the first floor of rue Marca, the photographs on the wall, of Crête des Tempêtes by Maurice Gourdon, and the picture of Russell with Comte de Sant Saud and his children in front of the Grottes de Belle Vue, the travel souvenirs, the music stand and an open music score.

'The door was opened by this tall old man with very blue eyes, fine wavy white hair and a high forehead. On his brown jacket was pinned the red ribbon of the Légion d'Honneur. What struck me most was his very gentle voice, and the courtesy this great old man of seventy-two showed in talking to a young man anxious for his opinions. He almost had an air of timidity at first. But this was nothing more than reserve and soon disappeared in the intimacy of master and disciple. His conversation was singularly alert and lively. His apparent timidity disguised strong convictions. He had a brilliant memory and could evoke in great detail even forty years later all the details of every rock and crevasse. They were the essential elements of his life. He judged men with a philosophical irony, though he was never unkind. He was too distant from society, having never had any great love for it, to hate it. Nature was the source of his happiness.'

Le Bondidier proved a fine disciple. He founded the Musée des Pyrénées in the Château de Lourdes, a collection in the same spirit as the poet Mistral's provençal museum in Arles, assembling humble artefacts, costumes, and tools to provide a history of the mountains. After Russell died Le Bondidier planned a statue in his honour, asking all his mountaineering friends to send him rocks from every summit in the Pyrenees, which were used to form the base of the bronze statue erected in the museum for Russell's centenary in 1934. Each stone represented a peak, but also the existential moment of arriving at the summit, an immense horizon suddenly revealed. Russell could thus quite literally have all the summits of the Pyrenees at his feet.

But Russell climbed less and less. His health declined and

he became weaker. He suffered from terrible insomnia, and he had always refused to walk or climb unless he had had a good night's sleep. Still he continued to hold court at Gavarnie every year, assuring his acolytes that he would never desert them. 'No, no, I will never quit Gavarnie,' he insisted. 'I am no more capable of it than the mountain of Marboré is capable of quitting.'

But Gavarnie too had changed, overwhelmed by thousands of tourists, particularly in charabanc loads from Lourdes, as Brulle described: '... a tide of progress changed Gavarnie, the tourists, the *auberges*, even the traditional storm of 20 August forgot to arrive. We did not live the life of the village any more, no longer sat in the chimney with the old folk, drinking a bowl of milk or a glass of Spanish wine.'

A Grand Hôtel had been built by the prospering Vergez-Bellou family of the Hôtel des Voyageurs, with a splendid view of the Cirque. Russell, 'the spirit of Gavarnie', gave the inaugural address but it is hard to believe his heart was in it. He spent most of his speech eulogizing the magnificent summer storms of Gavarnie. The hotel is a monstrous building, which still dominates the village, with its faux Swiss woodwork and ugly green shutters. At least Russell was never to see that the row of trees they planted round the garden gradually grew up to obscure the view of the Cirque.

On my first visit to Gavarnie I had been keen to see if anything remained of this grand hotel. But it is only open in the summer season, and when I walked into the grounds to take a photo I was summarily thrown out by a fierce blonde Frenchwoman. The next time, we succeeded in being served drinks on the terrace and could admire the view of the Cirque (the trees have been cut down now), but any original decoration had been ripped out in favour of mirrored glass and fake copper ceilings.

Russell still went regularly to Cauterets, at its most fashionable in the last quarter of the nineteenth century, with an express train from Paris and 20,000 visitors a year. He arrived by the new electric tramway, and often stayed in the magnificent new Hôtel d'Angleterre with visitors such as Lord Randolph Churchill, the mayor of St Petersburg, novelist Emile Zola and actress Sarah Bernhardt. (Her ocelot chewed the curtains, which had to be replaced every time she visited.) Russell went to the theatre, the balls and waltzes, and was a celebrity himself with his sojourns in the *grottes* recorded in the *Gazette de Cauterets* like the doings of visiting royalty. He was even the subject of a popular postcard.

Though he had made his adieux to Vignemale in 1900, and in 1901 was too ill to make the ascent, the following year he could not resist. He managed to climb as far as Belle Vue. 'But when I saw the peak sparkling, the air seemed alive, shivering with happiness, and the temptation became a torture. I tried to calm it by climbing Petit Vignemale, but it was worse, and the following day I climbed Vignemale again.' And again for the thirty-second time in 1902. In the *Gazette de Cauterets* he wrote, 'Adoring Beethoven, I am going to play my thirty-second variation, not on the piano, but on the sonorous skull of Vignemale.'

For Russell, climbing the same mountain many times was like interpreting a piece of music. He found the same infinitely subtle variety in his climbs of Vignemale, the quality of the ice and snow, the colours of clouds and sunsets, the blue of the sky, the sun, the wind, rain, hail, the temperature. He often equated the pleasure of music and mountains, what he called 'the melody of nature', but they were also for him similar processes, exploring a piece of music and exploring a mountain.

It was a great performance: 'It was the most luminous expedition I have ever made to Vignemale.' He recorded with satisfaction that there had been twelve to dinner in front of the caves. However, he returned very ill, and in great pain.

In 1903 he made it to the caves again but did not climb to the summit. In July 1904 he went to Belle Vue for seventeen days, the longest and sunniest time he ever spent there. Among his visitors was Roger Brulle, Henri Brulle's son, who took his photo. Henry stands proud and upright in bright sunlight, arms folded over his trusty tweed Norfolk jacket buttoned to the neck, pockets bulging. His beard is quite white, there are deep lines incised on his face, his eyes are more hooded – though they still have that distant view – and on his head he sports another hat, a crocheted beret with a pompom on top which looks Rastafarian in style and one suspects was rather highly coloured.

Russell stayed on for most of August, accompanied by the faithful Mathieu Haurine. On 31 July he was visited by Louis Robach, a young dentist and keen astronomer and photographer from Condom, who stayed to dinner. 'In the middle of the cave he had three small barrels of wine, and a great stock of provisions,' Robach recalled. 'He was astonished to find I was a vegetarian, and survived on bread and sugar and drank only water when walking.' They talked till midnight, with Russell bitterly deploring the invasion of the Pyrenees by crowds of sportsmen, 'incapable of sensing the beauty of the mountains'.

On 8 August Henry climbed to the summit for what really was to be the last time. It was as if he had to make it a symbolic number, thirty-three, the age of Christ when he was crucified. He was seventy. This final homage, two hours on the summit, filled him with emotion and permissible hyperbole. 'When for the last time I looked on the flamboyant snows, the white and splendid solitudes where for so many years I had tasted joys unknown on the plains, a great cloud passed over my heart.' He felt great sadness. There was a storm and hailstones, which he fancied were the tears of Vignemale at his leave-taking. 'It is finished,' he wrote, with biblical emphasis.

Meanwhile, like Toad of Toad Hall, the Baron de Lassus had found another passion, the automobile. He acquired his first car in 1903, which was driven up to the Col de Tourmalet in 1904 and to Gavarnie in 1906. Russell may have been in Gavarnie when Lassus roared up; certainly he visited Valmirande that same year. No doubt he courteously accepted a ride in his friend's vehicle and perhaps even took pleasure in the new sensation of speed.

But however Russell reacted, the car must have sounded a warning bell, if not a full-throated klaxon, bidding farewell to the Pyrenees Russell had known through much of the nineteenth century. 'When will the mountains be easily accessible with automobiles and *dirigeables*?' he wondered.

It hasn't taken long. Though even now the remote valleys of the Central Pyrenees remain unviolated by the motor car, elsewhere there have been many changes, not least along the coastal routes, where tens of thousands of heavy goods vehicles cross the Pyrenees daily, a rate that is increasing by 9 per cent a year. These are vital European routes connecting not just France and Spain, but Eastern European countries and Africa as well. They desperately need relief, and the only way to increase capacity is to create alternative routes across the Pyrenees. So far road routes have been made through the tunnels of Bielsa in the Central Pyrenees and the Col de Puymorens to the east.

Most controversial has been the nine-kilometre tunnel through the Col du Somport, one of the high passes of the Western Pyrenees at 1600 metres. It is at the head of the lovely Vallée d'Aspe, a route of passage from France to Spain for millennia; for the pilgrims to Santiago de Compostela, for trade and smugglers, for shepherds with their flocks, and later for the armies of Spanish, French and British who surged back and forth over the Pyrenees.

The Vallée d'Aspe was a favourite excursion of the English from Pau, who described it in picturesque detail: the waggons laden with Spanish wool, flocks of beautiful goats, and colourfully dressed peasants looking as if they were posed for a Murillo painting, with their sombreros, white leggings, cloaks and espadrilles, red gowns and white kerchiefs.

Russell loved it too, climbing the Pic d'Anie near the frontier one autumn day. 'It was the end of September, the forests were yellowing, violent gusts of wind carried away the leaves, there was a new powdering of snow on the mountains.' He could see the Pic d'Anie from Pau, 'a peak of gracious contours and proud attitude, dressed every night in gold and purple'.

After fifteen years of angry protests the tunnel finally

opened in 2003. I was there the year before and wanted to see the Vallée d'Aspe before the tunnel opened, so I drove up there one day from Pau with Paul Mirat. It was autumn then too, for me the most beautiful season in the Pyrenees, adding a poignancy which seemed appropriate to the expedition. There is the feeling that every warm golden day might be the last, and must be treasured. The cows are already on their way down from the mountains, ringing their bells, the rivers are freighted with dead leaves, whipped from the trees by a chill wind and the golden notes of the leaves are fading. Huge Spanish trucks pounded their way through the narrow valley, filling small village streets with traffic fumes and putting eagles to flight.

We stopped for lunch at the Hôtel des Pyrénées in Etsaut, halfway up the valley, a small old-fashioned hotel on the riverbank, where we enjoyed a classic béarnais meal of *garbure* soup of cabbage and bacon, and fresh river trout. Mirat explained the politics of Somport to me.

'Of course there is a problem with the traffic, something had to be done, but why not use the railway?' This had been closed down in 1975, and never reopened, making it easier to push through plans for a road tunnel instead.

'Why did they close the railway?'

'There was a train accident; the driver got out for a pee, and the train ran away and destroyed a small bridge. So the Spanish immediately started to build all over the train station at Zaragosa so it could not reopen.' The Spanish were very keen on the road option.

Eco warriors came from far and wide to join the struggle against the tunnel, emblematic of the desire to protect one of the last wildernesses in Europe. The environmental impact was of great concern, since increased traffic threatened several rare species: the royal eagles, wild vultures and the last bears of the Pyrenees who have taken refuge here; Camille, Canelle, Papillon, Pyrèn and Chocolat, as the bears are affectionately named, will all need to retreat higher still to escape the traffic fumes and risk of accidents.

Furthermore, the Aspe valley is very narrow, and most of the villages have only one street, through which any increased traffic must pass. Part of the problem now is that provision for deviations is well behind the schedule for the tunnel itself, and the road through many of the villages along the way remains unchanged. Anyway, there is only limited room for expansion; the road can only go behind the houses instead of in front. In the village of Bedous there is not even room for two trucks to pass each other. In 2003 the entire village council of Urdos, the last village before the tunnel, resigned because the road was still not wide enough for two vehicles to pass.

We went to see the headquarters of the protesters, in the abandoned railway station of Cette-Eygun, still festooned with signs – *Trop de Camions* (too many trucks) – but otherwise apparently deserted. An elderly dog lay beside the door but barely raised its head as we passed by. Eventually a long-haired sleepy hippie came and explained that everyone had gone, given up the struggle. Disappointed, we bought the protest T-shirt anyway.

At the other end of the spectrum is the energetic local mayor of Borce, M. René Rose, who is all in favour of progress and the increased opportunities the tunnel will bring. We went to visit him in his smart new *mairie*, one of the most chic I had seen in the Pyrenees, an imaginatively designed combination of metal staircases and plain glass in a medieval building. 'This is a beautiful valley but empty,' he explained sadly as he showed us the view of the shuttered village from the window. 'The valley is depopulating, the young leaving because there are no jobs. Apart from walks there are no tourist attractions. It is hard to make a living from agriculture. There are still houses inaccessible by car, and we need roads for shepherds so young people will continue the work. The valley is dying.'

After several more kilometres we saw the yawning hole that would be the tunnel and continued climbing till we reach the pass itself. Beyond was Spain. 'Will this tunnel be enough?' I enquired.

'No,' said Mirat. 'Now there are proposals for a new railway right through the central Pyrenees, through the valley of Argelès. All the local mayors are against it.' It was a valley that Russell particularly loved: 'The peaceful and fertile valley of Argelès, a paradise of green, and melodious torrents,' as he described it.

'And how will it go through the mountains?'

Mirat sighed. 'The tunnel will go right through Vignemale.'

22

Sunset in Biarritz

'Before a man studies Zen, mountains are mountains to him, and waters are waters, but when he obtains a glimpse into the truth of Zen through the instruction of a good master, mountains are no longer mountains, nor waters waters; later, however, when he has really reached the place of Rest mountains are again mountains, and waters waters.'

Zen saying

My final destination in the Pyrenees was Biarritz, right at the westernmost extremity of the chain. Henry Russell had always loved it, and wrote nostalgically about the happy family holidays he spent there as a child. He visited often in later life, revelling in the conjunction of nature, in being able to view the mountains from the sea and the sea from the mountains. He recommended the little mountain of la Rhune as the best place to see the Atlantic ocean from the heights of the Pyrenees. La Rhune is the mirror image of Canigou in the east, which offers an unparalleled view of the Mediterranean. Like Canigou it stands alone, sentinel at the western extremity of the chain. It too is visible from the shore, making the shore dwellers long for the mountains as the mountain folk long for the sea.

Henry Russell always liked to climb la Rhune. It was there he began the *Souvenirs*, with a description on the first page of climbing it on the shortest day of the year in the winter of 1865. He set off from the fishing port of Saint-Jean-de-Luz (he took a dip in the sea before dawn just to get himself in the mood) and in an hour he had covered seven kilometres to the base of the mountain. Three hours later he was on the summit. The air was still, the light and heat intense, and the immense view of the ocean reminded him of his exotic travels. 'La Rhune dominates one of the greatest maritime horizons in Europe,' he wrote, 'plain and sea and mountains all in one.' From the summit he could see to Spain, and the desolate glens of Navarre. To the east lay the silvery summits of the mountains, lit by the last dwindling rays of the sun; to the west the rocky coast and harbour of Saint-Jean-de-Luz, the long green line of the sea and the golden sands of Biarritz. 'There is no spectacle more imposing, nothing so vast or powerful as the sea seen from a mountain on a clear day.'

But the time had finally come when he could only sit on the shore and view his mountains from afar. 'After so much climbing what an ineffable pleasure it is to stop and dream on an autumn day in front of the seas of Biscay, contemplating the blue desert of the ocean, listening to the waves.' It was as if he always knew he would die there. 'When the fatal and cruel hour of final rest arrives, I will go and sit beside the ocean, in view of the Pyrenees, on the shore saturated with the spray of the sea, where in my youth I ran like the breeze,' he wrote in 1888.

It was winter when I travelled again the full length of the Pyrenees. I had contacted the Russell family for information and they had invited me to visit the Villa Christine in Biarritz. On the way I read Russell's guide, *Biarritz and the Basque Countries*, published in 1873. 'Biarritz is a charming village, fast becoming a small town . . . A gayer little place it would be difficult to find even in midwinter. It is capriciously and irregularly built, the houses looking as if they had fallen from the sky, the streets running up and down, right and left, but at almost every step letting you catch glimpses of the wild and blue ocean between two houses, or above them. It is the Bournemouth of the Bay of Biscay, but with the sun and colouring of Italy.'

What he most recommended was the sunset. 'Nothing can be grander than an autumn sunset on the Bay of Biscay, seen from the Biarritz cliffs; the tints are both so warm and so angry, that sea and land seem on fire, and the clouds are awful to look at.' The Western Pyrenees are the last to receive the rays of the sun before it sinks into the Atlantic. 'Every evening they receive the sun's adieux to Europe.' And Vignemale was the last to be extinguished. 'When the entire chain of the Pyrenees has disappeared into the austere shadows of dusk, Vignemale is still on fire.'

Henry was right about the sunset, as I discovered, strolling on the beach of the Grande Plage in the early evening. The soft sand was almost deserted as the dying sun blazed into the sea; a young couple, the woman plumply pregnant, were kissing and taking photos, a fair-haired boy sat alone on the sand, munching a baguette. I took off my shoes and socks to walk, feeling the fine floury sand cool beneath the soles of my feet, and imagined Henry running into the waves: '. . . the temptation to bathe is very great,' he reckoned and, naturally, recommended it at any time of year. But though I tested the water with my toes, December bathing in the Atlantic, even in Biarritz, was not for me.

Instead I retreated to the colonnaded porticoes of the exquisitely restored art deco Café de la Grande Plage with its splendid promenade overlooking the beach, and attempted at least to rival Russell's appetite, with a Basque meal of *chipirons* (small squid) with pepper and bacon and plain boiled potato, accompanied by a glass of dry fragrant Jurançon from the vineyards near Pau.

Russell particularly recommended a visit to the lighthouse for the view, and I could do no less, struggling up 256 steps to the beacon. Henry was right: 'The view is almost boundless, and the line of peaks from west to southeast is fully 150 miles in extent. Here you are sure to see, in autumn and winter, even in the calmest and loveliest weather, such a stupendous swell as is never witnessed even on the west coast of Ireland. The mass, height and length of these enormous waves are scarcely credible; they are hills of water, and their deafening roar is heard inland most distinctly at more than twenty miles! In fact, they make the coast tremble, and the rocks vibrate like bells.'

Perhaps it is the Ritz in Biarritz that still gives the name its cachet, but somehow it is a town that retains its glamour. It is the biggest resort on the French Atlantic seaboard, a great swathe of wide sandy beaches interpersed with rocky headlands, planted with exotic plants, waving pink tamarisk and purple, blue and white hydrangeas. Thanks to Napoleon III it is threaded with footbridges and promenades for strolling and viewing the thundering Atlantic surf. Its perfect situation between the Pyrenees and the sea makes for a mild climate, though rainy in winter and occasionally stormy in summer.

These days Biarritz is famous for surfing and I walked round to the biggest and most dramatic beach of all, the Plage de la Côte des Basques, where once the Basques would come on an annual pilgrimage to swim together, and now the surf set wait to catch the waves. These new Australian and American settlers have spiced up the genteel mix of retirees who form about a third of the population, and the annual bridge tournament in the revamped casino is closely followed by the international surfing championships. The old guard is still evident, however. I took tea later in the fine old Café Miremont on Place Clemenceau, all gilt chairs, Belle Epoque frescoes and finely wrought *patisserie*, and watched a very refined old lady in an ancient Chanel suit sipping tea and dipping biscuits for her poodle, while outside her black maid was waiting with her packages.

There is still plenty of evidence of the past here; the seaside architecture of Avenue Edward VII, Avenue de l'Impératrice and Avenue Reine Victoria reveals neo-Gothic castles, English villas, Andalusian haciendas and Swiss chalets. Russell's guide mentions several of the most lavish, with which he was obviously personally acquainted. Grandest of all was Marbella, a Moorish palace, lavishly decorated with marble, gold and ceramics, built by Lord Ernest Bruce, whose wife gave her name to the Milady Beach. The former Anglican church of St Andrews now houses the Musée Historique de Biarritz, a collection of documents, costumes and furniture tracing the history of the town. The English, inevitably, played a key role in the development of Biarritz.

Before the mid-nineteenth century Biarritz was a simple fishing village, in decline since the last whale was caught in the seventeenth century. By 1841 it had become popular for bathing, with new villas built in the centre of town and old fishermen's cottages and surrounding land snapped up. Hotels and cafés opened, soon followed by baths, a casino, billiard rooms, reading rooms and a ballroom. In 1843 Victor Hugo sounded a warning note: 'Biarritz is a lovely place. I have only one fear, that it may become fashionable.'

Rising prices in Pau prompted the British to try Biarritz as a health resort, encouraged by medical recommendation of the climate and also the arrival of the railway in nearby Bayonne in 1867. Soon Biarritz was the Brighton of Pau. The anonymous Pedestrian described the scene in the mid 1860s, on a summer afternoon when all the terraces, sands and promenades were occupied by visitors and the blue and white bathing tents were strung along the sands just as they are today. 'On the sands the centres of attraction are the bathing establishments – one of them being built in the form of a Swiss chalet, and another in the Moorish style – and these buildings, owing to their bold and picturesque character, contribute greatly to the beauty of the spectacle. Bathers in the most elaborate costumes of every colour and shape are seen smoking, reading, lounging, dipping, or chatting.'

He even spared a glance for the contrasting fashion sense of the locals: '. . . the fisherwomen near Biarritz are a very peculiar class. They are usually dressed from head to foot in blue serge, without shoes or stockings. They never walk, but are always on the run, balancing their large baskets on their heads, and uttering a curious, prolonged, shrill cry, which once heard can never be forgotten.'

Murray's 1877 guide recommended Biarritz for the new pastime of bathing: 'The chief resort being the Port Vieux, where French ladies and gentlemen "*en toilette de bain*" consume hours in aquatic promenades. The ladies may be seen floating about like mermaids, being supported on bladders, corks or gourds, attired in woollen trousers and tunics, and overshadowed by broad-brimmed hats.'

The English colonization followed its inexorable course. The first English church opened in 1861, under the patronage of the Colonial and Continental Church Society. By the 1870s there were two English churches and the Archbishop of Canterbury had to visit to smooth out the rivalry between the High Church Anglicans and the evangelicals. The inevitable English Club opened in 1872, followed by a fox hunt and the golf club in 1888, still the pride of Biarritz. By the 1880s Biarritz was a lively social whirl of grand receptions, dinners and dances. The Depôt Anglais ('English and American Store'), a huge emporium on Place Clemenceau, supplied its clients with everything they needed from London. The famous *épicerie* Felix-Potin subtitled itself 'Family Groceries' in English on the shop façade. Queen Victoria herself visited in 1889 after she had toured most of the cemeteries in the region, a favourite royal pastime. Pau too awaited her visit, planning to lodge her in the chateau, but she never arrived, a snub from which the town never really recovered. She was followed to Biarritz in the 1890s by Gladstone, who found it much to his taste.

Three times a week there was a mail coach, the Rocket, which took members of the Cercle Anglais from Pau to the Hôtel d'Angleterre in Biarritz. The journey generally took seven hours because they made so many stops, including the Hôtel de la Belle Hotesse in Orthez, which served an excellent lunch. This particular enterprise was initiated by James Gordon Bennett during his brief tenure of the Pau Hunt, and was particularly popular with the Americans, who liked to drive the coach themselves.

Ferdinand, Henry's brother, had a villa built in Biarritz

in 1896, and named it for his sister, Christine, probably after she died in 1898, in the Toulouse convent of which she had become Mother Superior, and where Russell had often visited her. But in Biarritz Russell more often stayed at the Hôtel d'Angleterre, which he highly recommended: '. . . a magnificent structure, 240 feet long, with twenty large salons, bathrooms and reading room, a garden, interpreters for every European language, and commanding a most superb sea view'. Though the hotel was long ago converted into sumptuous apartments the elegant façade still dominates the terrace overlooking the sea.

By the end of the nineteenth century Biarritz was in the whirl of the Belle Epoque, full of grand hotels, with the latest automobiles jostling the horses, carriages and donkeys on the streets. High society promenaded every morning on the Grande Plage, a moveable ramp whisking them from Place Bellevue to the beach in ninety seconds. They shopped at Biarritz Bonheur and took tea at the Miremont at four o'clock. There was a huge choice of sports and entertainment: golf, tennis, pigeon shooting, croquet, horses, polo, excursions and car rallies; even cinema. The Prince of Wales, who became Edward VII in 1901, came every year to stay at the Hôtel du Palais, and joined the Biarritz Hunt, which took off in full cry from the front of the Hôtel d'Angleterre. Henry Russell was an honorary member of the Biarritz Association (Gustave Eiffel was another) and I can imagine Henry then, strolling the promenade, as debonair and aloof as ever; no doubt, with his penchant for hats, sporting the latest straw boater.

I found the Villa Christine, a large late-nineteenth-century Basque-style villa in red brick, with ox-blood red shutters and a wooden veranda, just a few streets above

Place Clemenceau. It sits on the corner of a large leafy square featuring the usual *mélange* of Biarritz architecture, to one side a Gothic turreted mini-chateau named Esmeralda, on the other a pink house with a colonnaded Italian loggia and a Swiss chalet with carved wooden gables.

The family welcomed me to tea, and we talked about Russell's reputation, his mountain climbing and his caves. Although they are proud of their famous relative and would even like the street name changed to rue Henri Russell in his honour, they are anxious that people might think he was eccentric. To my disappointment they permitted me only a brief glance at family letters and documents. It was enough to see how Henry happily mingled English with French when he wrote, signing off 'with love', and referring to 'home'. However I did get to see Henry's ancient leather Gladstone bag, with his initials stamped in white on the side, which can be seen in so many photographs. Apparently he mostly used it to carry wine.

We looked at the dining room, kept as it was in Russell's day, the same solid square oak table and tall curved cane-backed chairs and the original iron radiator with a cunning little cupboard in the middle to keep the croissants warm.

From the top floor of the house Henry would have had a fine view of the sea across open land of sand and scrub, right down to the beach. Now there are too many houses in the way to see the sea but still I could imagine Henry in his last few days being able to watch the great waves of the Atlantic Ocean and the sun setting in the west.

As the sky darkened and the lights of Biarritz began to twinkle below, I tried to piece together Henry's last few months of life. He had begun to feel ill in Paris in the spring of 1908, where he complained of fatigue and loss of appetite (certainly a sign of malaise for Henry), and complained that he could walk no more than a kilometre. A visit to Gavarnie helped, the mountain air and views refreshing him, but by July in Pau he was so weak and thin he was unable to walk. 'A small child could throw me to the ground,' he grumbled. His brother Ferdinand came from Biarritz and immediately hurried to Eaux-Bonnes for Dr Meunier (old Dr Bagnell having finally died). They were told there was no hope for him, that he had a liver tumour which was developing rapidly and for which there was no cure, which might well have been a result of hepatitis contracted during his travels to the Far East as a young man. Ferdinand took his ailing brother to Biarritz.

As he left rue Marca for the last time, his neighbour, Dr Tissié, watched him from the window. 'Before climbing into the carriage, he looked for the last time at the house he was leaving for ever, and the window where I was standing to wave adieu. Pale, thin, tired, suffering, he saluted with a light movement of his head.' Thus Henry quitted rue Marca.

In November Henry wrote a postcard to Henri Brulle, in English. 'Most cordial thanks; but can't write, scarcely read or stand on my legs; absolute prostration; am sinking fast.' Soon he was confined to his room, and then to bed. Before he died he saw the new edition of the *Souvenirs* that he had been working on. On 13 January his dear young friend Baron de Lassus died in Paris at only thirty-nine. Perhaps the news hastened his own demise. Like Lassus he was consoled by religion and visited in his last days by his old friend Père Carrère, white-haired now, who had said mass for him on the summit of Vignemale. No doubt they spoke of it. In 1911 Carrère climbed again to the peak of Vignemale to say a requiem mass for Henry Russell. He later became vicar of the parish of Lourdes.

On 3 February a great event took place in Pau. The Wright Brothers, whose first flight took place in 1903 in North Carolina, had decided to establish the first school of aviation in Pau, because of the lack of wind. On 3 February 1909, Wilbur Wright took off and was airborne for five minutes and fifty-seven seconds. It was a momentous occasion, with huge crowds turning out to watch. It was the future. But it was also the end of an era. Before long everyone would be able to soar above the clouds and view the earth from the mountain tops. No doubt Henry would have heard the news, and understood. He died only two days later, before dawn on 5 February 1909. He was seventy-five.

He was buried in the Russell family mausoleum in the cemetery of Pau. His coffin was carried by four faithful guides and friends from Gavarnie, Célestin and Henri Passet, François Bernat-Salles and Mathieu Haurine. The day was cold, with glacial rain, and even flakes of snow as the Pyrenees bade Henry a last adieu.

Epilogue

Returning home on the train, I watched the Pyrenees go by and remembered the best moments of my own quest for the Sublime, the Picturesque and the Beautiful. For sublime it would be hard to beat sunrise and sunset on the Pic du Midi. I'll never forget surveying the world from the summit of Canigou, the first sight of the Cirque of Gavarnie or the view of Vignemale framed above the Lac de Gaube.

But I also remembered the quiet secret moments, like the walk I took one day with Monique to find the Cascade des Anglais outside Vernet-les-Bains. I had been intrigued by the faded old wooden sign pointing to a path above the cemetery, evidence of the days when Vernet was an English colony, and had imagined the ladies with their parasols, the gentlemen in straw boaters, making an afternoon excursion to see the waterfall. It is not far, about an hour and a half, a path marked out through the woods beside a river, with stone steps made here and there, even handholds where the path hugged close to the rocks of the gorge. We forded the river across flat stones and a sturdy tree trunk, and finally made a stiff scramble up the side of the gorge.

There was no-one there when we arrived, just us and the sound of the waterfall, crashing magnificently to a large pool below, sparkling and dancing in the sun, surging inexorably over a shelf of rock smoothed by time. The spray cooled our hot faces and we took off our boots and socks and bathed our feet in the clear icy water. Above us tenacious trees and ferns clung to the side of the rocks, which glinted red in the sunlight; Canigou's mysterious magnetism again. The path came to an end here; there was nowhere else for it to go, as the gorge beyond became steep and narrow and thickly forested. And anyway its objective was achieved. This was no mule path, no route to a rich pasture, it was simply a path to a waterfall. It had no other purpose but beauty. Somehow this idea, a path made for that single purpose, seemed as important as the waterfall itself.

Best of all, though, was the Wax Room, the Chambre des Certitudes, which we discovered one day a few miles from where we live. I had picked up a brochure in the tourist office in Prades; an artwork in the middle of nature which you had to find for yourself. I always liked the idea of landscape art, art you had to physically experience, like the Walter de la Maria lightning conductors in the middle of the Arizona desert. I think Henry Russell would have enjoyed those – you have to arrive and simply wait patiently till a storm hits and then watch the lightning dance across the poles.

We set out *en famille* to find the Wax Room, one bright day in spring, following a winding footpath across the plateau around the ancient priory of Marcevol, scrubby *garrigue* and huge rocks that tumble down the mountain-side every few thousand years, the air scented with wild herbs, no sound other than birds and wind. It is a wonderful wild open site, presided over by a clear distant view of Canigou on the other side of the Têt valley.

Somewhere in the great natural monuments of granite

that rose above us was another man-made cave, dug out by one as eccentric and inspired as Russell, a German artist named Wolfgang Laib, who had searched the Pyrenees for the right place for his cave: 'A place that only a few people could visit.'

Above us the mountainside rose steeply, and slowly we scrambled up the rocky escarpment, among twisted grey olive trees, clumps of thyme and lavender, dusty pink cistus and dry bunches of pale yellow everlasting flowers, all of which combined to produce a heady fragrance. Just when we thought we must have lost our way we saw in the cliff face a simple wooden door. It was like finding a door in a fairy tale. We opened it with the key we had collected from the café in Marcevol, and within was a cave completely plastered with golden wax, the hard rocky contours smoothed and transformed by the malleable substance. It was beeswax, which smelled like incense, like church. The surface of the wax was utterly smooth, the colour of pale egg yolk or gold, or even sun-kissed flesh. It looked warm and inviting as we entered but was cool to the touch. Caves always stay the same temperature, magically adapting to our needs, as Russell discovered. Today it was a hot day and the cave felt cool. On the top of Vignemale his caves were warm. We pressed our backs against the wax, bumpy over the natural shapes of the rock, and felt coolness seeping into us, marvelling at the task of plastering the entire space with wax, the heavy slabs swung up here by helicopter.

Theo and Miles set off to walk back (Theo said he sang a song to the artist all the way) and when they had gone I closed the door and sat in the darkness alone for a few moments. It was warm and still and smelled of candles and I felt completely safe. There is something terribly basic and primitive and moving about being a human alone in a cave. It is such a powerful metaphor. I thought of the caves at nearby Tautavel, where they found the bones of early man, and I thought of Russell alone in his cave with only a single candle in the middle of the storm, or watching the sunrise from the cave door.

When I opened the door again the light was so welcome I could have wept. It was like having one's sight restored. Framed in the entrance was Canigou, the peak still white with snow against a blue sky, a picturesque view of the mountain, an artistic vision imposed on nature. This was another cave constructed by a visionary with no other purpose than to contemplate beauty. Another Russell.

I felt a moment of perfect harmony, of balance between solitude and company, between light and darkness, poised between mother earth and father sky. It was immensely reassuring. I understood then that Russell's spirit was still there. Russell's Pyrenees were still there. However many tourists and climbers came, however many roads and tunnels were pierced, or planes and helicopters streaked overhead, the Pyrenees would never change. They are mountains, after all. There will always be space for the dreamers of the world.

THE END

Selected Bibliography

Anonymous, *A Peep at the Pyrenees by a Pedestrian*

Acland-Troyte, Reverend C.E. *From the Pyrenees to the Channel in a Dogcart*

Annan, Noel, *Leslie Stephen – The Godless Victorian*

Beraldi, Henri, *Cent Ans aux Pyrénées*

Besson, Francoise, *Pyrénées Romanesques, Pyrénées Poetiques dans le regard brittanique*

Blackburn, Henry, *The Pyrenees – A Description of Summer Life at French Watering Places with illustrations by Gustave Doré*

Boddington, Mrs, *Sketches in the Pyrenees*

de Botton, Alain, *The Art of Travel*

Stephen, Oscar Leslie (ed.), *Memoir: Victor Brooke*

Bunbury, Selina, *Evenings in the Pyrenees*

Burke, Edmund, *A Philosophical Enquiry into the Origin of our Ideas of the Sublime and the Beautiful*

Buxton, Edward North, *Short Stalks*

de Carbonnières, Ramond, *Observations faites dans les Pyrénées*

Chatterton, Lady, *The Pyrenees with Excursions into Spain*

Christiansen, Rupert, *The Voice of Victorian Sex: Arthur H. Clough*

Clifton-Paris, Thomas, *Letters from the Pyrenees, during three months pedestrian wanderings amidst the wildest scenes of the French and Spanish Mountains in the summer of 1842, with sketches by the author, taken on the spot*

Clark, R., *Victorian Mountaineers*

Colston, Mariane, *Journal of a Tour in France, Switzerland and Italy, during the years 1819, 1820, and 1821*

Costello, Louisa Stuart, *Béarn and the Pyrenees*

Erskine Murray, James, *A Summer in the Pyrenees*

Daumal, Rene, *Mount Analogue*

Dix, Edwin Asa, *A Midsummer Drive through the Pyrenees*

Duloum, Joseph, *Les Anglais dans les Pyrénées et les debuts du tourisme pyrénéen*

Ellis, Sarah, *Summer and Winter in the Pyrenees*

Eyre, Mary, *A Lady's Walks in the South of France*

Eyre, Mary, *Over the Pyrenees into Spain*

Fleming, Fergus, *Killing Dragons: The Conquest of the Alps*

Galton, Francis, *The Art of Travel. Or, Shifts and Contrivances Available in Wild Countries*

Gavarnie, Antonin Nicol, *Pau*

Gould, Sabine Baring, *A Book of the Pyrenees*

Honour, Hugh, *Romanticism*

Inglis, Henry David, *Switzerland, South of France and the Pyrenees*

Kipling, Rudyard, *Souvenirs of France*

Lacaze, Didier, *L'Aventure du Vignemale*

Macfarlane, Robert, *Mountains of the Mind*

Malcolm, John, *Reminiscences of a Campaign in the Pyrenees and South of France in 1814*

Maury, Luc, *Anne Lister Premiere Ascension du Vignemale*

Mirat, Paul, *Autrefois Pau*

Mirat, Paul, *Autrefois Pau L'Aviation*

Mumm, Arnold, *The Alpine Club Register*

Pérès, Jean-Louis and Jean Ubiergo, *Montagnes Pyrenees*

Ribas, Jospeh, *Petit Precis de Pyreneisme*

Radcliffe, Ann, *Mysteries of Udolpho*

Ribas, Joseph, *L'Aventure du Canigou Randonées Pyreneenes*

Ritter, Jean, *Le Pyreneisme avec Henri Russell et Bertrand de Lassus*

Ruskin, John, *Modern Painters*

Russell, Henry, *Souvenirs d'un Montagnard*

Sabatier, Georges, *Henry Russell Montagnard des Pyrénées*

Scott, O'Connor, V. C., *Travels in the Pyrenees*

Simpson, Joe, *Touching the Void*

Solnit, Rebecca, *Wanderlust: A History of Walking*

Spender, Harold and Llewellyn Smith, *Through the High Pyrenees*

Stephen, Leslie, *The Playground of Europe*

Stuart Mill, John, *Autobiography*

Taylor, Alexander, *The Climate of Pau*

Tennyson, Alfred, *In Memoriam*

Tennyson, Alfred, *The Works of Alfred Lord Tennyson*

Tennyson, Hallam, *Alfred Lord Tennyson – A Memoir by his Son*

Tucoo-Chala, *Pau Ville*

De Vaufreland, Henri, *Chroniques de la Vie Mondaine des Basses-Pyrenees*

Verne, Jules, *Around the World in Eighty Days*

Victor, R., *Mistress of Udolpho – Life of Ann Radcliffe*

Voyage aux Pyrenees – Ecrivains au 19ème siecle

Wilson, A.N., *The Victorians*

Whitbread, Helena (ed.), *I Know My Own Heart – Diaries of Anne Lister 1791–1840*

Whymper, Edward, *Scrambles Amongst the Alps 1860–69*

Wordsworth, William, *The Prelude*

Young, Arthur, *Travels during the Years 1787, 1788, and 1789, undertaken more particularly with a view of ascertaining Cultivation, Wealth, Resources, and National Prosperity of the Kingdom of France*

Periodicials and other sources: the *Alpine* journal, *Annuaire du Club Alpin Français*, *Pyrénées* magazine, *Revue des Pyrénées*, *Bulletin de Société Ramond*, *The Times*.